ARCHITECTS OF GLOBALISM

ARCHITECTS
OF GLOBALISM

BUILDING A
NEW WORLD ORDER
DURING WORLD WAR II

PATRICK J. HEARDEN

THE UNIVERSITY OF ARKANSAS PRESS
FAYETTEVILLE | 2002

06   05   04   03   02   5   4   3   2   1

Designed by Liz Lester

⊛ The paper used in this publication meets the minimum requirements of the American National Standard for Permanence of Paper for Printed Library Materials Z39.48-1984.

LIBRARY OF CONGRESS CATALOGING-IN-PUBLICATION DATA

Hearden, Patrick J., 1942–
     Architects of globalism : building a new world order during World War II / Patrick J. Hearden.
          p. cm.
     Includes bibliographical references and index.
     ISBN 1-55728-730-9 (alk. paper)
     1. United States—Foreign relations—1945–1953. 2. United States—Foreign relations—1933–-1945. 3. World War, 1939-1945—Diplomatic history. 4. World War, 1939–1945—Influence. I. Title.

E813 .H43 2002
327.73'009'045—dc21
                                        2002009380

For Carol

ACKNOWLEDGMENTS

Many friends have given me the benefit of their critical judgment. After reading a draft of my entire manuscript, Lloyd C. Gardner, Walter LaFeber, and Thomas J. McCormick provided me with valuable suggestions for revising the content, while William C. Lloyd and J. Michael Thorn made recommendations for stylistic improvements throughout my study. In addition, John C. Brogan, William B. Duddleston, James R. Farr, Elliott J. Gorn, and John L. Larson offered useful comments on various chapters, and my editor, Lawrence J. Malley, provided helpful guidance regarding the final revisions of my work.

During my long research trips away from home, A. Keene Byrd, James M. Hall, William R. Long, Robert H. Van Meter, and John S. Watterson supported me with their encouragement and hospitality, while Barton J. Bernstein, Melvyn P. Leffler, and David S. Painter called my attention to several unpublished sources. Many librarians and archivists working in historical depositories scattered across the United States aided me in locating important materials. The staffs at the Franklin D. Roosevelt Library, the Harry S. Truman Library, and the National Archives were especially helpful in facilitating my examination of their vast collections of primary documents. Moreover, John F. Doyle welcomed me into his home to investigate the private papers of his father-in-law, Leo T. Crowley.

Grants from the National Endowment for the Humanities, the Franklin and Eleanor Roosevelt Institute, the Harry S. Truman Library, and Purdue University helped finance my project.

PATRICK J. HEARDEN
Sturgeon Bay, Wisconsin

TABLE OF CONTENTS

PREFACE

The State Department during Pres. Franklin D. Roosevelt's administration assumed primary responsibility for the formulation of American plans for the post–World War II world. While drafting blueprints for a peaceful and prosperous international order, Secretary of State Cordell Hull and his top aides received a constant flow of reports about current developments around the globe. They also reviewed a wide array of political, economic, and historical studies that a large research staff had carefully prepared for a network of State Department planning committees. On a few occasions, however, War and Treasury Department officials did urge the president to take steps that would undermine the comprehensive program that State Department planners intended to implement after the war. But Secretary of War Henry L. Stimson, a distinguished Wall Street lawyer who had been secretary of state as well as secretary of war in past Republican administrations, failed to obtain presidential support for army and navy proposals for the annexation of Pacific islands to be taken from Japan. In contrast, Secretary of the Treasury Henry Morgenthau, a farming neighbor and personal friend of Roosevelt, did for a brief time gain approval from the White House for his scheme to deindustrialize Germany. Yet Roosevelt eventually backed away from the Morgenthau Plan, and the president ultimately sided with his State Department advisers in almost every important controversy regarding postwar issues.

Secretary Hull and his colleagues in the State Department advocated the creation of a liberal capitalist world system that would permit the American people to enjoy the fruits of prosperity within the framework of free enterprise. They did not want government bureaucrats in Washington to imperil the prerogatives of private ownership by planning the U.S. economy in an effort to achieve a permanent balance between domestic production and home consumption. Nor did they want the national government to accumulate a huge debt by spending borrowed money in an attempt to counter periodic downswings in the business cycle. If American farmers and manufacturers could sell their surplus goods in foreign markets after the war, Hull and the others believed that the United States would be able to maintain high levels of employment without resorting to centralized planning or deficit spending. They also thought that, if the principle of equal commercial opportunity prevailed throughout the world, other industrialized countries would be able to satisfy their economic needs without attacking their neighbors.

Prominent American business leaders provided strong backing for various aspects of the State Department campaign to promote the greatest possible degree of free trade among the nations of the world. Eugene P. Thomas, the president of the National Foreign Trade Council, pushed for the continuation of the reciprocal trade program to reopen the channels of international commerce after the cessation of hostilities. Eric A. Johnston, the president of the U.S. Chamber of Commerce, urged the extension of American credit to speed the postwar economic reconstruction of Europe. Thomas W. Lamont and Russell C. Leffingwell, both senior partners at J. P. Morgan and Company, used their prestige and influence in supporting the State Department drive to revive international commerce. While working for the Treasury Department after World War I, Lamont and Leffingwell had helped shape American financial policy at the Versailles Peace Conference. They had also helped establish the Council on Foreign Relations, an organization that prepared studies during World War II for the State Department to use in formulating plans for a peace settlement.

Furthermore, postwar planners in the State Department favored the establishment of an international security organization that would allow people in every part of the world to enjoy a long period of peace. Despite their willingness to use force if necessary to curb aggression, they did not entertain grandiose visions of the United States as a sole superpower that would alone shoulder the burden of policing the entire planet. Neither did they subscribe to the utopian dream that a single world government would soon replace the traditional nation-state pattern and ensure perpetual harmony among countries around the globe. Rather, they believed that if the United States and the other major powers constructed a strong international security organization, it might be possible to prevent the outbreak of a third world war for at least fifty years. But along with spokesmen for the army and the navy, they also thought that the United States must be prepared to defend the Western Hemisphere and project its military power across the Atlantic and the Pacific in case the system of collective security proved to be ineffective in maintaining peace.

The architects of globalism in the State Department articulated idealistic and humanitarian aims that were compatible with the economic and strategic objectives of the United States. They believed that the president would have less need to send armed forces overseas to check the spread of revolution and war if all countries were free to choose their own leaders and to engage in unrestricted commercial and financial transactions. They also thought that, if all nations were given a chance to manage their own political and economic affairs, the United States would have more opportunity to export surplus products to prosperous customers and to make profitable investments in stable countries. Assuming that what was good for their own country was good for the rest of the world, Hull and his associates sought to promote self-government and economic liberty abroad, not only due to their desire to help other countries but also because of their determination to protect the long-range interests of the United States.

Beneath the surface, however, sharp ego clashes and bitter personal rivalries provoked struggles within the State Department to shape American plans for the postwar era. Under Secretary Sumner Welles, an assertive career diplomat who tended to make quicker decisions than the more cautious Hull, worked closely during the early stages of the postwar planning process with Assistant Secretary Adolf A. Berle, a corporate lawyer who was valued by Hull because of his brilliance and creativity but was disliked by many of his cohorts because of his arrogant and overbearing personality. Assistant Secretary Dean G. Acheson, an astute and haughty corporate lawyer himself, did not get along with Berle, and the two assistant secretaries competed with each other for responsibility in the preparation of economic policies. To reduce the feuding between Acheson and Berle, Hull decided that both should report to Myron C. Taylor, a skilled negotiator who shunned publicity. Taylor had been the chairman of United States Steel before President Roosevelt selected him to serve as his special representative at the Vatican. Although he did not occupy an official position in the State Department, Taylor played an important part in drawing up plans for a better world.

Secretary Hull assigned key postwar planning roles to two other distinguished figures, Norman H. Davis and Isaiah Bowman, who also served without holding official posts in the State Department. A banker with ties to the House of Morgan, Davis had worked closely with Lamont and Leffingwell in providing financial advice to the U.S. peace commission at Versailles. Davis had also served as assistant secretary of the Treasury, under secretary of state, and chairman of the U.S. delegation for both the Geneva Disarmament Conference and the London Naval Conference. A patient and persuasive statesman with a keen intellect and a lively sense of humor, he became the president of the Council on Foreign Relations. Bowman was the president of Johns Hopkins University and a renowned geographer. A scientist with a superb ability to analyze political questions, he had served as the chief territorial specialist for the U.S. peace commission at Versailles. Bowman had been a founding member of the Council on Foreign Relations, and during World War II he directed territorial studies for both the council and the State Department.

But personal differences and competition for influence eventually led to a power shift in the State Department. While Secretary Hull maintained friendly relations with Bowman, Taylor, and Davis, he grew increasingly antagonistic toward Welles, a subordinate who occasionally had private talks with President Roosevelt and then made unauthorized speeches about U.S. foreign policy. Hull decided in early 1943 to take control of the postwar planning work, and later in the year he told Roosevelt that Welles could no longer remain in government service because of widespread gossip concerning his homosexual behavior. Welles quickly resigned. After replacing Welles as under secretary in the autumn of 1943, Edward R. Stettinius, formerly the chairman of United States Steel, kept Hull completely informed about his daily activities. When poor health prompted Hull to retire a year later, Stettinius became secretary, and the adroit business administrator with a warm personality immediately reorganized the State Department. He decided that the contentious Berle should be sent far afield to serve as U.S. ambassador in Brazil; that Joseph C. Grew, a tactful career diplomat, should become under secretary; and that William L. Clayton, the biggest cotton broker in the world, should be assistant secretary in charge of economic affairs.

Despite these changes in leadership, the same fundamental ideas about the postwar world continued to hold sway in the State Department throughout World War II. Clayton, Grew, and Stettinius, like Welles, Berle, and Hull, agreed on the need to establish a liberal capitalist world system. Even though Herbert Feis left his post as economic adviser in the State Department because he felt ignored and unappreciated, he never abandoned his commitment to the principle of equal commercial treatment. Neither did Leo Pasvolsky, a Brookings Institute economist who had worked in the Trade Agreements Division of the State Department before Hull selected him to oversee the entire postwar planning operation. Along with Bowman, Taylor, Davis, and the other top postwar planners working under the supervision of the secretary of state, Pasvolsky remained committed to the belief that free trade would provide a solid foundation for the creation of a peaceful and prosperous international community.

American blueprints for the postwar world, moreover, did not undergo a basic change when Roosevelt died from a stroke in the spring of 1945 and Harry S. Truman became president. Although he developed his own administrative style during his first six months in the White House, Truman worked hard to carry out the postwar plans that the State Department had drafted and Roosevelt had approved. The new president quickly selected James F. Byrnes, chairman of the War Mobilization Board and master of the art of compromise, to head the State Department. President Truman and Secretary of State Byrnes thought they would be able to induce the British to cooperate with American efforts to build an international trading network devoted to the doctrine of equal access to raw materials and commodity markets. Truman and Byrnes also believed they would be able to persuade the leaders of the Soviet Union to collaborate with the United States, Great Britain, and China in establishing a general security arrangement designed to deter aggression. Like their predecessors in the White House and State Department, Truman and Byrnes hoped that both the British and the Russians would be compelled by their need for postwar-reconstruction aid from the United States to support American proposals for the creation of a new world order.

INTRODUCTION | THE INTERWAR PERIOD

Shortly after the outbreak of World War I in 1914, Pres. Woodrow Wilson began thinking about the role that the United States should play in the eventual peace settlement. Wilson believed that American prosperity depended upon the exportation of surplus agricultural and industrial products. He also thought that, if international trade were conducted on a nondiscriminatory basis, all countries would be able to satisfy their economic needs without invading their neighbors. Wilson envisioned the establishment of a liberal capitalist world system based upon the principle of equal commercial opportunity. In addition, he contemplated the creation of the League of Nations, which would promote collective efforts to prevent future aggression. The president hoped to mediate a settlement between the Allies and the Central Powers before either side won a decisive victory and imposed terms that would destroy his dream of a peaceful and prosperous world order. But his efforts to persuade the British and French to stop fighting the Germans and accept his plans for a liberal peace ended in failure. When Germany resorted to unrestricted submarine attacks in 1917, Wilson decided to lead the United States into the war. He hoped that the introduction of fresh American troops would bring the conflict in Europe to a quick conclusion and provide the United States with the opportunity to help shape the future peace settlement.

Though he was confident that the large loans the United States had made to the Allies would strengthen his bargaining position, Wilson met stiff opposition when he arrived in Paris in 1919 to participate in the Versailles Peace Conference. He aimed to reintegrate Germany into the family of nations. If the German people were humiliated or impoverished, he feared, they might be driven into the clutches of communism. But the French wanted to cripple Germany in order to assure their future security. They intended to take the Rhineland and force the German people to pay huge war indemnities. After opposing the most extreme demands, Wilson agreed that the French army should occupy the Rhineland for fifteen years and that a reparations commission should handle the indemnity issue. Wilson also decided to compromise with regard to the colonial question. Before the United States entered the war, the Allies had signed a secret treaty to divide the overseas possessions of Germany among themselves. Wilson blocked their demands for outright ownership, but he agreed to let the great powers administer the detached German colonies under a League of Nations mandate. Although he had made many concessions that went against his principles, he succeeded in getting the Allies to accept his plans for the establishment of an international security organization.

But President Wilson encountered strong opposition when he returned home and sought to win support in the Senate for his League of Nations proposal. Under Article 10 of the league covenant, all member nations would be obligated to defend each other against aggression. Wilson insisted that this provision was essential for the establishment of a collective security system that would be effective in preserving world peace. But many senators believed that the approval of any treaty containing Article 10 would violate the constitutional prerogative of Congress to declare war. A large number argued against committing American soldiers to fight in future conflicts that might not have any relationship to vital U.S. interests, while others argued that no attempt to freeze the international status quo could succeed because historical change was inevitable. Although most Republican senators were willing to back a treaty without Article 10, Wilson refused to compromise. The president instructed his Democratic supporters to vote against any treaty that did not include Article 10. In the end, Wilson failed to obtain the two-thirds vote in the Senate needed to ratify the treaty providing for American membership in the League of Nations.

While steering clear of any political entanglements that would limit American freedom of action, the United States did play an active part in the economic affairs of the world during the 1920s. American farmers began experiencing hard times when the war ended and European demand for their crops declined. Realizing that they were producing more food and fiber than the home market could absorb, farmers quickly looked to foreign markets to find vents for the surplus products of their fields. American industrialists also found that home demand could not keep pace with the capacity of their factories to turn out goods. Some industrialists built branch factories overseas in order to get beyond tariff walls erected by foreign countries to shield their own manufacturers from keen American competition. The larger and more efficient manufacturers, especially those involved in capital-intensive industries, spearheaded a vigorous campaign to penetrate foreign markets. As a result, industrial exports from the United States more than doubled between 1919 and 1929, and important sectors of the American economy became ever more dependent upon foreign sales, even though overseas shipments represented less than 10 percent of the gross national product.

But Japan threatened to close the doors of China against American commerce. During the last third of the nineteenth century, Japan had embarked upon an ambitious modernization program that stimulated visions of imperial grandeur. The swift pace of industrial development enabled Japan to export finished goods in exchange for raw materials and foodstuffs, and the rapid expansion of overseas commerce allowed it to support a growing urban work force on a limited natural resource base. As the country experienced a dramatic population explosion, the well-being of the Japanese people became increasingly dependent upon foreign trade. Japanese leaders, realizing the vital importance of export outlets for their manufactured goods, soon began casting covetous eyes on the potentially vast markets in the Far East. They hoped, in particular, to obtain exclusive business concessions in China.

The United States, however, insisted that the Open Door policy must prevail in China. At the beginning of the twentieth century, U.S. diplomats had persuaded the leading European and Asian powers to pledge their support for the principle of equal commercial opportunity in China. American businessmen believed that, given a fair field and no favor, they would be able to capture a large share of the China market. Disturbed by Japanese demands during World War I for special economic privileges in China, the United States decided in 1922 to host a meeting of the great powers. The U.S. delegates at the Washington Conference succeeded in getting the Japanese to renew their promises to abide by the rule of nondiscriminatory trade in the Far East. In addition, American negotiators secured an agreement to limit the construction of warships in the United States, Great Britain, and Japan. They not only wished to save American taxpayers money by preventing a race for naval supremacy in the Pacific but also hoped that the naval limitation accord would set a precedent for an agreement to reduce the strength of land forces in Europe.

Though unwilling to join the League of Nations, the United States made a concerted effort to promote the postwar economic reconstruction of Europe. Policymakers in Washington did not believe that the United States could remain prosperous unless the European countries continued to serve as good customers for surplus American products. Neither did they think that Europe could recuperate from the devastating effects of four years of fighting if Germany remained impoverished. American states-men therefore urged the British and French to reduce their demands for war reparations so that Germany could resume its role as the center of coal and steel production on the European continent. They also encouraged the former belligerents to work out a disarmament agreement so that heavy military expenditures would not undermine European economic recovery and pave the way for another world war.

Business leaders in the United States participated in the campaign to stimulate the economic rehabilitation of Europe. American financers extended large loans to the Weimar Republic to help underwrite the Dawes and Young plans designed to scale down war reparations to the capacity of Germany to pay. The most internationally inclined members of the American business community also advanced schemes to refund the war debts that the Allies owed the United States in order to lighten the burden of payment on Britain and France. But more than anything else, the big bankers and large manufacturers interested in expanding American trade with Europe advocated a low tariff policy. These business internationalists realized that high U.S. import duties ran counter to the nation's postwar creditor position. They repeatedly pointed out that tariff barriers erected to protect the domestic market made it difficult for European countries to sell their wares in the United States and thereby earn dollars needed both to repay their war debts and to purchase American products.

But Republican political leaders, while insisting that the Allies pay off their war debts, refused to lower U.S. tariffs on European goods. On the contrary, in 1922 they sponsored the Fordney-McCumber Act, which raised import duties, to the delight of small manufacturers interested in safeguarding the home market. Rather than supporting a program of tariff reduction, Republican politicians favored a policy of credit extension. American bankers, unencumbered by government regulations on their overseas activities, made huge loans to foreign nations with small regard for the soundness of their investments. These loans permitted European countries to buy more merchandise than they sold when trading with the United States. Such loans likewise enabled Germany to pay the Allies' war indemnities, and these reparations in turn allowed Britain and France to pay interest on their growing debts to the United States. In other words, the payment of intergovernmental financial obligations as well as the shipment of American goods to Europe depended upon the continued flow of dollars across the Atlantic.

Sophisticated American bankers knew that this could not go on forever. As the European countries fell deeper and deeper into debt, the apprehension grew that they would never be able to service their financial obligations to the United States. American bankers became increasingly worried that they were sending good money after bad, and in 1928 they began cutting back on their overseas investments. After the Great Crash on Wall Street stunned American financial institutions in the following year, the export of capital from the United States slowed to a trickle. Soon there were indications that European nations would default on their debt payments to the United States. As the financial arrangements that had buttressed international trade collapsed, foreign demand for American products dried up. Thousands of factories in the United States shut down, millions of Americans lost their jobs, farm bankruptcies spread throughout the countryside, and bread lines appeared in the larger cities. The day of reckoning had finally arrived. As 1929 came to a close, the whole world plunged into a decade of depression.

The onset of the Great Depression drove countries all around the globe to make desperate efforts to protect their commercial interests both at home and abroad. The United States led the way in 1930, when the Smoot-Hawley Act elevated American tariff rates to record levels, and shortly thereafter Great Britain likewise succumbed to the forces of economic nationalism. The imperial preference system, organized at Ottawa in 1932, erected a high tariff wall around the entire British Commonwealth while establishing low import duties on goods exchanged within the huge British trading bloc. This meant, for example, that American exporters had to pay higher tariff rates than producers in the British dominions or colonies when making shipments to the United Kingdom. As other countries quickly joined in the scramble to shelter their domestic and overseas markets from foreign competition, it was not long before the channels of international trade were choked by a vast maze of currency devaluations, exchange controls, clearing agreements, import quotas, and tariff barriers. This virulent economic warfare caused a colossal commercial collapse. Between 1929 and 1933, the volume of world trade decreased 25 percent, and U.S. exports dropped almost 50 percent in quantity.

The rising tide of economic nationalism also led to a drastic decline in foreign demand for Japanese goods. The United States, which had been the largest consumer of Japanese exports, reduced its purchases from Japan by more than 40 percent between 1929 and 1930. Making matters worse, Europeans joined with Americans in raising tariff rates on Japanese products. Chinese nationalists, in the meantime, began to organize a boycott against the purchase of Japanese goods and to attack Japanese business interests in the province of Manchuria. As the United States replaced Japan as the biggest exporter of commodities to China, Japanese leaders rapidly concluded that the principle of equal commercial treatment had failed to meet the needs of their country. The Japanese army seized Manchuria in 1931, and civilian authorities in Tokyo decided to convert the province into the puppet state of Manchukuo, whose doors would be closed against American trade and investment.

American officials differed in their response to the Japanese move to carve out an exclusive sphere of economic influence in Manchuria. Secretary of State Henry L. Stimson wanted to suspend trade with Japan. If the Japanese were denied access to export markets and raw materials from across the seas, he argued, their industrial structure would quickly collapse. But Pres. Herbert C. Hoover ruled out the option of economic sanctions. Fearful that any attempt to badger the Japanese into withdrawing from Manchuria might lead to a military conflict in the Pacific, Hoover decided that the United States should employ moral suasion rather than economic coercion against Japan. The president hoped that public condemnation would ultimately persuade the Japanese to cooperate with the United States in upholding the principle of nondiscriminatory trade in the Far East. Stimson yielded to Hoover, and in 1932 he announced that the United States would not admit the legality of any forceful change in the territorial integrity of China. By refusing to recognize Manchukuo, the Hoover administration reaffirmed American economic interests in Asia without risking a war with Japan.

When Franklin D. Roosevelt became president in 1933, he promised to put the United States on the road to economic recovery. But he received conflicting opinions regarding what should be done to solve the twin problems of overproduction and unemployment. While members of his "Brains Trust" wanted to isolate the United States from the rest of the world and plan the American economy to create an internal balance between supply and demand, his State Department counselors argued that centralized economic planning would destroy the free enterprise system. Secretary of State Cordell Hull and his aides believed that the restoration of international trade would enable the United States to regain prosperity by exporting the surplus products of its farms and factories. They also thought that the revival of world trade would allow other countries to obtain essential foodstuffs and raw materials by engaging in peaceful commerce rather than military conquest. President Roosevelt shared their internationalist outlook. Although he temporarily experimented with New Deal measures to halt the downward spiral in the business cycle, Roosevelt hoped to achieve a full and enduring prosperity by embarking upon a quest to open New Frontiers in the markets of the world.

The State Department drafted reciprocal trade legislation to obtain the bargaining power needed to promote a revival in international commerce. The Trade Agreements Act, passed by Congress in 1934, authorized the president to make executive agreements that would decrease American import duties as much as 50 percent and provide the United States with reciprocal tariff concessions from other countries. The president did not have to submit these executive agreements to the Senate for ratification, but his authority to conclude them would expire after three years. Pleased with the provisions of the law, the State Department promptly began negotiating trade accords containing the most-favored-nation clause in its unconditional form. This meant that if the United States reduced tariff rates on certain articles imported from a given country, it would automatically lower duties on the same items coming from all other countries that gave Americans equal commercial treatment. The State Department hoped that the unconditional most-favored-nation formula would bring about a universal decrease in commercial restrictions and a vast increase in the volume of world trade.

President Roosevelt and Secretary of State Hull made the reciprocal trade program the centerpiece of U.S. foreign policy. Their primary objective in sponsoring the Trade Agreements Act and securing its renewal for another three years in 1937 was to open foreign markets to help the United States recover from the Great Depression. As other countries reduced their tariffs, American exporters would be able to expand their overseas business. When American tariffs were lowered in return, other countries would be able to increase their sales in the United States and thereby earn dollars needed to purchase American goods. Roosevelt and Hull believed that, besides helping the United States regain prosperity, the reciprocal trade program would help preserve world peace by enabling other countries to enjoy prosperity without using military force to satisfy their economic needs. Although many farmers and small manufacturers opposed the campaign to lower tariff barriers because they feared that cheap foreign goods would flood the American market, business internationalists throughout the United States provided solid backing for the reciprocal trade program. Prominent among these industrial and financial leaders were Alfred P. Sloan of General Motors, Thomas J. Watson of International Business Machines, Winthrop W. Aldrich of the Chase National Bank, and Thomas W. Lamont of the J. P. Morgan Company.

But the rise of the Third Reich presented a fundamental challenge to the American vision of a peaceful and prosperous world. The Treaty of Versailles in 1919 had forced the vanquished Germans to pay huge war reparations and to surrender valuable territorial possessions. These harsh terms sowed the seeds of discontent deep in German soil. Although Adolf Hitler had entered the political arena with hopes of reaping the bitter harvest, his National Socialist Party had failed to attract a large following as long as Germany remained prosperous. But the global depression hit the Weimar Republic particularly hard, and by 1932, one out of every three Germans was unemployed. Most Germans blamed the burdensome war indemnities for their economic troubles, and many looked to the charismatic Nazi leader to free them from the shackles imposed at Versailles. Such were the circumstances that enabled Hitler to become chancellor in 1933 on the promise that he would provide jobs for the German people and restore their fatherland to its place in the sun.

Dr. Hjalmar Schacht, the president of the Reichsbank, quickly developed a whole array of discriminatory trade methods to induce other countries to buy German products. He was able to obtain special commercial privileges for Germany by granting various countries preferential treatment with respect to bond payments, customs quotas, and exchange allocations. Determined to establish an extensive system of bilateral barter, Schacht also invented a special kind of currency, called "aski" marks, for international transactions. Regular reichsmarks could be converted into gold and thereby used to obtain other national monetary units like dollars, pounds, or francs for the purchase of American, British, or French merchandise. But aski marks had no gold value and could be used only to buy specified German goods. As the sole purchasing agent for the entire German nation, Schacht was in a strong bargaining position. He offered other countries a large slice of the German market for their raw materials and foodstuffs, but only on the condition that they would accept aski marks and thus be forced to buy German industrial products. Armed with the funny money he had created, Schacht directed a sustained trade drive to help German exporters outmaneuver their rivals, especially in the markets of southeastern Europe and South America.

At the same time, Hitler was making preparations to use military force to redraw the map of Europe. Hitler embarked upon a vast rearmament program as soon as he came to power in 1933, and before the year ended the Nazi dictator announced that Germany would withdraw from both the Geneva Disarmament Conference and the League of Nations. Two years later, in flagrant violation of the Versailles Treaty, Nazi soldiers marched across the Rhine River and reoccupied the demilitarized area along the western frontier of Germany. These actions created anxiety in the United States. While many American statesmen looked forward to the eventual return to Germany of territory taken at Versailles, none wanted to see a violent revision of European boundaries. U.S. diplomats knew that World War I had intensified class antagonism in Europe and had provoked a communist revolution that had swept away the existing social structure in Russia. They feared that another war of attrition would spark radical uprisings against the old order of capitalism throughout the entire continent.

American diplomats also worried that Japan would join forces with Germany in an attempt to partition the planet into exclusive spheres of economic influence. Their apprehension grew in 1937 when the Japanese launched a full-scale invasion of China and rapidly gained control of every important railroad, industry, and seaport from Manchuria to the Yangtze River. American statesmen became even more alarmed about the Japanese drive to monopolize the China market in 1938, when Tokyo boldly announced plans for the creation of a Greater East Asia Co-Prosperity Sphere linking Manchukuo and China with Japan. Despite their commitment to the Open Door policy in China, however, State Department officials remained cautious as the Japanese army pushed deep into the Middle Kingdom. They opposed calls for imposing economic sanctions that might escalate into a military conflict with Japan. Although they supported a huge naval construction program to prepare the United States for a possible showdown in the Pacific, their abiding wish was that the Japanese would withdraw their troops from China in return for access to markets and resources throughout the world.

The Roosevelt administration, reasoning in like fashion, hoped that the carrot of economic inducement and the club of military intimidation would keep Hitler from taking aggressive steps that might plunge Europe into the flames of war and revolution. On the positive side, Secretary Hull and his associates in the State Department sought to reintegrate Germany into a liberal capitalist international community so that the Third Reich could acquire food supplies and raw materials without recourse to either bilateral barter or territorial conquest. They hoped that Hitler would agree to abandon his discriminatory commercial practices and dismantle his mighty military machine in exchange for the opportunity to sell German industrial goods in an unrestricted world market. On the negative side, President Roosevelt and his foreign policy advisors sponsored an extensive rearmament program to prepare the United States for war and to dissuade Hitler from making any aggressive moves in Europe. They also hoped to deter the Nazis from attacking their neighbors by urging Congress to alter the Neutrality Act so that the U.S. government would be legally free to supply arms to countries fighting to contain Germany.

But the German Führer refused to abandon his dream of achieving mastery over Europe. After rejecting U.S. proposals that he disarm Germany and adopt liberal commercial principles, Hitler began to fulfill his territorial ambitions in Europe. He annexed Austria in March 1938, liquidated Czechoslovakia in March 1939, and then set his sights on Poland. Hitler knew that Britain and France could not obtain weapons from the United States because Congress had refused to lift the ban on the shipment of arms to belligerents. But the Nazi dictator did not want to risk a war with the Western powers until he could remove the danger of a conflict with Russia. Hitler strengthened his strategic position in August 1939 when he concluded a nonaggression treaty with the Soviet Union. A week later, at the beginning of September, he ordered his Wehrmacht to invade Poland, and after hesitating briefly, Britain and France declared war on Germany. Armageddon had arrived. The awesome Nazi army raced across the plains of Poland with incredible speed, and before the month ended, German soldiers had crushed all Polish resistance. Eager to have the Soviet Union share in the spoils of victory, Joseph V. Stalin promptly took advantage of his deal with Germany and dispatched Russian troops to grab the eastern half of Poland.

President Roosevelt and his State Department advisers, frustrated by their failure to prevent World War II, immediately turned their thoughts to the future. If Germany won a quick victory, they feared that Hitler would close the doors of Europe against American trade and investment. If the war became a stalemate, they worried that revolutionary upheavals would threaten capitalism everywhere on the continent. Thus, they decided from the very beginning of hostilities that the United States would have to play a major role in determining the nature of the postwar world. Perhaps the president could serve as a mediator and bring the conflict to a close before either the Nazis or the Communists emerged triumphant in Europe. Perhaps the United States would ultimately have to enter the war in order to have an influential voice at the peace table. The United States must, in any case, avoid making the same mistakes that had doomed American plans at Versailles. Whenever its second chance came, policymakers in Washington concluded, the United States must be prepared to help shape the eventual peace settlement to suit American interests and aspirations.

ONE | POSTWAR PLANNING BEFORE PEARL HARBOR

The outbreak of war in Europe gave American leaders cause for grave concern. Almost immediately after Adolf Hitler ordered his Wehrmacht to invade Poland on 1 September 1939, government officials and business executives in the United States began asking vitally important questions about how the military conflict would affect American economic and strategic interests. They also started contemplating the kind of international order that the United States would wish to see established following the termination of hostilities. On 12 September, the Council on Foreign Relations in New York offered to organize study groups that would examine these fundamental issues and submit their findings to the State Department. The proposal met with the approval of Secretary of State Cordell Hull, and on 16 September he appointed Leo Pasvolsky, an economist and loyal aide, as his special assistant to work on postwar problems.[1] Even as Nazi panzer divisions were storming across Poland, Pres. Franklin D. Roosevelt and his State Department advisers were already looking ahead to the time when they might have the opportunity to create a liberal capitalist world system that would make it possible for the American people to enjoy the blessings of peace and prosperity.

Shortly after the Poles surrendered, Hitler launched a peace offensive in hopes that the British and French would accept German domination of central Europe rather than engage in a fight to the finish. But the Allies rebuffed his peace overtures. They did not believe that a Nazi assault on their fortifications along the French border could succeed, nor did they think that Germany had enough resources to win a prolonged conflict. Assuming that time was on their side, the British and French intended to pursue a defensive strategy. They hoped that the German people, after realizing that victory was beyond their reach, would remove Hitler from power and accept terms that would promise a lasting peace.[2] Spurned by the Allies, the Germans suggested that the United States act as a mediator to bring the war to an end. But President Roosevelt refused to offer his services as a peacemaker when it became apparent that Berlin remained unwilling to propose terms that would be acceptable to London and Paris. After thoroughly examining the situation in October 1939, the State Department concluded that the time was not yet ripe for the president to try his hand at mediation. Roosevelt therefore decided to defer taking any action in hopes that a more opportune moment to initiate peace talks would come in the near future.[3]

But whether American policymakers would ever get the chance to help shape the peace settlement would depend, in part, upon the durability of the nonaggression pact that Hitler and Stalin had made on the eve of the war. Some American statesmen regarded the arrangement as a marriage of convenience that would eventually end in a divorce due to an inherent conflict of interest between Nazi Germany and the Soviet Union. Joseph E. Davies, the former U.S. ambassador in Moscow, viewed the advance of Soviet troops into eastern Poland as an attempt to establish a security perimeter to protect Russia from a possible Nazi attack in the future. "I doubt very much," Davies wrote Secretary of State Hull in October 1939, "that Russia has agreed to give military aid to Germany in the West."[4] But other American diplomats thought that Stalin and Hitler might bury their differences and split the European continent into permanent spheres of influence. A member of the original Brains Trust that had prepared Roosevelt for the presidency, Assistant Secretary of State Adolf A. Berle, was haunted by visions of a Teutonic-Slavic monster dominating the entire Eurasian landscape. "If this nightmare proves real," Berle fretted in September 1939, "you will have two men able to rule from Manchuria to the Rhine, much as Genghis Khan once ruled."[5]

President Roosevelt and his State Department advisers feared that, should the two dictators emerge triumphant, Hitler would put an economic stranglehold on the United States. A day after Nazi tanks and motorized units began roaring into Poland, Secretary of State Hull expressed anxiety that Germany, with the help of Russia, would win the war and then "prevent any Europeans from trading with us except on conditions which Berlin lays down."[6] State Department Economic Adviser Herbert Feis, who had served as the chief technical counselor for American delegates at several international conferences, was equally alarmed about the commercial future of the United States. "Hitler has become so decisive a factor in determining what lies ahead of every producer in this country," Feis warned in October 1939, "that the economist simply cannot think in terms of steady, ordinary development."[7] Just prior to his appointment as an assistant secretary of state, Breckinridge Long likewise worried that Nazi Germany, aided by raw materials from the Soviet Union, would overrun every country in Europe and "exclude us from practically all of those markets."[8] President Roosevelt gave vent to the same apprehension. "Our world trade," he warned in December 1939, "would be at the mercy of the combine."[9]

Determined to prevent such a disaster, President Roosevelt decided to support the Allied war effort from the very outset. Indeed, on the very day that Nazi soldiers began pouring into Poland, the president informed his cabinet that he intended to call a special session of Congress to secure a revision of the Neutrality Act. He wanted the prohibition against supplying arms to belligerent nations repealed to make it possible for Britain and France to obtain warplanes and munitions from the United States. But the president moved cautiously to avoid arousing suspicions that he would involve the United States in the European conflict. Realizing that the American people were reluctant to court danger, Roosevelt proclaimed that he had no intention of sending American boys to fight on the battlefields of Europe. His supporters in Congress carried the day despite claims from their opponents that an annulment of the arms embargo would constitute the first step on the road to war. The new Neutrality Act, signed by the president on 4 November 1939, repealed the arms embargo. Roosevelt was pleased. He hoped that American weapons would enable the British and French to hold their own against the Wehrmacht and that their blockade would produce an economic collapse in Germany and cause the downfall of the Nazi regime.[10]

But State Department officials feared that, even if the Allies did prove able to withstand the expected German assault on the Maginot Line, a long war of attrition would provoke revolutionary upheavals throughout Europe. Having earlier observed European affairs while serving as the U.S. ambassador in Italy, Breckinridge Long fretted in October 1939 that both sides would become so weak that "they could no longer resist the influences of Communism, which would spring not from without but from within the ranks of the hungry, discouraged people in each country."[11] State Department Counselor R. Walton Moore was equally concerned about the possible social and political effects of a protracted military struggle. "My own fear is that a war lasting a year or two years, or which may run on for even a longer time," Moore wrote a colleague in February 1940, "will place the people of Europe in such a terrible position as to produce revolutionary movements looking towards communistic policies."[12] Along with the rest of his associates in the State Department, J. Pierrepont Moffat, the chief of the Division of European Affairs, was filled with anxiety about "the probability of ultimate Bolshevism."[13]

Should a military stalemate create the material conditions for radical uprisings in Europe, American leaders feared that socialists or communists might come to power and close the doors of the continent against U.S. commerce. Alvin H. Hansen, an eminent professor of political economy at Harvard University, emphasized this point in a study prepared for the Council on Foreign Relations. "It may be expected that a European socialist commonwealth would, equally with the Nazi system, develop a highly self-sufficient and virtually closed economy," wrote Hansen in June 1940. "Trade with other areas would be probably limited largely to the same products which Nazi Germany would find it necessary to import. Moreover it may be expected that foreign trade purchases would be centralized in a single commonwealth controlled corporation and distributed throughout Europe from a common center." Hansen concluded that "the difference between the two systems might be relatively small so far as United States trade is concerned."[14] In other words, a stalemate culminating in the rule of radicals in Europe might hurt American commercial interests almost as much as a Nazi victory resulting in German domination of the entire continent.

Furthermore, the business internationalists who participated in the *Fortune* Round Table discussions warned that an extended war, even one ending in an Allied victory, would have profound consequences for the American economic system. "Although England and France have clung to the capitalist system, the outbreak of war has obliged them to regiment internal production and foreign trade to a large extent," the Fortune group lamented in January 1940. "There is a real danger, therefore, that as a result of a long war all the belligerent powers will permanently accept some form of state-directed economic system." If the Europeans continued their restrictive trade practices and if the Japanese employed similar commercial methods in the Far East, the United States might be forced into an economic vacuum. "What interests us primarily," the members of the group explained, "is the longer-range question of whether or not the American capitalist system could continue to function if most of Europe and Asia should abolish free enterprise in favor of totalitarian economics as a result of this war."[15] A few months later, the participants in the *Fortune* Round Table concluded that the United States should be prepared to use its financial power to induce other countries to abandon their stringent controls over foreign trade after the war.[16]

State Department officials were especially worried that, in the event of an Allied victory, Great Britain would employ discriminatory policies that would hamper the development of American commerce. Because of a shortage of dollars, the British were restricting their purchases from the

United States and buying more from countries in the sterling area, where they could pay in pounds. Cordell Hull warned in January 1940 that these British commercial practices might "extend into peacetime, perhaps permanently, to the detriment of American interests."[17] Norman H. Davis, the president of the Council on Foreign Relations and a frequent participant in State Department deliberations, made the same point two days later. "Whereas the British were now bent on fighting a military war," Davis observed, "there were too many evidences that they were at the same time laying the groundwork for fighting an economic war against us."[18] Pierrepont Moffat noted with equal dismay in February 1940 "the increasing evidence that Britain was planning a huge trading orbit within the pound-franc area designed to exclude us."[19] Disturbed by indications that the Allies were determined to create a European commercial union embracing preferential trade arrangements, Leo Pasvolsky lamented a month later that "such a course of developments would place before us some very serious problems."[20]

Concerned about British intentions but determined to lay the foundation for a peaceful and prosperous world after hostilities ceased, President Roosevelt and Secretary of State Hull embarked upon a campaign to secure the renewal of the reciprocal trade program. Hull invited Breckinridge Long to his office in December 1939 and asked him to lead the fight to get Congress to extend the Trade Agreements Act before it expired in June 1940. Hull told Long that the reciprocal trade program must form an elementary part of the eventual peace settlement.[21] Roosevelt agreed. In his State of the Union Address, delivered to Congress in January 1940, the president insisted that "the Trade Agreements Act should be extended as an indispensable part of the foundation of any stable and durable peace." Roosevelt emphasized his belief that the United States should play a leading role in the removal of international trade barriers after the war. "When the time comes," he declared," the United States must use its influence to open up the trade channels of the world in order that no nation need feel compelled in later days to seek by force of arms what it can gain by peaceful conference."[22]

Along with their conviction that the world could not enjoy a lasting peace unless restrictions on international commerce were relaxed, many American businessmen and statesmen believed that the salvation of capitalism in the United States depended upon the retention of the reciprocal trade legislation. The Business Advisory Council, comprising top corporate executives who conferred regularly with Commerce Department officials, aimed to open foreign markets for American commodities in order to avoid the need for government intervention in the economy to keep domestic production in line with home consumption. "The alternative to the present trade agreements program," the Business Advisory Council warned in January 1940, "is a greater dependency on self-containment" that would lead to "a degree of regulatory control destructive of free enterprise."[23] Secretary of State Hull concurred. During his testimony before the Senate Finance Committee in February 1940, Hull argued that the United States should engage in reciprocal trade with other countries rather than pursue an isolationist policy that would require centralized economic planning. "The question of the survival or disappearance of free enterprise," he declared, "is bound up with the continuation or abandonment of the trade agreements program."[24]

Secretary of Agriculture Henry A. Wallace, the founder of a huge seed corn business and the former editor of an influential farm magazine in Iowa, worked hard to obtain agrarian support for an extension of the Reciprocal Trade Act. The American Farm Bureau Federation, the National Grange, and the National Livestock Association had opposed the reciprocal trade bills in 1934 and 1937, and in the following years some farm representatives charged that the State Department aimed to lower import duties on agricultural products in order to gain tariff concessions in foreign markets for industrial goods.[25] During his testimony before the House Ways and Means Committee in January 1940, Wallace asserted that the reciprocal trade program could be "an extremely important factor in the economic reconstruction of the post-war world." He called attention to the fact that farmers in the United States were producing more food than the American people could eat, and he argued that reciprocal trade agreements would open foreign markets for surplus crops while affording American farmers adequate protection in the domestic market.[26] Though many agrarians remained skeptical of his assurance that their interests would be safeguarded, the powerful American Farm Bureau reversed its earlier position and backed the drive to maintain the reciprocal trade program.[27]

President Roosevelt and Secretary of State Hull were elated when Congress voted in April 1940 to extend the Trade Agreements Act for three more years. The senior officers in the State Department immediately congratulated their chief for winning "one of the most brilliant and hard-fought victories of his long career."[28] While expressing his gratitude for the renewal of the reciprocal trade program, Hull gave voice to his deep conviction that a revival of international commerce in the postwar period would enhance the prospects for domestic prosperity as well as world peace.[29] The president shared this belief. "Our nation cannot enjoy sustained and satisfactory prosperity," Roosevelt declared in May 1940, "unless adequate foreign markets exist for our exportable surpluses." Nor could future wars be averted, he argued, if the currents of world trade remained artificially clogged. Roosevelt promised that the advancement of liberal commercial practices would "continue to be a vital part and a dominant purpose of the foreign policy of the United States" so that when the war ended Americans would be ready to "contribute to the economic reconstruction of the world."[30]

Besides supporting the drive to renew the reciprocal trade program, leading bankers and exporters in the United States believed that the country must be prepared to resume lending money abroad to expedite the economic reconstruction of the postwar world. John Abbink, the president of Business Publishers International, argued that the United States must take the lead in financing economic rehabilitation. Addressing the Export Managers' Club of New York in March 1940, Abbink explained that loans from the United States would help other countries recover from the war and make them better customers for American products.[31] Pres. Winthrop W. Aldrich of the Chase National Bank asserted a few months earlier that the United States should also use its financial resources to help stabilize international exchange rates and thereby make it easier for countries to trade with each other.[32] Thomas W. Lamont and Russell C. Leffingwell, senior partners at the House of Morgan, agreed. They thought that the rapid accumulation of gold at Fort Knox would provide the United States with the opportunity to restore international monetary stability when peace returned. "We must use the gold," Leffingwell wrote Lamont in April 1940, "to help Europe in particular and the world at large to reestablish a gold exchange standard based upon the dollar."[33]

The two Morgan partners had already started thinking about the political and economic structure that might emerge in Europe after the war. In a memorandum prepared for Lamont in November 1939, Leffingwell dismissed the idea of a single European government. "The essential attribute of a federal government, or of any government, is the power to levy troops and taxes," Leffingwell asserted. "There is no chance whatever that I can see that any considerable state in Europe will surrender, except by conquest, to any other state or superstate, power to levy troops and taxes." But he did believe that the major European powers would have to cooperate with each other in preserving law and order on the continent. Leffingwell also envisioned the formation of a union among the European nations for the purpose of regulating tariffs. "A political United States of Europe is bunk," he concluded. "What Europe needs is a European customs union; and a regional political understanding for the maintenance of peace."[34] Lamont felt much the same way. "Some sort of economic zollverein in Western Europe is going to be essential," he wrote a British friend in January 1940. "But a political union is quite a different cup of tea."[35]

Business leaders and government officials in the United States were also beginning to grapple with the German question. After having served as a financial adviser to the American delegation at the Versailles Peace Conference in 1919, Lamont had helped draft the Dawes and Young plans to provide loans to Germany and to reduce Allied demands for reparations. But he had little faith in political mechanisms designed to prevent future wars because he doubted the German people would remain peaceful even if they removed their Nazi rulers in the event of defeat. "I cannot seem to differentiate between Hitler and the German people," Lamont complained in February 1940. "They are all imbued with the same idea of domination. I think it is born and bred in the flesh. It dates back at least from the time of Frederick the Great. How to change that attitude, how to cure that *idée fixe* is beyond me."[36] Henry Wallace also believed that the German people had a deeply rooted desire to dominate others. "Those who think that getting rid of Hitler will clear up the situation," he wrote Roosevelt in March 1940, "simply don't know what they are talking about." Yet even though he worried about the aggressive Prussian tradition, Wallace thought it might be possible for "the people of Germany to exorcise the evil spirit of militant imperialism."[37]

Encouraged by the long hiatus in military operations following the conquest of Poland in the autumn of 1939, State Department officials began thinking about the possibility of a peace settlement. Under Secretary of State Sumner Welles believed that the United States must be ready to participate in a peace conference well before the termination of hostilities in order to avoid making the kind of hasty decisions that he felt had been partly responsible for the deficiencies of the Versailles Treaty. In a memorandum for Secretary Hull on 18 December 1939, Welles argued that the time had arrived for the creation of a special State Department committee to formulate American plans for an eventual peace settlement. "It seems to me," he wrote, "that we must be prepared to determine in advance what, if any, contribution the United States itself can make in the

economic and financial fields, as well as in the field of limitation of armaments, when the peace negotiations commence."[38] Hull concurred. After
consulting with his principal associates on 27 December, Hull decided to
organize the Advisory Committee on Problems of Foreign Relations. It
was agreed at the very outset that the committee would study the problems of peace and reconstruction "with primary reference to the best
interests of the United States."[39]

The committee became the focal point of postwar planning in the State
Department during the winter lull in the fighting. Working under the
chairmanship of Sumner Welles, the committee included all of the high-
ranking members of the State Department. Welles quickly developed a
plan for an American peace initiative to bring the war to an end before a
spring offensive by Germany broke the silence on the western front. He
contemplated the formation of a conference of neutrals to be held in
Washington that would provide a mechanism for sponsoring a European
settlement. Welles was optimistic. He told his colleagues on 11 January 1940
that it was highly possible that a critical time would arrive within the next
few months when an organization of neutral countries might offer a peace
proposal.[40] His associates agreed that the president should call the meeting for the ostensible purpose of considering methods of maintaining participants' commercial rights during the war. "But the real and inevitable
discussion," Adolf Berle noted in his diary, "would be whether mediation
could not be proposed, together with possible peace terms, and with an
insistence that the neutrals sit at the peace table with equal right."[41]

The advisory committee was divided into two subcommittees that
met several times during January 1940 to discuss how the world could be
organized to prevent future wars. The members of the Subcommittee on
Political Problems, headed by Welles, concluded that the United States
should belong to a Pan-American group as distinct from a similar
European association that might arise from the defunct League of
Nations. In other words, they believed that political arrangements for the
preservation of peace should be made on a regional basis.[42] But the members of the Subcommittee on Economic Problems, headed by Leo
Pasvolsky, proceeded on the assumption that postwar commercial, financial, and monetary arrangements should be universal in scope.
Determined to lay the economic foundation for world peace, they quickly
prepared an outline of topics that might be discussed at a conference of
neutrals.[43] Pasvolsky explained that the United States would have to provide financial assistance to promote economic recovery in Europe and

thereby prevent social upheavals from creating political instability on the continent.[44] Eager to reopen the channels of international commerce, he pointed out that the main purpose for having consultations with neutral countries was to build the widest possible support for the principle of equal economic opportunity.[45]

After receiving authorization from President Roosevelt, the State Department made overtures to the governments of forty-seven neutral countries. Secretary Hull sent instructions on 10 February 1940 to U.S. diplomatic representatives in the neutral capitals to propose an exchange of views. The dispatch called for talks on "two basic problems connected with the establishment of a sound foundation for a lasting world peace, namely, the establishment of the bases of a sound international economic system, and the limitation and reduction of armaments."[46] Most of the replies were favorable, and many contained a request that the United States set forth its ideas as a basis for discussion. Realizing that other branches of the federal government had an interest in postwar economic arrangements, Pasvolsky recommended the creation of an interdepartmental committee for the purpose of developing an economic agenda for a neutrals conference.[47] Although the proposed interdepartmental committee was never formally established, Hull did confer with other cabinet members about helping with the conduct of economic consultations with the neutrals.[48]

President Roosevelt initiated three parallel moves, in addition to authorizing the overtures to the neutrals, to get the belligerents to make peace before the expected European bloodbath started in the spring of 1940. First, he appointed Myron C. Taylor, formerly the chairman of United States Steel, as his personal representative to the Vatican. Immediately upon his arrival in Rome, Taylor asked Pope Pius XII if he thought the time was ripe for the president to offer his services as a mediator to help end the war.[49] Second, Roosevelt asked James D. Mooney, the president of General Motors Export Company, to go to Germany to find out if the Nazi authorities were interested in participating in a postwar trading system that would assure their country equal access to world markets. After reaching Berlin, Mooney informed Hitler that the president would be happy to act as the mediator for peace negotiations if the belligerents requested his assistance.[50] Third, and most significant, Roosevelt dispatched Under Secretary of State Welles on a special mission to Rome, Berlin, Paris, and London to ascertain attitudes in the four capitals concerning the possibility of concluding a peace settlement.

Welles embarked upon his mission to Europe on 16 February 1940 in hopes of arranging peace talks that would result in a new international order based upon the formula of equal commercial treatment. Though not authorized to make any commitments that would bind his government, Welles was empowered to discuss the need for economic cooperation as well as military security. The under secretary carried to Rome and Berlin a State Department memorandum outlining American desires for the establishment of a global trading network devoted to the unconditional most-favored-nation doctrine. Welles delivered the same message to both Adolf Hitler and Benito Mussolini, the dictator of Italy. If the European powers could find the basis for a just political settlement, he explained, the United States would be willing to participate in discussions aimed at limiting offensive weapons and lowering trade barriers. But while Mussolini assured Welles that he favored liberal commercial relations, Hitler bluntly asserted that unrestricted trade could not cure every problem in the world. The Führer also insisted that Germany must maintain its preferential economic position in central and southeastern Europe.[51]

The Welles mission had, in fact, been doomed from the very outset. Even before the American representative started discussions in Berlin, Hitler had issued a secret order for all German officials to refrain from showing any interest in exploring the possibility of making peace. The Nazi dictator personally told Welles that there could be no peace in Europe until the German army had crushed the will of the Allies to destroy national socialism. Welles found that British and French leaders were equally convinced that they would have to achieve a decisive military victory in order to accomplish their objectives. Although Prime Minister Neville Chamberlain and Premier Edouard Daladier expressed willingness to negotiate with the Nazi regime, neither believed that Hitler would offer a practical plan that would guarantee the future safety of Britain and France.[52] Nevertheless, Welles still clung to the hope that the moment might arrive for the United States to mediate a peace settlement. "I believe there is a slight chance for the negotiation of a lasting peace," he wrote Roosevelt, "if the attack for peace is made upon the issue of security."[53]

When he returned home on 28 March 1940, Welles presented Roosevelt with two long memoranda summarizing his ideas regarding a peace settlement. Welles argued that an Allied attempt to dictate a harsh peace, designed to render Germany permanently incapable of aggression, would prove impractical on both political and economic grounds. If the victorious Allies insisted upon breaking up Germany into several independent states, he warned, the world would be deprived of the benefits of trading with an integrated German economy. Worse yet, he wrote, dismemberment "would inevitably lead to a resurgence of extreme German nationalism and hence would probably lead to another disastrous war." Welles also predicted that the enforced partition and consequent impoverishment of Germany would sow the seeds for radical uprisings in the prostrate country. "With the return of peace, German equipment, German skill, and German industriousness will require large external markets if the most serious unemployment is to be avoided," he explained. "Such unemployment, apart from the suffering it would involve, would provide a veritable forcing bed for communism."[54]

Welles concluded that a cooperative settlement, requiring considerable limitations on national sovereignty, would be necessary to achieve a durable peace. He argued that world security in the postwar era would depend upon the effective control of armaments, equitable methods for settling territorial disputes, and "in the final resort to the existence of sufficient force to discourage or rapidly to prevent any aggressive intention." To accomplish these objectives, Welles envisioned the creation of regional pacts in four or five different areas of the world. A regional council, consisting of representatives from the countries in each area, would be responsible for supervising national disarmament, maintaining a regional police force, and acting as a conciliator in disputes between member states. Welles explained that certain countries would have to belong to more than one regional pact. "If full world security is to be realized," he insisted, "it is of the utmost importance that the United States should" not only participate in a Pan-American security arrangement but "also join in the responsibility for peace in the Pacific region."[55]

But whereas he thought that security problems could best be solved on a regional basis, Welles believed that a world organization would be needed to support international action in the economic field. He pointed out that the major industrial countries, including the United States, would be faced with serious problems when they converted from the production of military hardware to the production of civilian goods. Welles foresaw the onset of another global depression unless there were international agreements to reduce trade barriers after the war. "Probably the greatest contribution to world recovery," he declared, "will be through a freeing of the channels of international trade." Welles was especially convinced of the need for international cooperation to deal with the colonial question. To reconcile countries deficient in food supplies and raw materials to a peaceful world order, Welles hoped that the existing imperial powers would institute an "open door" regime for trade and investment in their non-self-governing territories. He also hoped that they would accept the principle that the world organization should undertake an increasing degree of responsibility for the government and welfare of all dependent peoples.[56]

While Welles was in Europe and with Hugh R. Wilson, the former U.S. ambassador to Germany, serving as vice chairman, the Advisory Committee on Problems of Foreign Relations continued to prepare for a possible peace initiative. But the Subcommittee on Economic Problems decided in early March 1940 against further communication with the neutral governments until the Senate had passed a reciprocal trade bill.[57] In the meantime, positive responses from neutral capitals continued to pour into Washington, and by the time Welles returned home, the United States had received promises from Britain and France that they would discontinue their restrictive commercial practices at the earliest possible moment.[58] Encouraged by these developments, the economic subcommittee quickly drafted a broad statement on international trade for transmission to the neutrals. The twelve-point memorandum, completed just three days before the Senate renewed the Trade Agreements Act in early April 1940, succinctly expressed the American dream of a peaceful and prosperous world based upon liberal commercial principles. "International trade," the document proclaimed, "is vital both to economic well-being within, and enduring peace among, nations."[59]

But events soon overtook the vision. News reached Washington on 9 April that German troops had occupied Denmark and had landed at several points along the Norwegian coast. A few days later, at a meeting called by Welles, it was decided to postpone sending the paper to the neutrals because under the circumstances the Europeans were "too agitated to treat a document of this kind seriously."[60] Yet the Subcommittee on Political Problems continued to make plans for the postwar world. In a series of meetings between 16 April and 6 May, the members of the subcommittee discussed the establishment of a European political organization that would arbitrate disputes on the continent and command a regional police force. They also talked about the possibility of creating a political and economic union among the Danubian countries.[61] But all such discussion ended abruptly on 10 May when Hitler launched a ferocious assault against the western front. Plans for a conference of neutrals also died as German forces raced across Belgium, Luxembourg, and Holland. "There literally is not a neutral in Europe," Hugh Wilson lamented, "which can or will consult with us now."[62]

As Nazi troops made rapid advances toward Paris in the spring of

1940, President Roosevelt tried to dissuade Mussolini from joining hands with Hitler in hopes of recreating the old Roman Empire. The president, believing that the Italian dictator assumed that Germany would defeat Britain and France, told a member of his cabinet that Mussolini "is waiting until the last minute to get into the war so that he can collect after the peace to the utmost but with minimum risk and loss during the war."[63] Despite his pessimism about the chances of keeping Italy out of the fighting, Roosevelt sent four personal messages to Mussolini between 29 April and 30 May in a desperate attempt to discourage him from entering the conflict. The president made thinly veiled threats of American intervention if hostilities spread into the Mediterranean area. He also warned the Fascist leader that, if Italy became involved in the war, the United States would increase its rearmament program and redouble its efforts to ship military supplies to the Allies. But Mussolini was resolved to share in the spoils of victory, and on 10 June Italy declared war on Britain and France. Nazi soldiers marched triumphantly into Paris four days later, and on 17 June France asked Germany for an armistice.[64]

The Nazi blitzkrieg aroused grave apprehensions in the United States about the economic consequences of a German victory. As news of the German advances in Belgium came across the ticker tape during a cabinet meeting on 17 May, President Roosevelt interposed to ask Secretary of Agriculture Wallace to investigate what could be done for American farmers "if England and France were completely wiped out and we lost the entire European market."[65] Wallace went over to the State Department on the next day to discuss the problem, but he found that Secretary Hull "steadfastly refused to do anything but paint a very bad situation."[66] His aides were equally pessimistic. As the British hurried to evacuate their troops entrapped at Dunkirk, State Department officials feared that a triumphant Hitler would close the doors of the continent against American commerce. "If Germany wins this war and subordinates Europe," Assistant Secretary Long warned on 28 May, "every commercial order will be routed to Berlin and filled under its orders somewhere in Europe rather than in the United States."[67]

Spokesmen for the American business community feared that Hitler would not only monopolize the commerce of Europe but that he would also launch an economic blitzkrieg against the United States in the markets of the world. Prominent business leaders such as Bernard M. Baruch, W. Averell Harriman, and Lewis W. Douglas warned that individual American entrepreneurs would be unable to compete successfully in overseas markets against a regimented European industrial system operating under German direction.[68] Leading commercial and financial journals were filled with forebodings that Hitler would employ totalitarian trade tactics in a concerted drive to capture world markets. "If the German military machine is triumphant," *Bankers' Magazine* asked rhetorically, "won't our products be frozen out of world markets?"[69] Some business periodicals believed that the United States might be compelled to adopt Nazi barter methods to survive a trade war with a victorious Germany. "We may be forced to adopt some of the totalitarian ways of doing things," *Business Week* reasoned. "We may have to sacrifice some of the notions we have held about the rights of private property owners to dispose of their property as they see fit."[70]

State Department officials were particularly worried about a postwar Nazi trade drive in South America. In the past, when Schacht had served as the purchasing agent for less than 60 million Germans, the United States had maintained a comfortable lead over the Third Reich in competition for Latin American markets. But if Hitler acquired the power to purchase for more than 300 million Europeans, the Nazi bargaining position would be greatly enhanced. Assistant Secretary Berle quickly began developing plans for the creation of a colossal hemispheric cartel so that individual South American countries would not be forced to exchange their raw materials for aski marks, which could be used only to buy German industrial goods. "The logical riposte," he reasoned on 25 May 1940, "is to work up an agreement by which the twenty-one governments agree that so far as commercial relations are concerned they will deal as a bloc and not individually."[71] In other words, Berle wanted to put the surplus products of the entire Western Hemisphere in a vast export pool so that a huge European consumptive bloc could be met by an equally immense Pan-American productive unit.

Secretary of State Hull promptly created the Interdepartmental Group to Conisder Post-War Economic Problems and Policies. Leo Pasvolsky served as chairman of this informal group comprising representatives from the Departments of State, Treasury, Agriculture, and Commerce. During the first meeting of the Interdepartmental Group held on 27 May 1940, Pasvolsky explained that past thinking about postwar economic problems had been based upon the assumption that the Allies would win the war but that now it was necessary to make plans based on the premise of a German victory. The discussion then turned to the idea of organizing the Western Hemisphere into a gigantic economic bloc to serve as a counterpoise to the expected formation of a German-directed European commercial union. It was agreed that the members of the Interdepartmental Group would work as fast as possible to study what arrangements could be made "to implement cooperation between the countries of the Western Hemisphere in their economic relations with the outside world."[72]

President Roosevelt wanted a quick answer. Just one day after Nazi soldiers goose-stepped into Paris on 14 June 1940, he asked for the combined opinion of the secretaries of State, Treasury, Agriculture, and Commerce regarding the issue of inter-American economic relations.[73] The cabinet heads immediately referred the question to the Interdepartmental Group, but its members held conflicting attitudes. Some advocated a cartel that would act as a clearinghouse with control over all import as well as export transactions between the Western Hemisphere and Europe. Others proposed a more limited arrangement among the American republics, covering only the production and distribution of their main exportable commodities.[74] The cabinet heads favored the less comprehensive alternative, and on 20 June they recommended the establishment of an Inter-American Trading Corporation for the joint marketing of the principal export staples of the New World.[75] Roosevelt wanted to advance the cartel project without delay. During a White House conference on 27 June, he urged that it was "necessary to move forward at once in as much as if England blew up Germany would begin making effective trade agreements in Latin America and we would be on the scene too late."[76]

President Roosevelt and his State Department advisers, however, quickly abandoned the cartel scheme and reaffirmed their commitment to liberal trade principles. After concluding that the proposed marketing monopoly would endanger the American free enterprise system, they decided to use the National Foreign Trade Convention as a forum to preach the gospel of equal commercial opportunity. In a message read before the gathering on 30 July 1940, Roosevelt pledged his continued support for the tenets underlying the reciprocal trade program. "It is naive to imagine," the president admonished, "that we could adopt a totalitarian control of our foreign trade and at the same time escape totalitarian regimentation of our internal economy."[77] Meanwhile, State Department officials worked behind the scenes to counter the growing belief among businessmen that it might be necessary for the federal government to regulate foreign trade so that it could successfully fight a trade war with a German-dominated Europe. Their arguments did not fall upon deaf ears. The final declaration of the convention, following the advice offered by a State Department expert on commercial policy, gave "full support to the unconditional most-favored-nation principle."[78]

But German victories in Europe provided the Japanese with a golden opportunity to implement their plans for a new order in East Asia. Almost immediately after the fall of France in June 1940, the Japanese moved to shut off vital supply routes to the Nationalist forces that were resisting their efforts to subdue China. Japan pressured both the French into closing the Indochina border and the British into halting traffic on the Burma Road in hopes of starving the Chinese Nationalists into submission. Some members of the Roosevelt administration wanted to retaliate with economic sanctions to restrain Japan from making any more aggressive moves in Asia. But the president and most of the senior officers in the State Department opposed any action that might push Japan into invading the Dutch East Indies to obtain essential raw materials. While American leaders were debating the best means of deterrence without provoking further hostilities in the Pacific, the Japanese formally joined hands with Hitler and Mussolini in September 1940 in an alliance designed to intimidate Roosevelt. The three contracting parties to the Rome-Berlin-Tokyo Axis promised, without specifically mentioning the United States, to assist each other if any one of them were attacked by a power not yet involved in either the European war or the Sino-Japanese conflict.[79]

President Roosevelt and his State Department advisers waited to see how the Battle of Britain developed in the autumn of 1940 before taking a hard line against Japan. Secretary Hull urged caution as the Nazis launched wave after wave of attack planes in an attempt to bomb England into accepting German domination of Europe. But as the Royal Air Force fought successfully against the German Luftwaffe in the skies over Britain, Hull decided that the time had come for the United States to get tough in the Far East. Roosevelt concurred. During the closing months of 1940, therefore, the Roosevelt administration took several steps in an effort to restrain Japan without provoking a wider conflict in Asia while Germany was on the rampage in Europe. The U.S. government provided financial assistance to the Nationalists fighting to defend China while imposing an expanding ban on the export of strategic materials to Japan. The United States also strengthened American military forces in the Philippines to deter Japan from attacking the rich European possessions in the East Indies.[80]

But U.S. policymakers remained anxious about the outcome of the contest in Europe. Although the Nazis canceled their plans for an invasion of England after their failure to gain air supremacy, it became increasingly evident that the beleaguered British could not by themselves prevent Hitler and his Axis partners from dividing the world into exclusive spheres of economic influence. Government officials and business leaders in the United States agreed that the survival of American capitalism depended upon the defeat of Nazi Germany. Many with close ties to the president felt that the United States must sooner or later enter the war as an ally of Great Britain. Yet during his campaign for a third term in the White House in the autumn of 1940, President Roosevelt did little to enlighten the American people about the major foreign policy issues confronting the country. Roosevelt said nothing about the risk of war involved in his program of providing extensive assistance to Britain. Nor did he address the fundamental question of what the United States should do if the British proved unable to defeat Germany. Rather, he repeatedly promised that he would do his utmost to keep the nation at peace.[81]

After winning the election in November 1940, however, Roosevelt began maneuvering the country in the direction of war. He not only approved secret talks between American and British military planners, but he also sought authority to lend or lease war materials to any country fighting Germany. The Lend-Lease Act, passed by Congress in March 1941, empowered the president to have military articles manufactured in the United States for any country whose defense he deemed vital to American security. Although a prowar consensus rapidly crystallized in Washington during the next two months, Roosevelt remained devious because he knew that the overwhelming majority of Americans did not want to become involved in the European conflict. The president expanded U.S. naval patrols accompanying convoys across the Atlantic in April 1941 for the purpose of provoking Hitler into firing the first shot. Then he waited for a German submarine to attack an American destroyer. Roosevelt hoped that a naval incident in the Atlantic would generate widespread public support for a declaration of war against Germany. He also hoped that, if Germany could be prodded into taking the offensive, the Japanese would not feel obligated to help their Axis partner fight the United States.[82]

Closing ranks behind the president, business internationalists along the Eastern Seaboard argued that the United States must take the lead in establishing a liberal capitalist world system after the defeat of Nazi Germany. They were glad that massive military spending was stimulating industrial activity and creating jobs for many who had been without work. But they worried that the dual problems of overproduction and unemployment would reappear during the period of demobilization following the war. Hoping to avoid a postwar depression, American business journals repeatedly urged the exportation of surplus products to generate full employment and sustained prosperity in the United States.[83] Pres. Eugene P. Thomas of the National Foreign Trade Council vigorously expressed the outlook prevailing in the American business community. "It is necessary, looking ahead to what will be required of us at the close of the war," he declared in July 1941, "that our Government and business leaders take prompt steps to formulate plans for a postwar economic world order which will insure the resumption of normal, orthodox, international trade and investment."[84]

The need to negotiate a master lend-lease agreement provided the United States with an opportunity to extract commitments from Great Britain to adopt liberal commercial policies after the war. Two days before signing the Lend-Lease Act on 11 March 1941, President Roosevelt asked the Treasury Department to work out a quid pro quo for the shipment of American war materials to England. But rather than seeking postwar economic concessions from the British, Treasury officials proposed that the United States should eventually be repaid in equivalent amounts of tin, rubber, and other products from the British Empire. The State Department, in sharp contrast, wanted to use lend-lease aid as a lever to pry open the Ottawa imperial preference system. Pierrepont Moffat hurried home from his post as U.S. minister to Canada "to preach the gospel that unless we availed ourselves of the present situation to obtain a commitment from the members of the British Empire to modify the Ottawa Agreements after the war, we would ultimately be virtually shut out of our Dominion markets." Upon his arrival in Washington, Moffat found that Sumner Welles and Adolf Berle completely agreed with him. President Roosevelt also wanted to secure economic cooperation rather than material compensation from the British, and on 16 May 1941 he authorized the State Department to negotiate an overall lend-lease agreement with Great Britain.[85]

Assistant Secretary of State Dean G. Acheson called upon a group of Treasury officials on 4 June 1941 and explained how the State Department viewed the lend-lease question. If Americans wished to avoid becoming entangled once again in a serious war-debt problem, Acheson insisted, the United States should not make impossible demands for repayment in either cash or commodities for weapons sent to Great Britain. Instead of pressing for repayments that would deprive the United Kingdom of foreign exchange needed to buy American products after the war, the State Department intended to exploit the British need for American military supplies by demanding as a quid pro quo the abolition of imperial preferences that discriminated against the United States. Acheson explained that he and his colleagues had drafted a preliminary lend-lease accord "in the hope that if we sat down right away before we got too deeply committed in this war with the British they would be willing to go quite a way toward either cracking now or laying the foundation for cracking the Ottawa agreements."[86]

Many in Great Britain, however, aimed to keep the imperial preference system intact when the war came to a close. Complaining that Americans maintained protectionist measures while urging others to adopt liberal commercial policies, conservative leaders like Leopold S. Amery, Lord Beaverbrook, and Robert S. Hudson were determined to maintain a tariff wall around the British Empire. Treasury officials in London, though less committed to the preservation of the Ottawa agreements, believed that it would be necessary to employ discriminatory commercial tactics during the transition period after the war to enable Great Britain to reconvert to civilian production and regain its export trade. As a representative of the British Treasury, John Maynard Keynes, the eminent economist, traveled to Washington in May 1941 to work out the details of a lend-lease agreement. The State Department quickly presented him with a draft of a lend-lease accord that called upon Great Britain to pursue liberal commercial policies after the war. But Keynes was not willing to abandon imperial preferences or other discriminatory trading methods. He insisted that it would be necessary to employ exchange controls to extract preferential treatment for British exports in countries with which the United Kingdom had an unfavorable balance of payments.[87]

State Department officials reacted angrily to Keynes. "Despite the war the Hitlerian commercial policy will probably be adopted by Great Britain," Moffat lamented on 14 July 1941. "If and when we do become involved we shall give all and get nothing, other than a good screwing to our trade by Great Britain."[88] Berle also feared that the British would shut the doors of their empire against American products. "If this is worked out," he grumbled on 17 July, "the only economic effect of the war will be that we have moved a closed-economy center from Berlin to London."[89] On 28 July, Acheson handed Keynes a revised draft for a lend-lease agreement that Roosevelt had approved. Article 7 of the document stated that the terms of the final agreement "shall provide against discrimination in either the United States of America or the United Kingdom against the importation of any product originating in the other country." When Keynes complained that the clause seemed to ban exchange controls and imperial preferences, Acheson retorted that after receiving vast amounts of aid from the United States, the British must "not regard themselves as free to take any measures they chose directed against the trade of this country."[90] Acheson was an Anglophile in many ways, but his commitment to liberal commercial principles was much more important than his affinity for British culture in shaping his response to Keynes.

In a long memorandum on 4 August 1941, Harry C. Hawkins, chief of the Division of Commercial Policy, clearly articulated the anxiety in the State Department concerning the views that Keynes had advanced. "At some stage in the immediate post-war period we are likely to find ourselves in another acute economic depression," he explained. "Unmarketable surpluses of all kinds of goods will accumulate and export markets will be sought to relieve the situation and to stay the decline in the standard of living of our people." Hawkins feared that political pressure would force the American government to relinquish its liberal commercial policy if Great Britain embarked upon a bilateral trade program that discriminated against the United States. "Mr. Keynes apparently does not realize that there is grave danger that the adoption by Great Britain of export-forcing devices essentially similar to those employed by the Germans will necessitate the adoption of similar devices by ourselves," Hawkins warned. "If our postwar economic relations with the United Kingdom should consist of trade warfare involving a contest for markets with no holds barred, such bitterness would be created as to make very difficult, if not wholly impossible, the collaboration in the economic and other fields which is so essential to the reconstruction of the world on a peaceful basis."[91]

Apprehension in the State Department grew when Anglo-American differences over postwar commercial affairs provoked heated controversy during the Atlantic Conference, held 9–12 August 1941 off the Newfoundland coast. After obtaining the approval of President Roosevelt, Sumner Welles proposed that Great Britain and the United States should issue a joint statement that "they will endeavor to further the enjoyment by all peoples of access, without discrimination and on equal terms, to the markets and to the raw materials of the world." But

Prime Minister Winston Churchill replied that it would take at least a week before he could get permission from the self-governing members of the British Commonwealth to do anything that would prejudice the future of the Ottawa agreements for imperial preference. Welles was upset. "If the British and the United States Governments could not agree to do everything within their power to further, after the termination of the present war, a restoration of free and liberal trade policies," Welles asserted, "they might as well throw in the sponge and realize that one of the greatest factors in creating the present tragic situation in the world was going to be permitted to continue unchecked in the post-war world."[92]

But Roosevelt overruled Welles. Hoping to avoid any delay in issuing a public declaration of Anglo-American war aims, the president asked Churchill to try his hand at rephrasing the U.S. proposal regarding postwar economics so that he would not have to wait for approval from the dominion governments. Roosevelt told the prime minister that he could accept temporarily closed arrangements if the British made it clear that they stood for nondiscriminatory trade as an ultimate objective. Churchill then submitted a redraft that inserted the qualifying clause "with due respect for their existing obligations" before the joint pledge to promote equal access to the markets and raw materials of the world. This modification was designed to exempt the Ottawa agreements from the British commitment to sponsor liberal commercial practices. Welles was not satisfied, but Roosevelt told him that the British redraft "was better than he had thought Mr. Churchill would be willing to concede." Welles finally acquiesced, and the British revision of his earlier proposal became the fourth point in the highly publicized Atlantic Charter.[93]

Yet the Anglo-American controversy over postwar commercial policy had not been resolved. Greatly agitated by reports that British newspapers regarded point four in the Atlantic Charter as a loophole for preserving imperial preferences, Secretary of State Hull urged Churchill on 25 August 1941 to make a forthright public declaration indicating that the British and American governments had agreed to do everything in their power to promote liberal trade practices.[94] Churchill refused. Then Hull and his aides exerted pressure on the British to conclude a master lend-lease accord that would serve as a model for agreements with all other countries.[95] Lord Halifax, the British ambassador in Washington, finally presented a redraft of Article 7 on 17 October, but State Department officials thought that this proposal "was too vague and did not furnish a sufficient commitment."[96] They promptly began preparing a counterproposal designed to pin the British down, and on 2 December Acheson handed Halifax a revised draft that had been approved by the president. The new American formulation of Article 7 called for joint action directed "to the elimination of all forms of discriminatory treatment in international commerce and to the reduction of tariffs and other trade barriers."[97] But the British continued to balk.

At the same time that U.S. diplomats had been trying to prevent the British from drawing their dominions and colonies into a closed economic bloc, they had also been working to keep Great Britain from recognizing Eastern Europe as a Russian sphere of influence. Their apprehensions about the fate of Eastern Europe began when Stalin responded to the fall of France in June 1940 by sending Soviet troops to occupy Latvia, Lithuania, and Estonia. The State Department immediately protested the annihilation of independence in the three Baltic countries. "Our failure to recognize Soviet conquests just now," wrote Loy W. Henderson, the assistant chief of the Division of European Affairs, "may possibly place another card in our hands when, if ever, a conference regarding the future of Europe takes place."[98] But his colleagues feared that the British would bargain away Eastern Europe in an effort to induce Stalin to switch his allegiance from Germany to Britain. Ambassador Laurence A. Steinhardt reported from Moscow in October 1940 that the British had offered, pending consultations after the war, to give "de facto recognition" to the Soviet acquisition of eastern Poland, Bessarabia, Bukowina, and the three Baltic States.[99]

Though Stalin steadfastly refused to do anything that might arouse the wrath of Hitler, the British decided in early June 1941 to make another overture to the Kremlin. Prime Minister Churchill told Ivan Maisky, the Soviet ambassador in London, that if Germany invaded Russia, Great Britain would be willing to provide economic and military aid to the Soviet Union. Maisky replied that such help would be more welcome if preceded by British recognition of Soviet rule in the Baltic countries.[100] Sumner Welles promptly cautioned Ambassador Halifax that Great Britain should not attempt to achieve a rapprochement with Russia at the expense of the Baltic states. But his admonishment had little effect. Halifax told Welles that he "could conceive of a situation developing in which the British Government, in order to form close relations with the Soviet Union, might desire to take some steps with regard to recognizing the Soviet claims with regard to the Baltic States."[101] When Nazi troops attacked Russia on 22 June, Churchill seized the opportunity to dispatch a British military mission to Moscow. Stalin welcomed the

British emissaries, but he told them that wholehearted cooperation would require a political agreement.[102]

The German assault on the Soviet Union immediately raised questions about the future status of Poland. The Polish government-in-exile, which had been biding time in London, eagerly opened negotiations with Ambassador Maisky on 5 July 1941 in hopes of restoring the prewar borders of Poland. But Maisky indicated that the Kremlin would insist on boundaries closely corresponding to the Curzon Line, which the British had advocated at the peace conference in 1919 as the ethnographic frontier of Poland. The State Department feared that, in an effort to buy Russian friendship, Great Britain would press the Poles to make territorial concessions to the Soviet Union. "It is now evident that preliminary commitments for the postwar settlement of Europe are being made, chiefly in London," Adolf Berle warned Roosevelt on 8 July. "You will recall that at Versailles President Wilson was seriously handicapped by commitments made to which he was not a party and of which he was not always informed." Berle suggested that the British should be told that "we could not be bound by any commitments to which we had not definitely assented."[103]

The Roosevelt administration quickly acted to keep the British from making any secret deals with the Russians. On 11 July, the president instructed Harry L. Hopkins, his close confidant who was in London making arrangements for the Atlantic Conference, to inform Churchill that there must be no economic or territorial arrangements between Great Britain and the Soviet Union.[104] In a direct message sent to Churchill three days later, Roosevelt asked the prime minister to issue a public statement "making it clear that no postwar peace commitments as to territories, populations or economics have been given."[105] But Churchill made no reply. During the following weeks, the State Department received disturbing reports that the British were encouraging the Soviets to believe that after the war London would support the creation of a Pan-Slavic federation in Eastern Europe under Russian hegemony.[106] Sumner Welles revealed his apprehension at the Atlantic Conference when he met privately with Alexander Cadogan, the permanent under secretary of state for British foreign affairs. During their conversation on 9 August, Welles reminded Cadogan that Churchill had not yet replied to the American request for a public declaration affirming that no postwar commitments had been made by the British government. Cadogan then assured Welles that Great Britain had not entered into any agreements concerning frontiers or territorial readjustments.[107]

But the British decision to send Foreign Secretary Anthony Eden to confer with Stalin aroused renewed anxiety in Washington. The State Department worried that Eden would make territorial concessions to Russia in order to quiet Soviet demands for Britain to open a second front on the European continent. After getting approval from the president, Secretary Hull instructed the U.S. ambassador in London on 5 December 1941 to dissuade Eden from making any postwar commitments contrary to the Atlantic Charter pledge to respect the principle of national self-determination. "Above all," Hull stressed, "there must be no secret accords."[108] When Eden arrived in Moscow, Stalin proposed a secret treaty that would recognize Soviet territorial claims in Eastern Europe. Eden responded that the Russian proposal would cut across the Atlantic Charter and that Great Britain would not make any deals with the Soviet Union without first consulting the United States. The talks ended on an ominous note when Stalin remarked that he had thought that the Atlantic Charter was directed against the Axis powers but that it was beginning to look as if it were directed against the Soviet Union.[109]

President Roosevelt, though hoping to postpone consideration of territorial questions until after the war, had already concluded that the United States would have to join with Great Britain in the deployment of military force to ensure a lasting peace. During his private conversations with Churchill off the coast of Newfoundland in August 1941, Roosevelt explained that he "would not be in favor of the creation of a new Assembly of the League of Nations, at least until after a period of time had transpired and during which an international police force composed of the United States and Great Britain had an opportunity of functioning." Churchill observed that the extreme internationalists would demand a world security organization, but the president replied that "the time had come to be realistic."[110] After Hopkins argued that the American people desired some form of international organization, Roosevelt agreed to subscribe to "the establishment of a wider and permanent system of general security" as an ultimate goal. But he insisted that during the transition period following the war, the United States and Great Britain would have to disarm the Axis countries and police the world.[111]

Army and navy leaders soon began planning for the maintenance of a strong American military establishment to preserve order in the postwar world. Officials in the Navy Department believed that the powerful fleet of warships being assembled to defeat Hitler and his Axis partners should be maintained to deter future aggressors. On 27 October 1941, Under Secretary of the Navy James V. Forrestal, formerly the president of a big New York investment bank, explained that the United States must have a large postwar navy "to curb the ruffians of the world." Top army officers were also starting to think about their role in the deterrence of aggression after the war. On 12 November, Chief of Staff George C. Marshall recalled to active duty Brig. Gen. John M. Palmer to advise him on postwar plans for the army. Marshall and Palmer had bitter memories of the delays and confusion involved in the military demobilization following World War I and the subsequent failure to get congressional approval of War Department plans for a permanent armed force of 500,000 men backed by a system of universal military training. They were determined to avoid repeating past mistakes and to build public support for a strong peacetime army.[112]

The study groups formed by the Council on Foreign Relations were also engaged in postwar planning during the half-year preceding the Japanese attack on Pearl Harbor. Their clear articulation of American economic aims contemplated the establishment of a liberal capitalist world system based upon the principle of equal commercial opportunity. They looked forward to the reintegration of Germany and Japan into the global trading network, and they believed that the European powers should help lay the economic foundation for an enduring peace by giving all countries access to their colonial markets.[113] In their formulation of U.S. strategic goals, the study groups advocated the disarmament of the Axis nations and the deployment of Anglo-American sea and air forces to police the world. They also envisioned the eventual organization of a wider system of international security that would be based upon either a strong universal agency or a series of regional groupings working closely with the world association.[114] The Council on Foreign Relations promptly sent the State Department the studies that had been prepared by these groups.

The State Department had already started organizing its own research staff to investigate postwar problems. Secretary Hull created the Division of Special Research on 3 February 1941 and designated Leo Pasvolsky to serve as its chief. Pasvolsky gradually assembled a small staff of historians, economists, foreign service officers, and political scientists. Harley A. Notter, who had earned a Ph.D. in American history at Stanford University and had written a book on the foreign policy of Woodrow Wilson, headed the political section. Although the research division began operating without a superior committee to guide its work or to make use of its recommendations, its members pressed ahead with the preparation of studies dealing with various postwar subjects.[115] They proceeded on the central presupposition that the United States would enter the war and emerge victorious. "The most sweeping assumption which must of course be made in our work," Notter privately acknowledged on 24 September 1941, "is that Germany will be defeated and that England with participation on the part of the United States will win the war by a clear and uncompromising victory enabling us to disarm the enemy."[116]

The senior officers in the State Department, however, feared that they might lose control of the postwar planning process. They remained convinced that the American capitalist system could be preserved only through a policy of commercial expansion abroad and not through a program of economic reorganization at home. But some New Deal reformers advocated national economic planning in order to create a balance between supply and demand within the United States. Several agencies of the federal government had independently started working on the problem of how to avoid a depression when the time came to convert industrial plants back to peacetime production. The State Department was especially concerned about the activities of the Economic Defense Board, which had been established in July 1941 under the chairmanship of Vice Pres. Henry A. Wallace.[117] Although Wallace had been a staunch proponent of unrestricted international commerce, he was not adverse to federal spending on domestic programs to maintain full employment in the United States. Secretary of State Hull worried that government officials who wanted to expand the New Deal would gain control over the formulation of postwar economic policy. "If they really do get in the saddle," he fretted in September 1941, "they will adopt a closed economy and will not even try to prevent Britain from pursuing a policy of bilateralism."[118]

The State Department moved swiftly to consolidate its control over all phases of the preparatory work on postwar foreign policy. In early October 1941, Hull and Welles went to the White House and persuaded Roosevelt to authorize the creation of an Advisory Committee on Postwar Foreign Policy with the secretary of state serving as chairman and the under secretary of state as vice chairman. The Division of Special Research, together with other government agencies and outside organizations, would conduct research and draft memoranda for the advisory committee to use in making recommendations to the president. The mounting crisis in the Pacific caused a delay in implementing the proposal. But three weeks after Japan attacked Pearl Harbor on 7 December 1941, Roosevelt approved a list of names that Hull had suggested for membership on the board. The list included the following high-ranking State Department officials: Hull, Welles, Berle, Acheson, Feis, Hawkins, and Pasvolsky. It also included prominent figures from outside the State Department, such as Norman H. Davis, the president of the Council on Foreign Relations; Myron C. Taylor, the special U.S. envoy to the Vatican; Isaiah Bowman, the president of Johns Hopkins University; Anne O'Hare McCormick, a columnist for the *New York Times;* and Hamilton Fish Armstrong, the editor of *Foreign Affairs,* an influential magazine published by the Council on Foreign Relations.[119]

American planning for the postwar world had evolved in the year prior to Pearl Harbor. During the winter lull in the fighting after the German invasion of Poland in September 1939, President Roosevelt and his State Department advisers hoped to mediate a peace settlement based upon the principle of equal commercial treatment. But their plans came to naught when Germany launched a blitzkrieg along the western front. Fearing that the Germans might score a quick victory over Britain following the fall of France in June 1940, U.S. policymakers toyed with the idea of organizing the Western Hemisphere into a gigantic economic bloc that could compete with a Nazi-directed European commercial union. Government officials and business leaders in the United States were relieved when Germany failed to bomb the British into submission. But a consensus rapidly crystallized in Washington during the spring of 1941 that the United States would have to enter the war to prevent the Axis powers from dividing the globe into exclusive spheres of economic influence. Assuming that the Allied powers would be victorious, the State Department began assembling a group of political and economic advisers in the autumn of 1941 to draft plans for the president to implement when the time came to build a new world order. They were especially determined to prevent Great Britain from pursuing discriminatory commercial policies and to keep the Soviet Union from dominating the countries of Eastern Europe.

TWO | OPENING THE WORLD

As they began their deliberations shortly after the attack on Pearl Harbor, postwar planners in the United States had a clear conception of their broad economic objective. They were determined to establish a liberal capitalist world system based upon the principle of equal commercial opportunity. American leaders believed that a vast array of commercial restrictions and discriminatory trade practices had contributed both to the onset of the Great Depression and to the start of World War II. They hoped that a freer flow of trade, with all countries having equal access to raw materials and commodity markets around the globe, would provide the foundation for a peaceful and prosperous family of nations. Except in the financial and monetary fields, the State Department took the lead in making economic preparations for the postwar world. Secretary of State Cordell Hull and his colleagues received strong support from President Roosevelt as well as from influential business internationalists. Although they occasionally disagreed over the means to achieve their ends, American policymakers shared a basic outlook that shaped their plans for a new international economic order.

Government officials and business leaders became increasingly worried that the United States would once again suffer from the twin problems of overproduction and unemployment when war plants converted to civilian production and soldiers returned from the battlefields. But they had different ideas about how to avoid a postwar depression. Some thought that the national government should plan the American economy to create an internal balance between supply and demand. Others believed that the federal government should sponsor a massive public works program to generate millions of jobs. John Maynard Keynes, the influential British economist, had popularized the concept of deficit spending to counteract a downswing in the business cycle. If the government borrowed money and spent it to create jobs, Keynes argued, the resulting demand for goods and services would stimulate an upswing in the business cycle. The wartime experience of the United States supported his analysis. The federal government was borrowing money to buy weapons and pay soldiers, and the country was enjoying full employment and a rising standard of living.

Although some American business leaders were prepared to support a large federal spending program to avoid a postwar depression, many others criticized the ideas of Keynes and his disciples in the United States. Russell C. Leffingwell, a penetrating thinker who bore primary responsibility for financial analysis at the House of Morgan, articulated in vivid prose the prevailing view in the American business community. He repeatedly warned that government spending would act like a habit-forming drug that would be easy to start but hard to stop. "The conception of government spending as a balance wheel to be expanded in a depression and contracted in a boom is contrary to human nature," Leffingwell asserted in May 1943. "It becomes just a rivers and harbors scandal: just a pork-barrel. It is almost impossible to fire the employees who get jobs from the government. The chief spender finds it an easy way to buy votes. It corrupts our rulers and it corrupts the electorate."[1] Rather than becoming addicted to the narcotic of government spending after the war, Leffingwell reasoned, the United States should cultivate foreign markets to maintain domestic prosperity.

President Roosevelt also viewed overseas commercial expansion as a way to promote full employment without having to borrow huge sums of money to finance massive public works projects. Roosevelt had reluctantly agreed to increase government spending on domestic programs in order to counteract the recession of 1937–38, but he never became a convert to Keynesian economic doctrines. Concerned about the growing federal deficit as wartime expenditures mounted, Roosevelt told his budget director that he intended to commit the government to a debt-retirement program when the war ended.[2] The president aimed to generate full employment by opening foreign markets to absorb the surplus products of American farms and factories. "To increase jobs after this war," he declared in October 1944, "we shall have to increase demand for our industrial and agricultural production not only here at home, but abroad too." Roosevelt added that he thought the foreign trade of the United States could "treble after the war—providing millions of more jobs."[3]

Even those State Department officials who maintained a flexible attitude with regard to the question of deficit spending viewed commercial expansion abroad as a way of avoiding centralized economic planning at home. In his testimony before a special congressional committee on postwar economic policy and planning in November 1944, Assistant Secretary Dean G. Acheson clearly explained how the State Department hoped to solve the problem of domestic overproduction. "We could argue for quite a while that under a different system in this country you could use the entire production of the country in the United States," Acheson observed. "If you wish to control the entire trade and income of the United States, which means the life of the people, you could probably fix it so that everything produced here would be consumed here." But he warned that such an approach to the problem would destroy the American free-enterprise system. "Therefore, you find you must look to other markets and these markets are abroad," Acheson insisted. "The first thing that I want to bring out is that we need these markets for the output of the United States. If I am wrong about that, then all the argument falls by the wayside, but my contention is that we cannot have full employment and prosperity in the United States without the foreign markets."[4]

President Roosevelt and his State Department advisers wanted to expand the volume of international trade to lay the foundation for world peace as well as American prosperity. They believed that countries like Germany and Japan would have to export industrial goods after the war to earn foreign exchange required to pay for essential imports of food and raw materials. If such countries could not satisfy their economic needs by engaging in peaceful commerce, they might feel compelled once again to embark upon programs of imperial conquest. American policymakers realized that the removal of restrictions on international trade would not guarantee world peace. But they did not believe that any political or military agreements to maintain peace could succeed if the channels of international commerce remained clogged. The Special Committee on the Relaxation of Trade Barriers, in a report submitted in December 1943, succinctly summarized the State Department viewpoint: "A great expansion in the volume of international trade after the war will be essential to the attainment of full and effective employment in the United States and elsewhere, to the preservation of private enterprise, and to the success of an international security system to prevent future wars."[5]

State Department officials were determined to obtain British support for their plans to establish a new international order based upon multilateral trade. The United States and the British Empire combined accounted for more than half of the trade of the entire world. If the British decided to join hands with the United States in adopting liberal commercial policies after the war, other countries would have a strong incentive to participate in the global trading network. But if the British chose to close their empire tighter and to expand their vast sterling bloc, other countries might feel compelled to employ discriminatory commercial methods as weapons in the ensuing scramble for export markets. "One of the decisive factors in the economic future of the world," Leo

Pasvolsky of the Division of Special Research explained on 12 December 1941, "will be whether this country and Great Britain move, after the war, toward economic peace or toward economic war. Each of our countries is so important economically that if the policies of economic peace fail of adoption in one they will necessarily be doomed in the other and, therefore, everywhere in the world."[6]

Almost immediately after the attack on Pearl Harbor, the State Department resumed its efforts to negotiate a master lend-lease agreement with Great Britain. The American draft of Article 7 called upon the United States and Great Britain to cooperate in securing "the elimination of all forms of discriminatory treatment in international commerce" and to work together for "the reduction of tariffs and other trade barriers." The American draft also provided for the opening of detailed conversations between the two countries to reach an agreement on the best means of attaining these objectives. On 9 December 1941, the State Department instructed Ambassador John G. Winant to tell Prime Minister Churchill that an Anglo-American accord should be completed without delay because President Roosevelt would soon have to ask Congress for additional lend-lease aid for Great Britain. "It is of the utmost importance," the message emphasized, "that no factor such as the absence of a Lend-Lease Agreement between the two governments should operate to cause any reluctance in Congress to furnish the necessary funds." But the British tried to evade the issue, and on 29 December, Secretary of State Hull repeated the warning that another lend-lease appropriations bill would soon come up in Congress, and he would be asked to explain why the British had not signed the proposed agreement.[7]

When the British continued to balk, President Roosevelt decided to throw his own weight behind the State Department. Dean Acheson, after obtaining authorization from the White House on 29 January 1942, informed the British ambassador that the president wanted the United Kingdom to accept the American draft of Article 7 without further delay. Nevertheless, in a telegram sent from London a few days later, Ambassador Winant reported that the British cabinet had discussed the issue and had decided to make a counterproposal. Winant added that the British refusal to agree to Article 7 in its present form was due to a mistaken assumption that the president had little interest in the matter.[8] Roosevelt quickly corrected that misconception. In a personal message to Churchill on 4 February, the president urged that the British government promptly agree to the American draft regarding lend-lease. "I am convinced," Roosevelt

[handwritten margin note: explicit example of an early trade agreement]

warned, "that further delay in concluding this agreement will be harmful to your interests and to ours."[9]

But the British did not want to make a firm commitment that would require them to abandon all forms of discriminatory commercial arrangements. In a cable to Roosevelt on 7 February, Churchill stated that after its second meeting on the subject, his cabinet was "even more resolved against trading the principle of Imperial preference as consideration for Lease-Lend."[10] The British then proposed an exchange of notes that would qualify Article 7 and exclude the question of imperial preferences from future discussions concerning the implementation of the lend-lease agreement. Roosevelt made one more attempt to get the British to acquiesce. In a message to Churchill on 11 February, the president insisted that nothing should be excluded from future Anglo-American discussions regarding postwar commercial policy. But he also assured Churchill that the United States was not asking that the British government make "a commitment in advance that Empire preference will be abolished."[11] With that stumbling block removed, the United Kingdom joined with the United States on 23 February 1942 in signing a lend-lease agreement without any reservations diluting Article 7.

Shortly after the lend-lease agreement was concluded, however, the State Department received information that the British were reluctant to embrace liberal commercial principles because they feared that Congress would refuse to lower U.S. tariff rates even if they abandoned their discriminatory trade practices. "It seems almost certain," the U.S. embassy in London reported in April 1942, "that if we are not in a position to reduce our general tariff the British will insist on reserving the right to use discriminatory exchange controls with bilateral trading arrangements."[12] J. Pierrepont Moffat, the American minister in Ottawa, made a similar observation after his discussions in October 1942 with Canadian trade authorities. Moffat warned that Canada would not be willing to accept lower imperial preferences until the United States reduced its import duties.[13] But American diplomats hoped that the British would follow if the United States took the lead in lowering commercial barriers. "Provided that we are in a position to 'deliver the goods' in the matter of tariff reduction," the U.S. embassy in London reported in December 1942, "there is every reason to believe that our position on preferences and discriminations will be met."[14]

State Department officials believed that the British would view the upcoming debate in Congress over the renewal of the Trade Agreements

Act as an acid test of U.S. intentions concerning postwar commercial policy. "The British will consider it a great straw in the wind as to whether we are going on with a liberal policy or not," Ray Atherton, the chief of the European Division, noted in December 1942. "If we do not, England will adopt plans based on Keynes' plan for bilateral agreements."[15] Convinced that the British would regard the debate over reciprocal-trade legislation as a sign of future American commercial policy, Secretary of State Hull appeared before congressional committees in April and May 1943 to argue for another three-year extension of the Trade Agreements Act.[16] At the same time, Thomas W. Lamont of the J. P. Morgan Company used his influence to get Republican senators and representatives to back the renewal of the reciprocal trade program.[17] His efforts produced tangible results. With strong bipartisan support, Congress voted in June 1943 to extend the Trade Agreements Act, though only for two more years. President Roosevelt and Secretary Hull were pleased, and they both thanked Lamont for his help.[18]

The renewal of the reciprocal trade program set the stage for the opening of Anglo-American discussions on long-range economic policy to achieve the objectives set forth in Article 7 of the master lend-lease agreement. After receiving an invitation from the State Department, a delegation of senior British officials arrived in Washington in September 1943 to begin informal talks to explore ways of reducing trade barriers and eliminating commercial discriminations. The membership of the U.S. delegation, headed by Myron C. Taylor, was drawn primarily from the Advisory Committee on Postwar Foreign Policy.[19] The central point at issue was whether it would be possible to conclude at a large international conference a multilateral arrangement providing for comprehensive action with respect to tariffs, preferences, and quotas. The British argued that a multilateral approach would be necessary due to the difficulties they expected to encounter at home in dealing with preferences. But the Americans thought it would be hard to find a suitable formula for multilateral tariff reductions. As an alternative, they suggested the possibility of holding an international convention to secure a limited accord that would provide for the eventual elimination of all quotas but would leave action covering tariffs and preferences to bilateral negotiations based upon the most-favored-nation principle.[20]

After further study, however, the State Department concluded that the most promising method of creating a framework for the expansion of world trade would be the negotiation between as many countries as possible of a broad multilateral agreement on commercial policy.

"Simultaneous action on trade barriers everywhere," John M. Leddy of the Trade Agreements Division explained in February 1944, "would make it easier for each country to relax restrictions on its imports because of the certain knowledge that many other countries would, at the same time, be opening up outlets for its exports."[21] The Post-War Programs Committee agreed that a comprehensive commercial convention should be held as soon as possible. "The process of negotiating trade-barrier reductions on a country-by-country and product-by-product basis is necessarily time-consuming," the committee reasoned in March 1944. "The present need is for rapid and widespread action in the trade-barrier field for the creation now, before post-war trade can be crystallized behind existing trade barriers, of conditions in which each country will be relatively certain of its future export markets."[22]

Under-Secretary of State Edward R. Stettinius hoped to promote Anglo-American economic cooperation when President Roosevelt decided that he should go to London to compare notes with British leaders on various subjects.[23] While spending three weeks in England during April 1944 engaging in exploratory talks with Prime Minister Churchill and top officials from the Foreign Office and Treasury, Stettinius repeatedly pressed for the early resumption of Anglo-American economic discussions to implement Article 7 of the lend-lease agreement. But Churchill refused to give him any assurance that joint conversations regarding postwar commercial policy could be resumed anytime in the near future. When British officials expressed concern about their deteriorating financial position, Stettinius warned them that lend-lease aid would draw to a close at the end of the war.[24] The implications were clear. The United States and Great Britain would have to make some other financial arrangement so that the British could continue importing American goods after the war.

Stettinius and his State Department colleagues believed that the British would need American credits amounting to several billion dollars to overcome a serious balance of payments problem in the first years after hostilities ceased. They realized that the United Kingdom had already lost a substantial part of the income from overseas investments that had been used in the past to pay for essential imports. Anticipating that Great Britain would experience a reduction in proceeds from merchandise exports and shipping services in the immediate postwar years, State Department planners assumed that the British would need financial aid in order to purchase American products required for industrial reconstruction and social reform.[25] "It is therefore vital," Stettinius concluded after his conversations with British officials in London, "that our two Governments begin to plan now for financing arrangements, perhaps in the form of long-term credits, to ensure the continued flow of food and other necessary supplies from this country to Britain without a prolonged transition period of doubt and confusion which would work great hardships on the economics of both countries."[26]

But the British were reluctant to make any financial arrangements that would add to their burden of postwar debt. They hoped to receive large amounts of lend-lease aid during the phase two lend-lease period between the defeat of Germany and the end of the war in the Pacific. They also hoped to receive interest-free loans for postwar reconstruction from the United States. During a conversation in Washington in June 1944, British officials told Stettinius that their financial position would be so weak at the end of the war that it would be impossible for them to take on any interest-bearing obligations. Stettinius replied that the best they could expect from Congress would be a long-term credit at a very low rate of interest.[27] A month later, when a British official again referred to the difficulty that his countrymen would have in accepting any interest-bearing obligations, Stettinius said that with the vast resources of their empire, they should be able to find some way to service a debt in the neighborhood of $5–10 billion over a thirty-year period at 2 percent interest.[28]

Secretary of State Hull wanted to use financial aid, whether through the continuation of lend-lease shipments or the extension of low-interest credits, as a bargaining device to lure the British into adopting a liberal trade program. In a memorandum on 8 September 1944, Hull notified Roosevelt that Churchill might approach him about the seriousness of Great Britain's financial situation at their forthcoming meeting in Quebec. "It seems to me that it is in the interests of the people of the United States that we extend such credits and other financial assistance to the United Kingdom as may be necessary to reconstitute and restore what has traditionally been the largest market for American goods," Hull explained. "At the same time it is of fundamental importance to the interests of the United States and to the establishment of the kind of economic conditions which we hope to see prevail in the post-war world that we not blindly grant credits to the United Kingdom without taking into consideration the kind of commercial policy and trade practices which it may adopt."[29]

During his conference with Prime Minister Churchill at Quebec, however, President Roosevelt committed the United States to a generous phase two lend-lease program without obtaining any assurances that Great Britain would adopt a liberal postwar commercial policy. Churchill raised the issue on 14 September 1944 by saying he hoped the president would agree that, during the period between the end of the war in Europe and the defeat of Japan, it would be proper for Britain to continue receiving lend-lease supplies needed to reconvert to civilian production. The prime minister pointed out that the United Kingdom would have to reestablish its export trade so that it could pay for necessary imports. He therefore insisted that "the United States should not attach any conditions to supplies delivered to Britain on Lend-Lease which would jeopardize the recovery of her export trade." Convinced that the British were broke, Roosevelt quickly agreed with Churchill that the United Kingdom should receive about $6.5 billion in lend-lease aid during the first year of phase two. They also agreed that a joint Anglo-American committee should be set up to determine the exact amount of lend-lease material that would be shipped to Britain in light of the developing military situation.[30] *↳ president overrides Hull*

Hull was furious. He and his colleagues had been postponing discussion regarding phase two lend-lease aid for the United Kingdom in the hope of extracting a firm commitment from the British with respect to postwar commercial policy. But Roosevelt had given away that bait without bothering to consult the State Department. Though deeply disturbed and unable to sleep, Hull still hoped to regain some bargaining power.[31] "I note from your record of conversation with the Prime Minister," he wrote the president on 17 September, "that lend-lease aid during the war with Japan will exceed, in food, shipping, et cetera, the strategic needs of Great Britain in carrying on that war and will, to that extent, be devoted to maintaining the British economy. Would it not be well to make clear to the Prime Minister at this time that one of the primary considerations of the Committee, in determining the extent to which lend-lease might exceed direct strategic needs, would be the soundness of the course adopted by the British Government with a view to restoring its own economy, particularly with regard to measures taken to restore the flow of international trade?"[32]

In a long memorandum he handed the president two weeks later, Hull summarized the State Department position concerning phase two negotiations with the United Kingdom. "Naturally we don't know at this time the extent to which public opinion and Congress will support a program for the reduction of trade barriers, which in my opinion is indispensable to world peace," Hull wrote. "What is important, however, is that the British Government agree *now* that they will not be the obstacle if we are prepared to move along in that direction. In other words they should be prepared to go along with us to the extent that we find it possible to proceed, and they should make it easier, not harder, for us politically." Hull noted that he and his associates had made repeated efforts to get the British to fulfill their obligations under Article 7 of the lend-lease agreement. "My suggestion would be," he concluded, "that we not proceed too rapidly with the implementation of plans for lend-lease aid in phase two beyond the direct strategic needs of the Pacific war until we are able to ascertain a little more clearly the attitude of the British on these commercial policy questions."[33]

Rather than pressing the British for specific assurances regarding postwar trade, however, Roosevelt decided that the United States should proceed with phase two discussions with Great Britain from the perspective of helping reestablish the financial position of a good friend. The president wanted to furnish enough lend-lease aid to enable the United Kingdom to convert some of its industrial facilities to civilian production before the defeat of Japan. "The objective of the President," Secretary of the Treasury Henry Morgenthau explained on 20 October, "is to start England back on the road to recovery and its place in the sun."[34] With that goal in mind, American negotiators met with British representatives to work out a program of lend-lease aid. They proposed that Great Britain should receive $5.4 billion in lend-lease supplies during the first year after the end of hostilities in Europe. The amount proposed was $1.1 billion less than the sum that Roosevelt had promised at Quebec.

But the president quickly backed away from the proposed agreement after several of his advisers reminded him that Congress had made lend-lease appropriations solely for military purposes and not for industrial reconversion. "I am deeply concerned," a State Department official warned, "over the question of whether an arrangement along the lines proposed with the United Kingdom for phase 2 can be made to stand up before Congress and public opinion in this country."[35] In a meeting with Morgenthau and Stettinius on 21 November 1944, Roosevelt said that he did not want to make any commitment regarding lend-lease aid for Great Britain following the defeat of Germany. The president also indicated that he did not want any public announcement that Britain would get as much American help in the future as it had in the past. Any such promise to the British, he explained, would present a very serious political problem. After the meeting, Stettinius promptly informed British officials that the United States would continue sending their country lend-lease aid but that he could not give them a firm commitment as to the exact amount.[36]

Realizing that the lend-lease program would end with the close of hostilities in the Pacific, the State Department had already begun discussing the need to provide Great Britain with a large postwar loan. The

British would be faced after the war with a severe deficit in their balance of payments as well as a huge accumulation of debts to India and other countries in the sterling area. But the British were reluctant to borrow money to meet their financial obligations and to unfreeze blocked sterling accounts in the absence of any assurance that U.S. tariffs would be reduced. "The United States," aides to Secretary Hull explained on 4 November, "is concerned lest the British, in an effort to avoid the necessity of borrowing, should enter into bulk purchasing arrangements and other closed economic arrangements which would practically preclude the re-establishment of international trade and commercial policy along lines advocated by the United States." Before making any commitments to extend a large credit on easy terms to Great Britain, they concluded, the United States should obtain assurances that the British would not pursue discriminatory commercial policies after the war.[37]

Although illness forced Hull to resign on 30 November, his economic philosophy continued to guide State Department planning for the postwar world. "The President is determined," Stettinius explained after Roosevelt had asked him to replace Hull as secretary, "that we leave no stone unturned to re-vitalize the Department of State, particularly in view of the great burden that will be thrown upon us after victory."[38] Stettinius decided that William L. Clayton, the largest cotton broker in the world and an outspoken advocate of free trade, should become assistant secretary of state in charge of economic affairs. Harry L. Hopkins, who had a close personal relationship with both Stettinius and Roosevelt, agreed. "The State Department is unquestionably the place for Clayton," Hopkins cabled the president. "His views are identical with yours and Hull's."[39] Clayton had a deep understanding of commercial and financial issues, and Stettinius was delighted when Roosevelt agreed to appoint him to serve as the chief economic adviser in the State Department.

After the president approved his plans for the reorganization of the State Department, Secretary of State Stettinius decided to push for the resumption of Anglo-American discussions concerning postwar commercial policy. But he and his associates worried that Prime Minister Churchill might have obtained the false impression that Roosevelt did not have much interest in the removal of trade barriers and the elimination of discriminatory commercial practices. Stettinius therefore urged the president to send Churchill a letter indicating that he attached great importance to the prompt resumption, at a high level, of conversations between the United States and Great Britain to implement Article 7 of the lend-lease agreement. Roosevelt immediately agreed to do so. "I think it most important that these talks be re-invigorated," he wrote Churchill on 10 February 1945, "and I should like to suggest the prompt naming of full delegations on both sides, to be headed by a Chairman with the rank of Minister."[40] But the British refused to budge. "The War Cabinet," Churchill hastily replied, "do not wish to commit themselves at this stage of the war to sending a high-powered delegation to Washington."[41]

Convinced that the United States must take the lead in removing commercial restrictions after the war, President Roosevelt and his State Department advisers decided to ask Congress to renew the Trade Agreements Act on a permanent basis and to give them increased authority to reduce tariff rates. Because import duties on most items had already been cut by the 50 percent allowed under the original reciprocal trade law enacted on 30 June 1934, the Roosevelt administration wanted authority to lower tariff rates by 50 percent of those in effect on 1 January 1945. But congressional leaders informed State Department representatives in early March 1945 that they would have to abandon their fight to have the reciprocal trade program placed on a permanent footing if they wanted to obtain greater freedom to cut import duties in return for commercial concessions from other countries. After the State Department agreed to postpone its push for a permanent measure, a bill to extend the reciprocal trade law for another three years gained strong bipartisan support. The Trade Agreements Act, as eventually passed by wide margins in both the House and Senate, empowered the president to reduce tariff rates as much as 50 percent below existing levels.[42]

The State Department and the Executive Committee on Economic Foreign Policy had already started developing ambitious plans for a world trade conference. The executive committee, chaired by Assistant Secretary Acheson and comprising representatives from several departments and agencies of the federal government, worked during the summer and autumn of 1944 on a comprehensive program for international economic cooperation.[43] During a meeting on 5 March 1945, the State Department approved a document calling for "the negotiation, among as many countries as possible but including at least a nucleus of the major trading nations, of a multilateral commercial-policy agreement."[44] President Roosevelt died a month later, but American diplomats continued making preparations for an international-trade convention that they hoped could be held the following year. During a meeting in the State Department on 31 August 1945, Assistant Secretary Clayton stressed the need for prompt action "to assure that the countries to which we made loans would not take individual steps to raise their tariffs or to impose other restrictions on foreign trade before the International Trade Conference next spring."[45]

A week later, on 7 September 1945, Acheson sent Pres. Harry S. Truman a document setting forth a program that might form the agenda for a world conference on trade and employment to be held, if possible, early in the next year. The document, which had been approved by the Executive Committee on Economic Foreign Policy, contemplated the negotiation of a multilateral agreement with regard to the maintenance of employment, the relaxation of trade barriers of all kinds, the elimination of severely restrictive trade practices, the prohibition of discriminatory commercial treatment, and the establishment of an international-trade organization.[46] Truman approved the document two days later. State Department officials remained confident that American business interests would benefit from a general lowering of trade barriers throughout the world. "We are so efficient," Clayton explained on 10 October, "that it is not likely that any reasonable advance in wages will seriously curtail our ability to compete in world markets."[47] But an international consensus for a multilateral accord on commercial policy did not materialize until 1947, when a world conference produced the General Agreement on Trade and Tariffs. In the meantime, the State Department fell back on the traditional strategy of holding bilateral negotiations with individual countries in an effort to conclude reciprocal trade agreements based upon the most-favored-nation formula.[48]

As a part of their effort to create a liberal capitalist world order, State Department officials sought to extend the principle of equal economic opportunity to the field of international aviation. Assistant Secretary Adolf A. Berle played a central role in the preparation of U.S. plans for the expansion of commercial air traffic after the war. On 2 January 1943, Secretary Hull authorized Berle to establish an interdepartmental group to study international aviation questions. This group quickly evolved into the Advisory Committee on Civil Aviation with Berle serving as chairman.[49] From the very outset, its plans for postwar aviation were designed to open the skies of the world to commercial traffic. "The work of this Government's Interdepartmental Committee on Civil Aviation is still in its early stages," Berle reported to Hull on 11 March, "but the trend of its thought is toward a policy of providing that properly documented aircraft of any nation may reciprocally (but without rigid reciprocal limitations as to frequency of flights) use the airports of any other nation as freely as foreign vessels may enter seaports."[50]

In a memorandum prepared for Secretary Hull on 30 April 1943, Berle summarized the principal conclusions his committee had reached. The committee hoped to prevent a postwar struggle between the United States and Great Britain for exclusive air-transportation rights. If the U.S. government excluded British planes from the United States, Berle explained, the British government would attempt to block the entry of American planes into Europe and Asia. Thus, the committee concluded that the United States should initiate negotiations for an international agreement that would settle the problem of air navigation rights on an equitable basis. "The heart of a general navigation agreement would have to rest on agreement between the United States and the British Empire and Commonwealth of Nations," Berle emphasized. "It may fairly be assumed that once this agreement is reached, practically all countries in the world (with the possible exception of Russia) would accede." He and his colleagues believed that the postwar commercial interests of the United States would be best served by a multilateral agreement that would assure the widest generalization of air navigation rights.[51]

At the same time, the Advisory Committee on Civil Aviation tackled a tough political question: should the postwar foreign air traffic of the United States be placed in the hands of only one commercial firm or should it be divided among several American companies? Pan American Airways had built up a powerful lobby to push for exclusive control over all commercial air operations between the United States and the rest of the world. But an equally strong lobby was being organized by other domestic airlines and aircraft manufacturers to oppose the Pan American campaign for a postwar monopoly. "The Committee," Berle reported, "was of the view that American foreign aviation is too big a proposition for any single company; and that the monopoly principle used by other countries has in general produced inefficient service. It therefore proposes apportionment among a selected number of airlines, granting to each a particular zone in which it might be dominant." He added that the committee believed that the federal government should assume the task of protecting the commercial interests of all these airlines in their global operations.[52]

After reviewing the major questions related to international air transportation, President Roosevelt met with several members of the advisory committee on 10 November 1943 and outlined the policy that he hoped would prevail after the war. Roosevelt said that he had decided that American overseas aviation should not be handled by a single firm and that it would be better to have different U.S. airlines assigned to operate in different zones of the world. During this meeting, the president clearly indicated that he looked forward to a very free interchange of air traffic throughout the postwar world. He said that planes of every country should have the general right of innocent transit and the right of technical stop to get fuel and service at any airport in the world. He also stated that planes of each nation should have the right to land in any other country to conduct international, but not internal, business. If a Canadian firm wanted to run a line from Canada to Jamaica with stops in the United States at Buffalo and Miami, Roosevelt explained, it should be able to discharge cargo of Canadian origin at Buffalo or Miami, and it should be allowed to take on Jamaican-bound traffic in Buffalo or Miami, but it should not be permitted to pick up passengers or commodities in Buffalo and to discharge them in Miami.[53]

State Department officials feared that, if an international agreement on aviation policy were not reached before the end of hostilities in Europe, Great Britain would embark upon a campaign to obtain preferential air rights from other countries. "There is a danger that unless we move ahead in our study of post-war civil aviation problems," Hull warned Roosevelt on 29 November 1943, "we may find that the present fluid situation will become jelled in the minds of some of our Allies along lines that may not parallel your own thoughts."[54] Berle was especially worried. Reports coming into the State Department convinced him that the British Overseas Airways Corporation was attempting to make arrangements designed to exclude American planes from Europe, the Mediterranean, and the Near East.[55] At the same time, letters from Livingston Satterwaite of the U.S. embassy in London warned that British officials hoped to confine the United States to a fixed ratio of flying frequencies on overseas air routes. "They well know that they cannot compete on equal terms with us," Satterwaite wrote on 22 February 1944, "and they wish to guarantee percentages to their own aviation."[56]

Determined to give U.S. airlines the opportunity to take advantage of their technological superiority, the State Department proposed a series of bilateral aviation discussions to be held in the spring of 1944 with Great Britain, the Soviet Union, China, Canada, and several other countries. The State Department hoped these exploratory conversations would prepare the groundwork for an international civil-aviation conference later in the year. After obtaining approval from the president, Hull sent Berle on a mission to London for the purpose of discussing postwar commercial aviation with British officials. Berle flew to England on 29 March to hold informal conversations with Lord Beaverbrook and Prime Minister Churchill.[57] During these private talks, the British advocated the creation

[handwritten margin note: again, trying to get in bed [?] the Brits]

of an international aviation commission with power to fix rates and determine frequencies. But Berle insisted that an international agency should deal only with technical matters such as safety standards, traffic signals, and weather reports. In a subsequent conversation with Soviet aviation experts, Berle explained that the United States had rejected the British proposal for an international commission with authority to divide air traffic among different countries. "Questions of rates, frequencies, etc.," he declared, "should be decided not by the fiat of an international body but by the exigencies of free and open competition."[58]

In the midst of their campaign for freedom of the skies, President Roosevelt and his State Department advisers were angered by reports that Pan American Airways and the British Overseas Airways Corporation had negotiated a cartel arrangement dividing world traffic between themselves. Pan American would have the bulk of the North Atlantic and South American traffic, while British Overseas would have virtually all of the traffic across the continent of Europe.[59] Eager to implement the agreement, Pan American president Juan Trippe vigorously lobbied to have Congress make his airline "the chosen instrument" of the United States in the development of commercial aviation throughout the world. But Roosevelt and Berle worked behind the scenes to block his efforts. They met privately at the White House on 9 June 1944 with Bennett Champ Clark, the chairman of the Senate Subcommittee on Aviation. Although he acknowledged that Trippe could probably succeed in running a worldwide air-transportation business, Roosevelt said that he thought that the best policy would be to have "chosen instruments in particular fields," with different U.S. airlines assigned to different overseas routes. Senator Clark replied that he would encourage his subcommittee to support the policy the president favored.[60]

While pushing for an international aviation agreement that would conform to liberal commercial principles, the State Department began negotiating bilateral arrangements to obtain transit and landing rights from individual countries around the world. Berle advised Hull on 30 May 1944 that the United States should be prepared to move fast because the British were already making plans to secure landing rights along the air routes they coveted. "While we should continue to negotiate and press for generalized international agreements," he urged, "we should also endeavor to push forward, on a provisional basis, arrangements so that our aviation lines can enter the field as rapidly as military pressure is lifted." Rather than waiting for a multilateral agreement on aviation rights, Berle reiterated, the United States should immediately reach understandings with foreign countries for overseas air routes that would be open for American commercial development as soon as military operations along those routes ceased. "All arrangements," he concluded, "could be made subject to the overall international agreement as and when it emerges."[61]

The State Department promptly began negotiations with the Soviet Union to obtain permission for U.S. airlines to open commercial routes into Moscow. As a result of his discussions with the Russian aviation mission in Washington during June and July 1944, Berle thought that the Soviets intended to allow a limited number of foreign airlines to land in their territory after the war.[62] But the Russian aviation officials clearly indicated on 1 August that the Soviet Union would remain closed to foreign airlines. They proposed that international aviation across Soviet territory would be conducted by having passengers and freight transferred from foreign airlines to Russian planes at or near the Soviet border. Then the traffic would either be taken to a destination in the Soviet Union and discharged, or it would be carried to a point on the other side of the country and transferred from Russian planes to foreign airlines. Although he realized that it would be possible to establish a satisfactory international aviation system with the Soviet Union left out, Berle did not think that the State Department should accept the Russian position as final in view of "the fact that we base much of our hope for the future on open trade."[63]

Determined to open the skies for U.S. airlines, the State Department extended invitations in September 1944 to all allied, associated, and neutral countries to attend an international conference on civil aviation to be held in the United States. "The major conflict at the conference will be between interests who would like to cut up the air into great closed zones," Berle predicted, "and those who would like to see the air made a more or less universal medium of communication and transport service." Berle was confident that American representatives at the conference would be able to prevent the British advocates of closed blocs from excluding U.S. airlines from operating in Western Europe and the Near East. But he believed that the United States would have to accept some formula that would limit the number of landings its airlines could make on overseas routes.[64] On 27 October, President Roosevelt designated Berle chairman of the U.S. delegation to the International Civil Aviation Conference scheduled to open in Chicago a few days later. Fifty-two countries agreed to participate in the conference, but at the last minute the Soviet Union decided not to send a delegation.[65]

Shortly before the Civil Aviation Conference convened in Chicago on 1 November 1944, the British published a White Paper calling for the establishment of an international body with overriding powers to allocate routes and determine rates. Berle was distressed. On the first day of the conference, he decided to have lunch with Lord Swinton, the chairman of the British delegation. Berle pointed out that the White Paper was merely a restatement of the British position that the United States had clearly rejected during preliminary discussions in London in the previous spring. Lord Swinton then proposed that air traffic between the United States and Great Britain should be divided on a fifty-fifty basis. Berle replied that he simply could not accept an arrangement that would give Great Britain half of the traffic carried between the United States and the European continent on planes that happened to land at a British airport en route to their ultimate destination. After this sharp confrontation with Swinton, Berle moved swiftly to obtain promises of transit and landing rights for U.S. airlines from several key European countries.[66]

During the ensuing debates at the Chicago Conference, the American delegation held firmly to the position that commercial airlines should compete for international traffic in a free market. "The shippers and passengers should be able to choose the airlines they wish," Berle asserted on 18 November, "and the airlines should be able to put on as many planes as needed to carry the traffic." Thus, he and his colleagues advocated an escalator principle that would allow airlines to increase the frequency of their flights in order to carry additional passengers and freight if their planes were running close to capacity. But the British delegation insisted that the escalator principle should not apply to the acceptance or discharge of traffic at intermediate points on international routes. In their rebuttal, the Americans argued that restrictions placed on the number of commercial landings at intermediate points would make it impossible for airlines to run long overseas routes on a profitable basis. They believed that limits on intermediate traffic would prevent U.S. airlines from operating in Europe anywhere to the east of gateway cities such as Stockholm, Amsterdam, London, Paris, and Rome. But the British refused to yield. Lord Swinton said that he was bound by instructions from London and that he could not make any change in the position of his government.[67]

Hoping to break the impasse, President Roosevelt urged Churchill to telephone new instructions to the British negotiators in Chicago. "Your people are now asking limitations on the number of planes between points regardless of the traffic offering," he complained to the prime minister on 21 November. "The limitations now proposed would, I fear, place a dead hand on the use of the great air trade routes." When Churchill refused to change the British position, Roosevelt threatened him with a cut in lend-lease aid. "We will face Congress on that subject in a few weeks," he warned on 24 November, "and it will not be in a generous mood if it and the people feel that the United Kingdom has not agreed to a generally beneficial air agreement." But Churchill would not acquiesce. He feared that, if U.S. airlines were given equal opportunity to compete for overseas business, they would dominate commercial aviation throughout the postwar world. Despite two more messages from Roosevelt urging that an agreement be reached at the conference, Churchill insisted that further thought and consultation were needed before a final settlement could be made.[68]

With Roosevelt and Churchill at loggerheads, the American negotiators in Chicago had to take what they could get. The countries represented at the conference agreed to establish an International Civil Aviation Organization that would maintain statistics on air traffic, register aviation accords between individual countries, and handle other technical matters. They also adopted two documents—the Two Freedoms Agreement and the Five Freedoms Agreement—for the future consideration of all countries. Those choosing to sign the first document would grant each other the rights of innocent transit and technical stop. Those electing to endorse the second document would give each other additional rights to land for commercial transactions.[69] Berle gained the impression that most countries would sign the Two Freedoms Agreement, but he could only hope that the British and others would eventually endorse the Five Freedoms Agreement. In the meantime, Berle had reason to believe that Great Britain would be willing to conclude a bilateral air agreement with the United States. "I think that the British know that they have overplayed their hand and will be in a mood to negotiate," he reported to Washington on 2 December. "We have enough entries into Europe now, indeed, so that their naked lack of assent can no longer bar us from the European Continent."[70]

After the Chicago conference adjourned on 4 December 1944, the State Department continued to negotiate reciprocal aviation agreements with individual countries. Churchill was alarmed when he learned that the United States was about to conclude a bilateral air accord with Ireland. After the two countries signed an aviation agreement against his wishes on 3 February 1945, the prime minister asked Roosevelt to take the necessary steps to have the agreement annulled. But the president bluntly refused. "You will recall how earnestly I endeavored to secure your cooperation on the future of aviation during the Chicago Conference," he lectured Churchill on 15 March. "These bilateral aviation agreements were made necessary by the failure of that conference to reach a multilateral agreement permitting the natural development of aviation." Roosevelt noted that the agreement with Ireland was made in view of its obvious geographical importance for postwar U.S. air routes to Europe. "I think it only fair to tell you," he concluded, "that aviation circles in this country are becoming increasingly suspicious that certain elements in England intend to try to block the development of international flying in general until the British aviation industry is further developed."[71]

American civil aviation policy did not change when Roosevelt died and Truman became president. Stokeley W. Morgan, a State Department aviation expert, informed Truman on 5 June 1945 that the British were trying to prevent American planes from obtaining commercial rights to operate in the Near East and the Middle East. Truman said he would discuss the matter with Churchill at the forthcoming conference in Potsdam.[72] During a meeting between U.S. airline representatives and State Department officials on 7 September 1945, Morgan explained that "the British wanted an initial division of traffic between our two countries, but would be willing to permit escalation." When asked if the United States should accept a compromise that would allow American planes to make immediate flights to Great Britain and possibly to build up their business over time, several airline representatives suggested that financial aid should be used to pressure the British into signing an aviation accord that would permit an unlimited number of flights between the United States and Great Britain. "It was the general consensus," a State Department officer recorded, "that we should compromise with the British only as a last resort, and should use our bargaining position to the fullest extent in talks with the British on general economic matters."[73] Realizing that they had the upper hand, American policymakers were prepared to use the prospect of postwar financial assistance to induce the British to support their plans for international aviation.

Meanwhile, as the State Department was drafting blueprints for a liberal postwar commercial system, Treasury Department officials had been drawing up plans for the establishment of an international financial structure that would facilitate the expansion of world trade. Their basic goal was to create an international monetary system that would assure the maintenance of stable and predictable foreign-exchange rates. Under the gold standard that had prevailed before the Great Depression, the major trading countries fixed the value of their currencies in relation to gold. These countries allowed gold to move freely across their borders, and they agreed to convert their currencies into gold at the established price. But the gold standard broke down shortly after the onset of the global depression. The British abandoned it in 1931 to free themselves to devalue the pound and thereby make their products less expensive for others to buy. The United States and other countries soon left the gold standard too and joined the scramble to depreciate their currencies to gain a competitive edge in overseas markets. After watching how fluctuations in exchange rates had hindered world trade for an entire decade, Treasury officials were eager to lay the foundation for a return to international monetary stability after the war.[74]

On 14 December 1941, just one week after Pearl Harbor, Secretary of the Treasury Henry Morgenthau asked his special adviser on international finance, Harry Dexter White, to begin working on a plan for postwar monetary stabilization. White had earned a doctorate in economics at Harvard University, and although many of his colleagues disliked him, Morgenthau relied upon him because of his knowledge about international finance and trade. White quickly concluded that the restoration of world trade would depend upon the stability of foreign exchange rates and the availability of capital for economic reconstruction. In the spring of 1942, White proposed the creation of two separate agencies: an international stabilization fund and a world bank for reconstruction. The bank, as originally envisioned, was to make long-term loans at very low interest rates to help raise the productivity and living standards of its members. White explained that the institution was designed "to supply the huge volume of capital that will be needed virtually throughout the world for reconstruction, for relief, and for economic recovery."[75] But when he realized that Congress could not be expected to appropriate large sums of money for such a costly undertaking, White scaled back his proposal for a world bank. Its principal function would be to guarantee loans made by private banks to encourage them to invest capital abroad. It would not have to contribute its own money unless borrowing countries defaulted on their payments to private banks.[76]

After modifying his ambitious proposal for a world bank, White focused his attention on developing his plan for a postwar stabilization fund. His basic aim was to replace the gold standard with an international monetary agreement that would keep the currencies of the major trading countries at a constant value in relation to each other. Under his plan, member states would contribute varying amounts of money to the stabilization fund, and those making greater contributions would have more votes in determining fund decisions. Each member would be able to use its own currency to buy from the fund the currency of any other member. Besides supplying Great Britain and other countries with dollars needed to purchase American products, the fund would make sure that the currency of each member would be maintained at a predetermined value. "There would be agreement on the exchange rate which should prevail at the beginning," White explained to his Treasury colleagues in August 1943. "Thereafter, no exchange rate can be changed by the Fund without the permission of the country in question and without permission of three-quarters of the members' votes."[77]

The primary reason for establishing a postwar stabilization fund was to help Great Britain and other countries achieve a balance in their international payments without devaluing their currencies or employing various discriminatory practices that would choke the channels of world trade. In a letter to White in the autumn of 1942, Alvin H. Hansen, a director of economic and financial studies for the Council on Foreign Relations, argued that an international stabilization fund was necessary to prevent restrictive commercial measures from spreading throughout the world. "Unless we provide machinery which will insure an adequate supply of foreign exchange," Hansen warned, "many countries will quickly resort to severe restrictive policies, including quotas, exchange control, and bilateral clearing, in order to protect their balance of payment position."[78] White had already come to the same conclusion. Each country that became a member of the fund, he explained in the spring of 1942, would have to agree not only to maintain the value of its currency but also to abide by liberal commercial principles.[79]

After extensive preliminary discussions between U.S. and British Treasury officials, representatives of forty-four countries gathered at Bretton Woods, New Hampshire, in July 1944 for an international monetary and financial conference. A debate over the size of the quota that each country would have in the proposed stabilization fund dominated the first part of the proceedings. White insisted that the voting power of each fund member must be proportional to the size of its quota. He firmly rejected the idea that every member should have the same number of votes regardless of its contribution to the fund. During a meeting with the American delegation on the opening day of the conference, White explained that there would be a "demand on the part of the small countries, to get more votes, and we, on the other hand, don't want to budge, because the more votes you give the small countries, the less our proportion of influence in votes." The American delegation demanded that the United States must have a quota that was greater than 25 percent of the total. With more than a quarter of the votes, therefore, the United States could veto any proposed changes in currency values.[80]

The second major issue to be settled at the Bretton Woods Conference involved the degree of freedom that members of the monetary fund would have to alter exchange rates. On the one hand, the British wanted to have as much freedom as possible to depreciate the pound in order to give their exports a competitive advantage in overseas markets. On the other hand, the Americans sought to limit the freedom of member countries to devalue their currencies because they wanted to keep the international price structure stable and predictable. The exchange-rate debate ended with a compromise: members of the fund would be allowed to adjust the value of their currencies by 10 percent to correct a disequilibrium in their balance of payments. The delegates agreed that the value of the dollar would be fixed in terms of gold and that the value of all other currencies would be expressed either in terms of gold or dollars. After determining the initial value of all currencies, the fund would have the power to curtail the privileges of any member that changed the value of its currency by more than 10 percent. The fund would also have the authority to deny members access to its resources on the grounds that they were not acting in a responsible manner.[81]

After they had agreed on the rules that would govern the International Monetary Fund, the delegates at Bretton Woods began discussing the charter for the proposed International Bank for Reconstruction and Development. The delegates quickly decided that the main function of the world bank would be to guarantee loans made by private institutions for long-term projects after the war. It would authorize private banks to make loans for reconstruction and development, but its own funds would not need to be used except to cover possible defaults. Some delegates argued that the world bank could safely authorize loans up to 200 or 300 percent of its assets. But the Americans feared that Congress would regard such loans to be too risky. The delegates ultimately agreed that the bank should not guarantee loans that exceeded 100 percent of its capital. As in the case of the monetary fund, the United States would make the largest contribution of money to the international bank and therefore have the greatest influence in determining its overall policy.[82]

International bankers in New York, while receptive to the plan for a world bank, opposed the whole idea of a government-controlled stabilization fund. They feared that the proposed International Monetary Fund would eliminate the role that private bankers had historically played in preventing governments from pursuing inflationary policies. Under the gold standard, countries did not impose any restrictions on international capital transactions. If a particular government began spending huge sums on public works projects to achieve full employment, the value of its currency might fall and private investors might withdraw their capital. A government faced with such a situation would be compelled to adopt deflationary measures to attract the return of capital from the international banking community. But the International Monetary Fund would allow member states to impose restrictions on the transfer of capital. It would also provide them with an alternative source of credit so that they would be less dependent upon international bankers. If a government pursued inflationary policies and prohibited the withdrawal of capital, private investors could do nothing but sit and watch as inflation reduced the value of their assets.[83]

Thomas W. Lamont, the chairman of the board of the J. P. Morgan Company, was highly critical of the plan for the International Monetary Fund. Lamont feared that the proposed fund would make credits available to governments that were not being responsible in their financial behavior. "It is quite hopeless to expect to stabilize the currencies of a great community of nations," he warned in June 1943, "if the constituent members disregard their primary responsibilities."[84] Lamont argued that a better way to achieve international monetary stability after the war would be for American and British bankers to establish a dollar-pound exchange ratio that would serve as the basis for determining the value of all other currencies. "It should not be difficult for the American and British banking authorities, with the approval of their governments, to arrive at a workable stabilization ratio between the dollar and the pound," he explained in May 1944. "If once the Americans and the British reach a stabilization agreement as between themselves, all of the other active national currencies of the world can readily tie themselves to the dollar and the pound."[85]

Other New York bank leaders expressed their strong opposition to the monetary stabilization plan directly to the Treasury Department. In a letter to Secretary Morgenthau in June 1944, Pres. W. Randolph Burgess of the National City Bank articulated his fear that easy access to monetary-fund resources would accentuate inflationary tendencies after the war. Burgess argued that the most serious postwar exchange problem would arise from the weak British financial position. "They really need a direct credit of about two billion dollars," he wrote. "My own feeling is that the American people would rather meet the British needs directly and openly than through a plan that purports to be for monetary stabilization."[86] Winthrop W. Aldrich, the chairman of the Chase National Bank, agreed that the nub of the postwar financial problem would be the British lack of dollars to purchase American products. "What they really should get," he told Treasury officials in August 1944, "is a grant in aid of about thr[ee] billion dollars from this country to straighten out their exchange pos[i]tion." Aldrich believed that the problem should be faced squarely because it would be in the interest of the United States to have a strong British economy. "We have to re-establish Great Britain," he insisted, "for our own good."[87]

After the close of the Bretton Woods Conference, these eminent New York bankers tried to block the creation of the International Monetary Fund. Randolph Burgess used his position as president of the American Bankers' Association to organize broader opposition to the monetary fund.[88] A special committee, appointed by the association to study the Bretton Woods agreements, concluded in January 1945 that the fund should not be approved because "it would give credit automatically to countries which were not credit worthy."[89] In a report issued a month later, the American Bankers' Association endorsed the world-bank proposal but opposed the plan for a monetary fund. The bankers received strong backing from the *New York Times* and the *Wall Street Journal*. Both papers argued that monetary stabilization could be accomplished better by private bankers than by government bureaucrats.[90] In February 1945, in a personal letter thanking the publisher of the *New York Times* for his support, Thomas Lamont reiterated the argument that "the fatal flaw in the Monetary Fund—not the Bank which seems workable—is that it makes credit available regardless of merit and regardless of need."[91]

But these arguments failed to prevent the establishment of the International Monetary Fund. In a message to Congress on 12 February 1945, President Roosevelt urged that the Bretton Woods agreement should be approved without modification. Treasury officials not only defended the agreement during special House and Senate hearings, but they also made a concerted effort to convince American businessmen that the monetary fund would facilitate the sale of their products in foreign markets. In a speech before the Economic Club of Detroit on 26 February 1945, Secretary Morgenthau focused on the automobile industry to illustrate his point. Because the fund would help member countries keep their currencies stable, he explained, American car manufacturers would not have to worry that a sudden drop in the value of the pound or franc would make their products too expensive for prospective customers in Britain or France.[92] His argument had widespread appeal. Spokesmen for a variety of industries throughout the country agreed that the fund would help them expand their export business. Some bankers even began worrying that its defeat would prompt the British to pursue restrictive trade policies. Finally, in June 1945, Congress voted overwhelmingly to pass the Bretton Woods Act, which authorized U.S. participation in both the bank and the fund.[93]

State Department officials responded to the Bretton Woods agreement with mixed feelings. On the one hand, after expecting that the International Monetary Fund would make currencies interchangeable and prices more predictable, they were disappointed when the Treasury Department agreed to British demands that fund members be permitted to maintain restrictions on international currency transactions for as long as five years. They feared that their drive to create a liberal postwar commercial system would suffer a serious blow if Great Britain and other important trading nations continued to employ foreign-exchange controls for such a lengthy period. On the other hand, State Department officials supported, without any reservations, the establishment of the International Bank for Reconstruction and Development. They believed that the bank would encourage the flow of private American capital across the Atlantic and thereby enable European countries to buy more than sold when trading with the United States in the immediate postwar years. Moreover, they hoped that in the long run loans from the U.S. government as well as from New York bankers would help devastated European nations rebuild their industries and increase their exports so that they could earn dollars and keep on purchasing goods from the United States.

American policymakers had taken a series of interrelated steps to pave the way for the establishment of a new international economic order after the cessation of hostilities. Determined to lay the foundation for a peaceful and prosperous world, President Roosevelt and his State Department advisers repeatedly warned the British that they could not expect to receive American financial aid unless they adopted liberal commercial policies. State Department officials negotiated a master lend-lease agreement that obligated Great Britain to work for the reduction of trade barriers and the elimination of discriminatory commercial practices. During the war, however, the British refused to resume Anglo-American economic discussions to achieve these basic objectives. They also refused at the Chicago Aviation Conference to sign a general agreement that would open the skies of the world to commercial traffic. Meanwhile, at the Bretton Woods Conference, Treasury Department officials negotiated a multilateral agreement to create a solid financial structure for the expansion of world trade after the war. They hoped that the International Monetary Fund would help stabilize exchange rates and that the World Bank would facilitate the economic reconstruction of Europe.

THREE | RECONSTRUCTING EUROPE

President Roosevelt and his foreign-policy advisors planned on using American financial resources to promote the postwar economic rehabilitation of Europe. As they contemplated the future, the ravages of war were causing a tremendous amount of destruction and dislocation all across the European continent. Factories were bombed, farmlands were turned into battlefields, and millions of people were driven from their homes. In the short run, people in the war-torn countries would need food, clothing, medical supplies, and other essentials in order to survive. American policymakers aimed to send immediate relief to Europe not only for humanitarian reasons but also because they feared that widespread starvation and deprivation would sow the seeds for radical social upheavals. In the long run, the industrial countries of Western Europe would need a massive infusion of capital to rebuild factories, repair roads, and replace damaged machinery. Postwar planners in Washington intended to provide European countries with funds required for economic reconstruction so that they could resume the production and exportation of goods and thereby earn dollars needed to purchase American products.

Six months before the attack on Pearl Harbor, State Department officials had begun thinking about the possibility of using postwar relief as a bargaining chip to induce European governments to abandon their nationalistic agricultural policies. Leroy D. Stinebower of the Economic Advisor's Office suggested that wheat, sugar, and other commodities that threatened to glut the world market should be shipped to the devastated countries of Europe with firm strings attached. "These countries might never be called upon to pay for these commodities," he explained on 5 June 1941. "One quid pro quo of such a gift, however, might be an agreement not to produce these same surplus commodities under highly uneconomic conditions with the support of high tariffs, quotas, prohibitions, government subsidies, etc."[1] Assistant Secretary of State Dean G. Acheson concurred. "Our bargaining position vis-à-vis European countries in regard to any contribution we would want them to make toward basic solutions of the surpluses problem will be strongest at the time when their needs which we are offering to meet are greatest," he reasoned on 22 July. "One contribution which they can make to the long-range solution is to avoid the excessive economic nationalism which before the war caused them to erect preposterous tariff barriers."[2]

But State Department officials worried that the British would attempt to use postwar relief to pave the way for the creation of a European economic bloc under their domination. Assistant Secretary of State Adolf A. Berle sounded the alarm when Great Britain suggested the establishment of a central bureau in London to handle all the foodstuffs and other materials to be shipped to the continent in the immediate post-war years. In a memorandum sent to President Roosevelt on 9 July 1941, he warned that the British proposal for reprovisioning Europe was prompted not only by humanitarian motives but even more by a desire "to channelize the trade and economics of this area through London when the war is over."[3] Berle remained strongly opposed to the idea of funneling supplies to the liberated countries of Europe through Britain. "To do this," he grumbled on 25 September, "would be merely to move the German distribution and clearing system from Berlin to London with about the same effects." Berle concluded that the program to reprovision Europe should be international in character to keep Great Britain from creating "the nucleus of an extremely dangerous post-war cartel."[4]

Following an exchange of views between the State Department and the British Foreign Office, the Inter-Allied Committee on Post-War Requirements was established on 24 September 1941 under British auspices. The committee, with Frederick Leith-Ross serving as chairman, promptly began estimating the postwar relief requirements of the European countries suffering under the yoke of Nazi occupation. At the same time, the State Department instructed Ambassador John G. Winant to ask that the British government keep the United States fully informed regarding the development of plans for reprovisioning Europe. Winant reported from London on 3 October that Foreign Secretary Anthony Eden had assured him that the British government would consult the United States before any concrete decisions were made with respect to postwar relief. The next day, the State Department decided that an American observer should be present at all meetings of the Inter-Allied Committee on Post-War Requirements. This observer was authorized to participate actively in the deliberations of the committee after the Pearl Harbor attack. Recognizing the fact that the United States had formally entered the war, the British proposed on 3 February 1942 that the U.S. government should assume greater responsibility for the work of the committee.[5]

After the State Department received the British proposal, the Advisory Committee on Postwar Foreign Policy began considering the need for a more broadly based relief organization. The Subcommittee on Economic Reconstruction, chaired by Adolf Berle, met on 6 March 1942 to discuss the subject of providing relief to European countries upon their liberation from German occupation. When the meeting ended, Berle directed the State Department research staff to prepare a draft plan for a relief agency to be sponsored by the Allied countries. The members of the economic reconstruction subcommittee convened two weeks later to reconsider the relief issue, and on 4 April Berle presented their views to the full advisory committee. Speaking for the subcommittee, Berle recommended the establishment of an international relief council composed of representatives of all the nations that were united in the fight against the Axis powers. He also recommend the creation of a supervisory board headed by an American director and comprised of representatives from the United States, Great Britain, the Soviet Union, and China. After concluding that Americans should have adequate control over postwar relief activities, the advisory committee agreed that the United States should take the initiative in calling a meeting of the Allied countries to discuss the need for a new international relief organization.[6]

Prompted by fears that revolutions would sweep across Europe after the war, the State Department began conversations with Great Britain in June 1942 to explore the possibility of setting up a United Nations relief agency. Reports from Europe indicated that widespread hunger and deprivation were producing a dangerous revolutionary potential.[7] While some State Department officers worried about this threat, others believed that the prompt shipment of food and fuel to Europe would be sufficient to keep communism from spreading throughout the continent.[8] After consulting his State Department advisors in October 1942, President Roosevelt approved a plan they had worked out with the British for the establishment of an international relief organization. Further Anglo-American discussions culminated in the publication on 11 June 1943 of a draft agreement for the United Nations Relief and Rehabilitation Administration (UNRRA). After modifications to convince the smaller countries that the organization would not be dominated by the four major powers, the agreement was signed on 9 November 1943 during a formal ceremony at the White House.[9]

Some members of the Subcommittee on Economic Reconstruction had hoped to use the agency as an entering wedge to get funds from Congress for long-range reconstruction projects. They believed that the largest appropriations could be obtained by "defining relief broadly enough to include many things commonly regarded as reconstruction."[10] But the UNRRA agreement clearly stipulated that the international relief organization would not function in the field of postwar reconstruction. During its first session, which began on 10 November 1943 in Atlantic City, New Jersey, the UNRRA council elected Gov. Herbert H. Lehman of New York as the director general of the new organization. The council also passed a resolution stating that rehabilitation should be considered as coterminous with relief and not as the beginning of reconstruction. Five days later, when he asked Congress to appropriate funds to support UNRRA, President Roosevelt stressed that the scope of the agency would be limited to sending emergency aid to the liberated peoples of Europe. "UNRRA will not," he declared, "be expected to solve the long-range problems of reconstruction." With these assurances in mind, Congress passed a joint resolution on 9 March 1944 authorizing U.S. participation in UNRRA.[11]

The postwar planners in the State Department hoped to use relief expenditures to solve the problem of displaced populations. Having failed in his efforts to raise private funds to help finance a large migration of Jewish refugees from Nazi Germany prior to the war, Myron C. Taylor thought that it would be much wiser to ship food, clothing, medicine, and other basic necessities to Europe than to try to find new homes for millions of refugees scattered about the continent. "Immense amounts of money would be required for the resettlement of the large number of people involved," Taylor explained on 23 October 1942. "If the same amount of money were to be spent on relief, leaving these people where they are now, a more satisfactory basis for postwar recovery could be created." Norman H. Davis, who was simultaneously working in the State Department and serving as president of the International Red Cross, agreed that it would be "most unwise to contemplate the resettlement of large numbers of people in Europe after the war."[12] After lengthy discussions, the Special Committee on Migration and Resettlement concluded on 16 June 1944 that displaced persons should be returned to their home countries in an orderly manner at the earliest possible date. The Post-War Programs Committee promptly approved the recommendation, calling for the repatriation of European refugees in the immediate postwar years.[13]

After resolving the short-term issues of relief and resettlement, American postwar planners still had to wrestle with the more difficult long-range question of how to finance the economic reconstruction of Europe. Their desire to direct a stream of capital across the Atlantic was rooted in their belief that the maintenance of American prosperity depended upon European recovery. During the war, the United States was enjoying an economic boom due, in part, to the fact that lend-lease aid had enabled European countries to remain good consumers of American products. But government officials and business leaders feared that, after the termination of lend-lease, they would be faced with a postwar depression unless the nations of Western Europe could resume industrial production, regain export markets, and earn dollars needed to purchase goods from the United States. "Our problem," a member of the Subcommittee on Economic Policy explained in March 1942, "is how to create purchasing power outside of our country which would be converted into domestic purchasing power through exportation. In practical terms, this matter comes down to the problem of devising appropriate institutions to perform after the war the function that lend-lease is now performing."[14]

Foreign Economic Administrator Leo T. Crowley, a prominent businessman from Wisconsin, repeatedly emphasized the relationship between the restoration of industrial production in Europe and the creation of postwar jobs in the United States. "One of the surest ways to achieve full-scale employment here at home," he declared in a speech given in January 1944, "is to open up world markets." Crowley assured his audience that the economic revitalization of war-torn countries would generate a vast overseas demand for American products. "It will," he insisted, "raise the standard of living abroad and enlarge the capacity of the peoples abroad to buy what we have to sell."[15] In another address delivered in March 1945, Crowley argued that when the war ended, Americans would have to extend large loans to European countries to help finance their economic reconstruction. "We need a productive, thriving Europe as a market for our goods," he proclaimed. "It does no good to raise wheat or make automobiles for export if the foreign purchaser has no money to pay for our products. And he won't have money to pay for them unless he, too, is producing and selling."[16]

But while they agreed that Europe would need American financial aid, Crowley and other members of the Roosevelt administration soon found themselves in an extended debate over the relationship between lend-lease assistance and postwar economic reconstruction. Government officials realized that European countries would not be able to buy American materials needed for postwar reconstruction if they were required to repay debts resulting from lend-lease operations. "It therefore seems obvious," a State Department aide explained on 14 March

1942, "that the resulting monetary obligations, unless a major part of them are written off, are capable of becoming a major impediment to world trade after the war."[17] As lend-lease debit balances mounted against European countries, a consensus crystallized in Washington that no attempt should be made to seek full repayment in cash or in kind.[18] Leo Pasvolsky and some of his colleagues in the State Department wanted to go further and make lend-lease materials available for postwar rehabilitation.[19] When bills for the renewal of lend-lease came before Congress in 1943 and again in 1944, however, administration spokesmen assured legislators that they would terminate lend-lease assistance as soon as hostilities ceased. Many senators and representatives supported the bills, which passed by wide margins, because they understood that lend-lease materials would be used strictly for military purposes and not for postwar relief or reconstruction.[20]

In a conversation with Under Secretary of State Edward R. Stettinius on 19 January 1944, President Roosevelt said that he wanted the State Department to prepare a plan for financing long-range reconstruction projects that would begin after emergency relief measures ended. Stettinius promised that he would have the State Department conduct a study of the entire matter after Roosevelt indicated that he was against using lend-lease funds for postwar economic reconstruction.[21] Members of the State Department research staff promptly began to consider whether American financial aid for European industrial restoration should take the form of loans requiring full repayment. In a document prepared for the Post-War Programs Committee on 17 February, they noted that provision had already been made through UNRRA to finance, on a grant basis if necessary, the immediate relief needs of countries suffering extensive devastation. Thus, they recommended that long-term reconstruction financing should be made "on a loan basis with rates of interest and amortization tempered to the circumstances."[22] During a meeting on 26 May, with Assistant Secretary of State Acheson serving as chair, the Executive Committee on Economic Foreign Policy agreed that "reconstruction financing should take the form of loans with expectation of eventual full repayment."[23]

A few months later, Under Secretary Stettinius sent President Roosevelt a memorandum that summarized the State Department position with respect to such loans. Stettinius emphasized that when the war ended, the United States must be prepared to extend immediate financial assistance not only to promote the restoration of industrial production in Western Europe but also to encourage the adoption of liberal commercial policies throughout the entire continent. "The future economic pattern of Europe will be largely determined by the policies and procedures established during the period of reconstruction," he explained. "Whether postwar conditions lead back to bilateralism, restriction and anarchy, or are resolved in a manner which will permit the progressive growth and liberalization of trade and investment will depend in no small measure on the ability of the war-torn countries to obtain outside (i.e., mostly American) help in reconstruction."[24]

While drafting plans for a financial-aid program for Europe, the Roosevelt administration reviewed a request from the Dutch government for a loan from the Reconstruction Finance Corporation. Secretary of the Treasury Henry Morgenthau opposed a government loan to the Netherlands. "Holland is one of the relatively few foreign governments that at the appropriate time should have no difficulty borrowing from the private investment market at reasonable rates of interest," Morgenthau cabled Roosevelt on 2 May 1944. "I believe we ought to be very hesitant to give the impression that we are likely to compete with private investment markets for loans to good borrowers."[25] But the president was not dissuaded. "I am inclined to believe that granting a loan to Holland on good security in this country to be used for the purchase in America of reconstruction materials would not be an undesirable precedent," Roosevelt replied to Morgenthau a day later. "American industry in the post-war period may probably need all the foreign orders that can be safely accepted in order to benefit employment and dispose of surpluses."[26]

But with the backing of big New York bankers, Morgenthau and Secretary of State Cordell Hull joined forces to persuade the president to change his position. Morgenthau telephoned the White House on 6 June 1944 to inform Roosevelt that Winthrop W. Aldrich of the Chase National Bank had told him that private banks were willing to furnish the Netherlands credit for reconstruction.[27] Although Secretary of Commerce Jesse H. Jones wrote the president on 10 August in support of the Dutch loan application, Morgenthau and Hull advised Roosevelt that the U.S. government should encourage the Netherlands to seek reconstruction financing through normal banking channels. "It would be unfortunate," they warned, "if the government were subjected to the criticism that it was competing with the private banks and taking away business from them for which they have adequate facilities."[28] Roosevelt concurred. "I feel that every effort should be make to ascertain definitely the possibility of a private credit to the Netherlands Government before an agency of this Government undertakes to handle the loan," the president wrote Jones on 4 September. "In this connection, I am informed that a consortium of private banks is now prepared to extend a short-term credit on reasonable terms to the Netherlands Government."[29]

But the Roosevelt administration had not yet decided if lend-lease aid should be employed for the postwar economic reconstruction of Europe. Some State Department officers hoped to employ such funds to stimulate European industrial recovery. To gain broader support for their position, they asked Treasury officials to back their plans for lend-lease agreements with Belgium and Holland. "We have informed them we don't like the idea of using Lend-Lease funds for reconstruction purposes," Assistant Secretary of the Treasury Harry Dexter White explained on 8 September 1944, "and we didn't think that was the original intent and there'd be trouble with Congress."[30] The following day President Roosevelt issued a general order that prohibited all government departments from making any commitments to ship lend-lease supplies to any country after the collapse of Germany.[31] But Secretary of State Hull quickly sent the president a memorandum recommending that he approve a lend-lease agreement to ship industrial reconstruction goods to France after the European war ended. As Roosevelt was leaving to meet with Churchill in Quebec, Harry Hopkins sent him a note supporting the proposed agreement with France on the grounds that it would give him discretion over the use of lend-lease funds until the defeat of Japan.[32]

But the Treasury Department opposed the proposal for a lend-lease agreement that would enable the French to begin a large-scale program of economic reconstruction. On 14 September 1944, after receiving statements from military authorities that French industrial production would be of no help in fighting the war, Under Secretary Daniel W. Bell sent a telegram to Morgenthau, who had joined Roosevelt in Quebec. Bell argued that the only thing to be gained by signing the proposed agreement would be to present Congress and the American people with a *fait accompli*. "Quite contrary to the avowed purpose of the proposal to give discretion to the President," he concluded, "its practical effect will be to tie his hands with respect to our dealings with the French at the termination of the war in Europe much more than would otherwise be the case." The next day Morgenthau recommended that a decision on the matter be postponed, and Roosevelt agreed to reexamine the proposed agreement before taking any action. The president told Morgenthau that, although he was willing to make commitments to supply lend-lease materials to Great Britain for industrial reconstruction, he did not want his hands tied in his dealings with the French.[33]

Secretary of War Henry L. Stimson, who was widely respected for his integrity and candor, vigorously opposed the use of large sums from the lend-lease account for the postwar reconstruction of France. During a cabinet meeting on 13 October 1944, he expressed doubt about the legality of using such aid for economic rehabilitation unless it would contribute to the war effort. Stimson pointed out that he had participated in the committee hearings for the original Lend-Lease Act and in the subsequent debates over congressional appropriation to aid the Allies. As a witness to those proceedings, Stimson said, he knew perfectly well that Congress had been assured that lend-lease funds would be used only to help countries that were actually fighting enemies of the United States. Stimson explained that he was not at all against the idea of providing financial assistance for the economic reconstruction of Europe, but he argued that Congress should be consulted before lend-lease funds were employed for the purpose of postwar rehabilitation.[34]

Leo Crowley was in complete agreement with this viewpoint. "I do not wish to convey the impression that I do not recognize that in many instances it will be to the vital interest of the United States to assist other countries to rehabilitate themselves," he explained on 13 February 1945. "My point is that the necessity for economic aid to any other countries must be brought squarely to the attention of the Congress so that the Congress can provide the necessary means to carry out foreign economic aid programs for reconstruction purposes. This must be done directly and not by subterfuge or indirection through stretching the intent of the Lend-Lease Act."[35] After Roosevelt held his last cabinet meeting on 30 March, Crowley advised him that the lend-lease program should be cut back during the period between the defeat of Germany and the end of the war in the Pacific. Some State Department officials tried to get Crowley to ask Congress to appropriate $8 billion for lend-lease assistance, but he requested only $2.25 billion when he testified before the Senate Foreign Relations Committee. After being told by Crowley that the appropriations would not be used for postwar reconstruction, the committee voted unanimously on 4 April 1945 to extend the Lend-Lease Act for another year.[36]

Besides advocating the extension of financial aid for the industrial reconstruction of Europe, American postwar planners drafted blueprints for the creation of a gigantic economic union embracing most of the countries on the continent. Foremost in their thinking was the question of how the economic unification of Europe would affect the vital interests of the United States. "Time has indicated the desirability of some sort of comprehensive economic understanding among the European nations," Myron Taylor observed on 29 April 1942. "At the same time, we need to consider carefully how far our interests lie in promoting a strong European economic union as a world competitor."[37] In a memorandum prepared for the State Department on 14 September 1942, a Council on Foreign Relations study group came to the following conclusion: "The United States should favor the economic unification of Europe only if steps are taken to avoid the creation of an autarkic Continental economy. Positive American policy should aim at the interpenetration of Europe's economy with that of the rest of the world, as well as a lowering of economic barriers within Europe."[38]

The Advisory Committee on Postwar Foreign Policy soon began discussing the possibility of organizing an economic union among the European nations west of the Russian border. The Subcommittee on Economic Policy met on 20 November 1942 to consider a document that suggested the need for American financial assistance to assure the success of an economically unified Europe.[39] Adolf Berle explained that the discussion revolved around the question of whether the United States should attempt "to recreate the many clashing national economies in Europe" with their separate tariff and transportation systems, or whether it should "take advantage of the fact that the Germans have wiped the slate clean" and try to get the European countries "to fuse as an economic region" with reasonably open trade and transportation arrangements. Berle thought that the issue should be settled before American troops landed on the continent and the various European governments began pursuing their individual interests. In the event that the United States should decide to encourage the economic unification of Europe, he proposed the establishment of an inland transport authority to facilitate commercial transactions on the continent and the creation of a customs council that would lower tariff barriers within Europe as rapidly as possible.[40]

The State Department decided a half-year later to establish the Special Subcommittee on Problems of European Organization under the chairmanship of Hamilton Fish Armstrong, the editor of *Foreign Affairs* and an original member of the Advisory Committee on Postwar Foreign Policy. After preliminary meetings between Armstrong and the research staff began in May 1943, the subcommittee immediately started to review the possibility of organizing an economic union among European countries west of the Soviet Union.[41] At the outset, the group tried to determine the feasibility of an overall economic organization on the European continent. One research study indicated that European interest in unification was largely confined to prominent figures and that public opinion might not wholeheartedly support the idea.[42] Another study suggested that many countries might oppose the admission of Germany into a European economic union.[43] But whatever the obstacles, the subcommittee proceeded to examine the idea with great care.

The Division of Economic Studies, operating under the supervision of Leroy Stinebower, assumed the task of analyzing the potential consequences of a full European customs union. As they began their deliberations in July 1943, the members of the research staff reasoned that the removal of trade barriers within Europe would enable each country on the continent to specialize in the production of those goods that it could manufacture or grow most efficiently. In addition, they believed that access to markets across the entire European continent would encourage the growth of industrial plants and thereby create economies of scale.[44] The research staff also thought that the economic unification of Europe would have a tremendous effect on world trade. The staff observed that with "an external trade considerably larger than the United Kingdom or the United States," a European economic union would be "in a position to become the most powerful single influence over world commercial policies."[45]

The Division of Economic Studies, in a document prepared on 17 September 1943, discussed whether a full European customs union would be advantageous or detrimental to the long-term interests of the United States. If an economically integrated Europe maintained liberal commercial relations with the rest of the world, the research staff argued, the demand for surplus American products could be expected to increase steadily as the countries on the continent became more efficient and had more income. But the consequences for the United States would be appalling to contemplate if a European economic union sought to become self-sufficient or to make bilateral agreements that discriminated against American commerce. Not only would the industrial and agricultural goods of the United States be shut out of the immense European market, the members of the research staff warned, but also the peace of the whole world might eventually be endangered. "The longer the period one has in view," they wrote, "the more it is necessary to take into account the possible re-emergence of a dominant and aggressive element on the Continent which would attempt to shape the commercial policy of the union to fit in with its political and military ambitions."[46]

Although postwar planners in the State Department hesitated to recommend the establishment of a full European customs union, they did advocate the unification of transportation services on the continent. The Special Committee on Inland Transport, which began work on 9 October 1943, envisioned the creation of a central agency with authority over the waterways, railroads, and highways of Europe. In a memorandum completed on 3 January 1944, the research staff explained that the principal function of the proposed agency would be to eliminate "nationalistic transport practices" that prevented trade from flowing freely across the continent.[47] Discussions a few months later in London between State Department representatives and British officials culminated in a joint Anglo-American proposal for a European inland-transit authority. However, even though the Post-War Programs Committee approved American participation in the projected agency on 14 July 1944, more than a year elapsed before an international conference finally established the European Central Inland Transport Organization.[48]

While promoting the unification of transportation services on the continent, American postwar planners sought to dissuade European labor unions from advocating restrictive policies that would place new barriers in the way of world trade. The Atlantic Charter had raised the hopes among workers throughout Europe for "improved labor standards, economic advancement, and social security," and during a conference that opened on 27 October 1941, the International Labor Organization (ILO) passed a resolution calling for the achievement of these peace aims.[49] Carter Goodrich, the chairman of the General Board of the ILO and a research associate for the Council on Foreign Relations, worried that labor demands for full employment after the war might prompt European governments to raise tariffs against foreign goods in order to protect domestic jobs. "So far labor pronouncements on international economic policy have not gone very far beyond general endorsements of the Atlantic Charter," Goodrich observed on 8 December 1942 in a Council on Foreign Relations study. "Before labors' attitude becomes crystallized, our government should state its policies in such a way as to make it clear that the two parts of the slogan, 'full employment and a rising standard of living,' can be attained only in a world of freer trade and expanded production."[50]

The State Department hoped to convince European labor leaders that their desire for jobs and bread could not be satisfied unless their governments adopted liberal commercial policies after the war. In his testimony before a congressional committee on 30 November 1944, Assistant Secretary of State Acheson explained that the ILO should be brought into close relationship with the Economic and Social Council of the projected United Nations to ensure that their activities were "in fact harmonious and consistent with each other." He and his colleagues were especially concerned about ILO plans for a world conference that might advocate restrictive trade policies to promote full employment after the war.[51] On 30 March 1945, Secretary of State Stettinius sent President Roosevelt a memorandum recommending that "an effective full employment program should be formulated which would be favorable to the expansion of international trade in accordance with comparative efficiencies of production."[52] The Secretary's Staff Committee, eager to keep labor in line, decided six weeks later that preparations should be made for an international conference on trade and employment to be held after the war.

While seeking European labor's support for liberal commercial policies, the State Department was drawing up plans for the reintegration of postwar Germany into the world economy. A Subcommittee on Economic Policy document, completed on 28 March 1943, pointed out that Germany had made a significant contribution to the expansion of international trade before the Nazis began making bilateral barter arrangements and preparing for war by reducing their dependence upon overseas supplies of raw materials and foodstuffs. Prior to the Great Depression, Germany had exported large quantities of coal, steel, chemical products, electrical equipment, and other manufactured goods. At the same time, Germany had been dependent upon imports "for ninety percent of its textile fibers, eighty percent of its iron ore, half of its fat supply, twenty percent of its total food supply, nearly all of its petroleum, most of the steel hardening metals, and a substantial percentage of its consumption of copper, lead, zinc, and bauxite."[53] The State Department, with these figures in mind, hoped that after the war Germany would once again play a major role in the development of an expanding world economy.

The State Department also hoped that Germany would make a substantial contribution to the economic reconstruction of Europe by resuming normal trade relations with its neighbors and by paying them reparations in the form of industrial products to compensate for the damage caused by the Nazi war machine. In a study prepared for the State

Department on 27 May 1944, Percy W. Bidwell and his research associates in the Council on Foreign Relations argued that the U.S. government should reject any proposals for the economic treatment of postwar Germany that "would so weaken German production as to retard the restoration of a vigorous economic life in the European countries which depend on German markets and German supplies."[54] The Executive Committee on Economic Foreign Policy, chaired by Assistant Secretary of State Acheson, concurred. While advocating the imposition of far-reaching controls over the German economy after the war, the committee recommended on 4 August 1944 that German industrial production ought be sufficient not only to satisfy the minimum requirements of the German people but also to enable Germany to pay other European countries "maximum reparation[s] for the reconstruction of war-torn areas."[55]

In a report for the secretary of state on 1 September 1944, Leo Pasvolsky summarized the plans of the Post-War Programs Committee regarding the economic treatment of Germany. "During the period of reparation," he wrote, "the German people should be permitted to retain enough of their production to maintain a minimum prescribed standard of living." Pasvolsky explained that reparations should not be extracted from Germany for more than about five years because a longer time period might retard the reintegration of Germany into the global economy. While Nazi influence should be completely eliminated from German economic life, he continued, German industry should be restored to a reasonable level of production. "We should aim to create conditions under which Germany will contribute to the reconstruction of Europe and to the development of a peaceful and expanding world economy," Pasvolsky concluded. "Ultimately, Germany should be assimilated into the world economy without discrimination other than that necessary for security controls."[56]

American policymakers likewise aimed to incorporate Italy into a new world order based upon the principles of liberal capitalism. But as plans for the invasion and occupation of Italy were being discussed in the spring of 1943, American officials worried that the British would attempt to establish an Italian government that would remain under their influence after the war ended. Under Secretary of State Sumner Welles told a colleague on 12 May that, contrary to his hopes for a liberal government in Rome, "the British want control of Italy as part of their complete control of the Mediterranean."[57] Secretary of War Stimson joined with Secretary of State Hull in opposing British plans to install natives who would be friendly to the United Kingdom in high positions in the military administration of Italy. "They are straining every nerve," Stimson complained on 1 June, "to lay a foundation throughout the Mediterranean area for their own empire after the war is over."[58] Although they agreed with the British that Russian influence in Italy should be kept to a minimum, President Roosevelt and his foreign-policy advisors believed that the whole Mediterranean region should be open to American trade and investment.

When American and British troops landed in Sicily on 10 July 1943, Prime Minister Churchill was eager to support the reestablishment of the monarchy in Italy. His opportunity came two weeks later when Benito Mussolini was removed from power and King Victor Emmanuel III asked Marshal Pietro Badoglio to head a new government. Churchill was pleased to receive a message from Roosevelt on 30 July indicating that he was willing to deal with anyone in Italy who could "best give us first disarmament and second assurance against chaos." But Churchill did not like the accompanying suggestion that he join with the president in "saying something about self-determination in Italy at the proper time." On the next day, Churchill replied that he was not in the least afraid of seeming to recognize the king and Badoglio, provided they could get Italians to support the Allied war purposes. "Those purposes," he declared, "would certainly be hindered by chaos, bolshevisation, or civil war." Churchill added that he would deprecate any pronouncement about self-determination at the present time. In a follow-up message on 4 August, Churchill informed Roosevelt that an Italian representative had warned British officials that only the king and Badoglio could save Italy from "rampant Bolshevism."[59]

Although President Roosevelt looked forward to the establishment of a democratic government in Italy, he was willing to work with King Victor Emmanuel and Prime Minister Badoglio in waging war against the Nazis. Roosevelt informed Churchill on 20 September 1943 that he would treat the present Italian government as a cobelligerent if it declared war on Germany. But the president insisted that the Italian people must retain the right to choose what form of government they wished after the Germans were driven out of their country.[60] On the recommendation of Gen. Dwight D. Eisenhower, the commander of U.S. forces in Europe, Roosevelt decided that the existing Italian government should be permitted to carry on until Allied troops captured Rome. But the State Department registered strong opposition when Churchill suggested that the king and Badoglio should be allowed to return to Rome if the city fell into Allied hands. Believing that a new political order in Italy would be more inclined to seek guidance from the United States than Great Britain, Hull wrote Roosevelt on 25 January 1944 that the State Department had concluded that no political reconstruction under the present king was possible and that there should be no further delay in reorganizing the Italian government on a broad political basis.[61]

But Roosevelt directed the State Department not to take any action to change the existing Italian government until the military situation improved enough to risk alienating Italians who were assisting the Allied forces.[62] The time for a new political order in Italy finally came on 4 June 1944 when Allied soldiers marched into Rome. With tacit approval from Washington, Ivanoe Bonomi, an opponent of the Crown, formed a new Italian government and appointed Count Carlo Sforza, an American favorite, to the post of foreign minister. Sforza had previously warned Robert D. Murphy, the State Department advisor to General Eisenhower, that the retention of the king and Badoglio had enabled Italian communists to make large gains.[63] Despite arguments from Churchill against allowing a change of government in Italy, Roosevelt cabled the prime minister on 15 June that it would be a grave mistake not to permit the Bonomi cabinet to be promptly installed. The president argued that any interference in what appeared to be a representative government would have serious repercussions in Italy "to the detriment of the military situation and the profit of mischievous elements there."[64]

After the British grudgingly agreed to support the new Bonomi regime, the Roosevelt administration moved swiftly to provide Italy with economic assistance needed for relief and rehabilitation. Secretary of State Hull cabled Rome on 16 September 1944 to indicate his willingness to receive a technical mission from Italy to discuss economic and financial problems. During the next two months, the United States gave the Italian government $100,000,000 credit, and the U.S. military spent $120,000,000 in Italy for civilian relief.[65] This U.S. economic-aid program was designed to make sure that the first defeated Axis country would be integrated into a liberal capitalist international order. American policymakers did not want the British to establish an exclusive sphere of economic influence throughout the Mediterranean, nor did they want the Communist party to gain control of the government in Rome and bring Italy into the Russian orbit after the war. In a letter to Churchill on 11 February 1945, Roosevelt argued that it was in their joint interest to provide economic aid to Italy because "those who fish in troubled waters will be the only ones to gain from her present condition approaching despair."[66]

President Roosevelt and his State Department advisors also hoped that France would be integrated into a liberal capitalist world system. From the day that France fell into the hands of Hitler, American policy-makers held to the belief that the French people should have the right to elect their political leaders after the Nazis were expelled from their country. But U.S. officials became apprehensive about the ambitions of Gen. Charles de Gaulle, the head of the Free French forces and the symbol of French resistance to German occupation. In a memorandum sent to Roosevelt on 5 May 1942, Hull warned that there were numerous indications that de Gaulle and the French National Committee in London were endeavoring to create a provisional government that would rule postwar France.[67] H. Freeman Matthews, writing from his diplomatic post in London on 11 September, predicted that there would be a power struggle within the Free French movement. While de Gaulle and most of his early followers aimed to impose a right-wing regime on the French people, Matthews reported, most who had recently joined the movement intended to establish a left-wing government in Paris. "Each group," he concluded, "looks upon the other as a temporary necessity to be ousted once France is free."[68]

After Anglo-American forces invaded French North Africa on 8 November 1942, President Roosevelt and Secretary of State Hull were disturbed by reports that the British Foreign Office wished to assist de Gaulle in establishing a provisional government that would run postwar France.[69] In a memorandum he handed President Roosevelt on 10 May 1943, Hull pointed out that de Gaulle was seeking communist support in his drive to become the ruler of France. "We must," he concluded, "reach agreement with the British on the fundamental question as to the future of France and the manner in which the free expression of the French will as to their Government may be obtained."[70] When de Gaulle helped set up the French Committee of National Liberation in North Africa a month later, Roosevelt worried that de Gaulle might obtain control of the French troops in Morocco and Algeria.[71] "This government's position is that we will not tolerate, during our military occupation of North Africa, the control of the French Army by any agency not subject to the direction of the Allied Supreme Commander," he cabled General Eisenhower on 17 June. "Under no circumstances would we continue the arming of a force unless we had complete confidence in their willingness to cooperate in our military operations. Nor are we interested in the formation of any committee or government that in any way presumes to indicate that it will govern in France until such time as the French people select a government for themselves."[72]

In a message to Churchill on the same day, Roosevelt argued that the time had arrived for the United States and Great Britain to break with the French general. "We must divorce ourselves from DeGaulle," he declared. "My affirmative thought is that we should go ahead and encourage the creation of a committee of Frenchmen made up of people who really want to fight the war and are not thinking too much about politics."[73] But the British refused to discard de Gaulle. Worried that the United States might withdraw from European political affairs after the war and advocate the liberation of European colonies in Asia, Anthony Eden and his aides in the British Foreign Office wanted to maintain a close relationship with postwar France. Believing that the French people would rally behind de Gaulle when the war ended, British diplomats argued that the Allies should recognize the French Committee of National Liberation as the provisional government of France.[74] But Roosevelt and his advisers held to their anti-Gaullist position. After his conference with Churchill in Quebec ended on 24 August 1943, Roosevelt issued a statement insisting that the French people must be free to choose their own government upon their liberation from Germany.[75]

As American military leaders made final preparations for the invasion and occupation of France, Under Secretary Stettinius and several State Department officials traveled to London in April 1944 to discuss foreign-policy questions with British leaders. "We argued at length that in practice General Eisenhower would deal with the French Committee in all his pre-invasion planning," reported Matthews, now serving as deputy director of the Office of European Affairs. "We made it clear that neither the Department nor General Eisenhower has any intention of encouraging any rival group which may emerge in France, but we did feel that General Eisenhower's hands should not be tied to the extent of maintaining the Committee with American bayonets should it prove unacceptable to the French people." The talks brought out a distinct difference in American and British expectations with respect to what the Allies would find when they landed on French soil. "Whereas we consider that as France is liberated a period of some confusion, disorder, and even a limited blood bath are at least possible, the British attitude is one of convinced optimism," Matthews explained. "They not only hope, but believe, that the entire country will rally to the support of General DeGaulle and the Committee, and will accept their dictates without question."[76]

Prime Minister Churchill was caught in the crossfire. On the one side, the British Foreign Office wanted to recognize the French Committee of National Liberation as the provisional government of France. On the other side, President Roosevelt stood firm in his insistence that the French people should be free to choose their own government after their liberation from German occupation. Churchill was inclined to go along with Roosevelt. In addition to his personal dislike for de Gaulle, the prime minister placed a high value on maintaining close Anglo-American relations. He believed that the United States would be far more important than France to the future security and prosperity of Great Britain.[77] After spending a weekend with the prime minister in England, however, W. Averell Harriman, the U.S. ambassador to the Soviet Union, reported to Roosevelt on 29 May 1944 that Churchill was having a hard time restraining his own associates. "The Prime Minister promises he will faithfully follow your line regarding DeGaulle," Harriman cabled, "but warns that the Foreign Office and some members of his Cabinet are insistent on going further."[78]

But Anglo-American differences with respect to de Gaulle rapidly dissolved after Allied soldiers began their assault on 6 June 1944 along the beaches of Normandy. As American and British troops pushed into the interior of France, it became increasingly evident that the great majority of the French people embraced de Gaulle as their leader and freely accepted the civil administration that he had set up in liberated areas. American fears that de Gaulle would use force to establish himself as a dictator or that France would be engulfed by a bloody revolution gradually dissipated, and State Department officials finally convinced Roosevelt that refusal to support de Gaulle would retard the development of friendly relations with France. Accordingly, on 23 October 1944, the United States joined with Great Britain in recognizing the French Committee of National Liberation as the provisional government of the French Republic. Roosevelt immediately appointed Jefferson Caffery to be the U.S. ambassador in Paris, and the United States quickly began shipping lend-lease supplies to France.[79]

Despite their decision to support de Gaulle, U.S. officials had reason to worry that the virus of economic nationalism would infect France and then spread into neighboring countries. Simon L. Millner of the Foreign Economic Administration reported on 9 October 1944 that French leaders were making plans for the provisional government in Paris to nationalize basic industries and to control foreign trade. "Nearly all economic thought expressed by DeGaulle's government and in the Underground resistance circles," he warned, "is resolutely opposed to economic liberalism and orthodoxy."[80] Nevertheless, the State Department hoped to induce de Gaulle to adopt liberal economic policies, in part, by offering to rearm France with American weapons. "The furnishing of arms by the United States to France," Secretary of State Stettinius advised Roosevelt on 28 December 1944, "may provide this Government with a lever to exercise a certain measure of influence on French policy for a number of years."[81]

American policymakers had always included France, along with the other industrial countries of Western Europe, in their plans for a liberal capitalist new world order. Convinced that American prosperity would depend upon European recovery, they believed that the United States had a vital economic interest in helping France regain its strength and remain free from Russian domination. "It will hardly be possible for us to maintain our present standard of living if we lose too many of our world markets," Ambassador Caffery warned on 12 December 1944. "If France does not stand on her own feet again; does not remain independent and does not regain her strength and prosperity; France will fall under the domination of another power. If France falls under the domination of another power all the smaller countries of Western Europe will fall also. In that case it is very possible that we would lose a good part of our continental markets especially if the dominating power imposed another economic system throughout the continent."[82]

Postwar planners hoped to use American financial power not only to prevent the industrial countries of Western Europe from falling into the Russian orbit but also to promote close postwar economic and diplomatic relations with the Soviet Union. During a visit to Moscow in mid-October 1943, Donald M. Nelson, chairman of the War Production Board and former vice president of Sears, told top officials in the Soviet government that he looked forward to a mutually beneficial exchange of goods between the United States and Russia after the war. He said that the United States would have a vast surplus of industrial equipment that could be used to rebuild the Russian economy, while the Soviet Union had an ample supply of raw materials that the United States could use. Nelson emphasized that he was not speaking officially for his government but that he was simply expressing his own views as an American businessman. During conversations with Nelson, Foreign Minister

Vyacheslav Molotov and Commisar of Foreign Trade Anasthasias Mikoyan showed fervent interest in obtaining large quantities of capital goods from the United States for Russian economic reconstruction.[83]

So did Stalin when he met with Nelson on 15 October 1943 in the Kremlin. "Do you think American business would extend long-term credits to Russia?" Stalin asked. Nelson replied that he believed such credits would be forthcoming if satisfactory terms for repayment could be arranged. "We will guarantee our payments," Stalin declared. "Any obligation undertaken by this Government will be repaid." Then he indicated that Russia would want to buy the following items from the United States immediately after the war: steam and hydroelectric equipment to generate 250,000 to 300,000 kilowatts of power; 10,000 locomotives; 50,000 railroad cars; and 50,000 kilometers of track. After noting that Russia would be impoverished when the war ended, Nelson suggested a sliding scale of repayments that would remain small for the first five years and then mount as the Soviet economy progressively recovered. "I approve wholeheartedly," Stalin exclaimed. "We like to do business with the United States better than with the British. We like American material and American engineers. Everything you send us is of very good quality."[84]

Secretary of State Hull and W. Averell Harriman, the U.S. ambassador in Moscow, hoped to establish a sound economic basis for postwar collaboration with the Soviet Union. Harriman was the son of a great nineteenth-century railroad baron, and he had a diverse background in business, with interests in railroading, shipbuilding, mining, and banking. During the Conference of Foreign Ministers, which opened in Moscow on 19 October 1943, Hull gave Molotov a memorandum proposing that the United States should cooperate fully in the economic rehabilitation of the Soviet Union. Hull suggested that Soviet officials should begin conversations with U.S. diplomatic representatives in Moscow to determine the amount and kind of equipment that the Russians would need to repair the damage caused by the Germans.[85] During a discussion with Mikoyan on 5 November, Harriman said that the Russians should start thinking about what they would like to buy from the United States to rebuild their economy. He also mentioned the possibility that the Soviet Union might be able to obtain a credit to purchase materials that American factories would desire to sell when they changed over from military to civilian production.[86]

When the Big Three met a few weeks later in Teheran, there was some discussion about prospects for postwar economic collaboration between the United States and the Soviet Union. In response to a question from President Roosevelt on 28 November, Stalin said that in return for American equipment shipped to Russian ports after the war, the Soviet Union could provide the United States with a plentiful supply of raw materials.[87] Neither Roosevelt nor Stalin raised the question of American financial aid for Russian economic reconstruction during their talks. But in private conversations at Teheran, the president did discuss the subject with Ambassador Harriman and Harry Hopkins, and he authorized the ambassador to continue his direct negotiations with the Russians in Moscow. Harriman talked with Molotov on 31 December about the possibility of the Soviet Union obtaining a postwar credit from the United States for the purchase of American goods, and he promptly reported to Hopkins that Molotov had displayed "the keenest interest in the matter."[88]

Harriman believed that the U.S. government should furnish the Russians with a credit to obtain materials needed for reconstruction while restricting lend-lease shipments to supplies that the Soviets needed to fight the war. In a telegram to Hull on 9 January 1944, Harriman argued that a postwar reconstruction credit would not only promote close political relations with the Soviet Union but that it would also provide an outlet for American goods "at the time when our factories and labor are released from the production of war materials."[89] In a follow-up telegram to Hull the same day, Harriman suggested that the first credit should be relatively small, that the money should be used only to purchase goods and services from the United States, and that the specific procurements should be approved item by item in Washington. "The United States Government as a matter of general policy should retain control of the unallocated balance of the credit at all times," he advised. "There are many undetermined questions in our relations with Russia and therefore we should NOT put ourselves in a position where this credit could be used for purposes incompatible with the interests of the United States."[90]

But the State Department balked when Harriman reported that he had received a proposal from Mikoyan on 1 February 1944 that the U.S. government extend Russia a reconstruction credit of about $1 billion. Hull and his aides hesitated for two reasons. First, the Johnson Act prohibited both private and government loans to nations like the Soviet Union that had not paid their debts to the United States. Second, the Export-Import Bank did not have sufficient funds available to meet Russian needs for postwar financial assistance. State Department officials hoped that these difficulties could be overcome in the future, but they were not yet ready to ask Congress to repeal the Johnson Act and to increase the lending capacity of the Export-Import Bank. They decided, in the meantime, that some equipment that the Russians most urgently wanted for postwar reconstruction could be shipped from the United States under the authority of the Lend-Lease Act.[91] In a message to Harriman on 4 February 1944, Hopkins suggested that the Soviet Union could place lend-lease orders for materials that might be used either during the war or after the war. He explained that the Russians would be required to pay the United States later for any dual-purpose equipment that had not been delivered by the end of the war.[92]

But in his reply to Hopkins a few days later, Harriman pointed out that some equipment that the Russians desired could not reasonably be justified for war use because it could not be produced until long after hostilities ceased. The ambassador therefore recommended that the United States should begin working at once with the Soviet Union on a comprehensive reconstruction program that included items to be financed under a separate credit arrangement in addition to items to be supplied under the lend-lease agreement.[93] Although he agreed that lend-lease should be used as a stopgap to provide some postwar assistance to the Soviet Union, Harriman believed that a reconstruction credit could be employed not only as an economic measure to facilitate the sale of American products but also as a diplomatic lever to extract political concessions from the Russians. The ambassador stressed in a telegram to Hopkins on 13 February that the subject should be energetically pursued in the hope of finding a way to take prompt action. "If aid for Russian reconstruction is to be of real value in our overall relations with the Soviet Government as a benefit which they can obtain from us if they play the international game with us in accordance with our standards we must have a well forged instrument to offer them," Harriman reasoned. "Vague promises excite Soviet suspicions whereas a precise program offered now to them but kept always within our control to suspend will be of extreme value. Stalin must offer his people quick reconstruction to retain supreme leadership. We on the other hand want Russian business quickly during our period of conversion from war production."[94]

After Hull decided to establish an interdepartmental committee to study the subject, Morgenthau asked his aides in the Treasury Department to explore the possibility of extending a large credit to the Soviet Union to be repaid with shipments of strategic raw materials to the United States. Assistant Secretary Harry Dexter White headed the Treasury

Department investigation. In a memorandum to Morgenthau on 7 March, White reported that a $5 billion credit for the purchase of American products would be feasible because the Soviet Union could export strategic raw materials at an average annual value of at least $500 million. White argued that such a financial arrangement would be desirable as well as practical. "The U.S. will obtain access to an important source of strategic raw materials which are expected to be in short supply in the U.S. after the war," he explained. "The U.S. will also be assured an important market for its industrial products, since the U.S.S.R. represents one of the largest single sources of demand in Europe." White concluded that Soviet orders for American goods "could make an important contribution to the maintenance of full employment during our transition to a peace economy."[95]

Spokesmen for the American business community also regarded the Soviet Union as a potentially vast postwar market for the United States. No one did more to propagate this view in American business circles than Eric Johnston, the energetic president of the U.S. Chamber of Commerce. During a discussion with Stalin on 26 June 1944, Johnston indicated that he would do everything in his power to promote the extension of credits to the Soviet Union for the purchase of American machinery.[96] Stalin told Johnston that the Soviet Union would be able to provide the United States with large quantities of manganese, chrome, platinum, copper, tungsten, and petroleum. After spending eight weeks in the Soviet Union, Johnston reported to the members of the chamber of commerce that the Russians would need long-term credits to buy American goods and that they could repay their financial obligations by shipping raw materials to the United States. American business journals shared his enthusiasm for trade with the Soviet Union. In a typical expression of business opinion, one magazine described Russia as "the richest potential export market for American industrial equipment."[97]

Some U.S. diplomats, however, were pessimistic about the prospects for developing a mutually beneficial economic relationship with the Russians. George F. Kennan, the counselor at the U.S. embassy in Moscow, warned Harriman on 3 December 1944 that the Kremlin regarded foreign trade as a political weapon designed to make the Soviet Union more powerful than other countries. "It will view imports from our country only as a necessary means of hastening the achievement of complete military-economic autarchy of the Soviet Union," he predicted. "Once such autarchy has been substantially achieved, it is not sure that the Soviet

Government will be interested in large scale imports from the United States." Kennan also warned that Russian intentions had not yet been made sufficiently clear to warrant the assumption that "in furthering the military industrialization of the Soviet Union during the post-hostilities period we will not again, as in the cases of Germany and Japan, be creating military strength which might some day be used to our disadvantage."[98]

Despite their desire to facilitate the sale of American products to Russia after the war, President Roosevelt and his State Department advisers decided to withhold financial aid to the Soviet Union until Stalin demonstrated that he did not wish to dominate Eastern Europe. When Molotov proposed on 3 January 1945 that the United States extend the Soviet Union a $6 billion credit for the purchase of industrial equipment from American factories, Harriman advised that "at the appropriate time the Russians should be given to understand that our willingness to cooperate whole-heartedly with them in their vast reconstruction problems will depend upon their behavior in international matters."[99] President Roosevelt and Secretary of State Stettinius concurred. When Morgenthau proposed a week later that the United States offer the Soviet Union a $10 billion reconstruction credit, Roosevelt indicated that he wanted to postpone any discussion with the Russians about postwar financial assistance. "I think it's very important," Stettinius declared in reference to the credit request from the Russians, "that we hold this back and don't give them any promise of finance until we get what we want."[100]

Along with their decision to employ financial aid as a bargaining device to dissuade the Russians from establishing an exclusive sphere of influence in Eastern Europe, American policymakers were eager to help Western Europe attain economic stability as soon as possible. "The Soviet Government is attempting through the communist parties supported by it to penetrate the countries of Western Europe with the hope of expanding Soviet influence," Harriman cabled the State Department on 4 April 1945. "The development of sound economic conditions in these countries is the only hope of stopping Soviet penetration." He therefore recommended that the United States should distribute relief supplies to "our western allies and other areas under our responsibility first, allocating what may be left to Russia." Harriman also advised that U.S. economic policy should be oriented toward the development of friendly relations with the Soviet Union but always on a quid-pro-quo basis. "This means," he concluded, "tying our economic assistance directly into our political problems with the Soviet Union."[101]

The American approach to the problems of European relief and reconstruction did not change when Roosevelt died a week later and Harry S. Truman became president. In a memorandum for Truman on 16 April 1945, Secretary of State Stettinius emphasized "the disastrous political and economic results which may be expected if countries dependent on food imports, especially the liberated areas, have to go through another winter of want." Stettinius recommended that the president instruct the appropriate civilian agencies to explore ways to reduce food consumption in the United States.[102] In a memorandum for Truman two weeks later, Foreign Economic Administrator Crowley stressed that the United States must continue rationing food at home and help feed people in the liberated areas of Europe to "prevent unrest, chaos, and revolution."[103] Secretary of War Stimson also worried that a food shortage in the countries of Western Europe would have dangerous social and political consequences. "It is vital," he wrote Truman on 16 May, "to keep these countries from being driven to revolution or Communism by famine."[104]

President Truman agreed. "The needs of the liberated countries of Northwest Europe are grave—not only from a humanitarian point of view, but also because they necessarily involve many internal and international political considerations," he noted on 21 May in a private memorandum for the secretary of the interior. "To a great extent the future permanent peace of Europe depends upon the restoration of the economy of these liberated countries, including a reasonable standard of living and employment. United States economy, too, will be deeply affected unless these areas again resume their place in the international exchange of goods and services." Truman firmly believed that it was in the long-term interests of the United States to ship food supplies to the industrial countries in Western Europe. "A chaotic and hungry Europe," he concluded, "is not fertile ground in which stable, democratic, and friendly governments can be reared."[105] Twelve days later, in a direct appeal to the American people, Truman called for greater production and conservation of food in the United States so that more could be done to help feed millions of hungry Europeans.[106]

Furthermore, President Truman and his foreign policy advisers believed that, in addition to shipping food to European countries, the United States should help them rebuild their war-torn industries. During a conversation with Budget Director Harold D. Smith on 26 April, Truman said he realized that Congress strongly opposed the use of lend-lease funds for postwar reconstruction and that "if we use lend-lease for rehabilitation purposes we will open ourselves to a lot of trouble." But the president said that Crowley had suggested that a better way to make funds available for European reconstruction would be to increase appropriations for the Export-Import Bank.[107] On 6 June, Crowley informed the director of War Mobilization and Reconversion that Congress would be asked to authorize a substantial increase in the lending capacity of the Export-Import Bank so that European countries could barrow money needed to purchase American equipment. "It is vital to our political and economic interests that the supplies and services which foreign countries need urgently for rehabilitation and reconstruction be provided," Crowley explained. "If there is a drastic curtailment in the flow of such supplies and services, the consequences are likely to be grave political instability in Europe, a marked decline in employment and production in the United States, and the planting of the seeds of another war."[108]

In a memorandum for President Truman on 6 July, Crowley warned that Congress would be less disposed to support a comprehensive program of financial aid for European reconstruction if lend-lease funds were used for any postwar purposes. "It is important," he emphasized, "that in dealing with the postwar requirements of Europe, we develop a well-rounded coordinated over-all policy rather than attempt to do an unintegrated job through a misuse of lend-lease."[109] The president concurred. Truman decided to ask Congress to expand the lending capacity of the Export-Import Bank from $700 million to $3.5 billion so that sufficient funds would be available to meet the financial needs of Europe during the coming year. He also decided to ask Congress to repeal the Johnson Act so that loans could be made to countries that had not paid their debts to the United States. On 31 July, after only a brief debate, Congress passed legislation that complied with both of his requests.[110]

On 17 August, just three days after the cessation of hostilities in the Pacific, Truman directed the Foreign Economic Administration to take immediate steps to terminate the lend-lease program. Crowley promptly notified foreign governments that the United States would not enter into any new contracts to furnish goods or services to be financed with lend-lease appropriations. But he explained that foreign governments would be able to obtain supplies that were already in the pipeline (that is, in the process of manufacture in the United States, in storage waiting shipment, in transit, or in inventory abroad) if they agreed to pay for them on a cash or credit basis.[111] The decision to discontinue the lend-lease program meant that during the immediate postwar years, the U.S. government would utilize funds in the Export-Import Bank, along with private loans guaranteed by the International Bank for Reconstruction and Development, to provide financial assistance for the economic rehabilitation of Western Europe. But after it became clear that the job of reconstruction demanded more than interest-bearing loans, Truman decided to ask Congress to appropriate funds for the Marshall Plan so that the countries of Western Europe could obtain financial aid in the form of grants that did not have to be repaid to the United States.

During the war, American policymakers had decided that it would be necessary for the United States to take various steps to promote the economic rehabilitation of Europe. They made preparations to send food, clothing, and other essentials to war-torn countries on the continent as soon as the fighting ended to prevent widespread deprivation and radical social upheavals. They also made long-range plans for the United States to extend huge loans to help the industrial nations of Western Europe get back on their feet and regain their ability to buy American goods. As a central element in their program to foster the economic reconstruction of Europe, State Department officials aimed to permit the restoration of German industrial production to a level that would enable Germany to resume normal trade relations with its neighbors and to pay them reparations needed to rebuild their factories. Finally, the postwar planners in Washington intended to use financial aid as a tool not only to stimulate the sale of American products throughout Europe, and thereby prevent a postwar depression in the United States, but also to keep France and Italy from being drawn into the Russian orbit and to dissuade the Soviets from extending their influence across the continent.

FOUR | DECOLONIZING ASIA AND AFRICA

Determined to establish a peaceful and prosperous international order, President Roosevelt and his State Department advisors made a concerted effort to pave the way for the gradual decolonization of Asia and Africa after the war. They feared that the perpetuation of colonial monopolies in the postwar era, besides placing barriers against the expansion of American exports into large parts of the planet, might provoke some industrial countries to embark upon programs of military conquest to obtain essential foodstuffs and raw materials. American policymakers also feared that the continued exploitation of colonial peoples might stimulate a wave of violent revolutionary upheavals in underdeveloped areas around the world. They were particularly worried that the imperial activities of the British, Dutch, and French would give rise to a Pan-Asiatic movement that would endanger the commercial and financial interests of all Western nations in the Far East. Although they occasionally held conflicting views regarding the means that should be used to achieve their anticolonial ends, U.S. leaders agreed on the need to put European rule in Asia and Africa on the road to ultimate extinction.

Postwar planners in the United States were especially critical of the mandate system that had been created after World War I. The peacemakers at Versailles had decided to entrust individual countries with the responsibility for administering the overseas colonies of Germany as mandates under the authority of the League of Nations. While German possessions in the Pacific were turned over to Japan, those in Africa were distributed among the victorious European powers. The administrating nations were supposed to promote the welfare of the local inhabitants and to provide other countries with an equal opportunity to trade in these territories. But U.S. diplomats complained that the administrating powers were actually treating the mandates as colonies to be exploited for their exclusive benefit. Soon after the onset of World War II, State Department officials began drafting blueprints for a United Nations trusteeship system, based upon the concept of international accountability, that would promote home rule and nondiscriminatory trade in dependent areas throughout the postwar world.

President Roosevelt tried to get Prime Minister Churchill committed to the principle of national self-determination even before the Japanese attack on Pearl Harbor. During their historic meeting aboard ship off the Newfoundland coast, Roosevelt suggested that they issue a joint declaration laying down certain broad principles that would guide them in building a better world. Churchill immediately agreed. Article 3 of the resulting Atlantic Charter, released to the press on 14 August 1941, stipulated that the United States and Great Britain would "respect the right of all peoples to choose the form of government under which they will live." But a debate over the meaning of these words soon revealed a basic difference in Anglo-American attitudes toward the colonial question. In a speech before the House of Commons on 9 September 1941, Churchill insisted that Article 3 applied only to European nations living under Nazi occupation and that it had nothing to do with India, Burma, or other parts of the British Empire. Roosevelt later asserted, however, that he had always viewed Article 3 as having universal application. In a Memorial Day address on 30 May 1942, Under Secretary of State Sumner Welles clearly articulated the American position. "The principles of the Atlantic Charter," he declared, "must be guaranteed to the world as a whole."[1]

Hoping to ensure Indian support for the Allied war effort, President Roosevelt had already proposed that the British take immediate steps to permit the peaceful evolution of self-government in India. He and his advisors realized that Indian nationalists were not satisfied with British promises to grant their homeland dominion status after the war. Furthermore, as they watched Japanese forces drive the British out of Malaya and Burma, American leaders feared that the Indian people would refuse to resist if Japan invaded their country. "We should demand that India be given a status of autonomy," Assistant Secretary of State Breckinridge Long argued on 25 February 1942. "The only way to get the people of India to fight is to get them to fight for India."[2] The president decided to prod Churchill two days after the fall of Rangoon. In a message to the prime minister on 10 March, Roosevelt suggested that the Indians should be allowed to set up a temporary government (representing the different castes, occupations, religions, and geographical areas) with the understanding that they would have the opportunity soon after the war to create a permanent government for the whole Indian subcontinent.[3]

Aiming to placate the president while prolonging British sovereignty over India, Churchill promptly announced that he was sending Stafford Cripps to New Delhi to negotiate with the Indian nationalists. Cripps arrived at the capital in late March 1942 and offered dominion status for

India after the war, though subject to the right of any province to stand aside and establish a separate government. In other words, the Muslim minority would have the option of building their own nation in Pakistan. But the Congress party, dominated by the Hindu majority and led by Mohandas Gandhi and Jawaharlal Nehru, would settle for nothing less than immediate independence. Congress party leaders demanded the right to create a unified Indian state without conditions that would lead to partition. Rejecting the Cripps proposal, they charged that the British were cynically trying to provoke discord between Hindus and Muslims in order to perpetuate their rule over India. Louis Johnson, the personal representative of President Roosevelt in New Delhi, concluded that British officials in London were working to sabotage the Cripps mission.[4]

Roosevelt did not hesitate to blame the British when Churchill reported that the talks between Cripps and the Indian nationalists had broken down. In an angry message that Harry Hopkins delivered to the prime minister on 11 April 1942, Roosevelt expressed hope that Cripps would be instructed to remain in India and resume his efforts to reach an agreement. "The feeling is almost universally held that the deadlock has been caused by the unwillingness of the British Government to concede to the Indians the right of self-government, notwithstanding the willingness of the Indians to entrust technical, military and naval defense control to the competent British authorities," the president admonished. "If the present negotiations are allowed to collapse because of the issues as presented to the American people and India should subsequently be successfully invaded by Japan with attendant serious military or naval defeats for our side, the prejudicial reaction on American public opinion can hardly be over-estimated." But Churchill told Hopkins that he would rather resign than bow to American pressure to reopen the Indian question. "I do not feel I could take responsibility for the defense of India," he cabled Roosevelt the next day, "if everything has again to be thrown into the melting pot at this critical juncture."[5]

After Roosevelt was rebuffed by the prime minister, American policymakers adopted a more cautious approach toward Indian affairs. The president and his State Department advisors did not want to get into a serious dispute with Great Britain over India during the war. Nor did they want to do anything to encourage the civil disobedience campaign that the Congress party had decided to launch even though India remained in danger of an attack from Japan.[6] During a meeting of the Pacific War Council on 12 August 1942, the president stated that in his judgment India was not yet ready for home rule. "One thing is certain,"

Roosevelt emphasized, "open hostilities in India will slow up the United Nations war effort."[7] But if U.S. leaders were not inclined to exert further pressure on Churchill, they did express their concern when the British responded to the growing unrest in India by putting Gandhi and thousands of other Indian nationalists in jail. Secretary of State Cordell Hull decided on 17 September to ask Lord Halifax, the British ambassador in Washington, if there were any prospects for a resumption of conversations between his government and the Indian leaders. During their private discussion, Hull warned that a continued impasse might lead to widespread agitation in the United States against Great Britain and in favor of independence for India.[8]

Prominent journalists and politicians in the United States, aroused by reports about the situation in India, soon became highly critical of British imperial policy. In an open letter to the people of England, the editors of *Life* magazine declared on 12 October 1942 that the American people were not fighting against the Axis powers in order "to hold the British Empire together." Wendell Willkie, the Republican candidate for president two years earlier, returned home from a widely publicized round-the-world tour and made a bitter attack on British imperialism. In a national radio broadcast on 26 October, Willkie announced that the hundreds of millions of people living in Asia were "no longer willing to be Eastern slaves for Western profits." His speech quickly sent Churchill into a public rage. "We mean to hold our own," the prime minister proclaimed on 10 November. "I have not become the King's First Minister in order to preside over the liquidation of the British Empire."[9]

Eager to improve Anglo-American relations, the British Foreign Office proposed that the United States send a well-known and highly respected person to New Delhi. The British thought they were getting someone who could be convinced to sympathize with their position when President Roosevelt decided to dispatch former under secretary of state William Phillips to India as his personal representative.[10] Phillips was an Anglophile from a wealthy New England family, and during a long and distinguished career as a diplomat, he had earned a reputation for being a tactful negotiator with an ability to understand all sides of an issue. After consulting with the president, Secretary of State Hull instructed Phillips on 18 November 1942 that he should not place objectionable pressure on British authorities but that he could speak bluntly to them about the desirability of preparing India for independence at the earliest practicable date.[11] The Advisory Committee on Postwar Foreign Policy agreed with this approach to India. At a meeting held a few weeks later, the members of the Subcommittee on Political Problems unanimously concluded that the United States, while refraining from intervening in the Indian imbroglio during the war, should do everything proper to promote self-determination for the people of India after the war.[12]

But following his arrival in New Delhi on 8 January 1943, Phillips decided that immediate steps should be taken to assure the Indian people that they would be set free shortly after the cessation of hostilities. In a letter sent to the White House on 3 March, Phillips recommended that Roosevelt should try to get the British to make a cast-iron pledge to grant independence to India on a certain date after the war and to make a prompt transfer of substantial powers to an interim Indian government. He added that it might be necessary for the U.S. government to indicate that it stood behind British promises.[13] "India and China and Burma have a common meeting ground in their desire for freedom from foreign domination," Phillips wrote the president on 19 April. "Color consciousness is also appearing more and more and under present conditions is bound to develop. We have, therefore, a vast bloc of Oriental peoples who have many things in common, including a growing dislike and distrust of the Occidental." The only remedy for this disturbing situation, he argued, was to do everything "in our power to make Indians feel that America is with them and in a position to go beyond mere public assurances of friendship."[14] But Roosevelt was unwilling to press Churchill and risk alienating the British.

When he returned home to report to the president in May 1943, however, Phillips repeated his argument that the British should immediately establish a provisional Indian government with considerable authority over civil affairs and make a solemn pledge that India would be granted independence on a specified date after the war. He also had a chance to explain his ideas to Churchill, who happened to be in Washington at that time. But when the prime minister became angry and predicted a blood bath if Great Britain withdrew from India, Phillips concluded that it was hopeless to try to get Churchill to change his views on the subject.[15] Indeed, throughout the war, the prime minister remained firm in his belief that the people of India were unfit for self-government. "We cannot turn over the government of so vast an area and so many people to ignorant folk," Churchill told an American postwar planner in April 1944. "They marry young, they are immature mentally, they breed far in excess of reason seeming to think that to stretch their limbs out in the sun and let the light of Heaven shine on them is the chief aim of existence. How can you expect government from such people?"[16]

Even though Churchill refused to alter his attitudes toward India, President Roosevelt and his State Department advisers still hoped to prevent the development of an "Asia for the Asiatics" movement that would threaten U.S. economic and strategic interests in the whole region. "The discriminatory nature of our immigration and naturalization laws with regard to racial requirements is believed to be the most outstanding cause of resentment toward the United States by educated Indians," a State Department document noted in January 1945. "It has been Mr. William Phillips' opinion, in which the Office of Near Eastern and African Affairs concurs, that if allowed to increase, resentment on this and similar scores may at some later time result in open and hostile alignment by the people of India with other colored nations against the so-called Anglo-Saxon and kindred races."[17] Fearful of a rise in antiwhite sentiment throughout Asia, the president and the State Department made a concerted effort in March 1945 to get Congress to pass a bill that would extend immigration and naturalization privileges to the people of India.[18]

Although Roosevelt died on 12 April 1945, the State Department continued to push for the removal of the prohibition against Indian immigration in the then-current statutes. Under Secretary of State Joseph C. Grew, who had served as the U.S. ambassador in Japan for ten years, brought the matter to the attention of Harry S. Truman soon after he became president. In a memorandum for Truman on 9 June 1945, Grew warned that it might be difficult to expand American exports to India if the immigration laws of the United States continued to discriminate against the Indian people. "India has plans for post-war economic reconstruction which surpass anything seen anywhere outside Russia," he emphasized, "and the country is a great potential market for American goods."[19] Subsequently convinced of the need for his personal intervention, Truman urged an old friend in the Senate to expedite the passage of a bill that would permit about one hundred Indians a year to move to the United States. But Congress, faced with opposition from the American Federation of Labor and other organizations, waited a full year before it enacted a measure that allowed even a small number of Indians to settle in the United States.[20]

Earlier, before his decision to back away from a confrontation with Churchill over India, Roosevelt had begun thinking about how the United States could promote the gradual decolonization of other parts of the world. He was particularly eager to help the peoples of Southeast Asia get started along the road to independence. During a conversation with Soviet foreign minister Vyacheslav Molotov on 1 June 1942, the president revealed his budding ideas regarding colonial possessions. Roosevelt suggested that some form of international trusteeship would be the best method of administering various dependent territories until they were prepared for self-government. Although French Indochina, British Malaya, and the Dutch East Indies would each require a different lapse of time before they were ready to govern themselves, he explained, there was a surge toward independence in Southeast Asia, and the white nations could not hope to hold these areas as colonies in the long run. The president speculated that the nations exercising their responsibilities as trustees might be able to prepare some of these territories for self-government in twenty years, whereas it had taken the United States more than forty years to accomplish the same task in the Philippines.[21]

President Roosevelt and Secretary of State Hull liked to point to the American treatment of the Philippine Islands as a model of an enlightened colonial policy for the European powers to emulate. After acquiring the islands in 1898, the United States began preparing the Filipinos for self-government, and in 1934 the Tydings-McDuffie Act set 1946 as the date when the Philippines would become independent. The process was evolutionary rather than revolutionary. While talking with the Allied representatives on the Pacific War Council on 15 September 1942, Roosevelt said that no overnight change in government could take place in any backward country without causing trouble. "Certain processes must be accomplished bit by bit," he observed. "This is the thought that the United States entertained toward the Philippines ever since our occupation of those islands."[22] Writing in a similar vein to William Phillips two months later, Hull remarked that he thought the American record in the Philippines offered "a perfect example of how a nation should treat a colony or a dependency." Hull noted that both he and the president earnestly hoped that all dependent peoples would be prepared "for independence and for its bestowal in each instance at the earliest practicable date."[23]

The Advisory Committee on Postwar Foreign Policy had already started making an extensive investigation of the whole subject of non-self-governing territories. Under Secretary of State Welles, while serving as the chairman of the Subcommittee on Political Problems, vigorously argued that the period of European domination in Asia must end with the termination of hostilities.[24] During a meeting of the subcommittee on 8 August 1942, Welles told his colleagues that the United States should use its influence at the peace table to liberate the peoples of the Far East. Welles complained that the imperial powers had exploited the raw materials in their overseas possessions with little regard for either the welfare of the local inhabitants or the needs of other industrial countries, and he suggested that the entire problem of dependent peoples could be solved if the British could be persuaded to place their colonies under the control of an international board of trustees.[25] Following a lengthy discussion, the members of the subcommittee reached a tentative conclusion: "As a general principle the peoples of any Far Eastern country or territory under domination of European powers should be liberated after the war, and such possessions should be placed under some form of international trusteeship to assist the peoples concerned to attain political maturity and to control the raw materials of the area in the interest of all peoples."[26]

While developing the trusteeship concept in subsequent meetings, the political subcommittee discussed how colonial powers could be held accountable to the world organization that they planned to establish. Welles argued on 15 August 1942 that all colonial powers should be expected to submit to international supervision even if they continued to administer their overseas possessions. He thought that it would probably be best to permit the British and the Dutch, at least, to continue managing their own colonies, provided they recognized their responsibility to report to an international trusteeship authority.[27] During a meeting on 26 September, his colleagues agreed that "the smaller the number of territories placed under direct international control the better."[28] They drew the same conclusion with respect to non-self-governing territories in Africa as well as Asia. Although they favored direct international administration for the mandated territories in tropical Africa that had been taken away from Germany after World War I, the members of the subcommittee agreed on 3 October that the European powers should be allowed to continue governing their own African colonies but that they should be subject to the supervision of a trusteeship council.[29]

The Special Subcommittee on International Organization, also chaired by Under Secretary Welles, had already started drafting plans for the establishment of a United Nations trusteeship system after the war. Welles firmly believed that all members of the prospective United Nations should have an equal opportunity to buy raw materials, sell manufactured goods, and invest capital in territories that were to be placed under international surveillance.[30] During a subcommittee discussion on 2 October 1942, Welles graphically described the principle of equal economic opportunity as "the keystone of the whole structure of trusteeship for dependent areas." He suggested at the same meeting that, pending more careful investigation, French Indochina should be tentatively earmarked as a territory that would require international administration. Although he indicated that Secretary Hull feared that it might not be possible to secure British support for a system of international trusteeship, Welles said that he thought the chances of obtaining a satisfactory agreement with Great Britain were good if the United States refrained from presenting categorical demands.[31]

Working under his guidance, the special subcommittee soon produced a draft proposal for a United Nations trusteeship system. The document, completed on 21 October 1942, acknowledged that some dependent peoples, rather than aspiring to attain full independence, might prefer to remain in association with their present rulers if they were granted self-government. While direct international administration was to be avoided where possible, all non-self-governing territories were to be placed under international supervision. The countries serving as administrators would have the duty of submitting reports on local conditions, the international authority would have the right to inspect trust territories, and the indigenous peoples would have the right of petition.[32] When the political subcommittee considered the document on 14 November, Welles remarked that "the great practical difficulty in these recommendations is whether the present colonial powers" would be willing to admit that "they are responsible to the rest of the world for the way in which they administer" dependent areas.[33]

Stanley K. Hornbeck and the other Asian specialists in the State Department were busy working on a separate but related project. A Rhodes scholar with an acerbic personality, Hornbeck earned a Ph.D. in political science form the University of Wisconsin in 1909 and then taught in China for five years. Hornbeck viewed China as a potentially vast market for the United States, and while serving as the technical expert on the Far East for the U.S. delegation at the Versailles Peace Conference, he opposed Japanese retention of the Shantung Province. After entering the State Department, he served from 1928 to 1937 as the chief of the Division of Far Eastern Affairs and from 1937 to 1944 as the special political adviser with respect to Asian questions. Hornbeck argued vigorously that, if faced with American economic sanctions, the Japanese would withdraw their troops from China and not retaliate against the United States. Although he was proven wrong when Japan attacked Pearl Harbor in response to U.S. economic pressure, Hornbeck remained faithful to his lifelong commitment to the doctrine of equal commercial opportunity.

At the same time that Welles and his colleagues in the State Department were formulating the trusteeship plan, Hornbeck and the members of the Division of Far Eastern Affairs set out to draft a general proclamation on colonial policy. Their goal was to prepare a "World Charter" that would hold out the promise of eventual independence for colonial peoples everywhere and thus serve as the successor to the Atlantic Charter. The proposed declaration, to be espoused by all members of the future United Nations, emphasized that any colonial peoples who wished to become totally autonomous should be given the opportunity to achieve independence. Completed on 13 November 1942, the declaration was designed to commit the colonial powers not only to grant an increasing measure of self-government in areas under their care but also "to fix, at the earliest practicable moment, dates upon which the colonial peoples shall be accorded the status of full independence within a system of general security."[34]

But while Secretary Hull enthusiastically supported the proposal for a general declaration concerning dependent peoples, he decided to narrow the scope of the related project dealing with the specific issue of trusteeship. The two subcommittees headed by Welles had favored an arrangement that would place mandated areas and territories to be detached from the Axis powers under complete international administration and control. The Allied countries would continue governing their own colonies but under the supervision of the world organization. However, in a memorandum for the president on 17 November 1942, Hull advocated a less restrictive approach that would give the projected world organization responsibility for only mandated and detached areas. The Allied powers would manage their own colonies without any international supervision, although they would be expected to observe certain principles with respect to their dependent peoples and make public essential information regarding conditions in their colonies. Hull concluded that such a solution to the colonial problem offered a basis for "a forward movement of immense importance to peoples seeking independence" and for the maintenance of "good relations with our present associates."[35]

During a conversation a few months earlier with Lord Halifax, the British ambassador in Washington, Secretary Hull had suggested that the United States and Great Britain might issue a joint statement on the responsibility of colonial powers for helping dependent peoples attain freedom. British officials soon began drafting a declaration that could be submitted to the Americans for their consideration. Unified in their determination to maintain complete control of their vast empire, British leaders had no intention of giving the world organization any authority over their colonies. The British draft declaration on colonial policy, completed in January 1943, proposed the establishment of regional commissions to facilitate consultation and collaboration among colonial powers. There would be no international supervision, no accountability to the world organization, and no promise of eventual independence. The colonial powers would merely agree to work together in regional commissions to promote the advancement of dependent peoples. On 4 February, the British ambassador gave Hull a copy of the document.[36]

Although the British did not favor the establishment of international machinery to implement the principle of trusteeship, Secretary Hull still hoped to get them to support the idea of international responsibility for dependent areas. Thus, he asked Leo Pasvolsky, his special assistant charged with overseeing postwar planning, to prepare a response to the British draft. Pasvolsky and his associates produced a document, dated 9 March 1943, that combined both the proposal for a United Nations declaration on colonial policy and the plan for an international trusteeship system. The first part of the paper stated that it was the duty of colonial powers to prepare their possessions for self-government, to establish timetables for granting them full independence as soon as practicable, and to see that their resources were developed and marketed in the interest of the indigenous peoples and the world as a whole. The second part of the paper called for the creation of a United Nations trusteeship authority that would operate through regional councils in preparing mandated and detached territories for eventual independence. On 29 March, Hull presented Ambassador Halifax with a slightly revised version of the document.[37]

Prime Minister Churchill and the members of his cabinet, however, remained unified in their opposition to any American proposal that looked forward to the dissolution of the British Empire. At a meeting on 13 April 1943, the British cabinet ministers concluded that the American draft on colonial policy was unacceptable. They strongly objected to its emphasis on attaining independence and to its demand for timetables for achieving that goal. Colonial Secretary Oliver Stanley saw little chance of reaching an agreement with the United States on a joint declaration that would preserve British freedom of action. After consulting with both Churchill and Foreign Secretary Anthony Eden, Stanley decided to make a unilateral British proclamation on colonial policy. His statement, delivered before Parliament on 13 July 1943, merely endorsed the idea of regional commissions to facilitate voluntary cooperation among colonial powers, which would remain responsible for the administration of their own territories. There would be no derogation of national sovereignty, nor would there be any international accountability.[38]

But Hull still hoped to obtain British support for a United Nations declaration that would subject colonial powers to the pressure of world opinion. Hull wanted the colonial powers to agree to administer their dependent territories in accordance with certain specified principles. He also wanted them to cooperate with an international agency that would inspect each colony and make its findings available to the public. However, when he raised the subject during a conversation with Eden in August 1943, the British foreign secretary indicated that he did not like the American draft declaration because it stipulated that all dependent peoples should be prepared for independence. Eden stated that some backward areas in the British Empire would probably never have their own government. Rebuffed by the British, Hull decided to seek Russian backing for his ideas at the forthcoming Conference of Foreign Ministers to be held in Moscow. Hull met with the president just prior to his departure for Moscow. During their discussion on 5 October, Roosevelt said he thought that the inspection and publicity features of the American draft declaration "would be powerful means of inducing colonial powers to develop their colonies for the good of the dependent peoples themselves and of the world."[39]

After Hull left for Moscow, postwar planners in Washington turned their attention once again to the future status of Indochina. In a memorandum prepared for the Subcommittee on Territorial Problems on 29 October 1943, Isaiah Bowman advocated the restoration of French authority in Indochina but not without international oversight. Bowman wanted to draw France into an international agreement that would provide for outside inspection and publicity regarding the administration of Indochina along with all other colonial territories.[40] In a study prepared two weeks later for the Council on Foreign Relations, Rupert Emerson agreed that French rule in Indochina should be continued but subjected to international review. Emerson argued that the United Nations should promote equal economic opportunity as well as self-government in all colonial areas, including Indochina. "The fundamental premise must be," he concluded, "that no state having administrative jurisdiction over a colony is entitled to exercise that jurisdiction in such a way as to enrich itself or its nationals except as similar opportunities are equally open to other states."[41]

But while President Roosevelt agreed that the principle of nondiscriminatory trade should prevail in all dependent territories, he believed that France should be singled out and treated differently from the other colonial powers. Roosevelt thought that the colonial practices of France had been more oppressive than those of Great Britain and the Netherlands. Moreover, whereas he admired the British and the Dutch for their resistance against the Axis powers, he looked upon the French with contempt for their capitulation to Germany and Japan. Roosevelt viewed France as a decadent nation that would not regain its status as a first-class power for at least twenty-five years, and he saw no reason why the French should retain their overseas possessions after the war. Yet the president did not hesitate to assure officials in Vichy, the capital of Unoccupied France, that their colonies would be returned when the war ended. Hoping to keep the French government from even greater collaboration with Germany, Roosevelt instructed the U.S. ambassador in Vichy on 20 January 1942 to inform French authorities that the United States favored the restoration of their colonial empire.[42]

After the Allied invasion of French North Africa nine months later, however, Roosevelt quickly brushed aside the assurances that he had given to the Vichy government. During a meeting of the Pacific War Council on 9 December 1942, Roosevelt stated that France had done little to improve living conditions in Indochina and that the local inhabitants did not want to remain under French rule. The president added that, based upon information indicating that China had no desire to annex Indochina, plans could be made regarding the postwar disposition of the French colony. "It is perfectly refreshing," he exclaimed, "that none of the big powers wants Indo-China." When the New Zealand foreign minister asked if any commitments had been made concerning the French empire, Roosevelt falsely replied that "no firm commitment has been made."[43] He held to this position during a meeting on 7 January 1943 with the Joint Chiefs of Staff. After complaining that Robert Murphy had exceed his authority when he had assured French leaders in North Africa that their overseas empire would be restored, Roosevelt said that he was certain that some colonial possessions would not be returned to France and that he had grave doubts about the reestablishment of the French regime in Indochina.[44]

But the president and his State Department advisers were developing conflicting views with respect to the future of Indochina. During a discussion with Hull and Welles and a few other members of the political subcommittee on 22 February 1943, Roosevelt said that, while there was some question about what should be done with Indochina after the war, it was clear that the colony should not be retained by France. Neither Hull nor Welles directly challenged the president. After Eden arrived in Washington a month later to discuss postwar issues, however, Welles told the British foreign secretary that Indochina should be returned to the French, provided they agreed to prepare the local inhabitants for eventual independence and to give all countries an equal opportunity to trade in the colony. Yet at a meeting in the White House on 27 March, Eden learned that Roosevelt believed that Indochina should be taken away from France and placed under international trusteeship. Eden said that he thought the president was being too harsh on France, but Roosevelt replied that the French should be willing to give up some territory in return for postwar financial aid. When Welles reminded him about American pledges to support the restoration of the French empire, Roosevelt bluntly indicated that he would not be bound by any such promises.[45]

Neither Hull nor Welles expressed any reservations, however, when Roosevelt suggested to Eden that Korea should be placed under international trusteeship after the war. The members of the political subcommittee had already discussed a proposal to include Korea on a list of territories that would require direct international administration, and they carefully examined the idea after Eden returned to London. During a meeting of the subcommittee on 3 April 1943, Welles argued that Korea should be placed under the guidance of a trusteeship council comprising representatives of the United States, China, and the Soviet Union. He said that it would take a considerable period of time, perhaps twenty-five years, to prepare Korea for self-government. When the subcommittee returned to the subject a week later, Welles explained that Korea was not yet ready for independence because the country had been occupied for almost thirty-five years by Japan. "In order to make self-government possible," he concluded, "some period of transition would be necessary."[46] In line with his reasoning, a State Department memorandum on 15 April recommended that Korea should be temporarily administered as a trust territory.[47]

But President Roosevelt pressed ahead, without State Department approval, with his plans for dismembering the French empire. At a meeting of the Pacific War Council on 21 July 1943, Roosevelt stated his belief that Indochina should not be given back to France after the war. He said that the French had done absolutely nothing to prepare the Indochinese people for independence during almost a century of colonial rule and that it would be necessary to place them under international trusteeship until they were able to govern themselves. The president did admit, however, that Churchill disagreed with his ideas about Indochina.[48] Turning his attention to East Africa two weeks later, Roosevelt sent Hull a memorandum indicating that he did not think that the French had earned the right to keep their little colony in Somaliland after the war. He suggested that the proposed United Nations might compensate France in the form of postwar relief and rehabilitation as a quid pro quo for turning over

French Somaliland and the port city of Djibouti to Ethiopia.[49] In his reply on 10 August 1943, Hull warned Roosevelt that the French would not relinquish control of their desolate and torrid colony in East Africa "except under the heaviest of pressure and then only with the most violent reactions."[50]

Intent on outmaneuvering the British and the French, however, President Roosevelt sought to obtain Chinese and Russian support for his anticolonial ideas. The president made his first move at the Cairo Conference when he invited Chiang Kai-shek, but not Churchill, to come to his villa for a private conversation. During their evening meeting on 23 November 1943, Roosevelt asked if China wanted to acquire Indochina, and Chiang replied in the negative. Roosevelt then suggested that Indochina should be taken away from France and placed under international trusteeship until the local inhabitants could be prepared to govern themselves. The president also suggested that, upon their liberation from Japanese occupation, the Koreans would need to go through a period of international tutelage before they would be ready for self-government. During the next few days, Roosevelt discussed his plans for the postwar treatment of Japan with both Churchill and Chiang. The three leaders agreed that Japan must be stripped of all territories taken by force, that the territories stolen from China must be returned, and that "in due course Korea shall become free and independent."[51]

President Roosevelt made his second move to isolate the British and the French at the Teheran Conference when he decided to meet with Stalin before he talked to Churchill. During their private conversation on 28 November 1943, Roosevelt and Stalin saw eye to eye on the colonial question. They agreed that Indochina should not be returned to France and that a system of trusteeship should be established for the purpose of preparing the people of Indochina for independence within a period of twenty to thirty years. The next evening Churchill joined Roosevelt and Stalin in a discussion about the possibility of creating postwar military bases in the vicinity of Germany and Japan. Roosevelt and Stalin agreed that such bases should be constructed and held under international trusteeship, but Churchill feared that the American and Russian leaders aimed to build some of those bases on detached portions of the British Empire. Churchill firmly stated that the British did not desire any new bases or territory but that they intended to hold on to what they had. Specifically mentioning Singapore and Hong Kong, he warned that nothing would be taken away from Great Britain without a war.[52]

Roosevelt ignored Churchill and returned to Washington feeling satisfied that he had secured Chinese and Russian approval for his plans regarding Indochina. The president told a group of foreign diplomats on 16 December 1943 that he had been working very hard to prevent the restoration of French rule in Indochina. Because the Indochinese people had not been prepared for self-government by the French, he explained, they should be placed under a United Nations trusteeship and educated to govern themselves. Lord Halifax, the British ambassador in Washington, was disturbed by these remarks. He went over to the State Department on 3 January 1944 and reminded Secretary Hull about American statements favoring the restoration of French possessions after the war. During a meeting at the White House two weeks later, Halifax asked Roosevelt whether his observations on Indochina represented a considered view. The president replied in the affirmative, but he assured Halifax that the trusteeship plan would not be extended to either the British or the Dutch colonies. With respect to Indochina, Roosevelt said that Churchill should be reminded that "I have three votes to his one as we now stand."[53]

President Roosevelt responded with equal firmness when Secretary Hull called his attention to past American promises regarding the restoration of the French empire. "I saw Halifax last week," Roosevelt informed Hull on 24 January 1944, "and told him quite frankly that it is perfectly true that I had, for over a year, expressed the opinion that Indo-China should not go back to France but that it should be administered by an international trusteeship." Noting that both Chiang Kai-shek and Stalin had wholeheartedly endorsed his views, Roosevelt indicated to Hull that he was not worried about British objections to his trusteeship plan for the French colony in Southeast Asia. "The only reason they seem to oppose it is that they fear the effect it would have on their own possessions and those of the Dutch," he observed. "Each case must, of course, stand on its own feet, but the case of Indo-China is perfectly clear. France has milked it for one hundred years. The people of Indo-China are entitled to something better than that."[54]

Despite his assertion that each case should be judged on its own merits, however, Roosevelt was inclined to condemn the entire French empire. The president told the Pacific War Council on 12 January 1944 that the French administration of New Caledonia had been very bad and that France should not be permitted to regain control of these South Pacific islands after the Allies defeated Japan. The small part that France had played in the global conflict, he added, did not entitle her to a decisive voice in the peace settlement.[55] Roosevelt frequently talked about various French possessions as if he could dispose of them as he wished.

Even though he admitted that France had ruled Morocco very well, Roosevelt argued that the local inhabitants of that North African colony should not be forced to remain under French management. "I do not think," he wrote Hull on 24 January, "that a population, which is ninety percent Moors, should be permanently run by France."[56] In a follow-up memorandum two weeks later, Roosevelt suggested that Morocco should be placed under the custody of three trustees—one French, one English, and one American—until the Moors were ready to shift for themselves.[57]

His proposals to liquidate the French empire, however, met with resistance in both the State Department and the British Foreign Office. Responding favorably to a request from the French Committee of National Liberation for a military role in Indochina, Under Secretary of State Edward R. Stettinius suggested to Roosevelt on 17 February 1944 that he could approve the use of French forces in Indochina without limiting his options concerning the postwar status of that colony.[58] But the president told Stettinius a few days later that he did not want any French troops used in Indochina. "The operation should be Anglo-American," he insisted, "with an international trusteeship following."[59] Despite his determination to keep his options open, however, Roosevelt knew that he would have a hard time getting the British government to go along with his trusteeship plan for Indochina. During a meeting with a group of State Department officials on 17 March, Roosevelt said that he had not been able to get very far with British leaders on the Indochina issue. "The British suspect that if they give in on any colony of another country," he explained, "we will ask them to do the same with other places which are possessions of the British—for example, Burma and the Malay Peninsula."[60]

The British Foreign Office had already made preparations for a clash with the United States over the Indochina question. Alexander Cadogan, the permanent under secretary for foreign affairs, warned Anthony Eden on 2 February 1944 that President Roosevelt might someday conclude that Britain had no more right than France to regain colonial possessions that had been lost to Japan.[61] The Foreign Office and Post Hostilities Planning Committee promptly drafted a policy statement on Indochina. "A friendly and prosperous France is a strategic necessity to the Commonwealth and Empire as a whole," the document explained. "To deprive France of her economic stake in Indochina would weaken her severely. Any such deprivation would be passionately resented, with the result that the possibilities of friendly collaboration with France in post-war Europe would be jeopardized, and France would be encouraged to form a *bloc,* possibly with the Russians, opposed to an Anglo-American *bloc.*"[62] The British cabinet approved the statement on 24 February, but Prime Minister Churchill decided to delay any confrontation with Roosevelt over Indochina. "On this point," Churchill noted, "the President's views are particular to himself."[63]

But differences concerning the future of Thailand soon placed a strain upon Anglo-American relations. Viewing Thailand as an enemy state that should be punished for its collaboration with Japan, Prime Minister Churchill and the British Colonial Office looked forward to the possibility of acquiring Thai territory lying between Malaya and Burma. American policymakers, however, regarded Thailand as an enemy-occupied country that should be protected from any sinister British designs. After obtaining approval from President Roosevelt in March 1944, the State Department proposed a joint British-American declaration promising to restore the political independence and territorial integrity of Thailand at the end of the war. When British officials balked at issuing such a statement, U.S. diplomats urged them to make a unilateral declaration that their country had no territorial ambitions with respect to Thailand. But the British refused to make any commitments that would prevent them from either protecting their economic interests in Thailand or acquiring the Kra Isthmus for the postwar defense of Burma and Malaya.[64]

Differences regarding military strategy in Asia put an additional strain on Anglo-American relations. President Roosevelt and his military advisors aimed to defeat Japan by directing a powerful naval thrust toward Formosa and the Philippines and by developing China as a base for the support of the main advance westward across the Pacific. They wanted British forces in India to move eastward to support Chinese and American troops, commanded by Gen. Joseph W. Stilwell, in a campaign in north Burma to permit the construction of a supply road into China. But Lord Louis Mountbatten, the British admiral commanding Allied operations in Southeast Asia, prepared an alternative plan for an amphibious assault southward against Sumatra and Malaya. Stilwell and his advisor on political affairs, John P. Davies, vigorously opposed the Mountbatten proposal. In a dispatch to Washington on 16 January 1944, Davies argued that Mountbatten was "primarily concerned with the reoccupation, under British leadership, of colonial Southeast Asia."[65] Roosevelt promptly sent Churchill a message urging that Mountbatten should support Stilwell in an all-out drive to secure a land route into China. In his response on 25 February, the prime minister assured Roosevelt that British forces would not be withheld from the operations in north Burma.[66]

Yet Churchill, with strong backing from Foreign Secretary Eden, continued to advocate a British attack against Sumatra and Malaya in an effort to recapture Singapore. Determined to maintain the British Empire after the war, Churchill and Eden wanted their own forces to drive the Japanese out of their Southeast Asian colonies before the peace settlement. "If the Japanese should withdraw from our Malayan possessions, or make peace as a result of the main American thrust," the prime minister warned on 29 February 1944, "the United States Government would after the victory feel greatly strengthened in its view that all possessions in the East Indian Archipelago should be placed under some international body upon which the United States would exercise a decisive control." He added that the Americans would use their dominant position in the East Indies to "derive full profit from their produce, especially oil." But Churchill encountered firm opposition from his own military advisors, who argued that landings on Sumatra and Malaya could not be made for another year and that Great Britain would suffer a loss of prestige throughout Asia if it did not help the United States defeat Japan. Persuaded by these considerations, Churchill finally agreed that the British fleet should participate in the great American naval campaign in the Pacific.[67]

Though he realized that Churchill would refuse to place any British territory under international trusteeship, Roosevelt hoped that United Nations inspection tours would be sufficient to ensure enlightened administration in British and Dutch possessions after the war. He referred to Gambia during a press conference in early February 1944 to illustrate how the pressure of world opinion could be used to help relieve colonial peoples who were suffering from ruthless exploitation. The president charged that disease was rampant throughout Gambia and that for every dollar that the British had put into that West African colony, they had taken out ten. To remedy this situation, he said that a United Nations committee should go to Gambia and report to the world if the British did not improve the living conditions of the local inhabitants.[68] Roosevelt made the same point during a meeting in mid-March 1944 with Isaiah Bowman, who had just turned down an invitation from Hull to be an assistant secretary of state because he did not want to give up his position as president of Johns Hopkins University. After citing Gambia as an example of British exploitation, he said that it would be necessary to have an inspection commission "tell the world" how the colonial powers were treating their overseas possessions.[69]

With these thoughts in mind, Bowman accompanied Under Secretary of State Stettinius on a trip to London to learn more about British views regarding postwar colonial policy.[70] He soon found out that British officials remained unwilling to be held accountable to any international authority for the way they administered their colonial possessions. Prime Minister Churchill was especially blunt when he met Bowman. "We will not give up one acre of ground," he declared on 15 April 1944. "We haven't the least intention of breaking up the Empire or of letting it fall into ruin."[71] Colonial Secretary Stanley tried to steer Bowman away from the American idea of an international body that would inspect dependent areas and toward the British concept of regional councils without any executive powers. "We see no possibility of orderly government," he told the American visitor on 18 April, "if supervision is to be by an outside authority."[72] Hoping to placate Bowman a few days later, Stanley suggested that it might be possible for the world organization to establish a library that would receive annual reports from colonial powers on the administration of their overseas possessions.[73]

After Bowman returned from London, the State Department group that was preparing for a conference on world organization reexamined the whole problem of dependent peoples. Called the Informal Agenda Group, it decided on 10 May 1944 to modify the U.S. draft for a general declaration of principles designed to apply to all dependent areas. To get around the British objection to the goal of national independence in the original document, the revised draft stated that dependent peoples should be prepared for self-government.[74] The agenda group also drafted a proposal for territorial trusteeships to be included in the American plan for an international security organization. This trusteeship proposal, completed on 6 July, would apply only to mandated and detached territories. According to the document, the trusteeship system should promote self-government, nondiscriminatory trade, and international security. A United Nations council would be empowered to collect reports from administering authorities, receive petitions from dependent peoples, and conduct inspections of trust territories. But the Joint Chiefs of Staff argued on 3 August that any open discussion about trusteeships might adversely affect U.S. relations with Russia and that international consideration of the subject should be delayed until the defeat of Japan. Due to these overriding military considerations, the State Department removed the trusteeship proposal from the agenda of the conference on world organization to begin a few weeks later at Dumbarton Oaks in Washington.[75]

During the previous six months, differences of opinion about Indochina had developed within the State Department itself. Members of the Office of Far Eastern Affairs wanted to single out Indochina for special treatment. While some thought that Indochina should be placed under international trusteeship, others believed that it should be returned to France if that nation made specific political and economic commitments regarding its administration of the colony in addition to endorsing a general declaration concerning dependent areas. The people of Indochina, in either case, would be given the opportunity to attain independence within twenty-five years. Speaking for his colleagues in the Far Eastern Office, Joseph W. Ballantine argued on 10 March 1944 that the United States should formulate policies toward Indochina primarily in the light of American objectives in Asia and only secondarily with regard to possible repercussions in Europe. But members of the Office of European Affairs disagreed. In a document prepared on 1 July, they argued against either placing Indochina under international administration or imposing special conditions on the restoration of French authority over the colony. "A disgruntled, psychologically sick and sovereignty-conscious France," they warned, "will not auger well for post-war collaboration in Europe."[76]

Despite their differences concerning Indochina, however, the European and Far Eastern specialists in the State Department agreed on the need to promote the decolonization of Southeast Asia. Their thoughts were summarized in a memorandum, which Hull sent Roosevelt on 8 September 1944, suggesting that the European powers should make concerted public announcements about the future of their Southeast Asian colonies: "It would be especially helpful if such concerted announcements could include (1) specific dates when independence or complete (dominion) self-government will be accorded, (2) specific steps to be taken to develop native capacity for self-rule, and (3) a pledge of economic autonomy and equality of economic opportunity." Such commitments might have great value after the war not only in preserving the peace of Southeast Asia but also in opening in the densely populated countries of the region, "potentially important markets for American exports." But the memorandum warned that failure of the European powers to recognize the rising forces of nationalism in Southeast Asia could be disastrous. "An attempt to reestablish pre-war conditions will almost surely lead to serious social and political conflict, and may lead to the ultimate unifying of Oriental opposition to the West."[77]

Rather than attempting to extract public commitments from the European powers to decolonize Southeast Asia, however, Roosevelt concentrated his energy on preventing France from regaining control of Indochina. The president reacted negatively when he learned that the

British government had authorized the establishment of a French military mission to conduct operations in Indochina under the command of Admiral Mountbatten. In a memorandum sent to the State Department on 3 November 1944, Roosevelt insisted that no American approval should be given to any French military activities in Southeast Asia.[78] But the British explicitly asked the State Department three weeks later to approve their plans to deploy French forces in military operations aimed at liberating Indochina.[79] On 2 January 1945, Stettinius, who had just replaced Hull as secretary of state, informed Ambassador Halifax that Roosevelt did not want to make any commitments with respect to Indochina.[80] Halifax then decided to approach the president directly. In a conversation at the White House two days later, when Halifax explained that Mountbatten wanted to use French units for sabotage missions in Indochina, Roosevelt said that he could go ahead with his plans as long as he did not ask the United States to approve them. The president emphasized that he did not wish to see the restoration of French authority in Indochina.[81]

But his plan to place Indochina under international trusteeship ran counter to the thinking of his top foreign policy advisors. During a meeting with Harry Hopkins and the heads of the War and Navy Departments on 2 January 1945, Secretary of State Stettinius expressed the opinion that any American attempt to prevent the restoration of French rule in Indochina, or even to defer a decision on the subject until a general peace settlement, would probably fail in light of the determination of the British, Dutch, and Portuguese to regain control of their own colonies in Southeast Asia. The British, it was pointed out, were actively supporting French efforts to dispatch troops to Indochina. Noting that the United States had held back on several French matters in the past before finally changing its position to conform to British desires, Hopkins said that he believed that the French had come to feel that Americans were against their reemergence as a strong European nation. Hopkins suggested that the time had arrived for a complete review of U.S. policy toward France.[82] In a memorandum for the president ten days later, Stettinius recommended that "our policies toward Indochina should be consistent with our policies toward the other countries in Southeast Asia."[83]

But while President Roosevelt continued to single out Indochina for special treatment, he agreed with his State Department advisers on the need to establish an international trusteeship system. The president expressed surprise when Stettinius told him on 27 September 1944 that the State Department had not raised the trusteeship question at the Dumbarton Oaks Conference in deference to the wishes of the Joint

Chiefs of Staff. Roosevelt said that the navy was not sympathetic to his point of view on trusteeships but that he intended to persuade the navy to adopt his outlook.[84] The president made his position very clear on 15 November when he met with a group of postwar planners. After indicating that both the army and the navy believed that the United States should take over the Japanese mandates in the Pacific, Roosevelt stated that he was opposed to annexing these islands because it would be contrary to the Atlantic Charter. He said that it was his definite desire that the principle of international trusteeship should be firmly established and that the world organization should provide adequate machinery for administering trust territories.[85] Stettinius was pleased. "From a diplomatic standpoint," he explained after the meeting, "we are ready any moment to go into action."[86]

The State Department decided a month later to invite Oliver Stanley, the British colonial secretary, to Washington to discuss the whole issue of dependent territories. Churchill was apprehensive. "There must be no question of our being hustled or seduced into declarations affecting British sovereignty in any of the Dominions or Colonies," he insisted on 31 December 1944. "Pray remember my declaration against liquidating the British Empire."[87] Stanley did not disappoint Churchill. During a discussion at the State Department on 18 January 1945, the British colonial secretary argued that the goal for dependent areas should be self-government within the framework of empire rather than outright independence. He said that there should not be a large number of small independent countries scattered around the world and unable to fend for themselves. Stanley advanced the idea that powers having responsibility for administering dependent territories should voluntarily participate in regional commissions and make annual reports to the world organization. But he stated that the United Nations should not have the right to inspect dependent areas or to receive petitions from the local inhabitants.[88]

Although Roosevelt told Stanley that he intended to push his trusteeship plan for Indochina when he met with Churchill and Stalin at Yalta, State Department officials proceeded to draft a trusteeship proposal that would allow the French to regain control of Indochina. Their formula, to be advanced at the Yalta Conference, specified three different types of territories that would be included in the trusteeship system: first, existing League of Nations mandates; second, territories to be detached from current enemy states; and third, colonies that might be voluntarily placed under international trusteeship. John D. Hickerson, the deputy director of the Office of European Affairs, later explained to a British official that the

American trusteeship proposal had been designed by the State Department to permit a climb-down from the position that the president had taken in conversations about Indochina. Noting that the trusteeship formula would enable but not compel France to relinquish control of Indochina, Hickerson made it clear that the State Department disagreed with Roosevelt and had devised the third category as a face-saver.[89]

Secretary of State Stettinius and his aides succeeded at Yalta in getting their trusteeship formula accepted as the basis for future discussions concerning the problem of dependent areas. During a meeting with Eden and Molotov on 9 February 1945, Stettinius proposed that, prior to the conference to establish the United Nations, representatives of the five governments that would be permanent members of the Security Council should discuss the trusteeship question. But Churchill erupted in anger when Stettinius reported a few hours later that the three foreign ministers had agreed to his suggestion. "No one will induce me as long as I am Prime Minister," he declared, "to let any representative of Great Britain go to a conference where we will be placed in the dock and asked to justify our right to live in a world we have tried to save." After receiving assurances from Stettinius that his proposal had nothing to do with the British Empire, however, Churchill reluctantly accepted the American formula for creating trust territories. It was then agreed that both the preliminary discussions and the formal negotiations at the conference on world organization would be limited to a consideration of general principles without any reference to specific territories that might be destined for trusteeship.[90]

Though Roosevelt and Stalin had talked a day earlier about placing Indochina under international trusteeship, the president soon retreated from the strong anti-French position that he had maintained during the previous two years. There were disturbing indications in the weeks following the Yalta Conference that the Soviet Union planned to dominate Poland and other countries in Eastern Europe, and there were growing hopes in Washington that France would serve as a counterweight against the spread of Russian influence into Western Europe. But Charles de Gaulle warned the U.S. ambassador in Paris on 13 March 1945 that France might become a Russian satellite if the French people learned that the United States opposed the restoration of their Southeast Asian empire. "We do not want to fall into the Russian orbit," de Gaulle lectured. "I hope you do not push us into it."[91] Roosevelt quickly modified his position on Indochina. During a conversation on 15 March with Charles W. Taussig, a close advisor on colonial problems, the president said that he would be willing to allow the French to retain Indochina if they promised to assume the obligations of a trustee and agreed to prepare the local inhabitants for independence.[92]

After Roosevelt died on 12 April 1945, the State Department reexamined the Indochina issue in relation to American objectives in both Europe and Asia. The Office of European Affairs feared that the French would be less willing to support American goals in Europe if the United States imposed special conditions on the restoration of their authority in Indochina. But the Office of Far Eastern Affairs worried that American interests in Asia would suffer unless the United States extracted firm commitments from France regarding the implementation of liberal political and economic policies. In a memorandum for President Truman on 9 May, the State Department attempted to reconcile these two viewpoints. The memorandum recommended that, without placing any conditions on the revival of French rule in Southeast Asia, the United States should seek assurances from France with respect to the development of self-government and the establishment of equal commercial opportunity in Indochina. Truman promptly agreed that he should urge, but not demand, that the French carry out basic economic and political reforms as soon as they reestablished their authority in Indochina.[93]

The State Department was successful in shaping American policy not only toward Indochina but also toward the Japanese mandates in the Pacific. While agreeing that these islands should become part of a comprehensive overseas network of U.S. military bases, postwar planners in Washington advocated different means to achieve that end. President Roosevelt and Secretary of State Stettinius believed that the Japanese mandates should be included in the United Nations trusteeship system and then placed under exclusive U.S. administration. Secretary of War Henry L. Stimson and Secretary of the Navy James V. Forrestal, however, thought that the United States should annex those islands outright. Playing for time to make their case, Stimson and Forrestal sought to prevent any discussion of trusteeships at the conference on world organization to be held in San Francisco. But Roosevelt opposed their whole approach to the subject, and he was ready to rule against them when he suddenly died. After his funeral, Stimson and Forrestal quickly resolved their differences with Stettinius, and on 18 April 1945 President Truman approved their recommendation that the U.S. delegation at San Francisco should propose that certain areas be designated as strategic trust territories. Such an arrangement would enable the United States to exercise, under United Nations authority, complete control over a large number of strategic outposts needed to police the Pacific.[94]

The American trusteeship proposal, put forth at the San Francisco Conference a few weeks after Roosevelt died, became the basis for three chapters in the United Nations Charter dealing with dependent peoples. Chapter 12 provided for the establishment of an international trusteeship system. Certain areas could be designated as strategic trust territories and placed under the control of the Security Council. In addition to instituting nondiscriminatory economic policies in trust territories under their management, the administering powers would be obligated to promote their progressive development toward self-government or independence as the particular circumstances warranted. Chapter 13 provided for the creation of a central trusteeship council that would operate under the authority of the General Assembly. Besides considering reports submitted by the administrating powers, the trusteeship council could examine petitions sent by the local inhabitants and make periodic visits to inspect trust territories at times agreed upon by the administrating powers. The British had reluctantly yielded to U.S. demands for the articles calling for inspection tours and nondiscriminatory trade.[95]

While the two chapters dealing with trusteeships concerned only the mandates and a few areas to be detached from the Axis nations, Chapter 11 contained a general declaration that applied to all non-self-governing territories. The Russian and Chinese representatives at San Francisco wanted a declaration that would commit the European powers to prepare their colonies for independence. But the U.S. delegates convinced them to settle for a declaration that would be acceptable to the British. As a result, Chapter 11 obligated countries that endorsed the United Nations Charter to promote the development of self-government in all their dependent territories. American officials took comfort in the thought that self-government might lead to independence. Hoping that they could eventually persuade the European powers to place their colonies under international trusteeship, postwar planners in the United States looked forward to a gradual evolution toward independent nationhood in Asia and Africa. But it soon became evident that the European powers were determined to preserve their far-flung empires as long as they could. During the next two decades, however, the rising forces of nationalism swept away the old order of colonialism with unanticipated speed.[96]

FIVE | DEVELOPING THE MIDDLE EAST

Prior to World War II, the United States occupied an enviable position with respect to petroleum. The country possessed almost half of the known oil reserves in the world, and domestic producers were exporting large quantities of refined petroleum to foreign customers. At the same time, the abundant supply of domestic oil provided a cheap source of energy that helped American farmers and manufacturers compete successfully in overseas markets. The huge reserves of crude oil at home also guaranteed that American military forces would have sufficient fuel to defend the United States and to protect its economic interests abroad. Moreover, with the support of the State Department, American companies acquired rights to explore for oil in various countries around the globe. Geological surveys repeatedly indicated that the pools of petroleum lying beneath the desert sands of the Middle East held the greatest promise, and in 1933 King Ibn Saud granted the Standard Oil Company of California an exclusive concession to develop the underground reserves in vast stretches of Saudi Arabia. Other American companies, along with their European partners, obtained large interests in the petroleum resources of Iraq and Kuwait.[1]

During the fifteen-month period between the German invasion of Poland in September 1939 and the Japanese attack on Pearl Harbor in December 1941, however, American policymakers became increasingly convinced that the postwar security and prosperity of the United States would depend upon the development and protection of foreign oil fields. The spectacular achievements of the German Wehrmacht dramatized the crucial role of petroleum in modern warfare. Oil imports and synthetic petroleum substitutes enabled Nazi forces, spearheaded by dive bombers, tanks, and motorized infantry units, to overrun neighboring countries with amazing speed. At the same time, the growing demand for oil in the United States, combined with the rapid depletion of American reserves, led experts to predict that domestic consumption would far exceed domestic production soon after the fighting ended. Thus, American leaders concluded that it would be necessary to have access to an adequate supply of foreign oil to serve the postwar economic and strategic interests of the United States.[2]

Worried that the country would be faced with a serious oil shortage after the war, President Roosevelt decided in May 1941 to name Secretary of the Interior Harold L. Ickes the petroleum coordinator for national defense. Ickes was a dedicated conservationist with an abiding liberal faith that the federal government could be used to achieve great ends. Ickes promptly appointed Ralph K. Davies, the vice president of Standard Oil of California, as his deputy to manage the newly created Office of the Petroleum Coordinator. Davies soon warned his boss of an impending energy crisis. In a memorandum prepared for Ickes in October 1941, Davies pointed out that the ratio between domestic reserves and demand for oil in the United States had been steadily declining over the past decade. "The United States must have extra-territorial petroleum reserves to guard against the day when our steadily increasing demand can no longer be met by our domestic supply," he declared. "What a tragedy it would be if the United States, having by reason of the intensive liquidation of its own petroleum resources led the world to an age of mechanized life, transportation and warfare, should itself have lost the ability to compete in it."[3]

American leaders were already trying to find a way to protect the exclusive concession held by the California Arabian Standard Oil Company (CASOC), a jointly owned subsidiary of California Standard and the Texas Company, which was just beginning to develop the vast oil fields of Saudi Arabia. Following the outbreak of the war in Europe, King Ibn Saud began to experience serious financial difficulties primarily because of the curtailment of pilgrimages to the Muslim holy cities of Mecca and Medina. King Saud decided in the spring of 1941 to ask CASOC for $6 million in cash to cover his expenses. Fearing the loss of their concession, CASOC executives proposed that the U.S. government loan Saudi Arabia $6 million annually for the next five years. But President Roosevelt did not want to risk the possibility of any criticism from his political enemies. Rather than providing direct American aid, Roosevelt persuaded the British, who were receiving lend-lease supplies from the United States, to increase their financial assistance to the Saudi government. Fred A. Davies, the president of CASOC, was glad to be relieved of financial requests from Saudi Arabia. But he warned the State Department in November 1941 that if the British became the main source of income for King Saud, they might "attempt to extract certain *quid pro quos*."[4]

Amid escalating apprehensions that the British would attempt to obtain the right to drill for oil in Saudi Arabia, Secretary of State Cordell Hull decided in January 1943 to create a special board, the Committee on

International Petroleum Policy, in the State Department, and he asked Economic Advisor Herbert Feis to be its chairman. Feis had earned a Ph.D. in economics from Harvard University in 1921, and after entering the State Department ten years later, he remained steadfast in his support for the principle of equal commercial treatment. Almost immediately after the members of his petroleum committee began their deliberation, they recommended that the president should declare Saudi Arabia eligible for lend-lease aid. "In view of the financial assistance rendered to the Saudi Arabian Government by the British Government," a State Department official explained on 9 February, "there is a possibility that after the war the British may demand a *quid pro quo* at the expense of this American interest, which is considered necessary to preserve as a means of assuring the United States of an ample supply of oil in the event of exhaustion of domestic reserves."[5] Since King Saud had granted American military aircraft permission to fly over his country, President Roosevelt felt justified in announcing on 18 February that Saudi Arabia would receive lend-lease aid in recognition of its contribution to the Allied war effort.[6]

The Committee on International Petroleum Policy quickly began discussing the need for additional steps to safeguard American oil interests in Saudi Arabia.[7] In a report submitted to Secretary Hull on 22 March 1943, the committee recommended that the U.S. government should establish a Petroleum Reserves Corporation (PRC) with the authority to negotiate contracts for the option to buy oil from companies holding concessions in foreign countries. The report suggested that the first option contract should be with CASOC. The committee pointed out that the company was eager to make such an arrangement and that the government of Saudi Arabia would probably welcome the prospect of receiving increased royalties from petroleum exports. According to the proposal, the board of directors of the PRC would be comprised of representatives of the State, War, Navy, and Interior Departments. The board would be chaired by the State Department representative, and all acts of the corporation would be subject to the approval of the secretary of state. After consulting with his senior aides, Hull sent copies of the report on 31 March to Secretary of War Henry L. Stimson, Secretary of the Navy Frank Knox, and Secretary of the Interior Ickes.[8]

But Adm. F. J. Horne, the vice chief of naval operations, advocated bolder action. In a memorandum submitted to the Joint Chiefs of Staff on 31 May 1943, Admiral Horne urged the establishment of a government corporation to acquire ownership of petroleum reserves outside the

United States. He argued that its first act should be to obtain oil concessions in Saudi Arabia.[9] During a Joint Chiefs meeting on 8 June, Horne warned that the British had already approached King Saud in an attempt to acquire rights to drill for oil in his country. He explained that, while domestic petroleum reserves were sufficient for the present war, the United States would need access to foreign reserves to avoid a postwar oil shortage.[10] After a brief discussion, the Joint Chiefs approved the Horne proposal, and Adm. William D. Leahy sent their recommendation favoring its implementation to the president.[11] Roosevelt liked the idea.[12] He promptly directed Leahy to suggest to Hull that the U.S. government should make immediate efforts to obtain petroleum concessions from Saudi Arabia for the purpose of establishing a naval fuel-oil reserve similar to those already existing in the United States.[13]

Secretary of the Navy Knox had already advanced a similar plan to protect U.S. petroleum interests in Saudi Arabia. Knox not only worried about the depletion of domestic reserves, but he also feared that the British might get hold of the enormous pool of Arabian oil that belonged to American companies.[14] During a meeting at the State Department with Secretary Hull and Secretary of War Stimson on 8 June 1943, Knox proposed that the U.S. government should create a corporation to purchase a majority interest in the stock of CASOC. Hull said nothing. After the meeting, Knox and Stimson stopped at the Interior Department to discuss the proposition with Secretary Ickes, who had been named petroleum administrator for war. Ickes was heart and soul in favor of the scheme, and he hoped to persuade the president to support it.[15] But the next day Hull sent Herbert Feis over to the War Department to tell Stimson that the State Department opposed the proposal for government ownership of CASOC stock.[16]

After learning that Stimson sympathized with Knox and Ickes, Feis immediately warned Hull that the emergence in the Middle East of a petroleum company owned by the U.S. government might have repercussions that would actually lessen rather than improve the prospects of obtaining foreign oil reserves.[17] He explained that many State Department officials feared that, if the government proceeded to purchase CASOC stock, it would stimulate not only a movement to nationalize oil properties in Latin America but also a worldwide race to grab control of petroleum reserves and various other resources in violation of the principle of equal commercial opportunity.[18] Feis repeatedly warned Hull that, unless State Department officials controlled the operations of the proposed PRC, its overseas activities might imperil their whole postwar program for international economic collaboration.[19]

Accordingly, Hull decided on 14 June 1943 to send the president a memorandum arguing that the State Department should occupy an important place in the PRC and have prime responsibility for its negotiations with foreign governments. "It is essential," he explained, "that our own efforts in the period ahead be so directed as to achieve our ends without stimulating new restrictive moves on the part of other countries and creating intense new disputes." With regard to the recommendation that the U.S. government ask King Saud for petroleum concessions for itself, Hull pointed out that the most promising oil-bearing land in Saudi Arabia was already held by CASOC in an exclusive concession. As for the proposal that the PRC purchase CASOC stock, Hull observed that King Saud might oppose the entrance of the U.S. government into the business of developing the oil resources of his country.[20]

Representatives of the State, War, Navy, and Interior Departments then held a series of meetings in hopes of reconciling their differences. In a report sent to the president on 26 June 1943, they first recommended the establishment of the PRC with the stipulation that it should not embark upon any major overseas activities without receiving prior approval from the secretary of state. The report next presented two conflicting views regarding the method that should be employed by the corporation in obtaining oil reserves in Saudi Arabia: a proposal by Ickes that the PRC purchase 100 percent of CASOC stock; and a State Department proposal that the PRC negotiate option contracts to buy oil from the company. Roosevelt favored the bolder approach, and on 30 June he approved the creation of the PRC with the authority to acquire proven reserves of petroleum from sources outside the United States. A week later, Roosevelt appointed Ickes to head the PRC after Hull had declined to serve in that capacity.[21]

Ickes began negotiations on 2 August 1943 with Standard Oil of California and the Texas Company for the purchase of the subsidiary they had set up to produce oil in Saudi Arabia. Ickes first proposed that the two companies sell all the stock of CASOC to the PRC. When the two companies refused, he offered to buy a majority of the stock. But the companies remained firm in their refusal to sell their subsidiary to the government. As word of the PRC plan to acquire CASOC leaked out, powerful American oil barons started mobilizing against this unwelcome intrusion of the federal government into their domain. Petroleum industry spokesmen argued that the oil business should remain in private hands and that the role of government should be limited to helping American companies protect and expand their operations. As the opposition mounted during the autumn of 1943, Ickes quietly abandoned his plan to purchase CASOC stock.[22]

Ickes had also hoped to involve the U.S. government in petroleum affairs in Iraq and India. The PRC hastily drew up plans to help the Anglo-Iranian Oil Company build a pipeline from its oil fields in Iraq to the Mediterranean Sea. But King Saud had already complained that the oil resources of Saudi Arabia were not being developed as rapidly as those in nearby British-controlled areas, and the State Department feared that the use of American materials for the expansion of British petroleum operations in the Middle East would jeopardize the CASOC concession.[23] "This Department," Hull admonished Ickes on 13 November 1943, "believes that there should be a full realization of the fact that the oil of Saudi Arabia constitutes one of the world's greatest prizes, and that it is extremely shortsighted to take any step which would tend to discredit the American interest therein." Hull argued that the expansion of American petroleum facilities should have priority over any further expansion of British facilities in the region. "It should be kept clearly in mind," he emphasized, "that the expansion of British facilities serve to build up their post-war position in the Middle East at the expense of American interests there."[24]

The State Department also opposed PRC plans to construct an oil refinery in Bombay to produce fuel for the defense of India and for Allied military operations in the Far East. In a letter to the Joint Chiefs of Staff on 15 December 1943, Hull pointed out that the proposed refinery, while it would be owned by American interests, would be located in a British colony where restrictions had been placed on the marketing of American-produced oil. He likewise noted that the facility would not benefit an area where U.S. oil-producing interests were located. "The inadequate development of American-owned oil concessions in the Middle East would endanger the continuance of those concessions in American hands," Hull explained. "Thus for the direct protection of American interests in the Middle East it is believed that wherever possible and consistent with military requirements, refining facilities in that area should be so planned as to use oil produced by American companies in the Middle East and, where possible, should be located in the country of production."[25]

After the State Department blocked the Bombay refinery project, Commodore Andrew F. Carter of the Army-Navy Petroleum Board recommended on 17 January 1944 that the PRC build a pipeline from the Persian Gulf oil fields to the eastern Mediterranean. Ickes liked the idea because he thought a government-owned pipeline would protect American interests in Arabian oil against any British connivance. When the Joint Chiefs of Staff endorsed the proposal a week later, Ickes began negotiating an agreement with Gulf Oil, California Standard, and the Texas Company whereby the PRC would construct a pipeline to transport crude oil from their wells in Saudi Arabia and Kuwait in return for the right to buy a specific amount of oil at a favorable price. But the State Department did not want to put the government in the oil business and insisted that the pipeline should be turned over to private interests when the war ended. After Ickes agreed to review the ownership question following the war, Hull acquiesced, and Roosevelt approved the project.[26]

But most American oilmen objected to the proposed government pipeline. Although Gulf Oil, California Standard, and the Texas Company favored the project, which would save them the expense of building their own pipeline, their American competitors vigorously opposed the plan. Jersey and Socony, which had shares in an existing pipeline running from the Persian Gulf to the Mediterranean, worried that the proposed conduit would carry Arabian oil into European markets in competition with their Iraqi product. More important, domestic producers feared that the American market would be flooded by cheap foreign oil if Arabian petroleum took European markets away from oil produced in the Caribbean and Gulf of Mexico. The Petroleum Industry War Council, an influential lobbying organization, distributed more than ninety thousand pamphlets charging that the proposed government pipeline would undermine free enterprise in the United States. The intense campaign generated growing opposition to the plan in Congress. As a result, the project never came to fruition, and in 1945 California Standard and the Texas Company decided to build their own pipeline.[27]

In the meantime, the State Department had set out to reach an agreement with Great Britain for the orderly development of Middle Eastern oil resources. The Special Committee on Petroleum, established under the chairmanship of Herbert Feis on 15 June 1943, began drafting plans for an Anglo-American agreement that would assure all countries access to oil on equal terms and give producing countries a fair share of the profits accruing from the development of their fields. State Department officials hoped that the principles being formulated for petroleum might become the model for other raw materials. Concerned about promoting the long-range interests of the United States, they sought not only to protect the existing concessions held by American oil companies but also to provide them with an equal opportunity to compete for new concessions in the Middle East. Isaiah Bowman, a geographer with a wealth of information about the distribution of natural resources around the globe, warned that American farms and factories would be less competitive in foreign markets if they did not have an ample supply of cheap energy "We shall be commercially disadvantaged if we do not share in the benefits that flow from the discovery of new large oil fields," Bowman explained on 18 June. "Imagine our oil reserves at some future time reduced to such a point that development is markedly more expensive. Imagine that we shift to oil shale. This will certainly take more manpower and more dollars."[28]

During a meeting on 28 September 1943, the Special Committee on Petroleum concluded that a paramount reason for negotiating an agreement with Great Britain would be to secure the removal of various restrictions on the development of oil resources that were jointly owned by American and British companies operating in the Middle East.[29] The British had been favoring the development of certain oil fields at the expense of others in the region. For example, the Anglo-Iranian Oil Company, which was controlled by the British government, had rapidly developed its large field in Iran in order to provide revenue to the Iranian government. But at the same time, the British had used their majority interest in the Iraq Petroleum Company to hold back oil production in Iraq against the desires of their American and French partners, who each owned slightly less than a quarter share in the company. The British had also retarded the development of the rich oil fields in the nearby sheikdom of Kuwait. As part of the price for purchasing a half interest in the Kuwait Oil Company from the British, the Gulf Company had agreed not to sell any Kuwaiti oil in markets already served by the Anglo-Iranian Company.[30]

While State Department officials sought the immediate elimination of these restrictions and related pressures on Middle Eastern leaders to favor British over American petroleum interests, their long-range objective was to promote a basic shift in the geographical pattern of world oil production. James C. Sappington explained in a memorandum written on 1 December 1943 how he and his colleagues in the Petroleum Division of the State Department viewed the matter. "If oil flows abundantly from the vast reserves of the Persian Gulf region into the markets of the world, including European and other markets heretofore supplied by oil from this hemisphere (the United States and Caribbean Basin)," Sappington reasoned, "it is most probable that the draining of Western Hemisphere reserves will not proceed at so rapid a rate as in the past. If, in addition, Middle Eastern oil should enter the United States market to meet the postwar need for oil imports, the result should be a further conservation of the reserves of this hemisphere."[31]

Secretary Hull informed the British ambassador on 2 December 1943 that the United States was eager to undertake informal and preliminary oil discussions with his government. In a memorandum to the president a week later, Hull emphasized the importance of developing the enormous petroleum resources of the Middle East. "Because of the complex problems involved," he explained, "those resources, which are held to a substantial extent jointly by American and British interests, cannot be adequately developed unless the United States and British Governments reach an agreement providing for close cooperation." Hull concluded by advising Roosevelt that the proposed Anglo-American oil conversations should be under the clear supervision of the State Department. But Petroleum Administrator for War Ickes argued that he should be charged with the responsibility for directing the negotiations. As a compromise, Roosevelt decided that Hull should be the chairman and Ickes the vice chairman of an American delegation that would conduct oil talks with the British on a cabinet level.[32]

But the British said that it would be impossible to send high-ranking representatives to Washington for oil conversations during the coming months in view of the need to make final preparations for the invasion of Normandy. The British also indicated that they would not agree to participate in any petroleum conference unless the United States agreed, in advance, not to bring up the issue of oil concessions. Roosevelt was astounded. In a conversation with Under Secretary of State Edward R. Stettinius on 18 February 1944, the president stated that he did not want anything to be excluded from the proposed Anglo-American oil discussions. Roosevelt explained that he wanted to be free, for instance, to trade some American concessions in Saudi Arabia for some British concessions in Iran. Then with a stern voice, he instructed Stettinius to tell the British that high-level oil discussions must start in Washington at an early date and that nothing should be excluded from the agenda.[33]

Fearful that the Americans wanted to gain access to their oil reserves in the Middle East, the British sought to delay petroleum discussions with the United States. "There is apprehension in some quarters here," Prime Minister Churchill cabled Roosevelt on 20 February 1944, "that the

United States has a desire to deprive us of our oil assets in the Middle East." He warned that any announcement that Secretary Hull would lead a U.S. delegation in discussing petroleum issues with British officials would provoke demands in Parliament for an assurance that no questions involving the transfer of property would arise at the conference. In his reply two days later, Roosevelt expressed his own concern about reports that the British wished to "horn in" on American holdings in Saudi Arabia. The president argued that, due to the great importance of oil to the security and prosperity of the postwar world, Anglo-American petroleum talks should be held under the guidance of senior government officials. "It is my view that all of the discussions should take place in Washington," he concluded, "and that, in order that the broadest possible understandings may be reached, there should be no limitations on the petroleum problems to be discussed."[34]

After Roosevelt assured Churchill on 3 March that "we are not making sheep's eyes at your oil fields in Iraq or Iran," the British reluctantly acceded to American demands for oil conversations in the United States.[35] The Interdivisional Petroleum Committee in the State Department promptly drafted a paper outlining American objectives with respect to postwar oil questions. To serve the long-range interests of the United States, the paper called for the conservation of Western Hemisphere petroleum reserves together with a substantial expansion of oil production in the Middle East to keep pace with the expected increase in world consumption. The paper also advocated measures designed to safeguard existing petroleum concessions held by American companies and to give them an equal opportunity to discover and develop new oil fields overseas.[36] These objectives were then approved by the Post-War Programs Committee, and they became the basis for U.S. proposals when exploratory oil talks with the British began on 18 April 1944 in Washington. These discussions, conducted at the technical level, quickly resulted in an agreement to establish a joint Anglo-American petroleum commission that would help integrate Middle Eastern oil into world markets with a minimum of disruption.[37]

But a bitter debate broke out when the British delegation, headed by Lord Beaverbrook, arrived in Washington on 25 July 1944 to put the finishing touches on the petroleum agreement. Because the British anticipated an adverse foreign exchange position after the war, Beaverbrook introduced an amendment that would give the United Kingdom the right to exclude oil produced in "dollar areas" and to import petroleum solely from British-controlled sources.[38] The American delegates registered strong objection to the British proposal. Under Secretary Stettinius warned that, if the United Kingdom markets were closed to American-produced oil, public opinion in the United States might not support a generous settlement of lend-lease accounts. Stettinius firmly stated that he, acting for Secretary Hull, could not and would not consent to any arrangement that would sanction the exclusion of "dollar oil" from British markets. "Such an arrangement," he declared, "would be impractical, unfair, and wrong."[39] The deadlock was finally broken when the British withdrew the troublesome amendment with the understanding that they could terminate the petroleum agreement if no acceptable solution could be found for their foreign exchange problems.[40]

The Anglo-American petroleum agreement, concluded on 8 August 1944, established a framework for regulating the international oil business. The agreement embraced the following general principles: adequate petroleum supplies should be made available to all countries in a nondiscriminatory manner; producing countries should benefit fairly from the development of their oil deposits; existing concessions should be respected; all countries should have an equal opportunity to acquire drilling rights in new fields; and the development of petroleum resources should not be hampered by restrictions that would prevent the production of ample oil supplies to satisfy the economic needs of all countries. The agreement also provided for the creation of an international petroleum commission, charged with the task of promoting the orderly production and distribution of oil on a worldwide basis.[41] State Department officials were pleased with the agreement. Fearing that American oil reserves would be exhausted soon after the war, Petroleum Advisor Charles B. Rayner explained that he and his associates hoped to get Great Britain, and ultimately other countries, to adopt measures that would "establish a more equitable balance in the rate of exploitation between the highly developed petroleum resources in the Western Hemisphere and the less developed resources in the Eastern Hemisphere."[42]

Most oilmen in the United States, however, opposed the Anglo-American petroleum agreement after President Roosevelt submitted it to the Senate for approval as a treaty. Although the five major American international oil companies hoped that the arrangement would help them sell their Middle Eastern petroleum without disrupting world markets, domestic producers feared that an international petroleum commission would allow cheap foreign oil to flood the United States. Thus, the long-range

State Department goal of stimulating production in the Middle East to curb the drain on Western Hemisphere reserves clashed with the short-run financial interests of domestic oil companies. With more than twenty states involved in some aspect of the petroleum business, the voice of domestic producers echoed down the halls of Congress.[43] Tom Connally, the chairman of the Senate Foreign Relations Committee, denounced the agreement in December 1944 as "unfair to the American oil industry."[44] Faced with widespread opposition, Roosevelt decided in January 1945 to withdraw the treaty from the Senate for reconsideration and possible revision.

Petroleum Administrator for War Ickes immediately set out to overcome the opposition among oilmen in the United States to the Anglo-American agreement. After several conferences with oil industry leaders, Ickes produced a revised document that met with their approval.[45] But State Department officials objected to the new draft. They argued that a clause giving the American oil industry antitrust immunity would run counter to their efforts to curb cartels.[46] They also argued that a clause allowing Great Britain and the United States to limit petroleum imports might prejudice their broad campaign to reduce trade barriers.[47] State Department officials became increasingly unhappy as successive drafts progressively departed from their desire to encourage oil production in the Middle East.[48] Nevertheless, with several prominent oil executives at his side, Ickes flew to London in September 1945 to renegotiate the petroleum agreement. The British quickly approved the revised agreement, which embraced the basic principles contained in the original, but the Senate refused to ratify the resulting treaty.[49]

Meanwhile, postwar planners in Washington aimed to prevent both the British and the French from discriminating against American business interests in several countries in the Near East and North Africa. President Roosevelt decided in August 1943 to dispatch James M. Landis, the dean of Harvard Law School, to direct U.S. economic operations throughout the region. Landis soon encountered vigorous British efforts to retain a privileged commercial and financial position in the area. "We must," he warned State Department officials in June 1944, "expect a continuing discrimination by the British against our trade."[50] Working closely with Alexander C. Kirk, the U.S. minister in Cairo, Landis sought to expand the scope of American business activity in Egypt. But Miles Lampson, the British ambassador in Cairo, tried to block his efforts. Lampson told King Farouk in September 1944 that Great Britain was determined to maintain its domination of Egyptian markets after the war. American diplomats were disturbed. Hoping that Farouk would welcome American trade and investment, the State Department agreed in April 1945 to ship lend-lease supplies to Egypt.[51]

The State Department also took steps to keep Great Britain from reducing Ethiopia to a puppet state whose doors would be closed to American enterprise. In a memorandum to President Roosevelt in August 1943, Secretary Hull reported that the Ethiopian government had complained about British attempts to circumscribe its sovereignty and had requested the services of U.S. economic advisers. He explained that the State Department was arranging to send agricultural, mining, and transportation missions so that Ethiopia would be able to develop its resources "without resorting to the necessity of handing out disadvantageous concessions to the citizens of any nation."[52] In a memorandum a year later, Hull informed the president that Emperor Haile Selassie had asked for American rifles to maintain internal security but that the British had objected because they wanted to keep Ethiopia dependent upon their support. Hull advised that the arms should be sent "so that any future development of American interests would not be prevented by exclusive or preferential rights obtained by third parties." Roosevelt promptly authorized the War Department to send the arms to Ethiopia.[53]

American policymakers confronted additional challenges to the principle of equal economic opportunity in Syria and Lebanon. These two small countries in the Levant had been detached from the Ottoman Empire after World War I and placed under French administration as League of Nations mandates. During June–July 1941, a joint British and Free French task force occupied the two Levantine states to keep them out of German hands. Gen. Charles de Gaulle promised independence to Syria and Lebanon, but he insisted that France must retain its "preeminent and privileged position" in both countries. American diplomats were upset. Hoping to open the Levant to American trade and investment, the State Department decided in November 1941 to issue an announcement expressing sympathy for the aspirations of Syria and Lebanon for independence and stating that American treaty rights to nondiscriminatory economic treatment should be respected in both countries.[54] The French allowed elections to be held in July–August 1943, and nationalist regimes came to power in both Beirut and Damascus. After obtaining assurances that the Syrian and Lebanese governments would respect the existing rights of Americans to receive equal economic treatment, the State Department announced in September 1944 that the United States would recognize their independence.[55]

But the French soon began pressing the Syrian and Lebanese

governments for treaties acknowledging that France had a "privileged position" in their respective countries. During a discussion at the State Department in March 1945, a French diplomat said that, if the Open Door policy were followed in the Levant, other countries would be unable to compete because the United States had become such an economic colossus. Paul H. Alling, the deputy director of the Office of Near Eastern and African Affairs, retorted "that equality of opportunity was high on our list of war aims and that we had no intention of fighting this war and then abandoning our objectives."[56] But the French continued to demand treaties recognizing their "special position" in Syria and Lebanon. When the government in Damascus refused to acquiesce, de Gaulle rushed military reinforcements to Syria in May 1945, and fighting quickly broke out between French and Syrian troops. The British, after obtaining American approval, intervened with superior military forces and compelled the French troops to withdraw.[57] State Department officials were pleased when order was restored in Syria, and they continued to support the principle of equal economic opportunity in the Levant.[58]

While French efforts to dominate Syria and Lebanon were being rebuffed, British and Soviet actions in Iran posed a serious threat to U.S. interests in the Middle East. The British and Russians had been competing for influence in Iran since the nineteenth century, but after Reza Pahlavi became the shah in 1925, he looked to Germany as a counterweight to safeguard the independence of his country. Some two thousand German technical advisers had established themselves in Iran by the beginning of World War II, and on 25 August 1941 Great Britain and the Soviet Union invaded Iran to prevent the country from falling under Nazi control. While Soviet troops occupied northern Iran, where they could defend Russian oil fields located above the Iranian border, the British sent occupational forces into southern Iran, where they could protect their huge oil concession in that part of the country. The British also aimed to use the Trans-Iranian Railway, running from the Persian Gulf to the Caspian Sea, as a safe route for the shipment of war supplies into the Soviet Union. Rather than submit to the Anglo-Soviet occupation of his country, the reigning shah abdicated in favor of his youthful son. The new shah promptly agreed to cooperate with the Allies, and in a treaty with Iran signed on 29 January 1942 the British and the Russians pledged not only to respect the political independence and territorial integrity of Iran but also to withdraw their troops no later than six months after the end of the war.[59]

Despite these promises, President Roosevelt and his State Department advisers distrusted both the British and the Soviets. Their suspicions were reinforced by reports that the Russians were supporting a separatist movement in northern Iran and that the British were seeking a stranglehold on the Iranian economy. State Department officials had already expressed concern about plans to provide the Anglo-Iranian Oil Company with lend-lease materials for the construction of pipelines from the interior of Iran to the Persian Gulf. Wallace Murray, the chief of the Division of Near Eastern Affairs, warned his colleagues on 12 January 1942 that "vigilance may be needed to prevent these pipelines from falling into exclusive British use after the war."[60] Apprehensive about both Russian and British interference in their internal affairs, the Iranians turned to the United States for support. President Roosevelt shared their concerns, and on 11 March 1942 he declared Iran eligible to receive lend-lease assistance.[61] Later in the year, Roosevelt persuaded Churchill to ask the United States to take over the job of managing the Trans-Iranian Railway.[62]

At the request of the Iranian government, the United States also dispatched a large number of special advisers and administrators to Iran. One group of American military advisers assumed the task of reorganizing the Iranian army, while another group began training the Iranian police force in an effort to improve security in rural areas. The largest U.S. mission, headed by Arthur C. Millspaugh, involved sixty economic and financial supervisors. On 4 May 1943, the Iranian Parliament granted Millspaugh wide powers to direct such vital internal activities as the collection of taxes, customs, and harvests. Millspaugh was even permitted to attend sessions of Parliament when discussions focused on economic matters.[63] As Millspaugh explained on 1 December 1943, the purpose of his mission was to help Iran put its financial house in order and thereby "prevent Britain and Russia from having an excuse to take over the country."[64]

Gen. Patrick J. Hurley, while on a special mission for the president in the Near East, had already reported that Great Britain and the Soviet Union were preparing to vie for control of Iran after the war. "Britain's control would be for the purpose of keeping the monopoly of the oil resources which her nationals now own and of establishing a trade monopoly," Hurley explained in a cable from Cairo on 13 May 1943. "Russia's control would serve to secure her long desired access to a warm water port."[65] In a memorandum sent to Roosevelt on 16 August 1943, Secretary Hull and his aides in the Near Eastern Division of the State

Department likewise warned that either the British or the Russians, or both, might take action that would seriously abridge, if not destroy, Iranian independence. "The best hope of avoiding such action lies in strengthening Iran to a point at which she will be able to stand on her own feet," Hull wrote. "It is to our interest that no great power be established on the Persian Gulf opposite the important American petroleum development in Saudi Arabia."[66]

Washington officials hoped not only to protect the American oil monopoly in Saudi Arabia but also to arrange for the United States to share in the development of Iranian petroleum resources. In a memorandum for the president on 11 November 1943, James F. Byrnes, the director of war mobilization, urged that vigorous negotiations should be pressed for the purchase by the U.S. government of a one-third interest in the British oil concession in Iran. Byrnes argued that the United States should compensate Great Britain by building a pipeline from the Iranian oil fields to the Mediterranean, by constructing a new refinery near Haifa, and by not demanding repayment for petroleum already advanced to the British under lend-lease.[67] But the State Department wanted Americans to gain access to Iranian petroleum deposits without injecting the government into the oil business. The department responded favorably, therefore, when the Standard-Vacuum Oil Company asked if it should go ahead with its plans to seek drilling rights from the Iranian government. Since the United States had no agreement with Great Britain not to obtain oil concessions in Iran, Secretary Hull explained on 15 November 1943, there was no reason why Standard-Vacuum should not undertake negotiations with the Iranian government.[68]

President Roosevelt was already thinking about how the United States could prevent Great Britain and the Soviet Union from expanding their influence in Iran. In a conversation with Under Secretary of State Stettinius on 5 November 1943, Roosevelt talked about the possibility of setting up a trusteeship in Iran with Russian, British, and American representation.[69] The president introduced the idea during the Big Three conference in Teheran at the end of the month. During a discussion with Churchill and Stalin, he suggested that the three trustees could establish a free port at the head of the Persian Gulf and place the Trans-Iranian Railroad under international management for the purpose of providing Russia with a through route to warm water and promoting economic development in Iran.[70] Although neither Churchill nor Stalin expressed much interest in the proposal, they did agree to join with Roosevelt on

1 December 1943 in issuing a declaration promising some postwar economic assistance for Iran and advocating the maintenance of Iranian independence, sovereignty, and territorial integrity.[71]

Following the Teheran Conference, the Roosevelt administration moved to stop the British from gaining commercial advantages in Iran by serving as the middleman for the distribution of American lend-lease supplies. General Hurley complained to President Roosevelt that the United Kingdom Commercial Corporation was using lend-lease materials, paid for by American taxpayers, to establish a British trade monopoly in Iran. "The least we should demand," he advised Roosevelt on 21 December 1943, "is that we be permitted to do our own giving."[72] The president agreed. In a memorandum for Hull on 12 January 1944, Roosevelt indicated that U.S. administrators "should take complete control of the distribution of our own Lend-Lease supplies in the Middle East."[73] Hull took decisive action to put an end to specific British abuses in Iran and to maintain an open door for American enterprise throughout the Middle East. In a blunt note delivered on 20 June 1944, Hull informed Ambassador Halifax that the British could no longer transfer to third countries items similar to those that they had received from the United States under the lend-lease program.[74]

The United States, however, soon found itself in a race with Great Britain and the Soviet Union for oil concessions in Iran. While the British government was encouraging the Shell Oil Company to seek drilling rights in Iran, Richard Ford, the U.S. chargé d'affaires in Teheran, was supporting Standard-Vacuum and Sinclair Oil in their efforts to obtain permission from the Iranian government to explore for petroleum. "To gain this rich prize for American interests," Ford cabled the State Department in August 1944, "will require quick action." The Russians were also in a hurry. In early September 1944 a Soviet delegation arrived in Teheran and requested an exclusive petroleum concession in the five northern provinces of Iran. Many Iranians feared that the Russians wanted to detach the province of Azerbaijan, and on 9 October 1944 Prime Minister Mohammed Saed announced that his government had decided to postpone all oil negotiations until after the war. The State Department, like the British Foreign Office, accepted the decision without protest. The U.S. ambassador in Teheran simply informed the Iranian government that, whenever it was ready to consider applications for petroleum concessions, the United States would expect to receive no less favorable treatment than other countries.[75]

But the Russians were furious about the Iranian decision to defer oil discussions. The Soviet press immediately launched an intense campaign against Prime Minister Saed, and on 9 November 1944, he resigned in an attempt to get the Russians to drop their demands for a petroleum concession. Churchill and Roosevelt hoped to secure a satisfactory resolution of the Iranian issue at their forthcoming conference with Stalin in the Crimea. During a meeting at Yalta on 8 February 1945, British Foreign Minister Eden suggested that the Allies should agree to withdraw their troops from Iran as soon as possible and to refrain from seeking oil concessions while their soldiers remained on Iranian soil. Secretary of State Stettinius supported Eden, but the Soviets refused to accept his proposal. Although the war ended in August 1945, Soviet troops remained in Iran and began aiding separatists in Azerbaijan. The Iranian question was not settled until May 1946, when in response to strong American demands that they live up to their earlier promises, the Russians finally withdrew their soldiers from Iran.[76]

In the meantime, U.S. economic and strategic interests throughout the Middle East were endangered by the Zionist crusade to turn Palestine into a Jewish state. Zionism had become a factor in international politics during World War I, when the British government attempted to win Jewish support at home without alienating millions of Arabs in the Middle East. In November 1917 Foreign Secretary Arthur Balfour announced that the British government would endeavor to facilitate the establishment of a national home for Jewish people in Palestine but that nothing would be done to prejudice the religious and civil rights of non-Jewish residents. The British tried to gloss over the contradictory features of the Balfour Declaration after they assumed responsibility for administering Palestine as a League of Nations mandate. But the Arabs became aroused when Jewish immigration into Palestine increased after Hitler took over Germany, and in 1936 British troops put down a bloody Arab rebellion against the Jews in Palestine. Determined to maintain friendly relations with Arabs throughout the Middle East, the British government decided in May 1939, just three months before the outbreak of World War II, to issue a White Paper restricting Jewish immigration into Palestine to 75,000 over the next five years.[77]

The Advisory Committee on Postwar Foreign Policy began studying the Palestine question nine months after the attack on Pearl Harbor. Assuming that the United States and many other countries would refuse to open their doors to a flood of Jewish emigrants from Europe, Under Secretary of State Sumner Welles, the chairman of the Subcommittee on

Political Problems, suggested to his colleagues on 29 August 1942 that both economic incentives and military intimidation should be used to get the Arabs to hand over Palestine to the Jews. Welles hoped that leaders throughout the Arab world would agree to the forced resettlement of Arabs from Palestine to parts of Trans-Jordan and Iraq if the projected international security organization offered to irrigate those areas and encourage the formation of an Arab federation in the Middle East. "A bargain might be struck with the Arabs," he explained, "but the threat of force could be held over their heads." Arguing that a binational Palestinian state of Arabs and Jews could not be made to work, Welles concluded that the refugee problem that Hitler had created could only be solved by the establishment of an independent Jewish state in Palestine.[78]

But most of his colleagues believed that the creation of a binational Palestinian state would be the best way to provide a home for a limited number of Jewish settlers without arousing the enmity of the entire Arab world.[79] During a meeting of the political subcommittee on 5 September 1942, Isaiah Bowman denounced the idea of displacing Arabs to make room for a large Jewish immigration into Palestine. "We are in danger of running parallel to the Nazi geo-political ideas," he admonished. "Germany says she should have more *Lebensraum*. Then it is said concerning the Jews that we must provide them with a land, but those who have power are not proposing to give the Jews *their* land but someone else's land, to solve the problem. Those with power should not tell the Arabs that they have to suffer in order to settle other people's problems by giving up their territory." After listening to Myron C. Taylor, Anne O'Hare McCormick, and Green H. Hackworth express similar thoughts, Welles quickly dropped the idea of encouraging the establishment of a Zionist state at the expense of the Arab population in Palestine.[80]

Yet President Roosevelt remained sympathetic to the Zionist cause. On 3 December 1942, Roosevelt told Treasury Secretary Henry Morgenthau, his close Jewish friend who was concerned about the plight of war refugees, that he intended to move Arabs out of Palestine and provide land for them in some other part of the Middle East. Jews would be allowed to move into Palestine until they composed 90 percent of the population, he explained, adding that Palestine would then become an independent nation with Jews dominating the government.[81] Roosevelt had sent Col. Harold B. Hoskins to the Middle East to find out whether an agreement on Palestine could be arranged. In a memorandum prepared on 20 March 1943, however, Hoskins reported that a compromise could be worked out, though only if Palestine became a binational state with Jewish settlers making up no more than 50 percent of the population. "It is important for the American people to realize that in the Moslem world Arab feelings are uncompromisingly against the acceptance of a political Zionist state in Palestine," he emphasized. "The American people should be clearly informed that only by force can a political Zionist policy be made effective." Hoskins also warned that the continued Jewish agitation concerning Palestine would "add fuel to the anti-Semitic charges already rife that the primary loyalty of American Jews is to political Zionism, not to the United States."[82]

The political subcommittee returned to the subject of Palestine after Secretary of State Hull had replaced Welles as chairman. During a meeting on 27 March 1943, the members agreed on the desirability of establishing a Jewish homeland in Palestine, but only as part of a binational state in which equal political rights and economic opportunities would be accorded to Arabs and Jews alike. After concluding that a limited number of Jews should be permitted to move into Palestine, the members repeatedly asked Bowman, an eminent geographer, for an estimate of the future capacity of Palestine to absorb population. He answered that it would be conceivable to double the number of Jews that were then living in Palestine while increasing the number of Arabs by a smaller amount in an effort to achieve population parity between the two groups. Bowman went on to say that only at the close of the war would it be possible to determine the need to find overseas homes for Jews who were being persecuted in Europe. After living conditions in Europe were restored, he hoped many Jewish refugees might wish to return to their native lands.[83]

The Subcommittee on Territorial Problems, working under his chairmanship, agreed that Palestine did not have the capacity to absorb a large influx of Jewish refugees from Europe. "It should be made perfectly clear," Myron Taylor argued during a meeting on 30 April 1943, "that there is no room for them there."[84] William Yale warned his colleagues on the territorial subcommittee a month later that the introduction of a large number of Jewish refugees into Palestine would probably lead to "a prolonged and bitter Jewish-Arab war."[85] During a meeting on 11 June 1943, Adolf Berle hoped that a solution to the problem of Jewish refugees could be found without creating overcrowded conditions in Palestine and sowing the seeds for future bloodshed. "If the refugees were permitted to immigrate in small numbers into many foreign countries," he reasoned, "it would serve as a safety valve which would relieve the pressure on Palestine." Berle added that "the re-immigration of Jews to their original homelands would relieve some more pressure."[86]

Isaiah Bowman and his State Department associates urged President Roosevelt to keep the Palestine question in abeyance until the end of the war. "If we must make promises," Bowman advised Roosevelt on 22 May 1943, "promise both Arabs and Jews that there will be deliberate consultation on the questions involved *after the war*."[87] American diplomats repeatedly warned that there was a deep-seated Arab hostility to the Zionist program for the establishment of an exclusive Jewish state in Palestine. "If this government should have anything to do with giving effect to such a program, we should incur the enmity of the Arab peoples, whose friendship is vital to us," a State Department memorandum declared on 27 May. "It is recommended that the Arabs and Jews first endeavor to reach a friendly settlement between themselves, by their own efforts. If this endeavor is unsuccessful, our influence should be exerted toward a solution, reached after full consultation with both Arabs and Jews."[88]

President Roosevelt soon acted on this advice. In a message to King Ibn Saud in June 1943, Roosevelt expressed hope that Arab and Jewish leaders would be able to settle their differences with respect to Palestine before the end of the war.[89] The president also dispatched Colonel Hoskins a month later on a second mission to the Middle East. Roosevelt instructed Hoskins to ask King Saud whether he would enter into friendly conversations with Pres. Chaim Weizmann of the Jewish Agency for Palestine. But the king told Hoskins during a discussion in August 1943 that Weizmann had attempted to bribe him and that he would not meet with anyone connected with the Jewish Agency. When Hoskins returned to Washington and reported to the president on 27 September, he once again emphasized his belief that a Jewish state in Palestine could only be established and maintained by military force.[90]

President Roosevelt told Hoskins that he had been searching his own mind for a solution to the Palestine problem. Roosevelt mentioned that he had been receiving an increasing amount of information indicating that many European Jews would prefer to return to their countries of origin rather than to migrate to Palestine after the war. With regard to Jewish refugees who might wish to move out of Europe, the president said that he was working on the possibility that some of them could be resettled in South America. Roosevelt further stated that his own thinking leaned toward the idea of establishing a United Nations trusteeship to handle Palestine. He talked about making Palestine "a real Holy Land for all three religions, with a Jew, a Christian, and a Moslem as the three responsible trustees." Roosevelt acknowledged that it might be difficult to get the Jews to accept such a plan. But if the Muslims and Christians of the world would agree, he hoped that the Jews could also be persuaded to go along.[91]

President Roosevelt and his foreign-policy advisers, however, were soon distressed by the introduction of Senate and House resolutions calling upon the U.S. government to work to open Palestine to the free entry of Jews so that they could reconstitute Palestine as an independent Jewish commonwealth. Fearing that the adoption of these resolutions would "play hell" with the enormous American petroleum concession in Saudi Arabia, Secretary of State Hull telephoned Army Chief of Staff George C. Marshall on 5 February 1944 and suggested that he might wish to urge the measures' defeat on military grounds.[92] Secretary of War Stimson was informed by his staff the next day that the passage of the congressional resolutions might jeopardize plans for the construction of an oil pipeline across Saudi Arabia as well as precipitate serious disturbances requiring the diversion of Allied combat forces from Europe to the Middle East.[93] In a letter sent on 7 February to Tom Connally, the chairman of the Senate Foreign Relations Committee, Stimson warned that any public hearings on the pro-Zionist resolutions might be detrimental to the Allied war effort. After this letter was published at the request of the State Department, the resolutions were quashed in Senate and House committees.[94]

The mere introduction of the pro-Zionist resolutions on the floor of Congress, however, had provoked sharp protests from King Saud and several Middle Eastern governments. Warning that "Ibn Saud holds top cards," Wallace Murray urged Under Secretary of State Stettinius to alert President Roosevelt that "we might lose the oil."[95] But Arab apprehensions were further aroused on 9 March 1944 when Roosevelt met with Rabbis Stephen S. Wise and Abba H. Silver. The press reported that the president had authorized these two Zionist leaders to announce that "when future decisions are reached full justice will be done to those who seek a Jewish National Home." Roosevelt immediately attempted to control the damage caused by his effort to court Jewish political support. In a message on 13 March, he assured King Saud that the U.S. government believed that no decision to alter the present status of Palestine should be reached without full consultation with both Arabs and Jews. Roosevelt also authorized the State Department the next day to send the governments of Egypt and Iraq messages repeating the assurances he had given to King Saud and indicating that his comments favorable to a national home for Jews did not mean that he advocated an exclusive Jewish state in Palestine.[96]

At the same time, the Roosevelt administration took steps to protect the exclusive American petroleum concession in Saudi Arabia from any British encroachment. The State Department received reports in March 1944 that S. R. Jordan, the British minister in Jidda, was working to weaken the American position in Saudi Arabia. Murray and his colleagues in the Division of Near Eastern Affairs feared that King Saud might succumb to British intrigue if he received more financial aid from Great Britain than from the United States.[97] "If Saudi Arabia is permitted to lean too heavily upon the British," Hull warned Roosevelt on 3 April, "there is always the danger that the British will request a *quid pro quo* in oil." To prevent such a possibility, Hull recommended that the United States and Britain should subsidize King Saud on an equal basis. Roosevelt agreed, and in July 1944 the two countries worked out a joint supply program for Saudi Arabia. But Minister Jordan continued his efforts to undermine U.S. interests in Saudi Arabia. The State Department finally demanded his removal, and the British Foreign Office reluctantly transferred him from Jidda.[98]

But the Palestine question, contrary to the desires of American diplomats, could not be kept out of domestic politics as the presidential campaign heated up in the United States. When the Republicans and Democrats held their conventions in the summer of 1944, they both incorporated pro-Zionist planks in their party platforms. Moreover, in October the two candidates, Democratic incumbent Roosevelt and Republican challenger Thomas E. Dewey, each made unequivocal statements promising that, if elected, he would help bring about the establishment of Palestine as a Jewish commonwealth. During a high-level meeting in the State Department on 15 November, however, Wallace Murray reported that these pro-Zionist declarations had caused an alarming deterioration in U.S. relations with Arab countries. Murray also pointed out that the Russians were opposed to Zionism. "If they should choose to capitalize on the difference between their attitude on this subject and the attitude of the United States and British Governments," he warned, "the Soviets might be able to assume a predominant position in the Arab world."[99]

In a memorandum for Roosevelt a month after his re-election, newly appointed Secretary of State Stettinius noted that the bipartisan endorsement of a Jewish state in Palestine during the presidential campaign had given rise to a wave of anti-American protests in the Middle East. Some Arab leaders had called for a complete boycott of American trade, while others had suggested that economic concessions should be withheld from countries that did not respect Arab rights. If this trend were to continue, he warned, it might endanger "the future of the immensely valuable American oil concession in Saudi Arabia." Stettinius also feared that the U.S. position in the whole region would be weakened vis-à-vis both Great Britain and the Soviet Union. "The Russians are showing a growing interest in the Arab world and are quite plainly anxious to expand their influence in the area, particularly toward the Persian Gulf," he explained. "Such expansion would, of course, be in the direction of the oil fields in Saudi Arabia and Bahrein as well as those in Iran, Iraq, and Kuwait."[100]

Determined to maintain the American oil monopoly in Saudi Arabia, the State Department sent President Roosevelt a memorandum on 22 December 1944 recommending the extension of long-range financial assistance to the Saudi government. "The vast oil resources of Saudi Arabia, now in American hands under a concession held by American nationals," the memorandum declared, "should be safeguarded and developed in order to supplement Western Hemisphere oil reserves as a source of world supply." The memorandum pointed out that King Saud had indicated that he would adopt a more independent attitude toward third countries if Saudi Arabia were assured adequate financial support from the United States. Because lend-lease aid could not be promised on a long-term basis, the memorandum proposed that the president should ask Congress to appropriate funds to meet the urgent financial requirements of the Saudi government, that U.S. military personnel should build airfields and roads in Saudi Arabia, and that the Export-Import Bank should make loans for the development of Saudi resources. Roosevelt promptly approved these recommendations.[101]

The president felt confident that he would be able to solve the Palestine problem when he had a chance to talk with King Saud after the Big Three meeting in Yalta. During a conference with Secretary of State Stettinius on 2 January 1945, Roosevelt said that he intended to show the king a map indicating that Palestine was only a very small part of the Near East and to say that he could not see why a portion of Palestine could not be given to the Jews with the understanding that they would not move into adjacent areas.[102] Stettinius made no comment, but a week later he warned Roosevelt that King Saud had recently stated that he would feel it an honor to die in battle as a champion of the Arabs in

Palestine.[103] On 17 January, in response to an inquiry from Roosevelt as to what he might say to the king, James Landis advised the president that the Arabs would never accept the idea of Palestine as a Jewish commonwealth but that it should be possible to sell the concept of a national home for Jews. Landis added that there was even hope for achieving a compromise on the immigration question because Palestine lacked the economic capacity to absorb a large number of Jews.[104]

On his return home from the Yalta Conference, President Roosevelt stopped in Egypt at the Great Bitter Lake to talk with King Saud. They met for five hours on 14 February 1945 aboard the USS *Quincy*. During their conversation, Roosevelt tried to get the king to agree to a compromise that would permit some of the displaced European Jews to find homes in Palestine. But King Saud would not condone further Jewish immigration into Palestine. He said that, although the Jews and Arabs residing in Palestine had learned to live together in peace, if European Jews with foreign financial backing and higher standards of living continued to move into Palestine, they would make trouble for the Arab inhabitants. "Arabs would choose to die rather than yield their lands to the Jews," the king warned, adding that, as a Muslim leader, he would take the side of his co-religionists if the Arabs surrounding Palestine proclaimed a holy war against the Jews. The president was given pause. Roosevelt quickly assured Saud that he "would do nothing to assist the Jews against the Arabs and would make no move hostile to the Arab people."[105] After his sobering discussion with the king, Roosevelt told a State Department adviser that a Jewish state in Palestine could be established and maintained only by military force.[106]

Although the president returned to Washington empty handed, his foreign-policy advisors continued their efforts to protect American petroleum interests in the Middle East. The State, War, Navy, and Interior Departments all agreed on the need to help King Saud cover his budget deficits so that Saudi Arabia would not turn to Great Britain for financial assistance.[107] During a meeting with a small group of congressional leaders on 8 March 1945, Assistant Secretary of State Dean G. Acheson and Under Secretary of the Navy Ralph A. Bard explained that it would be necessary to find some means of providing King Saud with $50 million over the next three years in order to maintain a strong influence over him.[108] The State Department also tried to calm the storm in the Middle East after President Roosevelt told Rabbi Wise that he still stood by his earlier pledge to support a Jewish homeland in Palestine. In a note dispatched on

22 March 1945, Under Secretary of State Joseph C. Grew instructed U.S. diplomats in Baghdad to reassure Iraq that the president still believed that no decision regarding Palestine should be reached without full consultation with both Arabs and Jews.[109]

The Palestine issue remained unsettled when Roosevelt died suddenly on 12 April 1945 and Harry S. Truman became president. "It is very likely that efforts will be made by some of the Zionist leaders to obtain from you at an early date some commitments in favor of the Zionist program which is pressing for unlimited Jewish migration into Palestine and the establishment there of a Jewish state," Secretary of State Stettinius warned Truman on 18 April. "There is continual tenseness in the situation in the Near East largely as a result of the Palestine question and as we have interests in that area which are vital to the United States, we feel that this whole subject is one that should be handled with the greatest care and with a view to the long-range interests of this country."[110] Truman proceeded with caution. On 29 May, he approved a State Department plan to offer financial assistance to Saudi Arabia with the idea that King Saud would provide a substantial oil reserve for the future use of U.S. military forces.[111] In response to a State Department recommendation on 16 June, moreover, Truman indicated that he would refrain from making any commitments to Zionist leaders.[112]

The State Department hoped that it might be possible to work out a compromise that would permit a limited number of Jewish refugees to enter Palestine without provoking a violent Arab reaction and thereby jeopardizing American petroleum interests in the Middle East. In a memorandum prepared on 31 August 1945, members of the Division of Near Eastern Affairs noted that Zionists were demanding that one million Jews be admitted into Palestine as rapidly as possible but that Arabs would probably use armed force to oppose such a mass immigration. They warned that the security requirements would be considerable if Palestine were opened to large-scale Jewish immigration while it remained a British mandate under the League of Nations and before it received a new status in keeping with the concepts of the United Nations. "The United States should refrain from supporting a policy of large-scale immigration into Palestine during the interim period," they advised. "The United States could support a Palestine immigration policy during the interim period which would carry restrictions as to numbers and categories."[113]

President Truman agreed. In a letter to Prime Minister Clement Attlee on 18 September 1945, Truman suggested that Great Britain allow an additional 100,000 Jewish refugees to enter Palestine. "The American people," he wrote, "firmly believe that immigration into Palestine should not be closed, and that a reasonable number of Europe's persecuted Jews should, in accordance with their wishes, be permitted to resettle there."[114] A month later, Truman and Attlee decided to establish a joint Anglo-American committee to study the possibility of finding places for Jewish refugees to settle in "countries outside Europe (including Palestine)."[115] They hoped that this could be accomplished without bloodshed. When Sen. Joseph H. Ball of Minnesota presented Truman with a Zionist resolution demanding the immediate opening of Palestine to unlimited Jewish immigration, the president expressed his views in an unsent response. "We will have to negotiate awhile," Truman wrote on 24 November. "I don't think that you, or any of the other Senators, would be inclined to send a half dozen Divisions to Palestine to maintain a Jewish State."[116] But the failure of his efforts to find a peaceful solution to the Palestine question marked the beginning of a long period of violence characterized by recurrent clashes between Arabs and Jews in the Middle East.

The architects of globalism in the State Department had paved the way during World War II for the development of the vast petroleum resources of the Middle East. By shifting the geographical center of oil production to the Persian Gulf, they hoped to provide an ample supply of cheap energy that would serve the military needs of the United States and enable American manufacturers and farmers to maintain their competitive edge in world markets without depleting the petroleum reserves of the Western Hemisphere. They repeatedly used the lend-lease program to protect the huge American oil concession in Saudi Arabia and to promote the principle of equal economic opportunity throughout the Middle East. The postwar planners in the State Department also warned Roosevelt and Truman again and again that, if they supported the Zionist crusade to turn Palestine into a Jewish state, Arab leaders might retaliate against vital American petroleum interests and declare a holy war against the Jews. But to their dismay, Truman eventually decided to back the creation of Israel as a Jewish state. "The whole mess in Palestine," Isaiah Bowman grumbled in December 1947, "is largely our fault for playing politics with Jewish ambitions and withholding from the American people the ultimate consequences of this action in American lives."[117]

SIX | PRESERVING WORLD PEACE

President Roosevelt and his State Department advisers worked together during World War II to lay the foundation for the establishment of an effective system of international security. They aimed not only to keep the United States safe from any future military attack but also to prevent the outbreak of another global conflict for as long as possible. Their plans for the creation of a peaceful world order rested upon two fundamental propositions. First, the American people and their representatives in Congress must agree that the United States should participate in the implementation of international arrangements to preserve world peace by the use of force if necessary. Second, the Soviet Union must agree to join with the United States, Great Britain, and China in disarming the Axis powers, in policing the planet during the transitional period immediately following the war, and in building a permanent international organization to promote an enduring peace. Believing that Russian cooperation would be essential for maintaining world peace, U.S. policymakers hoped to persuade Soviet leaders to seek security by pursuing a policy of international collaboration rather than by embarking upon a program of territorial expansion along their European and Asian borders.

Secretary of State Cordell Hull was determined not to repeat the same mistakes that had prevented the United States from joining the League of Nations after World War I. Ever mindful that President Wilson had failed to obtain broad domestic backing for his effort to promote collective-security arrangements at the Versailles Peace Conference, Hull warned the Advisory Committee on Postwar Foreign Policy on 2 May 1942 that it was of the "utmost importance to have the support of American public opinion."[1] Hull quickly resolved to do everything possible to avoid any partisan controversy that might once again block American participation in an international organization to maintain world peace. On 27 May, he invited Sen. Tom Connally, a Democrat from Texas, and Sen. Warren R. Austin, a Republican from Vermont, to become members of the advisory committee. Hull reached out in a radio address two months later in an attempt to influence people throughout the country. "It is plain," he declared, "that some international agency must be created which can—by force, if necessary—keep the peace among nations in the future."[2]

The Subcommittee on Political Problems, chaired by Under Secretary of State Sumner Welles, had already begun formulating plans for the establishment of an international security organization that would be able to act without delay. "We ought to make the assumption," Welles explained on 14 March 1942, "that Russia will agree to cooperate with the United States and Great Britain."[3] During a meeting two weeks later, Welles summarized the tentative conclusions that the subcommittee had reached: the world organization should include representatives from all the Allied countries; an executive committee should be comprised of representatives from the four major powers (the United States, Great Britain, the Soviet Union, and China) together with selected representatives from different regions of the world; and various commissions should be created with representation from each member nation. Although they agreed that the four major powers should make the important political and military decisions, the members of the subcommittee wanted to foster a sense of participation among the smaller countries. "Speaking frankly," Welles admitted, "what was required was a sop for the smaller states."[4]

The Subcommittee on Security Problems, under the chairmanship of Norman H. Davis, who had earlier headed the U.S. delegation at the Geneva Disarmament Conference, soon began discussing the issue of arms limitation. When the subcommittee met for the first time on 15 April 1942, Davis said that it would be necessary to have both an international inspection system to determine if the disarmament regulations had been violated and an international enforcement mechanism to punish the violator. "International inspection is important," he reasoned, "because if each nation knows that its violation of the disarmament regulations will be detected at an early stage, it will be much less likely to perpetuate the violation."[5] During a meeting of the security subcommittee two weeks later, Davis suggested that the United States, Great Britain, and the Soviet Union should come to a formal agreement establishing both a maximum and a minimum level for the military forces that each should maintain. "With such an agreement each of them could safely reduce armaments," he argued. "Without it there is danger that the British and American people will insist on a reduction of armaments for reasons of economy and leave the Russians as the only power with a large military force." Davis concluded that "the real hope of keeping the peace rests in the combination of these three powers."[6]

President Roosevelt was thinking along similar lines. Norman Davis informed his colleagues on 20 May 1942 that he had recently talked with the president about the work of the security subcommittee. During their conversation, Roosevelt said that in the last analysis, the United States, Great Britain, Russia, and China must control the peace settlement and maintain world security. These four nations, he explained, would have to determine what armament reductions should be made. Then they would need to conduct inspections to detect armament violations and to deploy their forces to control the sea and the air. The president also expressed the opinion that France, along with Germany, should be disarmed and kept disarmed.[7] In a letter written a year earlier, Roosevelt had reminded Assistant Secretary of State Adolf A. Berle to keep the question of disarmament in mind while he was developing plans for the postwar world. "Don't forget that the elimination of costly armaments is still the keystone—for the security of all little nations and for economic solvency," he advised. "Don't forget what I discovered—that over ninety percent of all national deficits from 1921 to 1939 were caused by payments for past, present and future wars."[8]

President Roosevelt conveyed his ideas about postwar security to Soviet foreign minister Vyacheslav Molotov during private conversations in the White House. While serving cocktails before dinner on 29 May 1942, Roosevelt told Molotov that he could not visualize the creation of another League of Nations with a hundred different signatories because there would be too many countries to satisfy. The president said that he thought that the United States, Britain, Russia, and possibly China should police the world and enforce disarmament by instituting a system of inspection. These four powers should maintain sufficient armed forces to curb aggression, and all other nations should be disarmed. If any country menaced the peace, it could be blockaded and then bombed if it still refused to acquiesce. Roosevelt explained that his aim was to establish an era of peace that would last at least twenty-five years.[9] During another confidential discussion three days later, Molotov told the president that he had reported to Moscow the American proposal that the "Big Four" should act as the policemen of the world. Molotov said that he had received a reply from Stalin that the Soviet government approved the idea and would fully support it.[10]

Although Norman Davis agreed with President Roosevelt about the need for postwar collaboration among the four major powers, he was troubled by his determination to disarm all the other countries. During a meeting of the security subcommittee on 18 September 1942, he cautioned his colleagues against making the assumption that after the war the Soviet Union would be willing to pursue a policy of close cooperation with the United States and Great Britain. Davis said that in all probability the Russians might be bent upon an expansionist program that would destroy the territorial status quo in Central and Western Europe. "If this were true," he warned, "it would be very greatly to our disadvantage if in the peace settlement we had insisted upon the drastic disarmament of Germany's neighbor states on the continent."[11] Davis reiterated his apprehensions about Russian ambitions two weeks later when he had lunch with Isaiah Bowman, a political subcommittee member who occasionally attended the security subcommittee meetings. "If Germany and France and Italy and all the rest are disarmed," he asked, "will Russia go along? If she won't what is the effect to be? Bolshevism all over Europe?"[12]

While sharing his anxiety regarding the Soviet Union, his colleagues on the security subcommittee also worried that restrictive trade practices could sow the seeds for future wars. "It might not be impossible, but it would be very difficult to create a system of postwar security," Gen. George V. Strong proclaimed during a subcommittee meeting on 23 October 1942, "unless at the same time economic arrangements were being made which would improve the welfare of all countries." Norman Davis agreed that economic opportunity would be necessary to provide a sound basis for military security. "As an aftermath of the war there would be so much misery and suffering that it would be impossible to maintain security merely by relying upon the use of military force," he reasoned. "Only through international political cooperation and through liberal economic and financial policies could these desperate peoples of the war-torn states be given any hope for the future."[13] During a subcommittee discussion a week later, Adm. Arthur J. Hepburn said that he was pleased to see that his colleagues believed in the need for economic agreement among the nations of the world to serve as a foundation for achieving peace. "No progress can be made," he declared, "unless effective steps have first been taken to remove the basic economic tensions which form such an important background of modern war."[14]

Turning their attention to the transitional period between the termination of hostilities and the creation of a permanent international organization, the members of the security subcommittee concluded on 30 October 1942 that immediate steps should be taken to cement an agreement among the four great powers to collaborate in maintaining world peace. "Unless such an agreement could be reached," Admiral

Hepburn declared, "it would be almost impossible realistically to plan any security arrangements for the future." Myron Taylor emphasized that "every effort in that direction should be made now in the period of military adversity." General Strong concurred. "At the present time the United States is in a position of tremendous power," he asserted. "It can dictate, if necessary, to any or all of the other three United Nations, forcing them to accept our leadership by threatening to divert the flow of American materials to other more cooperative nations." Warning that this power to dominate would rapidly disintegrate as the war drew to a close, Strong argued that the United States should negotiate a four-nation security accord before the military situation improved and an ultimate victory seemed inevitable. Norman Davis vigorously endorsed these views. Hoping to obtain commitments that would restrain the Russians after the war, he suggested that the contemplated agreement should contain a clause reaffirming the principles of the Atlantic Charter.[15]

Though convinced that a four-power security pact should be concluded at the earliest possible moment, the members of the security subcommittee held different opinions concerning the prospects of reaching a satisfactory understanding with the Soviet Union about postwar questions. They discussed at their meeting on 11 December 1942 the chances of persuading the Russians to accept some limitations on their armaments and their territorial demands along their frontier in Eastern Europe. Explaining that he did not believe that Soviet leaders were still bent on destroying other governments in order to bring about a world revolution, Norman Davis said that he thought that Russian cooperation with respect to postwar affairs might be readily forthcoming. "An immense amount of economic reconstruction would be necessary," he reasoned, "and the Russian government would undoubtedly prefer to devote its funds and energy to pacific rather than military ends." But Myron Taylor was somewhat less optimistic regarding the probable nature of postwar Russian diplomacy. He thought that the Soviet intervention in the Spanish Civil War had foreshadowed the kind of indirect interference in the internal affairs of other countries that might characterize future Russian foreign policy.[16]

When the security subcommittee reexamined the Russian question one week later, Norman Davis thought the attitude of Soviet authorities would be influenced by whether or not they believed they would have to depend primarily upon their own resources in the event of a future military attack from the West. "If there were a strong international security organization," he suggested, "the Russian demands might be less extensive." But if they did not think that they could count on American and British help in repelling an assault on their country, Russian leaders might feel compelled to establish a security perimeter by subjugating neighboring states in Eastern Europe. Davis pointed out that the United States would not go to war with the Russians should they, on the basis of their claim that the Baltic states had freely chosen to become a part of the Soviet Union, insist on maintaining their hold on these small countries. Nevertheless, he expressed hope that the United States might be able to diminish the Russian desire to absorb the Baltics by negotiating a four-power agreement to preserve world peace.[17]

Reverting to a more pessimistic attitude toward Russia during a security subcommittee discussion on 15 January 1943, Davis worried that the Soviet Union would possess the only strong army on the European continent if both Italy and France were disarmed following the elimination of German military power. Davis suggested that it would be very much in the interests of the United States to have Italy as an ally should there be a third world war. "Therefore, it may not be wise to weaken Italy too much, but to go only far enough to be sure that she could not combine with another power and start another war in the future," he reasoned. "If Western Europe is disarmed, it would be opened thereby to possible invasion by Russia in the years to come." Davis said that the ideal solution would be to secure a disarmament agreement between the Soviet Union and the other major powers before the American and British forces were demobilized. "Russia will be the real problem," he warned "and we must face that issue very soon."[18]

Turning to the subject of an international police force, Davis noted that the security subcommittee had come to the conclusion that such a force would be impracticable unless it were stronger than the military forces of any one nation. "It seemed more practicable to consider some plan whereby the four great powers would agree to uphold and enforce the decisions of the international political organization," he continued. "Certainly the United States would not place its forces under any international security organization which would be stronger than the combined military forces of this country."[19] When the topic came up for discussion again on 19 February 1943, Davis said that it was high time the security subcommittee should register its view that an international police force was not desirable. "An obligation among the four great powers was needed to stop any rearming without discussion," he insisted. "Then there should be an obligation that we should contribute to the forces required to put an end to this rearming."[20]

A week later Davis informed the members of the security subcommittee that he had discussed this subject with the president. Roosevelt had expressed the opinion that the four great powers would have to work together to preserve world order, and he had agreed entirely with Davis that an international police force would be impracticable. Davis reported that the president was reconsidering his views with regard to France. Roosevelt had earlier told some people that France should be kept disarmed after the war, but he was now weighing the question of what would happen if France and Germany were both disarmed and Russia decided not to cooperate with the United States, Great Britain, and China in maintaining peace. Davis said that France presented a serious problem the security subcommittee must attempt to solve. "It appeared necessary to have France participate in the military sense," he explained, "but we could not make our former mistake of making France too strong as to her armaments, and then permitting her to make alliances." Davis cautioned that the United States, while trying to prevent the French from threatening the peace, must be careful to keep them as friends in case the Russians were not fully cooperative after the war.[21]

At a meeting of the political subcommittee on 20 February 1943, Davis asked how the Russians could be assured that the U.S. government would not repeat what it had done in 1919 and refuse to make any commitments to maintain world peace. It would be a very strong trading point, he argued, if the Russians could be assured that the United States would participate in an international organization and help in keeping the Axis powers from rearming and threatening the peace. Sumner Welles expressed complete agreement with this line of reasoning. He said that the present policy of the Soviet Union was based upon the assumption that the United States would once again reject any form of international responsibility. "Consequently," Welles observed, "Russia feels that she has got to look out for herself insofar as her future security is concerned." To make sure that she would be secure if Germany were allowed to gain strength again, Russia aimed to take the territory that she deemed necessary for her own defense. "Our bargaining position would be greatly increased," he concluded, "if we were in a position to say that we would cooperate in maintaining the peace of the world."[22]

Isaiah Bowman expanded on these ideas in a memorandum, prepared on 6 March 1943, which received careful consideration in the security subcommittee. Assuming that the United States would not fight either to stop the Soviet Union from taking part of Poland or to give Finland the port of Petsamo, Bowman argued that the U.S. government should negotiate an agreement that would satisfy Russian interests in Eastern Europe. "Russia has need, first, for a western border strengthened by the tangible additions that improve Russia's position militarily," he explained. "I would begin by agreeing with her on her western border and make the best terms possible." Bowman suggested that the United States should try to persuade the Russians to take a moderate course of action with respect to Eastern Europe by promising them postwar economic assistance and by issuing a declaration that would give them some assurance of American willingness to join a general security system. "Negotiation should follow and not precede such a declaration," he emphasized. "And the time is now."[23]

When Bowman read his memorandum to the security subcommittee on 12 March 1943, he found that its members unanimously agreed on the need for an immediate approach to Russia. Norman Davis indicated that he and Myron Taylor had been working for early consultations with the Soviet Union for a long time but that President Roosevelt and Secretary of State Hull had decided to proceed gradually in this matter. Davis then revealed his growing impatience with their caution. He said that it was so important to conclude an agreement with the Russians that it might even be necessary to accede to their desires in the Baltic region.[24] During the next two weeks, the members of the subcommittee reiterated their eagerness to reach an agreement with the Soviet Union before it was too late. Davis argued that the United States was in a better position to negotiate now than after American troops landed in Europe. "When this happened," he warned, "Russia would be in a position to dictate maters by threatening to make a separate peace, or even by merely failing to fight whole-heartedly."[25] Davis hoped that an accord with the Soviet Union would forestall the unauthorized occupation of territory in Eastern Europe. "Some commitment was needed," he concluded, "so that Russia would not be permitted to run loose."[26]

In the midst of these private deliberations, and without any encouragement from either the White House or the State Department, Sen. Joseph H. Ball of Minnesota drafted a resolution calling for the United States to take the initiative in setting up a permanent international organization during the war. His resolution, introduced into the Senate on 16 March 1943, proposed that the new world body should have the power to carry on the war, to occupy territory liberated from the Axis countries, to provide machinery for the peaceful settlement of disputes, and to create an international police force to suppress any future attempt at military aggression. Both President Roosevelt and Secretary Hull were disturbed by the strong and specific character of the proposal. They feared that, if Ball and his supporters pushed for immediate Senate approval, they might provoke a fierce reaction among isolationists and make it more difficult to obtain broad public backing for U.S. participation in a world security organization. They also feared that, if the resolution passed by only a narrow margin after a long and bitter partisan debate, it would reinforce Soviet worries that the United States would refuse after the war to cooperate in preserving the peace.[27]

Roosevelt and Hull worked closely with Tom Connally, the chairman of the Senate Foreign Relations Committee, in an effort to obtain an agreement on a resolution that his colleagues would endorse by an overwhelming vote. The State Department quickly prepared a brief resolution declaring that the Senate advocated U.S. participation in an international organization to ensure peace, and on 22 March 1943 Hull read the proposal to Connally and two of his associates on the Senate Foreign Relations Committee. Roosevelt also tried his hand at drafting a resolution, and three days later he sent the chairman his version, which went as far as proposing the creation of a world organization with sufficient forces to curb aggression. Connally promptly decided that his committee should delay action on the Ball proposal and then report out a less detailed resolution designed to avoid controversy and to secure adoption by a wide margin. Hull later helped Connally draw up a compromise resolution to be introduced in the Senate in place of the Ball proposal.[28]

Meanwhile, the Special Subcommittee on International Organization, chaired by Sumner Welles, had been working for several months on a charter for a world security association. On 26 March 1943, Welles and his subcommittee submitted a draft constitution for an international organization. The document called for the creation of a three-tiered body. At the top, an executive committee representing the United States, Great Britain, the Soviet Union, and China would be responsible for the maintenance of international security. At the second level, a council comprising these four big powers and seven other states representing different regions of the world would determine whether or not there was a threat to peace and take all steps necessary to restrain any act of aggression. At the bottom, a general conference made up of all members of the world organization would assist in the application of measures required to restore peace. The draft constitution made no provision for the establishment of an international police force, but it did obligate all member states to make available to the world body forces and facilities that would be needed to suppress aggression and to maintain peace.[29]

Under Secretary Welles kept Roosevelt fully informed about the work of the various subcommittees planning for the postwar world, and when the president discussed the projected United Nations with Anthony Eden on 27 March 1943, his remarks corresponded with the views of his State Department advisers. Roosevelt told the British foreign secretary that an executive committee consisting of representatives of the Big Four would make "all the more important decisions" because these powers would have to police the world for many years to come. At the other end of the scale, a general assembly representing all members of the international organization would meet about once a year to let the smaller countries "blow off steam." In the middle, an advisory council made up of the Big Four plus six or eight other representatives from different geographical areas would meet from time to time to settle international questions. Roosevelt emphatically stated his conviction that the United Nations must be organized on a worldwide basis and not on a regional basis. He specifically declared that the United States could not be a member of any independent regional body such as some kind of European Council of Nations, which Prime Minister Churchill had recently proposed in a public address.[30]

In closely related talks with Eden, Secretary Hull stressed the need for the United States and Great Britain to make every effort to encourage the Soviet Union to seek future security by pursuing a policy of international cooperation rather than a program of territorial expansion. Hull decided to begin the process immediately. He invited Maxim Litvinov, the Russian ambassador in Washington, to confer with him at the State Department just after Eden left for London. During their meeting on 31 March 1943, Hull told Litvinov that he wanted to keep the Soviet government informed about his discussions with the British foreign secretary. Hull explained that he and Eden had agreed that the Big Four must remain united after the war to prevent the world from once again heading toward military destruction. In another conversation with Litvinov a month later, Hull argued that national self-preservation depended upon international collaboration. "Of course," he said, "Russia or the United States could isolate itself and ward off outside attacks for a few years. But the inevitable result would be a considerable drain on the economic strength of the country pursuing such a policy. And in time a more or less chaotic world, led by unscrupulous dictators, as at present, would get out of hand."[31]

While Hull was working on Litvinov, Roosevelt was trying to arrange a one-on-one meeting with Stalin to discuss postwar issues. Roosevelt wanted to meet Stalin without the presence of Churchill in hopes of establishing a close personal relationship with the Russian leader and convincing him that the United States and Great Britain were not ganging up on the Soviet Union. Roosevelt emphasized his strong desire for such a meeting by sending Joseph E. Davies, a former U.S. ambassador to Russia, on a special mission to Moscow. Davies carried with him a letter, signed by the president on 5 May 1943, proposing a confidential meeting with Stalin sometime during the summer. Stalin told Davies that he would like to meet with the president but that he could not say when he might be able to leave Moscow in view of the expected German offensive on the eastern front. When Churchill expressed his distress upon learning about the proposed meeting, Roosevelt dishonestly claimed that Stalin had advanced the idea. Then he argued that the meeting should be held because Stalin would be more frank in discussing his postwar ambitions if the two could confer alone. Later, though, Roosevelt agreed to a Big Three conference without a prior meeting between just Stalin and himself.[32]

In the meantime, Secretary Hull had created the Informal Political Agenda Group to guide the work of all the subcommittees planning for the postwar world. This group of senior officials—including Myron Taylor, Norman Davis, Isaiah Bowman, Leo Pasvolsky, Sumner Welles, and Edward Stettinius (after he replaced Welles as the under secretary of state)—frequently accompanied Hull when he went to the White House to discuss foreign policy with the president.[33] On 15 May 1943, Taylor sent each member of the agenda group a memorandum arguing against U.S. participation in any regional supervisory council for Europe even if it remained subsidiary, and did not become independent, to the world organization. Taylor also circulated an informal draft protocol of a four-power security agreement stipulating that the United States, Great Britain, the Soviet Union, and China would take the lead in establishing a universal organization to maintain world peace.[34] A week later, while chairing a meeting of the political subcommittee, Hull stressed his belief that there must be a combination of the four great military powers in order to deter future aggression. "The aggression that led to the present war was made possible by a lack of determination on the part of the powers that sought to keep the peace," he declared. "Japan and Germany plunged recklessly ahead because they felt that no one would resist them."[35]

During a luncheon on 22 May 1943 with a small group of American officials at the British embassy in Washington, Prime Minister Churchill outlined his thoughts on how to prevent aggression by Germany or Japan in the future. Churchill contemplated a postwar international structure that would stand like a three-legged stool, with a supreme world council resting on three subordinate regional councils, one each for Europe, the Western Hemisphere, and the Pacific. He indicated that the United States, Great Britain, Russia, and possibly China would be responsible for maintaining peace. These major powers, together with certain other powers, would form the world council and sit on the regional councils in which they were directly interested. Churchill explained that it would be important to recreate a strong France because the prospect of having no strong country on the map between Britain and Russia was not attractive. He added that it would be necessary for France to assist in the policing of Europe. Churchill attached great importance to the regional principle. "It was only the countries whose interests were directly affected by a dispute who could be expected to apply themselves with sufficient vigor to secure a settlement," he argued. "If countries remote from a dispute were among those called upon in the first instance to achieve a settlement the result was likely to be merely vapid and academic discussion."[36]

The political subcommittee promptly decided to reconsider the whole issue of regionalism. While agreeing that regional arrangements might be useful in dealing with purely local problems, the subcommittee members believed that the universal body should have original jurisdiction over broad international disputes and appellate jurisdiction over all regional disturbances. They thought there would be grave dangers in having the world organization rest upon a foundation of regional associations.[37] "We found that the fatal weakness of a primary dependence upon a regional system in attaining an over-all international organization arises from the natural differences that exist among regions," Isaiah Bowman explained on 12 June 1943. "If primary reliance is placed upon regions, their cultural, economic, political and military differences will probably grow in time as their power and conflicting economic interests grow, and region will be arrayed against region." Bowman pointed to the field of international trade to illustrate the dangers inherent in regional arrangements. "If a powerful European Council demands certain trade relationships with South America," he warned, "we shall find that political influences will follow and they will not be for the general good of the world."[38]

The members of the political subcommittee also feared that there might be a reversion to isolation in the United States unless they exercised great caution in formulating proposals for a world organization. Although there seemed to be a growing public desire for international collaboration, they worried that the American people might refuse to participate in a world organization if its activities appeared to restrict their sovereignty too much or to extend too far beyond the field of security. They concluded on 19 June 1943 that the four major powers should reach an understanding with respect to the character of the world organization during the war while the American people still agreed on the need for international cooperation to maintain peace.[39] A letter from W. Averell Harriman, soon to become the U.S. ambassador in Moscow, gave them cause for encouragement. "As you know," Harriman wrote President Roosevelt on 5 July, "I am a confident optimist in our relations with Russia because of my conviction that Stalin wants, if obtainable, a firm understanding with you and America more than anything else—after the destruction of Hitler."[40]

Myron Taylor continued to push the idea that the United States, Great Britain, the Soviet Union, and China should quickly conclude a four-power pact as the first step toward the establishment of a world security organization. "I am not one of those who believes that a mere declaration of American sentiment would be adequate," Taylor explained on 8 July 1943 in a memorandum that he promptly sent to both Hull and Roosevelt. "I should prefer a fundamental approach to the question of firm agreement among these four nations, urgently presented to the Senate for ratification, with the hope that it may be removed from political controversy in the year to come." Taylor believed that such an agreement, backed by the constitutional authority of the federal government, would help convince other countries that the United States would participate in a United Nations Organization for the preservation of peace. "Our failure to enter the League leaves a reasonable doubt as to our sincerity now," he warned. "To promote the world organization, therefore, some positive step must be taken now to assure the world of our adherence."[41]

Secretary Hull thereupon decided to launch two closely related projects. First, he asked his senior aides to formulate provisions for a four-power agreement to be concluded at the earliest possible moment. Second, Hull authorized the establishment of a State Department group under the direction of Leo Pasvolsky to prepare a draft charter for a world organization based upon global rather than regional principles.[42] The Tentative Draft Text of the Charter of the United Nations, completed by Pasvolsky and his aides on 14 August 1943, made no provision for an executive committee and gave the council the primary responsibility for maintaining international security. The United States, Great Britain, the Soviet Union, and China would be permanent members of the council, and three other members would be elected by the general conference for annual terms. Thus, the Big Four would always outnumber the smaller countries on the council. Procedural questions before that body would be decided by a simple majority vote. Any action taken by it to enforce peace would require a two-thirds majority of the members present and voting, including three of the four permanent members. But no party to a dispute, not even a permanent member of the council, would be allowed to vote in any decision taken to promote a peaceful settlement.[43]

While the State Department research staff had been drawing up the text for a United Nations charter, Hull and his Informal Political Agenda Group had been drafting a proposal for a security pact among the four major powers. They pressed ahead quickly. On 10 August 1943, Hull took Welles, Bowman, Davis, and Pasvolsky to the White House to discuss with the president the type of agreement they should attempt to negotiate. A draft protocol, prepared by Myron Taylor three months earlier, had been couched in the form of a treaty that would need to be ratified by all the signatory governments. But Roosevelt and the group that he called "my postwar advisers" decided that the agreement should take the form of a declaration that would require no ratification and would come into effect at once. The following day their conclusions found expression in the Tentative Draft of a Joint Four-Power Declaration, which Hull intended to push with great vigor during the forthcoming Anglo-American Conference in Quebec.[44]

The document called upon the governments of the United States, Great Britain, the Soviet Union, and China to make the following joint declaration: that they would cooperate in creating a peaceful international order after the war; that they would act together in all matters relating to the surrender, disarmament, and occupation of enemy and enemy-held territory; that they would take all measures necessary to enforce the requirements imposed upon the enemy; that they would establish at the earliest practicable date a general international organization to preserve world peace; that they would, pending the inauguration of a general system of security, consult and act jointly for the purpose of maintaining peace on behalf of the community of nations; that they would establish a technical commission to advise them on problems involved in the employment of force to curb aggression; that they would bring about a general agreement for the regulation of armaments after the war; and that they would not employ their military forces within the territory of other states except for the purposes envisaged in the declaration and after joint consultation and agreement.[45]

On 7 August 1943, in a message informing Russian leaders about the forthcoming Anglo-American discussions, Churchill had urged that he and Stalin should meet with Roosevelt as soon as possible. Stalin replied three days later that a conference among the heads of the American, British, and Russian governments should be arranged at the first opportunity but that at the present time he could not travel to any distant point due to the existing military situation on the eastern front. To expedite an examination of important questions, however, Stalin suggested that the foreign ministers of the United States, Great Britain, and the Soviet Union should meet in the near future. Roosevelt and Churchill were encouraged. They soon began a long process of arranging with Stalin times and locations both for a preliminary conference at the foreign-minister level and also for a Big Three meeting. After cabling each other a great many times, the three government chiefs finally agreed to hold a foreign ministers' conference at Moscow in October 1943 and a meeting among themselves in Teheran the following month.[46]

Meanwhile, during the political phase of the Quebec Conference, which took place between 17 and 24 August 1943, American and British leaders discussed the agenda for the upcoming foreign ministers' meeting. Eden argued that there would be little likelihood of improving relations with the Soviet Union unless some agreement could be made with respect to Russian territorial claims in Eastern Europe. But Roosevelt stated that, if Molotov raised any frontier question, the U.S. representative would evade the subject.[47] Roosevelt and Hull wanted to postpone consideration of difficult territorial issues until the final peace settlement. They hoped that, if the United States showed a willingness during the war to take part in a collective effort to prevent future aggression, it might be possible after the war to persuade the Russians to exercise restraint in dealing with their neighbors.[48] With this thought in mind, Hull showed British leaders the American draft of a four-power declaration. Eden said that he liked the document, and Churchill agreed that Hull should send a copy of the proposed declaration to Moscow with the hope that the Soviet government would give it favorable consideration.[49]

During the previous half-year, Roosevelt and Hull had continued working with leaders from both of the major American political parties in developing a congressional resolution pledging support for U.S. membership in a world security organization. Their contacts with important figures such as Republican senator Arthur H. Vandenberg of Michigan and

Democratic representative J. William Fulbright of Arkansas soon yielded positive results. On 8 September 1943, at a conference on Mackinac Island, Republican leaders issued a statement declaring that their party favored U.S. participation in a postwar international organization to prevent aggression and to attain a lasting peace. Two weeks later, on 21 September, the House of Representatives passed by an overwhelming margin a resolution, sponsored by Fulbright, endorsing the creation of international machinery with adequate power to maintain world peace. Roosevelt attempted to get Senate leaders to pass a similar resolution before Hull proposed a four-power declaration at the Foreign Ministers' Conference in Moscow. But Roosevelt and Hull were disappointed when action in the Senate was delayed due to a debate over how strongly such a resolution should be worded.[50]

Then, in the diplomatic field, Roosevelt and Hull were even more dismayed when Foreign Minister Molotov sent word that the Soviet government objected to the inclusion of China in the proposed four-power declaration.[51] On 5 October 1943, just two days before his departure for Moscow, Hull and a few of his principal aides went to the White House to discuss the problem with the president. Roosevelt insisted that Hull should do everything he could to conclude a four-power and not a three-power pact. The president said that it would be disastrous to leave China out because it would enable the British to act as a broker juggling American and Russian interests.[52] As Hull was preparing to leave Washington on 7 October, he asked his colleagues if they had any last-minute thoughts. Bowman replied that he believed that bargaining with Russia was the only hope, and Pasvolsky urged that primary consideration should be given to what the United States could do to provide economic help for Russia after the war.[53]

During the Foreign Ministers' Conference held in Moscow between 19 and 30 October 1943, Hull concentrated his efforts on getting the American draft of a four-power declaration accepted. He emphasized the need to take steps during the war to lay the foundation for international cooperation after hostilities ended. When Molotov objected to the inclusion of China in the proposed declaration, Hull hinted that if China were left out, the United States might divert to China some of the war supplies that it was sending to the Soviet Union. Molotov promptly agreed to allow China to join in signing the declaration the next time the subject came up for discussion. After making sure that China would be included in the declaration, Hull agreed to a few minor alterations that Molotov and Eden had suggested in the wording of the original draft. Then, at the last session of the conference, the three foreign ministers and the Chinese ambassador in Moscow signed the Four-Nation Declaration.[54]

While avoiding any discussion at Moscow of specific territorial issues, Hull did suggest that it would be in the best interest of Russia to refrain from taking independent action with respect to its frontier claims in Eastern Europe. "After the war, you can follow isolationism if you want, and gobble up your neighbors," Hull lectured Molotov. "But that will be your undoing. When I was young I knew a bully in Tennessee. He used to get a few things his way by being a bully and bluffing other fellows. But he ended up by not having a friend in the world." After warning Molotov about the negative consequences of unilateral action, Hull called his attention to the economic benefits that could be expected to flow from international cooperation. He gave Molotov a memorandum proposing that the United States should provide material and equipment that Russia would need to repair damage caused by the ravages of war. "Our productive capacity will be sufficiently great," the document explained, "to enable us to play a substantial part in rehabilitation and reconstruction in the USSR."[55]

American leaders believed that the Moscow Conference had prepared the ground for postwar collaboration among the major powers. In a telegram to the president on 31 October 1943, Hull reported that Stalin had talked and acted 100 percent in favor of the program of international cooperation outlined in the Four-Power Declaration.[56] Roosevelt and his entourage at the White House were also excited. "We are all elated at the success of the Moscow Conference," Harry Hopkins wrote the U.S. ambassador in London, "although, naturally, there are still many headaches to be ironed out."[57] In a cable to Roosevelt on 5 November, Ambassador Harriman reported from Moscow that he thought the conference had strengthened a tentative decision among Soviet leaders to work with the United States and Great Britain in settling postwar problems. "Before the conference I doubt if they had any intention of allowing the inclusion of China as an original signatory of the Four-Nation Declaration," Harriman observed. "Their acceptance of China is a clear indication that they are genuinely satisfied with the way things went and are ready to make important concessions to further the new intimacy."[58]

The Moscow Conference also helped solidify support in Congress for a postwar program of international collaboration. When the Four-Nation Declaration was released to the press, the Senate was in the midst of a debate over the wording of a resolution favoring U.S. participation in a world security organization. The news prompted the feuding senators to resolve their differences quickly, and on 5 November 1943 they passed by a huge margin an amended version of a resolution sponsored by Connally. The resolution called upon the United States to help establish and maintain an international authority with power to preserve world peace. When Hull returned from Moscow five days later, he was lauded as a national hero. The president greeted him at the airport as his plane touched down in Washington, and he was invited to address a joint secession of Congress. "As the provisions of the Four-Nation Declaration are carried into effect," Hull told an applauding Congress on 18 November, "there will no longer be need for spheres of influence, for alliances, for balance of power, or any other of the special arrangements through which, in the unhappy past, the nations strove to safeguard their security or to promote their interests."[59]

President Roosevelt had already departed for the Big Three meeting in Teheran with the hope that Stalin would support American plans for postwar collaboration. During a private discussion with Stalin on 29 November 1943, the second day of the conference, Roosevelt advocated a world organization with three main parts: an assembly of all the United Nations that would discuss general problems and make recommendations for their solution; an executive committee, made up of the Big Four and six representatives from various regions, that would deal with all non-military questions; and an enforcing agency, the "Four Policemen," that would have the power to deal immediately with any threat to peace. Stalin expressed the opinion that European countries would resent having China act as an enforcing authority even if it somehow emerged from the war as a powerful nation. As an alternative, he suggested the establishment of regional committees in Europe and the Far East with the United States, Great Britain, and the Soviet Union belonging to both. But Roosevelt said that he doubted Congress would agree to participate in a purely European committee that might be able to compel the United States to send troops to the continent. In another private conversation on 1 December, the last day of the conference, Stalin told Roosevelt that he had changed his mind and had come to agree on the need for a worldwide security organization.[60]

At the Teheran Conference, Roosevelt made a concerted effort to build a bridge of trust between Stalin and himself. Thus, he tried to allay any suspicions that the Russians might have had about a prearranged Anglo-American agreement on postwar matters. Besides avoiding long private meetings with Churchill while holding a series of one-on-one talks with Stalin, the president frequently sided with Stalin and emphasized his differences with Churchill when the Big Three met together. Roosevelt also tried to avoid getting bogged down in any quarrels over specific territorial questions that could jeopardize his attempt to court Stalin. If relations among the Allies deepened into feelings of mutual trust during the war, he hoped, Soviet frontier claims in Eastern Europe might be adjusted satisfactorily after the defeat of the Axis countries. Roosevelt was confident when he left Teheran that Stalin would be a cooperative partner in establishing a system of postwar security. In a joint press release issued after the conference ended, the Big Three expressed their determination to work together to construct a lasting peace.[61]

On 9 December 1943, a week before President Roosevelt arrived back in Washington, the Informal Political Agenda Group decided to prepare a proposal for an international security organization. The group then comprised Cordell Hull, Edward R. Stettinius, Norman H. Davis, Myron C. Taylor, Isaiah Bowman, Leo Pasvolsky, Benjamin V. Cohen, James C. Dunn, Green H. Hackworth, and Stanley K. Hornbeck. During later meetings dealing with military questions, the armed services were represented by four participants—Gen. George V. Strong and Adm. Arthur J. Hepburn for the Army and Navy Departments and Gen. Stanley D. Embick and Adm. Russell Willson for the Joint Chiefs of Staff. The agenda group met seventy times over a seven-month period until it became part of the U.S. delegation for conducting formal conversations with British, Russian, and Chinese representatives to work out a preliminary agreement for a postwar security organization. This time of concentrated activity began on 21 December, when Roosevelt asked Hull to provide him with a proposal for an international organization to maintain world peace. Responding to this request, Hull and several members of the agenda group hastily drafted a plan based upon the studies that the various subcommittees had conducted during the past two years.[62]

The tentative plan, transmitted to the president on 29 December 1943, set forth the basic ideas that might be embodied in the charter of a world security organization. The brief document called for a small executive council with sufficient power to settle disputes and to repress aggression, a general assembly to provide a broad framework for international collaboration, a world court to promote justice, and various agencies to facilitate cooperation in economic and social fields. The drafters, unable to reach definite conclusions on a number of important questions, had listed alternative ways that they might be answered. In a covering memorandum attached to the document, Hull explained to Roosevelt that the plan was based on two central assumptions: "*First,* that the four major powers will pledge themselves and will consider themselves morally bound not to go to war against each other or against any other nation, and to cooperate with each other and with other peace-loving states in maintaining the peace; and *Second,* that each of them will maintain adequate forces and will be willing to use such forces as circumstances require to prevent or suppress all cases of aggression."[63]

The agenda group immediately began discussing the ramifications of a proposal that would require members of the world organization to contribute their quota to an international force that would operate under the authority of the council. In a memorandum prepared on 2 January 1944, Myron Taylor argued that the first test of strength of the international organization would come when the time arrived to apply and continue to apply restraints on Germany. "Unless we agree to contribute to the forces intended to prevent the development of a dangerous situation the organization might become little more than a debating society— hamstrung from the outset," he warned. "In my opinion unless measures, such as we are considering are adopted, are made workable and become effective, the age-old trouble with Germany will in due course be repeated in some form." Taylor was emphatic. "Without a plan backed by the availability of such contribution of forces as are adequate," he declared, "the whole structure of the world organization fails in its most vital aspect, i.e. in *enforcement of its decrees.*"[64]

But Taylor raised two disturbing questions. In the first place, he cautioned that any plan that obligated the members of the world organization to contribute military forces, as requested by the council to prevent or suppress aggression, might conflict with the Monroe Doctrine. "Will we," Taylor asked, "consent to Russian, Chinese, European or African forces invading South or Central America or our own adjacent islands?" In the second place, he cautioned that any treaty, even if ratified by the Senate, that committed the United States to employ armed forces at the behest of an international authority but without the approval of the House of Representatives might violate the Constitution. "The plan envisages action which may in fact be *war,* our entry into war without Congressional sanction!" Taylor exclaimed. "The question follows: Does Congressional action, not Senate action alone, become a prerequisite to our participation in a World Organization which has the power to call our military forces into action to prevent aggression, to preserve peace, or to subdue violence wherever it appears?"[65]

When Secretary Hull took the agenda group to the White House on 3 February 1944, he gave President Roosevelt a document outlining the fields of work of the Post-War Programs Committee. Roosevelt examined the list of topics carefully and showed great interest in the size and complexity of the job that his State Department advisers had undertaken, especially as compared to the hasty preparations that the Wilson administration had made for the Versailles Peace Conference twenty-five years earlier. Hull and his colleagues assured the president that their work had been carried to the point that they were now ready to place before him a policy recommendation on any one of the subjects they had studied. After indicating that he was pleased with the progress his postwar advisers had made, Roosevelt observed that "we are unquestionably better prepared than the British."[66]

Then Roosevelt authorized Hull to go ahead with preparations for the creation of a world organization on the basis of the tentative plan the agenda group had drafted. But the president explained that he did not want to be presented with any proposal that would obligate the United States to send troops to Europe after the war. He indicated that the principal American contribution to the preservation of world peace should be made by naval and air forces operating in the Western Hemisphere and the Pacific Ocean. Roosevelt emphasized that he wanted "to make sure that we would not be called upon to furnish armed forces without our consent."[67] A week after the president had approved the general approach taken in the tentative plan, the State Department informed the British and Soviet governments that it was ready to proceed with an exchange of views regarding the nature and functions of the projected international organization. Great Britain responded on 16 February by circulating a summary of topics as a suggested agenda for discussions, and the United States promptly dispatched an outline of topics in the form of questions that might be addressed. The Soviets were not yet prepared to circulate a paper indicating their preliminary views, but they later agreed to use the American and British lists as a basis for discussion.[68]

Secretary of State Hull and his colleagues, while endeavoring to lay the foundation for a close postwar relationship with the Soviet Union, were not always sure how best to proceed. On the one hand, Hull believed that the United States should ignore minor incidents that might disturb relations with the Russians. "They have been subject to so much abuse and suspicion from other nations," he explained on 8 February 1944, "that it would take some time before they lose their sensitivity."[69] On the other hand, Ambassador Harriman thought that the United States should be firm if the Soviet Union took steps that might imperil the movement toward international collaboration. He argued, in a telegram from Moscow on 16 March, that the Russians viewed forbearance as a sign of weakness but that they respected firmness. "We may well look forward to a Soviet policy of playing the part of a world bully," the ambassador warned, "if we don't follow this procedure of firmness now in connection with each incident."[70] In a telegram sent to Moscow two days later, Hull replied that he and his associates were in entire accord with the views that Harriman had expressed.[71]

Under Secretary of State Stettinius and four other State Department officers soon embarked upon a mission to London not only to compare notes with British leaders about overall planning for the postwar era but also to talk about future relations with Russia. During their conversations with British officials between 7 and 29 April 1944, Stettinius and his aides stressed the need for the United States and Great Britain to work for continued cooperation with the Soviet Union after the cessation of hostilities. "We emphasized, " Stettinius reported to Secretary Hull, "that the outlook for a post-war world without such prospect of Russian partnership would indeed be grim." Stettinius and his associates were happy to find that British policymakers seemed to share their strong desire for harmonious relations between the Soviet Union and the Western Allies following the surrender of Germany. Like their American counterparts, the British thought that a reluctance to confront the Russian people with the need to tighten their belts once again in preparation for another war would prompt Stalin to collaborate in the establishment of a world security organization.[72]

But the Joint Chiefs of Staff worried that an eventual world conflict could grow out of a clash between Russian and British interests in Europe. "Since it would seem in the highest degree unlikely that Britain and Russia, or Russia alone, would be aligned against the United States," they reasoned in a memorandum for the State Department on 16 May 1944, "it is apparent that any future world conflict in the foreseeable future will find Britain and Russia in opposite camps." The Joint Chiefs feared that the United States might be drawn into a war that it could not win even though it would be in no danger of defeat and occupation. "It is apparent that the United States should, now and in the future," they concluded, "exert its utmost efforts and utilize all its influence to prevent such a situation arising and to promote a spirit of mutual cooperation between Britain, Russia and ourselves. So long as Britain and Russia cooperate and collaborate in the interests of peace, there can be no great war in the foreseeable future."[73]

During their conversations in London, Stettinius and his aides had drawn Prime Minister Churchill into a discussion about a postwar security organization. Churchill took out a sheet of paper and drew a tripod headed by a supreme council acting on the authority of the United States, Great Britain, and the Soviet Union. Churchill said that he could not bring himself to use the phrase "The Four Great Powers" because China was not a great power. When he referred to the Chinese as "the pigtails," Stettinius reminded him that President Roosevelt believed China would be a great power in fifty years and then it would be very important to have friendly relations with that nation. "But," Churchill replied, "I have little confidence in the pigtails, first as to their power to unite and second as to their worth in the future." Then the prime minister drew three circles below the supreme council to indicate the subsidiary position of regional councils for Europe, Asia, and the Americas. The purpose of these lower councils, he explained, was to have regional affairs settled regionally and thus to avoid having every nation poking its fingers into the business of every other nation around the world.[74]

But Stettinius quickly discovered that the views of the British Foreign Office were similar to those of the State Department. Taking issue with what Churchill had said, Foreign Secretary Eden told Stettinius that it would be a mistake to rely upon regional councils to settle international disputes. Eden and his colleagues in the Foreign Office also told Stettinius that they were eager for the United States, Great Britain, and the Soviet Union to begin formal talks to prepare for the establishment of a world security organization. After agreeing that such talks should be held in Washington as soon as possible, Stettinius and Eden planned to make a joint statement indicating that tripartite conversations would commence in the near future. But Hull flatly rejected their proposal. Besides fearing that relations with Russia would be damaged if the Soviets learned that Anglo-American discussions concerning an international organization had taken place in London, Hull felt very strongly that no public announcement about these conversations should be made before he had time to consult with congressional leaders. Stettinius therefore informed British officials that a date for tripartite talks could not be set until Hull gave the word.[75]

While these Anglo-American discussions were going on in London, the agenda group drafted the Possible Plan for a General International

Organization. The document, dated 24 April 1944, proposed an executive council consisting of the four major powers and four other nations elected by the general assembly for annual terms. To assure the maintenance of world peace, the members of the organization were to provide armed forces and military facilities at the request of the executive council. Moreover, at the earliest possible moment after the organization came into existence, the member nations were to conclude an agreement regarding the armaments and forces that they would make available to help put down aggression. The document recommended that the executive council should make decisions by a majority vote—including the concurring votes of all permanent members—on the following categories of questions: the settlement of disputes; the regulation of armaments and armed forces; the determination of threats to peace, breaches of peace, and acts obstructing the maintenance of peace; and the application of enforcement measures.[76]

Thus, the plan for a world organization gave the permanent members of the executive council a veto power with respect to all security questions. Recalling that the United States had refused to enter the League of Nations in 1920 due to fears that an international agency might order its troops into action, the drafters of the document were determined not to arouse renewed apprehensions that Americans might be compelled to go to war against their wishes. Secretary Hull and his aides believed that congressional approval of U.S. membership in the United Nations could be obtained only if the United States retained the right to veto any proposal calling for the collective application of military force or economic sanctions to curb aggression. But American postwar planners could not decide whether the vote of a council member directly involved in a dispute should be counted. Some argued that the principle of unanimity among the permanent members should be maintained in all situations, while others thought that it would not be just if a nation could exercise a veto in a dispute to which it was a party. Unable to resolve their differences, they decided to leave the question open for future consideration.[77]

The drafters of the document were also vague on the difficult question of who would have the authority to commit U.S. forces in any collective action to suppress aggression. According to the system of checks and balances established in the U.S. Constitution, the executive and legislative branches of government had different prerogatives with respect to military affairs. Hull and his colleagues acknowledged that the constitutional right of Congress to declare war must be safeguarded in cases where force would be used on a major scale. But they believed that the president should have the power to deal with minor breaches of the peace without having to obtain permission from Congress on each occasion that he ordered American forces to participate in a police action.[78] John W. Davis, a distinguished legal expert, assured them that the president had the authority under the Constitution to use force without securing a formal declaration of war from Congress. But they remained worried that the Senate would refuse to ratify a treaty sanctioning American entry into the proposed world organization on the grounds that any commitment to deploy U.S. forces would violate the constitutional right of Congress to declare war.[79]

Secretary Hull had previously asked Tom Connally to appoint a bipartisan Senate committee to discuss the State Department plan for a world security organization. Hull hoped to avoid a repetition of the executive-legislative split that had prevented U.S. participation in the League of Nations. After careful consideration, Connally chose eight senators who would confer with Hull, and it soon became clear that the key figure in the group was Arthur Vandenberg, the senior Republican member of the Senate Foreign Relations Committee. During his first meeting with the Committee of Eight on 25 April 1944, Hull stressed the importance of postwar cooperation with Russia and the need to keep the entire issue out of domestic politics. Then he gave each senator a copy of the Possible Plan for a General International Organization and asked them to examine the document before their next meeting.[80] Both Connally and Vandenberg were delighted with the draft. Vandenberg liked the idea that the Big Four would dominate the world organization, and Connally was especially pleased that the United States would possess a veto power with regard to all security matters. "The United States," Connally reasoned, "should not be forced into a future war merely because the other council powers agreed to it."[81]

But during subsequent meetings between Hull and the Committee of Eight, Senators Vandenberg and Robert M. LaFollette Jr., a Progressive from Wisconsin, raised a serious objection. Until he knew that the final peace settlement would be just, Vandenberg insisted, he could not commit himself to support any proposal for a postwar organization that would enforce the peace agreement. Hull countered that the creation of a world organization would facilitate the working out of a good peace rather than a bad peace. Hull wanted the Committee of Eight to issue a statement that he could send to other governments to demonstrate that the Senate would support U.S. participation in a postwar organization. But Vandenberg and LaFollette held to their position that it would be unfair to commit the American people to support a peace that might be odious. During their final meeting on 29 May 1944, Vandenberg told Hull to go ahead and secure an agreement with the Allied governments on a plan for a world organization but to wait until after the peace settlement before implementing it. Hull immediately made a public announcement that he was encouraged by his conversations with the senators and that he was ready to proceed with discussions about plans for a world organization with Great Britain, the Soviet Union, and China.[82]

President Roosevelt and Secretary Hull followed up on this statement with additional remarks designed to win broad public backing for U.S. membership in a world security organization. During a talk with reporters on 30 May 1944, Roosevelt said that he favored the creation of international machinery to prevent the recurrence of war "without taking away the independence of the United States in any shape, manner or form." He aimed at pleasing conservatives with his emphasis on maintaining U.S. sovereignty. At a press conference two days later, Hull sought to reassure liberals by asserting that the U.S. government was working to see that "all nations, especially the small nations, are kept on a position of equality" in the contemplated world organization. Hull and his aides decided to prepare another statement for public consumption, and on 15 June the president released it to the press under his own name. "We are not," the paper declared, "thinking of a superstate with its own police forces and other paraphernalia of coercive power." Roosevelt and Hull were taking a middle ground. They advocated the establishment of a world organization that held out the possibility of achieving an enduring peace without surrendering American freedom of action.[83]

Along with their attempts to mold public opinion, Roosevelt and Hull worked behind the scenes to secure bipartisan support for U.S. membership in an international organization to maintain peace. Hull held additional meetings in his office with leaders of the two major parties in both the Senate and the House of Representatives. At the same time, Assistant Secretary of State Breckinridge Long was conducting a quiet campaign to induce the Democratic and Republican national conventions to adopt planks supporting the creation of a world security organization. These efforts produced satisfactory results. On 27 June 1944, the Republican convention adopted a platform favoring "participation by the United States in postwar cooperative organization among

sovereign nations to prevent military aggression." The Democratic platform, drafted at the White House and adopted on 29 July, likewise called
for the United States "to join with other United Nations in the establishment of an international organization based on the principle of the
sovereign equality of all peace-loving states."[84]

President Roosevelt and his State Department advisers drew encouragement not only from these indications of domestic support for U.S. entry
into a world organization but also from signs that the Soviet Union would
cooperate in establishing a general system of postwar security. In a cable
dispatched from Moscow on 12 June 1944, Ambassador Harriman reported
that he just had a heartening conversation with Stalin. The ambassador
told Stalin that Roosevelt was pleased with the progress that had been made
in U.S. relations with Russia, and Stalin replied that he too was gratified
that "we are going along a good road."[85] In a memorandum sent from the
Bretton Woods Monetary and Financial Conference on 23 July, Treasury
Secretary Henry Morgenthau happily reported that at his request the
Russians had agreed to raise their subscription of capital stock in the proposed International Bank for Reconstruction and Development. Assistant
Secretary of State Dean G. Acheson regarded this demonstration of Soviet
willingness to collaborate with the United States as "a matter of great political significance."[86] These straws in the wind gave American policymakers
reason to believe that they would be able to obtain Russian as well as
domestic backing for their postwar security plans.

SEVEN | ESTABLISHING THE UNITED NATIONS

During the spring of 1944, President Roosevelt and his State Department advisers decided upon an overall strategy for promoting the establishment of an international security organization before the war ended. The first step would be to hold a preliminary conference, restricted to a small number of diplomatic officials and technical experts from the United States, Great Britain, the Soviet Union, and China, to draw up a tentative charter for the projected world body. If their representatives could reach a general agreement during private discussions, the four major powers would publish a set of basic proposals for the consideration of the smaller nations throughout the world. The final step would be to convene a full conference of all the Allied countries to amend the tentative charter that had been drafted by the Big Four. Although policymakers in Washington hoped that this entire process could be completed during the autumn of 1944, disagreements over a few key issues prevented the United Nations from being launched until the following year.

Secretary of State Hull began making arrangements for a conference among the four great powers to develop proposals for a new world organization on 30 May 1944, when he met in his office with the ambassadors from Great Britain and the Soviet Union. After announcing that the United States was ready to proceed with talks about postwar security plans, Hull said that he hoped their governments would agree to start these conversations in Washington as soon as possible. He also urged that China should be allowed to take part in the discussions. But Hull realized that the Russians, since they were not yet at war with Japan, might object to Chinese participation. Accordingly, the next day he suggested that the conference could be held in two separate phases: the first phase would involve the Soviet Union along with Great Britain and the United States; the second phase would involve China together with Great Britain and the United States. Generalissimo Chiang Kai-shek immediately cabled President Roosevelt to express his gratification that the United States had proposed that China should be included in the discussions.[1]

The British ambassador informed Hull on 12 June 1944 that his government was ready to participate in the projected Washington talks and that Alexander Cadogan, the permanent under secretary for foreign affairs, would head the United Kingdom delegation. A month later, the Russian chargé d'affaires gave Hull an *aide-mémoire* indicating that his government was prepared to take part in the first phase of the proposed conference and that Andrei A. Gromyko, the ambassador in Washington, would head the Soviet delegation. But the note revealed that the Russians wanted to exclude from the negotiations any consideration of economic matters or procedures for the peaceful settlement of disputes. In a prompt reply the State Department insisted that mechanisms for the pacific adjustment of disputes must constitute an integral part of any effective scheme for international security. The State Department added that the American representatives would expect to discuss economic and social issues at the forthcoming meeting. After the Russians agreed not to limit the scope of the negotiations and the British agreed to permit the Chinese to participate in the second phase of the conversations, Hull publicly announced on 17 July that in the near future the four major powers would hold a two-series conference in Washington to discuss plans for an international security organization.[2]

The next day, after informing the British, Russian, and Chinese governments that Under Secretary Edward R. Stettinius would head the U.S. delegation, Secretary Hull sent those three governments copies of a State Department draft of Tentative Proposals for a General International Organization. The document, dated 18 July 1944, was a slightly revised version of the one that Hull had recently given to the bipartisan group of senators. Besides stipulating that the executive council should consist of eleven members instead of eight, the new draft stated that France should become a permanent member of the executive council after a freely elected government had been established in Paris. It also suggested that provisions would need to be worked out with respect to voting procedure to take care of cases in which one or more of the permanent members of the executive council were directly involved in a dispute.[3] After receiving from the three other major powers memoranda containing ideas that were similar to their own proposals, State Department officials were optimistic that the Big Four could quickly reach an agreement that would provide the basis for a full conference to establish a general organization for the purpose of maintaining world peace.[4]

But their spirits were suddenly dampened by signs that Thomas E.

Dewey, the Republican candidate for president, would attack their proposals for an international security organization in an effort to defeat Roosevelt, the Democratic incumbent, in his bid for a fourth term in the White House. In a press release on 16 August 1944, Dewey stated that he was deeply disturbed by some reports concerning the Big Four conference about to begin at the magnificent Dumbarton Oaks estate in Georgetown. "These indicate," he said, "that it is planned to subject the nations of the world, great and small, permanently to the coercive power of the four nations holding this conference." Secretary of State Hull worried that American liberals who wanted to protect the interests of the small countries might lose their enthusiasm for the projected world organization. In a public statement issued the next day, Hull declared that the fears that had been expressed by Dewey were "utterly and completely unfounded." He was determined to prevent concerns about the small nations from becoming a major issue in the presidential contest. Later that day Hull told newspaper reporters that he would welcome a conference with Dewey to discuss plans for postwar security in a nonpartisan way.[5]

Dewey immediately asked John Foster Dulles, his adviser on foreign affairs, to represent him in conversations with Hull. When they held their first meeting on 23 August 1944, Hull gave Dulles a copy of the State Department plan for an international organization and a memorandum highlighting the position the small countries would occupy in the proposed world body. The memorandum explained that no decisions on security matters could be made by the executive council without the concurrence of a least some of the representatives of the small nations. Dulles seemed to be satisfied with the part that the small counties would play in the proposed United Nations, and during their second discussion a day later he told Hull that he thought the State Department plan was excellent. After their third and final meeting the following day, they issued a joint statement indicating that Hull believed that the subject of future peace must be kept entirely out of politics and that Dewey agreed, though with the understanding that there could be full nonpartisan discussion about the means of attaining a lasting peace. Hull now had reason to hope that partisan clashes during the presidential race would not undermine public support for U.S. membership in the United Nations.[6]

In the meantime, Secretary Hull assembled a group of experts to represent the United States at the Dumbarton Oaks Conference. The American delegation, headed by Edward R. Stettinius, comprised the following civilian and military advisers: Isaiah Bowman, Benjamin V.

Cohen, James C. Dunn, Gen. Stanley D. Embick, Gen. Muir S. Fairchild, Joseph C. Grew, Green H. Hackworth, Adm. Arthur J. Hepburn, Stanley K. Hornbeck, Breckinridge Long, Leo Pasvolsky, Gen. George V. Strong, Adm. Harold C. Train, Edwin C. Wilson, and Adm. Russell Willson. In keeping with his bipartisan approach, Hull asked Henry P. Fletcher, the general counsel for the Republican National Convention and a man who had wide diplomatic experience, to join the negotiating team. The group held twelve meetings before the conference opened to review and reconsider the American proposals.[7] At the last minute Hull directed Stettinius to discuss personally with the president as well as himself any questions that required high-level decisions. Stettinius promptly made arrangements to meet after each afternoon secession with Roosevelt at 5:00 P.M. and Hull at 6:00 P.M. to report on developments at the conference.[8]

Shortly after the Dumbarton Oaks Conference got underway on 21 August 1944, Hull resumed his consultations with the bipartisan committee of eight senators. The secretary sent each committee member a copy of the revised State Department plan for an international security organization, and on 23 August he met with the senators to discuss it. During their conversation, attention focused on a key question: could the U.S. representative on the executive council vote to use force on instructions from the president without encroaching upon the constitutional prerogative of Congress to declare war? Senators Arthur H. Vandenberg and Robert M. LaFollette argued that U.S. forces could not be employed in behalf of the United Nations without the consent of Congress on each occasion. Hull vigorously disagreed. The world organization would not be able to preserve the peace, he maintained, unless the president had discretionary power to decide whether or not U.S. forces should participate in collective efforts to curb aggression. Hull added that he presumed the president would consult with congressional leaders before instructing the American representative on the executive council to vote for the use of force to deal with any important security problem.[9]

But Senator Vandenberg was not satisfied. In a long letter to Hull on 29 August, he reiterated his argument against the employment of U.S. forces without the approval of Congress. Vandenberg suggested that it might be all right for the president to authorize the use of force to deal with minor problems in the Western Hemisphere, but he insisted that the American representative on the executive council must not commit the United States to participate in a major military operation without congressional sanction as required by the Constitution. Hull was very upset. He quickly asked Green Hackworth, the legal adviser in the State Department, to prepare an opinion on the subject. Two days later, Hackworth submitted a memorandum arguing that, once the Senate ratified a treaty stipulating that U.S. forces would be made available to the United Nations for collective action, the president would have the right to authorize the use of these forces without obtaining congressional approval on each occasion. Hull promptly sent this opinion to the Committee of Eight.[10]

Amid indications that other Republican senators might join Vandenberg in fighting for a congressional veto on the use of U.S. forces assigned to the United Nations, Hull redoubled his efforts to avert a partisan rift during the coming presidential campaign. Hull asked an intermediary on 11 September to inform Dewey and Dulles about the movement to call for congressional approval of every application of force by the international security organization. If Republican leaders did not nip this movement in the bud, he warned, it might endanger the whole program for world peace. During a telephone conversation with Dewey the next day, Hull expressed his fear that a lively public controversy over the issue might lead the Russians and the British to believe that the State Department would not be able to obtain Senate backing for its own plan. Hull met later that day with the Committee of Eight and proposed a compromise. If the Senate ratified a treaty authorizing U.S. entry into the United Nations, he suggested, it could later decide whether or not Congress would have to approve the use of American forces on each occasion. Hull was relieved when Vandenberg and his Republican colleagues agreed to postpone debate on this fundamental question.[11]

This solution to the problem depended upon the willingness of the Russians to drop their proposal for an international air corps that might deter aggression by providing the United Nations with the power to retaliate without delay. Shortly after the Soviet phase of the Dumbarton Oaks conversations began, the Russian delegation argued that members of the world organization should place at the disposal of the executive council planes and pilots that could be used without waiting for authorization from the various governments. President Roosevelt and his postwar advisers, however, preferred to have member states keep their armed forces as separate contingents that would stand ready to repel aggression at the request of the council. During a private discussion on 29 August, Stettinius explained to Gromyko that the operation of the international air corps would infringe upon the constitutional right of Congress to declare war. The Russians eventually withdrew their suggestion and accepted an American proposal that called for member states to conclude separate agreements to make armed forces available to the United Nations. These special agreements would be subject to ratification by the signatory countries in accordance with their own constitutional processes.[12]

But the question of voting procedure in the executive council could not be settled so quickly. In a preconference memorandum, the British government had argued that council members should not be permitted to vote if they were involved in a dispute under consideration. The American negotiating team remained divided with respect to this issue on the eve of the conference. Some believed that council members should be free to vote on all matters, while others thought that countries should abstain from voting in cases involving themselves. During a meeting with several of his associates in the State Department on 19 August, Hull decided that no party to a dispute, not even a great power, should be allowed to vote in such a case before the council.[13] President Roosevelt approved this position during a brief discussion with a few members of the U.S. delegation three days after the conference opened. "Our people," he remarked, "would understand the principle that a man should not sit in judgment on his own case."[14]

During a Joint Steering Committee meeting at Dumbarton Oaks on 28 August 1944, Stettinius informed the heads of the British and Russian delegations that the U.S. government had come to the conclusion that the vote of a country involved in a dispute should not be counted during executive-council deliberations. Cadogan said that the British government agreed. If the great powers at Dumbarton Oaks insisted upon voting when the council was considering disputes affecting themselves, he warned, the smaller countries would object to their plan for a world security organization.[15] But Gromyko and the other Soviet representative stated that they considered the American position "to be in violation of and a retreat from the principle that major decisions of the proposed international organization should be reached on the basis of unanimity among the Great Powers." They also indicated that the Russian government might later make a proposal for the establishment of a special voting procedure to govern instances when a state with a permanent seat on the council was involved in a dispute.[16]

Then Gromyko dropped a bombshell. He told the Joint Steering Committee that all sixteen republics in the Soviet Union should be initial members of the United Nations. This would give the Russians control of sixteen votes in the general assembly. When Stettinius reported to the president at 5:00 P.M. that afternoon, Roosevelt was alarmed about the proposal for multiple Soviet memberships. "My God!" he exclaimed, "You must explain to Gromyko privately and personally, immediately, that I can never accept this proposal. This might ruin the chances of getting an international organization adopted by the United States Senate." Roosevelt added that Stettinius should tell Gromyko that it would be just as logical for the U.S. government to demand a seat in the general assembly for each of the forty-eight states. When Stettinius explained the Russian viewpoint with respect to voting in the executive council, the president reiterated his belief that the American position was entirely correct and must not be altered. He instructed Stettinius to tell Gromyko that "this was a matter on which we would have to be consistent and that we hoped his government would find it possible to agree with us."[17]

Stettinius met privately with Gromyko the following morning to discuss the most difficult issues facing the delegates at Dumbarton Oaks. When Gromyko stated that the principle of unanimity among the major powers must be preserved, Stettinius replied that the president did not think the American people would support a plan that permitted a party to a dispute to vote on its own behalf. Stettinius also explained that both Roosevelt and Hull feared that, if the Russian delegation pressed for the admission of all sixteen Soviet republics into the United Nations, the success of the conversations at Dumbarton Oaks might be jeopardized. Gromyko quickly agreed that there should be no further reference to the subject of multiple Soviet memberships in the general assembly during the present meetings. But the president remained worried that any discussion of the topic before the establishment of the world organization would imperil the whole project. Therefore, in a personal message drafted on 31 August, Roosevelt asked Stalin for assurance that Russia would not raise the question until the United Nations had been launched and the general assembly had full authority to deal with it.[18]

Secretary of State Hull asked Gromyko to come to his office that same day for a private talk. During their conversation, Hull stated as plainly as possible his objections to the proposal for multiple Soviet memberships in the United Nations. He argued that large countries, such as the United States and the Soviet Union, would not require more than one vote in the general assembly to voice their opinions. Before their discussion ended, Hull also emphasized his strong belief in the need for international economic cooperation to prevent the recurrence of military conflict after the

ECOSOC,

defeat of the Axis powers. He said that an economic and social council should be established as a basic component of the United Nations because peace and prosperity were inextricably linked with each other. The Russian delegation at Dumbarton Oaks had been contending that economic and social problems should be handled outside the general framework of the world security organization. A week after Hull and Gromyko had discussed the matter, however, the Russians accepted the American proposal for the creation of an economic and social council to operate under the jurisdiction of the general assembly.[19]

But the delegations at Dumbarton Oaks remained divided over the fundamental issue of voting procedure in what they began calling the security council. Hoping that Roosevelt would be able to get the Russians to accept the American and British position on this point, Stettinius arranged to bring Gromyko to the White House early in the morning on 8 September to meet with the president in his bedroom. Roosevelt told Gromyko that in the United States, when a husband and wife fell out, both could state their case to a judge but neither could register a vote. He added that the principle that parties to a dispute could not vote on their own behalf had been imbedded in American law by the founding fathers. At this stage in the conversation, Stettinius handed the president the draft of a cable that he might send to Stalin. The proposed message asked Stalin to instruct Gromyko to agree that the vote of a member involved in a dispute should not be counted in the council. Roosevelt approved the cable but wanted it redrafted to underscore his belief that neither the U.S. Senate nor the smaller nations would support a world organization plan that violated this principle. The next day the revised message was dispatched to Moscow.[20] But Stalin would not bend to please the president. In his reply to Roosevelt on 15 September, Stalin insisted that "the council should base its work on the principle of agreement and unanimity between the four leading powers on all matters."[21]

Nevertheless, Hull and Stettinius still hoped that both the British and Russian governments would approve a compromise voting formula that had been drafted by the U.S. delegation at Dumbarton Oaks. According to this formula, members of the security council could not vote in cases involving the peaceful settlement of disputes affecting themselves, but any enforcement action would require the consent of all the permanent council members even in cases affecting one of them. Hull regarded this formula as the maximum concession that could be made to the Soviet Union.[22] But during a telephone conversation on 17 September, Stettinius informed Roosevelt that neither the British nor the Russian governments would accept the compromise formula and that prospects for settling the voting issue at the conference seemed bleak. "The wisest course to pursue," he suggested, "would be to adjourn the meetings at Dumbarton Oaks in some graceful way as promptly as possible." Roosevelt agreed.[23] Stettinius then proposed that at the conclusion of the meetings, the four participating countries should release simultaneous communiqués stating that good progress had been made at the conference but that some items remained open for future consideration. The president suggested that Hull should work through Dulles to get Dewey to endorse the proposed communiqués.[24]

But since Hull feared that Americans might turn their back on the world organization if the Dumbarton Oaks conversations were terminated without an agreement on voting procedure in the security council, Stettinius met once again with Gromyko and Cadogan on 18 September to try to break the impasse. Gromyko told Stettinius that his government would never consider joining an organization in which a major power involved in a dispute did not have the right to vote on it. "Ed," he explained in a friendly but firm voice, "there is no chance whatsoever of the Soviet Union changing this position on the matter of voting in the Council now or six months from now or a year from now." During the course of the conversation, Gromyko said that he did not think his government would even agree to attend a general United Nations conference until the great powers had reached an agreement on the voting question. Cadogan likewise stated that he did not believe the British government would agree to participate in a general conference unless the Big Four were in full agreement on all basic issues.[25]

Although some members of the American delegation at Dumbarton Oaks wanted to make further concessions to end the deadlock, Hull thought that it would be better to bring the Russian phase of the conference to a close and to leave the issue of voting in the security council for future consideration.[26]His determination to bring a new world organization into existence without caving in to Russian demands was strengthened by assessments that Ambassador W. Averell Harriman made about Soviet intentions. "If a world organization is established under which there will be required the agreement of all permanent members for the consideration of any dispute regardless of whether or not one of them is involved," Harriman warned Hull on 19 September, "the Soviet Government will ruthlessly obstruct consideration by the Council of any matter in which it feels that its interests are affected and will insist, especially in disputes with its neighbors, that the question be settled by the Soviet Union with the other country or countries involved."[27] Nevertheless, Harriman thought that Stalin and his principal counselors placed the highest priority on maintaining friendly relations with the United States. In a cable dispatched from Moscow the following day, Harriman advised that Hull should be patient but firm with the Russians when discussing matters deemed vital to American interests. "I am satisfied," he assured Hull, "that in the last analysis Stalin will back down in such cases."[28]

Secretary of State Hull had come to the same conclusion. While conferring with the entire U.S. delegation in his office on 19 September, Hull said that he was convinced that Soviet leaders had decided to embark upon a course of international cooperation. He thought that their decision was based, in large part, upon economic considerations. "All Russia's interests caused her to take this course," the secretary asserted. "It is only through international cooperation that she can advance her general economic interests, her industrial development, her social welfare—all of her permanent interests." Even if the Russians got off the track, he reasoned, their economic needs would eventually force them to come back into line. Hull emphasized that the United States should be patient and friendly when dealing with the Soviet Union. He reminded the delegates that the main task was to get an international security organization established, even though it might take longer to achieve that objective than they wished.[29]

American policymakers soon decided that the only feasible alternative would be to end the Russian phase of the Dumbarton Oaks Conference and to refer the voting question to the heads of state. During a heated discussion with the U.S. delegation on 20 September, Stettinius argued that failure to reach a quick agreement on all points would not prevent the establishment of a world organization to maintain peace. Nor would adjournment of the conference, he added, jeopardize the continuation of friendly relations with the Soviet Union.[30] The next day Stettinius and Hull brought several of their delegates to the White House to discuss the situation with the president. Roosevelt and Hull both stated that it was not necessary to reach an agreement at the present time either by forging a compromise or by accepting the Russian position. They concluded that the best solution would be to terminate the talks with the Soviet delegation as rapidly as possible and to leave the voting question open.[31] During a conversation a few days later, Harry Hopkins agreed with Stettinius that the next step would be for Roosevelt and Churchill to meet with Stalin to settle the voting issue.[32]

On 27 September, after waiting six days for Gromyko to receive instructions from Moscow, the Joint Steering Committee met for the last time. Gromyko reported that the Soviet Union was agreeable to the publication of the Dumbarton Oaks proposals for a United Nations charter. He also said that the Russian government approved the insertion of a provision, which the American delegation had put forward, relating to the promotion of human rights and fundamental freedoms. After Gromyko announced a few other concessions that he had been authorized to make, the committee agreed to include in the text of the proposed charter a statement indicating that the question of voting procedure was still under consideration. But an ominous note was sounded when Gromyko warned that his government would not be willing to participate in a general United Nations conference unless the U.S. and British governments agreed to the Russian proposals concerning voting in the security council and multiple Soviet memberships in the general assembly. With respect to the voting question, he reiterated the Russian contention that the principle of unanimity of the four great powers must be carried out unconditionally.[33]

The Russian phase of the Dumbarton Oaks Conference ended on 28 September 1944, and the Chinese phase began the following day. The conversations with the Chinese delegation, headed by Wellington Koo, proceeded smoothly and led to no major alterations in the tentative sketch for a United Nations charter. Although they suggested a number of minor changes, the Chinese were willing to accept the current draft as the basis for future discussions and to present their own views at a full United Nations meeting. Negotiations with the Chinese were quickly completed, and on 9 October the Dumbarton Oaks proposals were released to the press. In an accompanying statement President Roosevelt expressed his gratitude that "so much could have been accomplished on so difficult a subject in so short a time."[34] His State Department advisers were also pleased with the progress that had been made. "We have just finished the Dumbarton Oaks talks," Joseph Grew wrote his old headmaster at Groton, "and while the result is not all that I had hoped for, nevertheless I think we have laid a useful foundation on which an effective world organization for the maintenance of security and peace can eventually be erected."[35]

Roosevelt had hoped to keep all questions about the United Nations plan out of the presidential campaign, but Sen. Joseph H. Ball directly challenged both the Republican and Democratic candidates to take an unambiguous stand on a basic issue that had not yet been settled. "Should the vote of the United States' representative on the United Nations security council," Ball asked on 12 October, "commit an agreed upon quota of our military forces to action ordered by the council to maintain peace without requiring further congressional approval?" When Dewey failed to answer this question in a major speech on foreign policy six days later, Roosevelt decided to come out squarely for an international organization with the power to act quickly and decisively to prevent another world war. If a policeman saw a robber break into a house, the president reasoned in an address delivered on 21 October, he should not have to call a town meeting to obtain a warrant before he could arrest the burglar. "So to my simple mind," Roosevelt declared, "it is clear that, if the world organization is to have any reality at all, our American representative must be endowed in advance by the people themselves, by constitutional means through their representatives in the Congress, with authority to act."[36]

The results of the general elections on 7 November 1944 showed that most Americans who went to the polls looked forward to the creation of a world organization that would stand ready to repel aggression. Although Roosevelt won a fourth term in the White House by only a narrow margin in popular votes, the races for seats in the House of Representatives and the Senate revealed that a bipartisan consensus had crystallized in favor of his postwar security plans. Many leading isolationists from both parties went down to defeat, while several outspoken internationalists scored impressive victories. After the ballots were counted, Republicans and Democrats alike interpreted the outcome as an indication that a majority of the American people wanted the United States to play an active part in world affairs. Even anti-Roosevelt newspapers and magazines agreed that the president had been given a clear mandate to continue working for the establishment of an international organization to promote a lasting peace.[37]

On 21 November, just two weeks after the elections, Secretary Hull dictated a letter from his hospital bed in the Naval Medical Center at Bethesda to inform Roosevelt that he had decided to resign from the State Department due to poor health. The president hoped that he could persuade Hull to remain on the job, but he told Stettinius that even if Hull did resign it might be possible to have him preside over the conference that would give birth to the United Nations. Roosevelt said that Hull had a better standing in the United States than he did and that it would be important to have Hull identified with the world organization to help obtain Senate authorization for U.S. membership.[38] In a letter expressing his hope that Hull would soon be back on his feet, the president suggested to Hull that he remain at his post for two more months so that they could complete three terms in office together. "When the organization of the United Nations is set up," Roosevelt added, "I shall continue to pray that you as the Father of the United Nations may preside over its first session." But Hull insisted that his resignation take effect immediately, and on 27 November, Roosevelt announced that Stettinius would succeed Hull as secretary of state.[39]

With Stettinius at the helm, the State Department launched a vigorous drive to solidify public support for U.S. entry into a new world organization to prevent future wars. Stettinius had served as vice president in charge of public relations at General Motors before he became chairman of the board at United States Steel. During a two-week period between 5 and 19 December 1944, Stettinius sent five different groups on the road to talk with community leaders in sixteen cities across the country. These State Department teams, comprised of high officers as well as staff members, delivered prepared speeches, held panel discussions, and conducted question-and-answer sessions on the Dumbarton Oaks proposals. After securing the appointment of Archibald MacLeish as a new assistant secretary for public and cultural relations on 20 December, Stettinius asked him to direct the campaign to promote the State Department plans for postwar security. MacLeish, a poet who had been working in the Office of War Information, energetically sought out church, labor, business, and professional groups and urged them to sponsor public meetings that would disseminate information about the United Nations project. He also arranged for a series of national radio broadcasts and for the production of a short documentary film to persuade as many people as possible of the need for an international organization to maintain peace.[40]

State Department officials held several meetings with congressional leaders in a parallel effort to maintain bipartisan backing for the establishment of a world security organization. On 24 November, Stettinius and some of his subordinates met with the Committee of Eight to discuss the questions the Dumbarton Oaks negotiators had failed to settle. They gave the senators a candid explanation of their differences with the Soviet Union over voting procedure in the security council. On 4 December, Stettinius and his aides similarly briefed a group of Republican and Democratic leaders in the House of Representatives about the issues that had been left open at Dumbarton Oaks. Stettinius covered much of the same ground during a discussion with Dulles a few days later. After the meeting, both Dulles and Dewey released public statements promising to support Roosevelt in his efforts to lay the foundation for an enduring peace and to treat the subject of international organization in a nonpartisan way.[41]

In hopes that a full United Nations conference could be held in the near future, the State Department had already drafted a new compromise formula for voting in the security council with the following provisions: first, that decisions on procedural matters should be made by an affirmative vote of any seven of the eleven members on the council; second, that decisions on all other matters should be made by an affirmative vote of seven members, including the concurring votes of those with permanent seats on the council; but, third, that any party to a dispute should abstain from voting when the council was attempting to arrange a peaceful settlement. Like the compromise that the American delegation had suggested at Dumbarton Oaks, the proposed formula required the consent of all permanent members before the council could employ force in response to any threats to the peace or breaches of the peace.[42]

During a meeting at the White House on 15 November 1944, Stettinius handed the president a memorandum explaining the voting procedure the State Department thought should be followed in the security council. "This proposal should be acceptable to this country, since no party to a dispute would sit as a judge in its own case so long as judicial or quasi-judicial procedures are involved," the memorandum stated. "It should be acceptable to Soviet Russia because it meets her desire that no action be taken against her without her consent."[43] After examining the memorandum, Roosevelt said that he had come to the conclusion that it would be necessary to arrive at a compromise solution. "It is unlikely," he reasoned, "that this country, in the final analysis, would agree to our not having a vote in any serious or acute situation in which we may be involved." After reviewing the compromise formula attached to the memorandum, the president approved it as the position that should be taken by the U.S. government. Henceforth it constituted the preferred formula of the United States for resolving the contending positions among the major powers on the voting question.[44]

In a telegram to Churchill on 5 December, Roosevelt sought British support for the American position on security council voting. The president explained that under this formula, which he hoped Great Britain and the Soviet Union would approve, the principle of unanimity among the permanent members would be preserved with respect to all decisions pertaining to the determination of a threat to the peace and to all actions relating to the suppression of aggression. "I am certain therefore that these powers should not insist on exercising a veto in such judicial or quasi-judicial procedures as the international organization may employ in promoting voluntary peaceful settlement of disputes," Roosevelt declared. "I am certain that willingness of the permanent members to abstain from the exercise of their voting rights on questions of this sort would immensely strengthen their own position as the principal guardians of the future peace and would make the whole plan far more acceptable to all nations."[45]

Returning to his post in Moscow after having spent a month in the United States, Ambassador Harriman delivered the same message to Stalin. During their conversation in the Kremlin on 14 December, Harriman said that the president believed that Stalin was basically right with respect to his views toward voting in the security council on matters connected with the enforcement of peace. But Roosevelt thought it was equally important, the ambassador continued, that any power involved in a dispute should refrain from voting when the council was attempting to find a peaceful solution to the problem. Harriman explained that the president hoped that the major powers could reach a quick agreement on a voting formula so that a general conference could soon be convened for the purpose of creating a world security organization. Before answering the president, Stalin replied, he would need time to consult with his colleagues, especially with Foreign Minister Molotov, who would be laid up for a week or ten days due to a minor stomach operation.[46]

While they eagerly waited for a response from Stalin, President Roosevelt and his State Department advisers remained devoted to the doctrine that world peace depended upon continued collaboration among the major powers.[47] But in his reply to Roosevelt on 26 December, Stalin wrote that he could see no possibility of agreeing to the proposal that parties to a dispute should refrain from voting in connection with security council efforts to bring about a peaceful settlement. Molotov told Harriman on the same day that the principle of unity among the great powers must be preserved from the very inception of a dispute without any exceptions. Molotov did agree, however, that the matter should be kept open for personal discussion between Stalin and Roosevelt.[48] In reporting his conversation with Molotov two days later, Harriman stated that he thought that the Russians objected to the U.S. voting proposal because they wanted to remain free to settle disputes with their neighbors without any outside interference. "They believe that the court is packed against them," he explained. "Therefore, in settling disputes of this character they appear to be insisting upon the right of unilateral action."[49]

Roosevelt soon indicated that he was thinking about retreating from the position he had taken on voting in the security council. Expressing concern about the possibility of not being permitted to vote if the United States got into a row with Mexico, he told Secretary of War Henry L. Stimson on 31 December that he was beginning to see some merit in the Russian position.[50] The president made the same point in a conversation with Stettinius two days later. "If the shoe were on the other foot," he said, "the American people would be very reluctant to see the United States deprived of a vote if it were involved in a dispute with Mexico." But Stettinius pointed out that the real issue was whether or not a great power could prevent the complaints of a little country from being considered by the international organization. After Stettinius explained that this was quite different from any question about the application of force to compel the settlement of a dispute, the president agreed to make time for a full discussion of the matter.[51]

During a meeting with Stettinius and some of his aides on 8 January 1945, Roosevelt said that he was determined to press for a decision on the voting issue at his forthcoming conference with Churchill and Stalin but that he was perplexed about how to approach the problem. Roosevelt asked whether, in view of the fact that Stalin had turned down his proposal, they had found another voting formula. In replying to this question, Leo Pasvolsky said that discussions with congressional leaders, with many individuals and groups throughout the country, and with representatives of the American republics and other nations had convinced State Department officials that the unanimity rule needed to be modified so that a party to a dispute would not be permitted to vote when the security council was trying to promote a peaceful settlement. The president then asked what would happen if a controversy arose between the United States and Mexico with respect to oil. Pasvolsky answered that the council would presumably attempt to bring about a conciliation but that it could not take any substantive action without U.S. consent. After saying that something like the formula that had been devised in the State Department was necessary, Roosevelt stated that he would make every effort to persuade Stalin to accept the American position.[52]

When he conferred with the Committee of Eight on 11 January 1945, Roosevelt told the senators that he would try to resolve the points at issue with Stalin before the international conference met to consider the Dumbarton Oaks proposals. But the president surprised two State Department representatives who were present at the meeting when he revealed his inclination to abandon the voting formula that he had just promised to push. After saying that he thought Stalin would yield on his request for membership of all sixteen Soviet republics in the general assembly, Roosevelt told the senators that he might have to give way on the Russian demand for unanimity among the major powers in the security council. "The president leaned strongly toward the belief," the State Department officials reported to Stettinius, "that unanimity was as a practical matter inevitable and might as well be conceded as a formal matter."[53]

The State Department and the British Foreign Office found themselves in the same predicament with respect to the question of voting procedure in the security council. Both had reached the conclusion that it was imperative to obtain Russian agreement to the voting formula that had been proposed by the United States. But neither President Roosevelt nor Prime Minister Churchill seemed to believe that this was a matter of great importance. Although the British cabinet decided on 11 January to accept the American voting formula, Churchill said that he was reluctant to debate the issue with the Russians. "I cannot undertake," he told his colleagues in the cabinet, "to fight a stiff battle with them on the subject."[54] On 31 January, during a brief plane stop at Naples while en route to the Yalta Conference, Stettinius learned from Harry Hopkins that Churchill was not firmly committed to the U.S. position even though he had approved it. Stettinius and Hopkins flew to Malta that afternoon, and the next morning Stettinius discussed the situation with Foreign Secretary Eden aboard a British warship. After declaring that he liked the American formula very much, Eden said that Churchill did not yet fully understand it and that the Foreign Office had more work to do to bring the prime minister around. Stettinius remarked that he and his colleagues would also have to work on the president.[55]

On 4 February 1945, shortly after their arrival in Yalta, Stettinius and Eden made a concerted effort to persuade both Roosevelt and Churchill to support the voting formula that the State Department had proposed. Roosevelt promptly agreed when Stettinius suggested that he should not refer to the proposal as the "compromise" formula because it was the preferred position of the United States. During a subsequent discussion with Stettinius and Eden, however, Churchill said that he was inclined to accept the Russian view on voting procedure because he thought that the preservation of world peace depended upon the maintenance of unity among the three great powers. Eden was upset. If he went over to the Russian position, Eden bluntly warned Churchill, there would never be a United Nations conference due to adverse reactions in Great Britain and the smaller countries throughout the world. Churchill finally said that he thought the American formula made sense after Stettinius explained how it would be applied if a dispute arose between the United States and Mexico. "You made an extremely important point," Eden told Stettinius later. "I believe this is the first time the prime minister realized what the question is all about."[56]

On 6 February, the third day of the Yalta Conference, Stettinius presented the American proposal for voting in the security council. Unless freedom of discussion was permitted in the council, Stettinius asserted, the establishment of an international organization to save the world from another war would be seriously jeopardized. Agreeing that a major power should not be able to prevent the council from considering a dispute, Churchill came out strongly in favor of the American plan. But Stalin insisted that the primary task was to maintain unity among the major powers. He said that his colleagues in Moscow could not forget what had occurred after war broke out in December 1939 between Russia and Finland. At that time the League of Nations, at the instigation of Britain and France, had expelled the Soviet Union and mobilized world opinion against the Russians. Although Roosevelt acknowledged the need for unity among the great powers, he suggested that full discussion in the council would demonstrate their confidence in each other and in the justice of their policies. The president then agreed to give Stalin more time to study the question.[57]

The negotiators at Yalta soon settled their differences with regard to the establishment of a new world organization. On 7 February, Molotov suddenly announced that the Soviet Union would accept the American formula for voting in the security council. Molotov also stated that his government would no longer press for the inclusion of all sixteen Soviet republics but would be satisfied with the admission of just two or three as original members of the general assembly. Acknowledging that the countries in the British Commonwealth would be represented as separate entities in the United Nations, Churchill said that he had great sympathy for the Soviet request. Roosevelt at first resisted, but he soon decided to accommodate the Russians. The president confided to Stettinius that he doubted a few extra Soviet votes in the general assembly would make any difference because real power would reside in the security council. The next day Roosevelt and Churchill agreed that, at the general conference to form the world organization, the United States and Great Britain would join the

Soviet Union in asking that the Ukraine and White Russia be granted seats in the general assembly.[58]

But some members of the American delegation at Yalta warned Roosevelt that his concession to Stalin might create a political storm in the United States. James F. Byrnes and Edward J. Flynn both feared that the Irish communities in the large eastern cities would be especially critical if they learned that the United States had only one vote in the general assembly compared to three votes for the Soviet Union and six votes for the British Commonwealth. When Byrnes urged the president to propose that the United States be granted as many votes as the Soviet Union, Roosevelt sent Stalin and Churchill similar letters asking for their support at the forthcoming United Nations conference if he should request additional votes to give the United States parity in the general assembly. This might be necessary, he explained, to ensure the wholehearted assent of Congress and the American people for participation in the world organization. Both Stalin and Churchill immediately replied that they would back a proposal to provide the Unites States with extra representation in the general assembly, but Roosevelt insisted that the subject remain secret.[59]

On 12 February 1945, a day after their final meeting, the Big Three made a public announcement that a conference to create a new world organization would be held in San Francisco. The communiqué explained that invitations to attend the conference, scheduled to open on 25 April, would be sent only to those countries that by 1 March had declared war on the common enemy. The communiqué also stated that a formula for voting in the security council had been approved and would be publicized once the other permanent members, France and China, expressed their agreement. But there was no mention of the pledge to support an American or Soviet request for three votes in the general assembly. Speaking before a joint session of Congress shortly after his return from Yalta, the president stressed the need for U.S. participation in an international security organization. "There will soon be presented to the Senate of the United States and to the American people a great decision that will determine the fate of the United States—and of the world—for generations to come," Roosevelt declared. "We shall have to take the responsibility for world collaboration, or we shall have to bear the responsibility for another world conflict."[60]

Meanwhile, on his way home from Yalta, Stettinius flew to Mexico City to head the U.S. delegation at the Inter-American Conference on Problems of War and Peace. His primary objective was to gain Latin American backing for the Dumbarton Oaks proposals to be considered at San Francisco. When the meetings in Mexico City commenced on 21 February 1945, however, Stettinius encountered strong opposition. The Latin American delegations complained that the proposals for a new world organization not only favored the great powers at the expense of the small nations but also placed global concerns above regional interests. There were widespread fears, shared by some members of the U.S. delegation, that the European countries would intervene in the affairs of the Western Hemisphere. Nevertheless, Stettinius was successful in securing the adoption of a resolution that endorsed the Dumbarton Oaks proposals as a basis for establishing a general international organization to achieve peace. Reflecting the wishes of the other American republics, the resolution urged that the powers of the general assembly should be increased and that Latin American countries should be given adequate representation on the security council.[61]

But another resolution, sponsored by Columbia with the prior approval of President Roosevelt, gave rise to a serious debate within the U.S. delegation. It called for an inter-American security pact that would require each signatory nation to render immediate assistance in the event of an attack against the territorial integrity or political independence of a member state. Gen. Stanley Embick, representing the Joint Chiefs of Staff, argued in favor of the Colombian proposal for a binding system of hemispheric defense. But Leo Pasvolsky regarded the resolution as a threat to the supremacy of the world organization, while Senators Warren Austin and Tom Connally viewed it as an encroachment on the constitutional prerogative of Congress to declare war. After the resolution was modified at the insistence of the United States, it was adopted on 6 March as the Act of Chapultepec. The signatory nations agreed that measures, including the use of armed force to prevent or repel acts of aggression against an American state, would be taken in accordance with the constitutional procedures of their respective governments. They also agreed that their regional security arrangements should be consistent with the purposes and principles of the future world organization.[62]

Before the close of the Mexico City Conference on 8 March 1945, the participants resolved their differences with respect to Argentina. The United States hoped to isolate Argentina because it had been attempting to create an anti-Yankee bloc of nations in South America. But the other American republics feared that, if the United States succeeded in toppling the pro-Nazi regime in Buenos Aires, it might engage in similar acts of unilateral intervention throughout the hemisphere. Despite their concerns about possible Argentine designs on neighboring countries, the Latin American delegations advocated a policy of reconciliation toward Argentina. Roosevelt and Stettinius eventually decided to accept a compromise in order to preserve inter-American unity. Under their plan, approved by the conference, Argentina would qualify for membership in the United Nations if the Buenos Aires government declared war on Germany or Japan and adhered to the Act of Chapultepec. Thus, the meetings ended on a cheerful note. But as Stettinius prepared to return to Washington, he worried that the Latin American nations might align with each other in support of regional goals at the San Francisco Conference.[63]

President Roosevelt and Secretary of State Stettinius had already determined the make-up of the small but carefully balanced delegation that would represent the United States at the United Nations Conference on International Organization. Hoping for continued bipartisan support for their postwar security plans, they selected two Senate leaders—Tom Connally, a Democrat, and Arthur H. Vandenberg, a Republican—and two members of the House of Representatives—Sol Bloom, a Democrat, and Charles A. Eaton, a Republican. They also chose two prominent figures, who held strong internationalist views, from outside the halls of Congress—Cmdr. Harold E. Stassen, formerly the Republican governor of Minnesota but currently on active duty in the navy, and Dean Virginia C. Gildersleeve of Barnard College in New York. While Stassen could speak for the millions of men in the armed forces of the United States, Gildersleeve could express the concerns of American women who had been demanding a voice at the peace table. The president rounded out the U.S. delegation by naming Stettinius as chairman and Hull, who was still recuperating at the naval hospital in Bethesda, as senior adviser.[64]

After the White House announced the names of these individuals on 13 February 1945, Stettinius gradually assembled a large group of advisers to help the delegates prepare for the conference and to give them guidance at San Francisco. He selected eleven advisers to represent the State Department: some provided technical information on specific topics, but five served as general advisers and senior negotiators. Determined to maintain bipartisan backing for U.S. entry into a world organization, Stettinius convinced Roosevelt to invite Dulles to join the State Department advisory team. Roosevelt also approved a list of seventeen other advisers, recommended by Stettinius, to represent various departments and agencies of the U.S. government. On the military side, the advisers represented the War and Navy Departments and the Joint Chiefs of Staff. The civilian advisers included representatives of the Agriculture, Commerce, Interior, Labor, and Treasury Departments as well as the Foreign Economic Administration and the Bureau of the Budget.[65]

In keeping with this bipartisan approach, Stettinius and several State Department aides discussed their plans for the San Francisco Conference with three different groups of Senate and House leaders from the two major parties. These meetings, held on 15 and 16 March, devoted considerable attention to the agreements that had been made at Yalta with respect to voting in the security council. While the decision to require seven affirmative votes rather than a simple majority of six would give small nations greater influence in the council, Pasvolsky explained, the decision to require the affirmative vote of all permanent members on enforcement questions reflected the fact that these large powers would bear the responsibility for preserving the peace. Stettinius emphasized that the voting formula he had advanced at Yalta meant that the armed forces of the United States could never be sent into action without the consent of the U.S. government. By accepting this formula, he noted, the Russians had indicated their willingness to allow any international dispute, even if their own interests were involved, to be brought before the bar of world opinion. Stettinius said that he had returned from Yalta with the deep conviction that the Russians were eager to cooperate in setting up an effective international security organization.[66]

But Stettinius and Roosevelt harbored private fears that the agreement at Yalta to support either a Russian or an American request for three votes in the general assembly would undermine public backing for the world organization. When Roosevelt informed the U.S. delegates about this arrangement on 23 March, he understated the strength of his commitment to Stalin. They should not feel bound by his pledge, the president said, because he had only told Stalin that he would vote for multiple Soviet memberships if he were a delegate. But a week later, after someone leaked the story to the press, reporters charged that the deal would destroy the principle of equality among the United Nations. Stettinius moved quickly to quiet the public outcry. After securing approval from both the president and the American delegation, Stettinius announced on 3 April that the United States would not ask for more than one vote in the assembly but would support a Soviet request at San Francisco for three votes. Most reporters applauded the decision not to seek extra votes for the United States.[67]

The sudden death of President Roosevelt on 12 April 1945 did not alter American plans for the establishment of an international security organization before the war ended. Shortly after taking the oath of office that evening, Pres. Harry S. Truman decided that the conference on world organization should be held as scheduled. Truman also decided that a statement should be made to reassure the Allied countries that he would carry out the policies of his predecessor.[68] "President Truman has authorized me to say," Stettinius announced, "that there will be no change of purpose or break of continuity in the foreign policy of the United States Government."[69] Stalin was moved when he learned that Roosevelt had died. After expressing deep sorrow over the death of the president, Stalin told Ambassador Harriman on 13 April that he wanted to work with Truman as he had with Roosevelt. Harriman then suggested that Stalin should assure the world of his desire for continued international collaboration by sending Molotov to the United States not only to see Truman but also to attend the United Nations conference. Stalin agreed. After first securing a formal request from the White House, Stalin announced that Molotov would go to Washington to confer with the new president and then go on to San Francisco to head the Soviet delegation even if he could only stay for a short time.[70]

When the United Nations Conference on International Organization opened in San Francisco on 25 April 1945, Molotov immediately proposed that the Ukraine and White Russia should be permitted to take part in the proceedings. Truman instructed Stettinius to second the Russian proposal. But the Latin American delegations threatened to vote against the seating of the two Soviet republics unless Argentina was also admitted to the conference. Although Truman was not in favor of having Argentina represented at San Francisco, Stettinius realized that the work of drafting a United Nations charter could not begin until he could get the Latin Americans to support the Russian proposal. "We are going to have to make a deal," Stettinius told the president over the telephone on 27 April. "You make it any day," Truman replied. "You have to get that thing going." With strong Latin American backing, Stettinius succeeded a few days later in getting Argentina along with the two Soviet republics admitted to the conference.[71]

But the negotiators at San Francisco had a harder time reaching an agreement with respect to the question of regional security arrangements. While the Russians proposed that their security treaties with Britain and France should be exempt from the provisions of the United Nations charter, the Latin Americans sought a similar exemption for the Western

Hemisphere. The issue produced a heated debate among the representatives from the United States. In a letter to Stettinius on 5 May, Senator Vandenberg advocated an exemption for the inter-American defense system in order to prevent the world organization from interfering with regional security arrangements in the Western Hemisphere. "We can't expect our Allies to depend upon an untried peace league for their defense against a resurgent Axis," he argued, "until it has demonstrated its adequate capacity to serve this defense function." But some of his colleagues feared than an exemption for the inter-American system would encourage the formation of other regional blocs and destroy the world organization. "There will be four or five armed camps," Pasvolsky warned on 7 May, "and another world war."[72]

Stettinius and his advisers hoped to resolve these differences by proposing that the charter should be worded in a way that would safeguard the inter-American system without undermining the world organization. Fearing that the Senate would refuse to authorize U.S. participation in an international body that would supplant the Monroe Doctrine, they hastily developed the idea that countries in any region should be able to exercise their inherent right to collective self-defense if the United Nations failed to protect them from aggression. Their compromise plan concerning regional methods of peacekeeping satisfied U.S. military leaders who worried that the world organization might either disintegrate or prove ineffective. After discussing the situation with Truman on 15 May, Stettinius persuaded the Latin Americans to support the proposed compromise on regional security arrangements by assuring them that the United States would be willing in the near future to sign a treaty providing that an attack against any American state would be regarded as an attack against every American state. The major powers approved the compromise proposal a few days later, and its language became the basis for Articles 51 and 52 of the United Nations Charter.[73]

Shortly after the controversy about regional defense arrangements had been put to rest, a debate over voting procedure in the security council produced a deadlock in the proceedings at San Francisco. The dispute involved conflicting interpretations of the voting formula that had been accepted at Yalta. The Soviet delegation, headed by Gromyko after Molotov returned to Moscow, argued that under the Yalta formula a permanent member could exercise a veto to prevent the council from even considering a question. But the U.S. and British delegations insisted that the Yalta formula permitted freedom of discussion in the council and provided that a veto could only be employed to block enforcement action. On 26 May, Gromyko decided to refer the matter to Moscow, and for the next five days the conference came to a standstill while he waited for instructions. Finally, on 1 June, Gromyko announced that his government still demanded that it must be able to use a veto even to keep an issue from being introduced into the council for discussion. The American delegates were dismayed. They warned Gromyko that the Senate would not authorize U.S. entry into a world organization that embraced the Soviet view.[74]

Hoping to break the impasse at San Francisco, Stettinius decided that Hopkins, who was in Moscow on other important business, should discuss the veto issue directly with Stalin. Truman immediately approved the idea, and on 2 June Stettinius dispatched a cable asking Hopkins and Harriman to raise the question with Stalin. "Please tell him in no uncertain words," Stettinius emphasized, "that this country could not possibly join an organization based on so unreasonable an interpretation."[75] In a cable to Truman four days later, Hopkins reported that he and Harriman had just had a fruitful talk with Stalin about the debate over voting in the security council. "Stalin had not understood the issues," Hopkins explained. "After considerable discussion in which Molotov took an active part, Stalin overruled Molotov and agreed that the American position was acceptable to him."[76] The American delegates at San Francisco were elated when Gromyko announced on 7 June that his government agreed with their view. "The result of your efforts has electrified the conference," Stettinius cabled Hopkins. "There is no question now but what we will have a successful outcome with a good charter."[77]

The resolution of the veto question cleared the way for the delegates at San Francisco to finish drafting a charter for the world organization. The document contained the basic ideas, with only a few modifications, that had been set forth at Dumbarton Oaks. While the general assembly would be restricted to discussing problems and recommending solutions, the security council would be able to impose military or economic sanctions but only with the unanimous consent of the great powers. The United Nations Charter, approved at the final session of the conference on 26 June 1945, called upon the members to sign a separate agreement to supply forces needed to repel aggression. It also provided for the establishment of an economic and social council as well as a new international court of justice. In his address that brought the conference to a close, President Truman gave voice to the basic American belief that peace could not be maintained in an impoverished and unfair world. "Experience has shown how deeply the seeds of war are planted by economic rivalry and social injustice," he declared. "Artificial and uneconomic trade barriers should be removed— to the end that the standard of living of as many people as possible throughout the world may be raised."[78]

After the representatives of fifty Allied countries signed the United Nations Charter, the Senate moved swiftly to authorize U.S. membership in the new world organization. The brief hearings conducted by the Senate Foreign Relations Committee revealed strong bipartisan support for the document. In his testimony before the committee, Stettinius justified the veto provision by arguing that the great powers must act together to maintain peace and that, if any one of them embarked upon a course of aggression, a major war would occur in any case.[79] The committee, with only one dissenting vote, recommended that the charter should be approved without any amendments or reservations. After a perfunctory debate, the full Senate ratified the charter on 28 July by an overwhelming margin of 89 to 2. Stettinius had reason to be especially pleased with the results of his long efforts. Although Byrnes had already replaced Stettinius as secretary of state, Truman appointed Stettinius to serve as the first U.S. representative to the United Nations.[80]

But few Americans regarded the new international security organization as a panacea that would rid the world of war. While three out of four Americans believed that the United States should belong to the world association, only one out of five thought that the United Nations could preserve the peace.[81] The postwar security planners in the State Department shared these apprehensions. From the very outset, they were especially worried about how Russia would act in the future. "Will she adhere to the Charter; will she keep any treaty which she signs; or will she be abusive and coercive in all her relations with the rest of the world, and especially with the small and relatively weak countries on her borders?" Isaiah Bowman had asked during the discussions at Dumbarton Oaks. "We do not know the answers to these things. Until the answers can be given we would do well to be cautious."[82] Although he and his State Department colleagues hoped for the best, they always believed that the United States must be prepared for the worst.

EIGHT | PROJECTING AMERICAN POWER

Postwar planners in Washington agreed on the need to maintain a powerful U.S. military establishment after the defeat of Germany and Japan. They thought that the United States must be prepared not only to repel an attack against its own shores but also to protect its overseas commercial and financial interests. Believing that American military weakness had encouraged the Axis powers to embark upon a campaign to partition the planet into closed economic blocs, they hoped that American military strength would discourage aggression in the future. Civilian officials joined with military leaders in embracing the doctrine of deterrence. They reasoned that the best way to prevent war would be to possess an awesome array of weapons that would intimidate potential aggressors. Because neither Congress nor the American people could be expected to support a large peacetime army, security planners in Washington urged the establishment of a system of universal military training that would provide a huge reserve of men ready for active duty in the armed services. They also advocated the acquisition of an extensive network of overseas naval and air bases that would enable the United States to project its military power throughout the world.

President Roosevelt and his State Department advisers believed that many key strategic points around the globe should be placed under international trusteeship and administered as military bases by the powers that would be responsible for policing the postwar world. During a conversation with Soviet foreign minister Vyacheslav Molotov on 1 June 1942, Roosevelt said that "there were, all over the world, many islands and colonial possessions which ought, for our own safety, to be taken away from weak nations." The president suggested, as a specific example, that the Pacific islands that Japan had received as mandates after World War I should be placed under some form of international trusteeship.[1] During a meeting of the Subcommittee on Security Problems two months later, Norman H. Davis argued that the United States should be authorized by the world organization to administer the Japanese mandates as trust territories. "For political reasons it would not be desirable for the United

States to annex these islands in any direct form, no matter how desirable for strategic reasons such a step might be," Davis explained. "If the United States limited itself to the acquisition of strategic bases, refusing to take any additional territory under its flag, the charge of imperialism could scarcely be made against us."[2]

As he looked ahead to the postwar era, President Roosevelt envisioned the "Four Global Policemen"—the United States, Great Britain, the Soviet Union, and China—utilizing airpower to deter aggression in behalf of the world security organization. He instructed the Joint Chiefs of Staff on 23 December 1942 to make a study, without considering the issue of current sovereignty, to determine what air bases might be needed by an international police force. The Joint Strategic Survey Committee, comprising Generals Stanley D. Embick and Muir S. Fairchild and Adm. Russell Willson, promptly began examining the question in preparation for an eventual peace settlement. In their report to the Joint Chiefs three months later, the committee members recommended that, from among the islands that would come under American control in the process of defeating Japan, the United States should select and fortify a line of naval and air bases stretching from Hawaii westward across the Pacific. "These are required primarily for national defense," they concluded, "but will also be available for use by any international military force."[3]

Although the Joint Strategic Survey Committee had skirted the issue of international trusteeship, President Roosevelt soon provided British foreign secretary Anthony Eden with a clear picture of his ideas regarding overseas military bases. While talking with the president on 22 March 1943, Eden said he hoped the United States would annex the Japanese mandated islands in the Pacific. But Roosevelt was not about to take the bait and give the British an excuse to keep their colonial possessions. After telling Eden that the United States did not want the Japanese mandates, he said that these islands, along with many others in the Pacific, should be placed under some kind of trusteeship and converted into military bases for the defense of the United Nations. Roosevelt once again revealed his recipe for peace in the Pacific when he met with Eden a week later. After reiterating his belief that the Japanese mandates should become the responsibility of the world security organization, the president suggested that the French Marquesas and Tuamotu Islands should pass under international trusteeship and be used as landing fields for air routes from the Caribbean to Australia and New Zealand.[4]

The General Board of the Navy had already begun preparing a comprehensive study of postwar security questions. In its first report on 20 March 1943, the board argued that the United States and Great Britain, as the only two countries that would have preponderant naval strength, should hold conversations "looking towards a division of responsibility for maintaining order over the water areas of the world." It noted that these two countries would need many overseas bases to carry out their police duties.[5] In its second report a week later, the committee recommended that the United States should assume possession of the islands that would be taken from Japan in the North Pacific. "None of the islands in question possesses natural features of value from other than the military standpoint," its members asserted. "The transfer to the United States of any or all of these islands with all that is implied therein cannot constitute territorial aggrandizement."[6] In its third and final report the following week, the board recommended that the sovereignty of a long list of British and French islands in the South Pacific should be transferred to the United States.[7]

While the navy was developing ambitious plans for transforming most of the Pacific basin into an American protectorate, Roosevelt continued to think in terms of placing important strategic points throughout the world under international trusteeship. On 23 June 1943, he sent Secretary of the Navy Frank Knox a memorandum suggesting that the United Nations should lease Dakar and a port in Liberia and that U.S. and Brazilian forces, acting as agents for the world organization, should maintain naval and air bases in these areas.[8] The president expanded on his ideas during a conversation a few months later with Adm. William D. Leahy and several State Department officials. After saying that security points in many parts of the world might be placed under international trusteeship, Roosevelt specifically mentioned the need for American military bases on the west coast of Africa as well as on several islands in the Atlantic and Pacific.[9]

The Joint Chiefs of Staff soon sent the president its finished study on postwar air bases. Completed on 6 November 1943, the paper and accompanying maps divided the prospective sites into two categories: those essential for defending the United States and those necessary for policing the rest of the world. An outer and inner ring of air bases would shield the United States against future attacks from any direction. In the Atlantic the outer defense line would run from Iceland through the Azores, Madeira, the west coast of Africa, and Ascension Island, while the inner line would run from Greenland through Labrador, Newfoundland, Bermuda, Trinidad, French Guiana, and Brazil. The outer perimeter in the

Pacific would run from the Aleutian Islands through the Bonin Islands, the Philippines, New Britain, the Solomons, Fiji, Samoa, Tahiti, Clipperton Island, and the Galapagos, while the inner string of bases would run from the Gilbert Islands through Ecuador or Peru and then through Guatemala and Mexico. Hoping to avoid the charge of imperialism, the Joint Chiefs indicated that the United States would not annex any foreign territory. Rather, the required bases were to be leased either by the United States or by the world organization for the use of an international police force.[10]

Though President Roosevelt liked the findings of this study, he thought that it could be improved from both a political and a military perspective. He believed, as did his civilian advisers, that the political issue of sovereignty could best be handled by placing overseas bases under international trusteeship. During a meeting with the Joint Chiefs on 15 November 1943, Roosevelt referred to a recent State Department memorandum on the subject of trusteeship and suggested that this form of administration would be an excellent way to govern territories taken from Japan.[11] Roosevelt turned his attention to strategic concerns when he met with the Joint Chiefs a few days later. After saying that he agreed on the whole with their paper on postwar air bases, the president indicated that the outer perimeter in the Pacific should be extended to include the Marquesas and the Taumoto Archipelago. He pointed out that in the future, planes based on these islands would be able to bomb Mexico, the Panama Canal, and the west coast of South America.[12]

After these meetings with the Joint Chiefs, the president was ready to discuss the need for postwar bases with foreign leaders. Roosevelt arrived at Cairo on 23 November 1943 for conversations with Winston Churchill and Chiang Kai-shek. Among other things, the three leaders agreed that "Japan shall be stripped of all the islands in the Pacific which she has seized or occupied since the beginning of the First World War." Roosevelt and Churchill then proceeded to Teheran to confer with Stalin. During a discussion on 28 November, the president told Churchill and Stalin that certain areas of strategic importance should be taken away from France and placed under international trusteeship. He specifically mentioned New Caledonia and Dakar. Returning to the topic of postwar bases the next day, Roosevelt stated that strategic points in the vicinity of Germany and Japan should be held under trusteeship. Churchill warned that he would resist any effort to take territory away from the British Empire, but Stalin agreed with the idea of placing certain strategic areas in the hands of the world organization.[13] Speaking for the president in a follow-up talk with Eden and Molotov, Harry Hopkins said that the three great powers would have to decide who would control the bases needed to enforce the peace.[14]

The Joint Chiefs of Staff had already asked President Roosevelt to direct the State Department to undertake negotiations with a large number of foreign countries to acquire postwar bases for U.S. military aircraft.[15] On 7 January 1944, not long after he had returned from Teheran, Roosevelt sent Secretary of State Cordell Hull a letter outlining American requirements for air bases and instructing the State Department to begin negotiations to obtain them.[16] The president was especially interested in the acquisition of air bases on both the bulge of Africa and the bulge of South America. During a conversation with a group of State Department officials on 17 March, Roosevelt explained that U.S. military authorities believed that the most direct threat to the future security of the Western Hemisphere would come from an attack across the Atlantic Narrows. He therefore hoped to obtain air bases along the coast of Brazil as well as in Dakar and the Cape Verde Islands.[17] On June 19, Hull informed Roosevelt that the State Department had concluded an agreement giving postwar rights for American military planes to use eight bases in Brazil.[18] The president expressed his delight two days later in a note to the U.S. ambassador in Rio de Janeiro. "I feel that this is a model," he wrote, "setting a pattern for the maintenance through cooperative measures of security of the Hemisphere after the war."[19]

Roosevelt and his advisers sought a vast network of overseas military bases as part of their regional plan for policing the postwar world. During a meeting of the Subcommittee on International Organization on 14 August 1942, Under Secretary of State Sumner Welles said that after the war U.S. forces should not become involved in local disputes all over the world. "The main concern of the United States would be to enforce peace in the Atlantic and Pacific areas," he observed. "For this purpose our naval and air forces would probably be sufficient."[20] The Joint Chiefs of Staff agreed. "In both the immediate and ultimate phases of the international organization," they explained, "U.S. military commitments should be limited so far as possible to the Western Hemisphere and the Far East."[21] While discussing U.S. plans for a world security organization with Stalin on 29 November 1943, Roosevelt said that he could foresee the possibility of sending American naval and air forces to Europe after the war but that any land armies needed to keep peace on the European continent would have to be provided by Great Britain and the Soviet Union.[22]

Indeed, the president indicated on numerous occasions that he expected British and Russian forces to assume primary responsibility for preserving order in Europe while the United States shouldered the major burden for maintaining peace in the Western Hemisphere and the Far East. During a meeting with his State Department advisers on 3 February 1943, Roosevelt said that he did not want them to draft a world organization plan that would bind the United States to send troops to Europe. He explained that the United States would make its chief contribution to the cause of postwar security by employing naval and air forces in the Western Hemisphere and the Pacific. "The meaning was plain," Isaiah Bowman commented after the meeting with the president. "He thought our public would be unwilling to send troops abroad but quite willing to send ships and airplanes on limited missions at limited costs."[23] Roosevelt made his position equally clear in a message to Ambassador John G. Winant in London. "After the surrender of Germany," he cabled Winant on 9 October 1944, "it is my intention to return from Europe to the United States as many of our troops as possible and at the earliest practicable dates."[24]

Although President Roosevelt believed that about one million American soldiers would have to remain in Germany for a year or two after the war, he refused to accept any military responsibility for the future stability of France or Italy. Roosevelt told the Joint Chiefs of Staff on 19 November 1943 that British rather than American troops should police France. Admiral Leahy, the former U.S. ambassador in Vichy, agreed. "Possibly there will be civil war in France," he warned. "It would be much easier for the United States to handle conditions in Germany." Thus, the president wanted American troops to have access to the North Sea so that they could leave Germany without having to pass through France.[25] In a message to Churchill on 7 February 1944, Roosevelt indicated that he was unwilling to police France or Italy after the war. "After all, France is your baby and will take a lot of nursing in order to bring it to the point of walking alone," he cabled Churchill. "It would be very difficult for me to keep in France my military force or management for any length of time."[26]

While Roosevelt and the Joint Chiefs of Staff wanted an extensive system of overseas bases to ensure American strategic domination in the Western Hemisphere and the Far East, they disagreed over the best way for the United States to exercise its authority over the Japanese mandates in the Pacific. In a memorandum for the president on 4 July 1944, the

Joint Chiefs recommended that the mandated Pacific islands should be placed under the sole sovereignty of the United States. "Their assured possession and control by the United States are essential to our security," the Joint Chiefs argued. "Together they constitute a single military entity, no element of which can be left to even the partial control of another nation without hazard to our control of that entity."[27] In his reply a few days later, Roosevelt agreed that no other nation should be given any control over the islands in question, but he reminded the Joint Chiefs that the United States had promised not to seek additional territory as a result of the war. "I am working on the idea that the United Nations will ask the United States to act as Trustee for the Japanese Mandated Islands," he explained. "With this will go the civil authority to handle the economic and educational affairs of their many inhabitants, and also the military authority to protect them."[28]

President Roosevelt and his State Department advisers hoped to have the Japanese mandates placed under the exclusive trusteeship, but not the sovereignty, of the United States. They did not want the United States to appear as a typical imperialist power, nor did they want to give other countries an excuse to grab territory in various parts of the world. "The solid argument for not trying to secure sovereignty," Assistant Secretary of State Adolf A. Berle noted in his diary on 26 July 1944, "is that we do not wish to open an annexation scramble in the Pacific."[29] During a conversation with several State Department officials a few months later, Roosevelt said that the army and navy had been urging that the United States should take outright possession of the mandated islands in the Pacific. The president stated that he was opposed to such a procedure because it would be contrary to the Atlantic Charter and because he did not think it would be necessary for security purposes.[30] While discussing the need for postwar military bases with Secretary of State Edward R. Stettinius on 2 January 1945, Roosevelt said that the trusteeship principle should be applied to a number of islands in the Pacific.[31]

Secretary of War Henry L. Stimson, however, decided to employ his impressive powers of persuasion in an effort to get the president and his State Department advisers to change their position on the trusteeship question. In a memorandum for Secretary of State Stettinius on 23 January 1945, Stimson argued that the United States must have absolute authority in the Japanese mandated islands. "Acquisition of them by the United States does not represent an attempt at colonization or exploitation," he declared. "Instead it is merely the acquisition by the United States of the necessary bases for the defense of the security of the Pacific for the future world."[32] Stimson continued his campaign for direct American ownership of the Japanese mandates after Stettinius left for the Big Three conference at Yalta. During a meeting with Secretary of the Navy James V. Forrestal and Under Secretary of State Joseph C. Grew on 8 February 1945, Stimson observed that the United States would need to have possession of specific islands in the Pacific not for economic gain but for the sole purpose of maintaining peace. Forrestal agreed. "We are talking about sand spits," he noted. "There would be no economic advantage."[33] But to their dismay, Stimson and Forrestal soon learned that the trusteeship formula put forward by Stettinius and approved at Yalta would apply to the islands to be detached from Japan.

Stimson therefore altered his tactics after the Yalta Conference by endeavoring to make sure that trusteeship provisions would impose almost no limitations on U.S. authority over strategic outposts in the postwar era. During a meeting with State and Navy Department officials on 20 February 1945, Stimson argued that, at least for areas with little economic but great strategic value, "there must be created a form of trusteeship closely akin to ownership." He said that with regard to the Japanese mandates, the United States must have the right not only to control and fortify them but also to prohibit other countries from building military bases on any nearby islands. Under Secretary of State Grew and Assistant Secretary of State James C. Dunn agreed that it would be wise to work for "the establishment of forms of trusteeship so complete in their control as to accomplish substantially the same result in respect of such security outposts as might be accomplished by actual acquisition."[34]

An interdepartmental committee on dependent areas soon began drafting plans for the creation of a special category of trusteeship for places of high strategic importance. The committee, chaired by Leo Pasvolsky of the State Department, comprised Admiral Willson and Generals Embick and Fairchild of the Joint Strategic Survey Committee, Abe Fortas of the Interior Department, and Charles W. Taussig along with Nelson A. Rockefeller and Benjamin Gerig from the State Department. After several meetings, these civilian and military representatives proposed the establishment of two different types of trust territories: strategic and nonstrategic. Fortas suggested that it would be easier to justify giving strategic areas a special status on grounds of world security rather than national defense. Admiral Willson agreed. When Taussig discussed these ideas with the president on 15 March 1945, Roosevelt said that for security reasons all or part of a strategic trust territory could be designated as a closed area and thereby exempt from any international agreements.[35]

However, even after the State Department drafted a trusteeship proposal that made special arrangements for the administration of strategic areas, Stimson and Forrestal still feared that U.S. military forces might not be granted sufficient control over the air and naval bases that they would need in order to police the Pacific. The trusteeship plan, which the State Department hoped would be adopted at the United Nations Conference in San Francisco, would transfer sovereignty over the Japanese mandates to the world organization. Then the United States would be asked to administer these islands as strategic trust territories. After reviewing the situation on 30 March 1945, Stimson and Forrestal agreed upon a course of action. First, they would try to get the whole subject of trusteeship removed from the agenda at San Francisco by arguing that there should not be any international discussion of the issue prior to the defeat of Japan. Second, they would attempt to get the president or the secretary of state to make a public statement indicating that the United States intended to take full title to the Japanese mandates for the purpose of maintaining peace in the Pacific.[36]

But the State Department, with strong backing from the Interior Department, urged Roosevelt to overrule his military advisers. In a memorandum for the president on 5 April 1945, Secretary of Interior Harold L. Ickes warned that, if the United States insisted upon exercising full sovereignty over the Japanese mandated islands, the British might respond by claiming absolute title to certain oil-rich areas in the Middle East. He also warned that failure to reach an agreement on trusteeships at the San Francisco Conference would sow the seeds of suspicion and distrust.[37] In a cable sent to the president at his retreat in Warm Springs, Georgia, on 9 April, Secretary of State Stettinius argued that the trusteeship proposal that had been drafted by his aides would give U.S. military forces sufficient control over strategic points in the Pacific. Stettinius also asserted that, if the State Department plan for dependent areas were not submitted at San Francisco, American efforts to establish a trusteeship system would be jeopardized.[38] Determined to promote the decolonization of Asia and Africa, Roosevelt cabled Stettinius the next day that he approved his message in principle and that he would settle the matter when he returned to Washington.[39]

But his civilian and military advisers were left to resolve their differences on trusteeships when Roosevelt suddenly died two days later.

After attending the memorial services for the president at his home in Hyde Park, New York, on 16 April, Stettinius told Stimson and Forrestal that the State Department would be willing to meet them halfway but it could never agree to sponsor a policy of annexation at the San Francisco Conference. "They both now realize that we cannot agree to annexation," Stettinius informed Dunn and Pasvolsky. "They both are now in the mood to reach an agreement on the basis of some middle ground."[40] War and Navy Department representatives immediately joined with State Department officials in drafting a policy directive for President Truman to give the U.S. delegates before they left for San Francisco. The memorandum recommended the establishment of a trusteeship system that would assure the United States control over strategic areas required for postwar security purposes as well as provide for the social, economic, and political advancement of the inhabitants of dependent territories.[41] When the heads of the State, War, and Navy Departments met with Truman on 18 April, Stettinius explained that he and his colleagues hoped to exercise control over strategic bases in the Pacific and yet at the same time avoid being charged with territorial aggrandizement.[42] Then Stimson told Truman that the United States would administer these strategic outposts for the benefit of all the freedom-loving countries in the world. After listening carefully to Stettinius and Stimson, the president approved their recommendation for a trusteeship policy that later found expression in Chapter 12 of the United Nations Charter.[43]

Along with the Japanese mandates, the Philippine Islands figured prominently in American plans for postwar security in the Pacific. The Tydings-McDuffie Act of 1934, which had promised that the Philippines would be granted independence in 1946, had provided for the maintenance of only a few U.S. naval bases and fueling stations on the islands. American desires to acquire additional bases in the Philippines grew during the war, but military leaders in Washington feared that they might lose their opportunity to obtain these bases when they learned in September 1943 that Sen. Millard E. Tydings, a Democrat from Maryland, intended to introduce a bill to give the islands immediate independence. Secretary of War Stimson warned Tydings that such legislation would make it very difficult to arrange for the acquisition of military bases that would be needed to protect the Philippines.[44] In November 1943, after consulting with Stimson and others, Tydings introduced Senate Joint Resolution 93, which authorized the president to proclaim Philippine independence after the liberation of the islands. The resolution, which was approved by both houses of Congress the following spring, also authorized the president to negotiate for the acquisition of military bases in addition to those specified in the Tydings-McDuffie Act.[45]

The liberation of the Philippines by U.S. forces under Gen. Douglas MacArthur, the supreme Allied commander in the Southwest Pacific, led to the renewal of discussions about the future of the islands. After the first American troops reached Manila on 3 February 1945, Stimson sent MacArthur a telegram asking if he thought it was time for the United States to send a high commissioner to the Philippines. The general responded by indicating that he not only opposed the appointment of an American commissioner but also favored the recognition of Philippine independence as soon as Japanese forces were cleared out of the islands. When Stimson discussed the matter with Secretary of the Navy Forrestal and Secretary of the Interior Ickes on 8 February, he was relieved to find that they disagreed with MacArthur. The three secretaries believed that there should be an interim period between the liberation of the Philippines and the establishment of independence and that a high commissioner should be dispatched to negotiate for additional military bases while the islands were still under American control.[46]

Stimson took it upon himself to urge U.S. military leaders to make up their minds regarding the best places to build naval and air bases in the Philippines before it was too late. On 20 February 1945, Stimson told Adm. William F. Halsey, the commander of the Third Fleet in the Pacific, that he wanted the navy to prepare careful plans for the establishment of postwar bases in the Philippines. "There will be a demand that we shall declare the Philippines independent," he warned Halsey, "and it will be much more difficult after that to negotiate for the bases."[47] The next day Stimson alerted Chief of Staff Gen. George C. Marshall and his aides about the danger of an early declaration of independence for the Philippines. He urged the army officers that they should get together with their counterparts in the navy to develop "clear and well-supported plans for naval and air bases in the Philippines as promptly as possible."[48]

President Roosevelt and his State Department advisers agreed on the need for postwar U.S. military bases in the Philippines. But they did not want to postpone granting independence to the islands any longer than necessary; neither did they wish to send a high commissioner to the Philippines. Meeting with Stimson and Forrestal on 3 March, Under Secretary Grew explained that the State Department thought it would be unwise to appoint a high commissioner because the Filipinos might take it as an indication that the United States did not intend to fulfill its commitment to grant them independence. But Stimson said that he, Forrestal, and Ickes believed that it would be necessary to dispatch a high commissioner to negotiate for the establishment of military outposts before the Philippines became independent. After acknowledging that it would be necessary to have some U.S. official in the Philippines, Grew suggested that the man to be sent should be called a special representative of the president of the United States rather than bearing a title that might arouse suspicions about American intentions. Stimson and Forrestal thought this would be a practical solution to the problem.[49]

The State, War, and Navy Departments continued working together with regard to the Philippines after Roosevelt died. During a meeting with Stettinius, Stimson, and Forrestal on 18 April 1945, Truman said he was going to discuss the future of the islands with Philippine president Sergio Osmena the next day. Stimson immediately said that in his opinion it would be much better to arrange for the establishment of U.S. military bases now than to negotiate for them after the Philippines were independent.[50] Everyone seemed to concur, and after the meeting ended Stimson discussed his ideas with President Osmena.[51] When they went to the White House to confer with Truman on 19 April, Stimson explained that he and Osmena both thought that the United States and the Philippines should settle certain issues before severing their close relationship. Stimson also explained that he and Osmena agreed that the settlement of such issues would be greatly facilitated by the appointment of an American official with the power of a high commissioner but with a different title so that the Filipinos would not fear that the United States was going to renege on its promise to grant them independence.[52]

President Truman promptly decided to appoint a special commission, to be headed by Senator Tydings, that would go to Manila and report on conditions in the Philippines. Tydings was eager to arrange for the establishment of U.S. naval and air bases in the Philippines before the islands became independent. "Filipino politics being what they are," he wrote Truman on 25 April, "it may be much more difficult to obtain agreement on the military bases we need several months from now than in the approximate present."[53] In a letter to Truman a week later, Stimson suggested that he and Forrestal should prepare for transmission to Osmena a list of locations where the army and navy wanted to have bases in the Philippines. "The one important thing," Stimson emphasized, "is that the matter should be settled before independence is announced." The president quickly expressed his agreement.[54] After receiving assurances from Truman that the Philippines would be granted independence at the earliest possible date, Osmena went to the White House on 14 May and signed an agreement to provide sites in the Philippines for the establishment of all the naval and air bases that the United States desired.[55]

Although agreeing on the need for overseas naval and air bases, U.S. military leaders held conflicting opinions toward proposals to unify the armed services after the war. Members of the army air force became vigorous advocates of a single defense department that would preside over three individual branches of service. In their view an independent air force would have equal status with the army and navy.[56] The army came to accept the idea that unification would reduce duplication and make the armed forces more efficient. "There should be one department after the war for the land, air, and naval forces," Secretary of War Stimson declared in April 1944. "Cooperation between military forces could never be as effective as combination."[57] But the navy strongly opposed unification. Secretary of the Navy Forrestal and the admirals feared that in a unified defense department the army and air force would work together to strip the navy of its air and ground units. Although the Joint Chiefs of Staff presented a merger plan in April 1945, the navy was able to prevent unification of the services until long after the war ended.[58]

Despite their bitter differences regarding proposals for unification, however, army and navy representatives did agree that the United States should maintain a powerful military establishment after the war. American military leaders, like the postwar planners in the State Department, were committed to the doctrine of deterrence. They repeatedly argued that the United States must remain strong in order to discourage any aggressive moves by a future Hitler. "Those that hate war," Forrestal declared in April 1945, "must have the power to prevent it."[59] Should deterrence fail, military spokesmen reasoned, the United States must be prepared to help suppress aggression before it developed into another global conflict. "Adequate military force, applied in sufficient time against an aggressor nation," Chief of Naval Operations Ernest J. King asserted in a memorandum for Forrestal, "is the most effective means of defense and of preventing a world war from developing from its nascent state."[60]

Admiral King ordered his staff in August 1943 to begin formulating plans for a large postwar navy. During the next eighteen months, they developed plans for a peacetime fleet that would require more than 500,000 officers and sailors.[61] "In view of the nebulous assumptions that have to be made as to post-war conditions," King reported to Forrestal in February 1945, "it is necessary to leave a pretty wide margin of safety in estimating the size of a post-war Navy."[62] In a memorandum that he sent to Forrestal three weeks later, King explained that the primary task of the navy would be "to maintain command of the sea in the western part of the North and South Atlantic Oceans including the approaches thereto, and in the entire Pacific Ocean including the approaches thereto."[63] King assured Forrestal that American warships would be ready to move swiftly "to any part of the world in support of our national policies." Before the war ended, his staff concluded that the United States would need a postwar naval force comprising 50,000 officers, 500,000 seamen, and 110,000 marines.[64]

While the navy had determined the force level that would be required to patrol vast stretches of the Atlantic and Pacific, no decision concerning the size of the postwar army had been made before hostilities ended. Chief of Staff Marshall and his aides in the Special Planning Division of the army feared that Congress would refuse to provide financial support for the maintenance of a large peacetime force. But they hoped that a small regular army, backed by a huge reserve of trained men, would be cheap enough for Congress to fund and strong enough to defend the United States.[65] Determined to obtain maximum effectiveness at minimum cost, Col. Gordon E. Textor and his colleagues in the Special Planning Division produced a tentative plan in January 1945 for a postwar army of only 330,000 soldiers but backed by a program of universal military training that would provide a hefty reserve force of 4,500,000 men. "What we are doing at the moment is to base the plan on the assumption we have universal military training," Textor told the Top Policy Group in the navy. "If it looks like the pendulum will swing the other way, we will have to get up the other plan."[66]

Secretary of War Stimson and Secretary of the Navy Knox were early proponents of universal military training. In letters to the chairmen of the House and Senate Military Affairs Committees dated 12 August 1943, Stimson advocated the enactment during the war of legislation to institute a permanent system of military instruction for all physically qualified males in the United States.[67] Taking advantage of the contacts he had made while serving as the publisher of the *Chicago Daily News,* Knox sent similar letters a few months later to several prominent news commentators. "To my mind it is exceedingly important that this subject be written into law before the end of the war," he explained to Arthur Krock of the *New York Times,* "first because the system would provide for the prospective emergency in military personnel which will come at the end of hostilities, and second, because I think it would be more readily passed while the public is more thoroughly conscious of the importance of such a measure."[68] After speaking in favor of compulsory military instruction before the Boy Scouts' Council in Cleveland on 14 January 1944, Knox planned to discuss the question with the presidents of several major universities, but illness prevented him from doing so.[69]

After Knox died suddenly from a heart attack, Forrestal succeeded him as secretary of the navy and joined with Stimson in continuing the campaign for universal military training. "Unless we get it while the war is still in progress," Forrestal wrote the chairman of the House Committee on Naval Affairs, "I for one am very skeptical whether it will ever become law."[70] Hoping to win the support of organized labor, Stimson held a large conference in his office on 10 November 1944 to discuss the need for compulsory military instruction after the war. Those present included Pres. William Green of the AF of L, Pres. Philip Murray of the CIO, and the presidents of four railway unions; Representatives Clifton A. Woodrum and James W. Wadsworth of the House Select Committee on Post-War Military Policy; Forrestal and Admiral King representing the navy; and Stimson and General Marshall speaking for the army. Setting the tone at the beginning of the two-and-a-half-hour meeting, Stimson emphasized that Marshall and his staff regarded universal military training as absolutely essential for the future safety of the United States.[71]

In a cabinet meeting later that day, President Roosevelt indicated that he was thinking about asking Congress to pass a bill that would require young men to undergo a year of training for both civilian and military purposes. But Stimson and Forrestal urged the president to endorse a straightout military training program. Based upon impressions gained from their discussion with the labor leaders, Stimson and Forrestal said that they believed unions would be more likely to support a bill that involved military training only rather than one that included civilian training. Secretary of Labor Frances Perkins and several other cabinet members concurred. At the close of the meeting, Roosevelt told Stimson that he wanted the War Department to send him material for a speech to Congress on the subject of compulsory military instruction.[72] But Stimson advised the president a week later that the message should not be delivered until the new Congress convened.[73]

In the meantime, the War and Navy secretaries decided to meet with prominent education leaders in hopes of securing their support for universal military training.[74] Stimson asked Secretary of State Stettinius if he could come to the conference, to be held on 29 December 1944, to help convince the educators that a permanent system of military instruction was needed to provide the foundation for world peace. Although Stettinius could not attend the meeting, he asked Under Secretary of State Grew to go in his place.[75] Stimson was pleased to have State Department support when the presidents of fifteen colleges and universities assembled in his office. After some of the educators said they thought a postwar military training program would not be in accord with plans for a world security organization, Grew joined with Stimson, Forrestal, King, and Marshall in arguing that the success of the United Nations would depend upon the availability of an adequate number of soldiers and sailors prepared to subdue any act of aggression.[76]

Two days later Stimson reported to Roosevelt that the educators were in favor of compulsory military training on a strictly military basis and that they did not want any kind of civilian training mixed with it. He also said that representatives of the State, War, and Navy Departments had drafted a statement on universal military training for the president to use in his annual message to Congress.[77] When Roosevelt delivered his State of the Union address on 6 January 1945, he advocated a compulsory system of military instruction without mentioning anything about postwar conscription for civilian purposes. The president said that in due course he expected to deliver a special message to Congress on this important subject.[78] But Stimson and his aides in the War Department had already decided that the push for postwar military instruction should be delayed while they fought for a national-service law that would give the government power to assign all U.S. citizens to jobs deemed necessary to win the war. Fearing that Congress and the American people would become confused if both issues were debated at the same time, Stimson advised Roosevelt on 12 January that he should withhold his promised message on the subject until the current manpower and production shortages were solved. The president replied that he intended to wait for about two months before asking Congress to pass legislation requiring universal military training after the war.[79]

After Congress refused to enact a national-service law, Stimson and Forrestal resumed their campaign for universal military training. The death of President Roosevelt delayed but did not derail their efforts. Less than two weeks after his funeral, officials from the State, War, and Navy

Departments met with the representatives of more than forty women's organizations to discuss the need for compulsory military instruction.[80] Stimson took it upon himself to brief President Truman on the subject. In a memorandum on 30 May 1945, Stimson informed Truman that the Joint Chiefs of Staff regarded universal military training as the keystone upon which to build the future security of the United States. Stimson then explained that the program jointly recommended by the War and Navy Departments would require all able-bodied young men between the ages of seventeen and twenty to undergo one continuous year of military training. "It is believed," he concluded, "that such a program will enable the United States to maintain an adequate military system and at the same time reduce to a minimum the size of the regular armed forces."[81]

The House Select Committee on Post-War Military Policy, under the chairmanship of Rep. Clifton Woodrum of Virginia, conducted hearings on the subject during the next few weeks. In their testimony before the Woodrum Committee, officials from the State, War, and Navy Departments endorsed the plan for a year of continuous military training after the war. They argued that compulsory military instruction was needed to defend the United States, to help the United Nations maintain world peace, and to discourage other countries from embarking upon a path of aggression.[82] Under Secretary of State Grew, for example, said that he did not believe that Japan would have attacked Pearl Harbor if the United States had been prepared to fight. "My experience has taught me," he declared, "that aggressors are not deterred by latent superior strength but shrewdly try to obtain their end by attacking when they consider their political opponents unprepared."[83] Despite these arguments, however, the hearings showed that many educational, religious, labor, and agricultural leaders opposed compulsory military training for all young men qualified for service.[84]

As the Woodrum Committee considered the question, President Truman developed his own plan for universal military training. His proposal was designed to cause as little disruption as possible to the education or employment of the trainees. Rather than being compelled to take a year of continuous instruction, the trainees could choose to receive instruction for a few months each summer over a period of four years after they left high school.[85] Congressman Woodrum liked the idea. Although he did not think it would be possible to pass legislation requiring a continuous year of military training, he believed it would be possible to pass a bill allowing instruction over four brief periods as the president had in mind. Woodrum informed the White House on 21 June 1945 that his committee would simply recommend that Congress should enact some form of compulsory military training. But he said that, in his opinion, the president should not send a message on the subject to Congress until it reconvened in the autumn.[86]

The campaign for universal military training came to a climax a few months later. War Department officials held to their position that there should be one year of continuous instruction. "In training, as in education, the processes of learning are not well served by piecemeal instruction offered during isolated periods," they argued. "But the most important consideration is that nothing less than a continuous year of military training will convince the world that we are earnest in our determination to have an effective security program."[87] In a message to Congress on 23 October 1945, Truman urged the establishment of a military training system that would provide a large reserve prepared to reinforce the regular armed forces in times of danger. He recommended that all eighteen-year-old men should receive a full year of instruction and then serve in the reserve for the next six years.[88] "The surest guarantee that no nation will dare again to attack us," Truman declared, "is to remain strong in the only kind of strength an aggressor understands— military power." But, despite the president's desire to deter aggression by demonstrating American readiness, Congress refused to create a peacetime system of compulsory military training.[89]

Along with their desire for a large reserve force that could be rapidly mobilized if Congress decreed an emergency, U.S. policymakers wanted a sophisticated intelligence organization that could provide accurate information about military preparations in other countries. The State, War, and Navy Departments, plus the Office of Strategic Services and other government agencies, had been operating independently in the field of foreign intelligence. But there was a growing awareness of the need for greater cooperation after the war in gathering military intelligence on a worldwide basis.[90] In a memorandum prepared on 25 October 1944, Isador Lubin, a special assistant to President Roosevelt, proposed the establishment of an overall foreign intelligence service that would operate under the guidance of an interdepartmental board. "What I have in mind is an organization that would collect, analyze, and disseminate intelligence on the policy and strategy levels," Lubin explained. "It should objectively and impartially serve the needs of the combined diplomatic, military, and economic services of the Government."[91]

After reading the memorandum, Roosevelt forwarded it to the State Department for analysis and comment. Secretary of State Stettinius responded to the president on 15 December 1944 in a memorandum that acknowledged the need for a permanent foreign intelligence service. Stettinius recommended the establishment of an interdepartmental board, to be chaired by a State Department official, that would be responsible for coordinating foreign intelligence activities among the various departments and agencies of the U.S. government.[92] But the president favored the idea of an independent organization that would be responsible for gathering military intelligence. In a memorandum for Stettinius on 17 January 1945, Roosevelt indicated that he believed the future security of the United States required the creation of an overall foreign intelligence organization. "At the end of this war there simply must be a consolidation of Foreign Intelligence between State and War and Navy," he emphasized, "and I think it should be limited to military and related subjects."[93]

William J. Donovan, the director of the Office of Strategic Services, had already proposed the establishment of a centralized intelligence agency for the postwar era. His plan, sent to Roosevelt on 18 November 1944, called for the creation of a central authority that would coordinate U.S. intelligence operations and report directly to the president.[94] But when someone leaked his plan to the press a few months later, the enemies of the president charged that Roosevelt intended to build up a secret police similar to the Gestapo in Nazi Germany.[95] Even some friends of the president worried that there might be unforeseen dangers inherent in the proposal. In a conversation with Secretary of the Navy Forrestal on 29 March 1945, Admiral King warned that a single intelligence agency might over a long period acquire far more power than anyone at present intended and that it might be hard to take that power away.[96] Roosevelt decided to proceed with caution. In a memorandum on 5 April, he simply asked Donovan to meet with representatives of the various executive units engaged in intelligence work in order to obtain a consensus of opinion regarding his proposal.[97]

President Truman inherited the problem when Roosevelt died a week later. During a conference at the White House on 26 April 1945, Budget Director Harold D. Smith told Truman that it was very important to have a well-organized intelligence system but that it was also important to refrain from rushing into a program that would produce harmful rivalries between the various agencies involved in intelligence. Truman agreed.[98] After the war in the Pacific ended, however, a debate ensued concerning the best way to organize a unified intelligence service. Donovan urged Truman to approve his plan for a single agency.[99] But while the secretaries of state, war, and navy agreed on the need for this, they argued that such a bureau should report to them rather than directly to the president.[100] The controversy continued for more than a year. Eventually, the Central Intelligence Agency was organized along the lines Donovan had originally proposed.

Besides assuming that information from overseas intelligence operations would give them sufficient time to mobilize their military forces, U.S. policymakers believed that scientific research would provide them with an array of awesome weapons to deter or defeat any future aggressor. The development of radar and rockets, plus the tremendous resources devoted to building an atomic bomb, had indicated that scientific readiness would be a crucial element in military preparedness after the war. Stimson and Forrestal realized that scientific innovation would revolutionize future warfare, and on 9 November 1944 they asked the National Academy of Science to establish the Research Board for National Security to oversee the postwar development of new weapons for the army and navy. Although the project was soon terminated due to a controversy about government authority over scientific activity, the close wartime collaboration between civilian scientists and military leaders had established a pattern for postwar weapons research and development in the United States.[101]

The decision to build the atomic bomb had far greater postwar implications than the development of any other weapon during World War II. After learning that British scientists believed that atomic bombs could be built rapidly enough to help determine the outcome of the war, President Roosevelt suggested to Prime Minister Churchill in October 1941 that atomic research in their countries should be "coordinated or even jointly conducted." American and British scientists soon began exchanging basic information on the subject. During a private discussion in June 1942, Roosevelt and Churchill agreed that the United States and Great Britain should fully share the results of their atomic research as "equal partners." But American scientists persuaded Roosevelt in December 1942 that information about the manufacture of nuclear weapons should be withheld from the British. Since the United States was doing most of the work to develop the atomic bomb, they argued, Great Britain should not be allowed to share equally in the commercial application of atomic energy after the war.[102]

But the British urged Roosevelt to reverse his decision to restrict the interchange of nuclear information because they wanted their own arsenal of atomic weapons to strengthen their postwar strategic position with respect to the Russians. When Churchill came to Washington in May 1943 to discuss military strategy, he convinced Roosevelt that the exchange of information about the atomic bomb should be resumed. The president instructed American scientists two months later to "renew, in an inclusive manner, the full exchange of information with the British." According to a secret agreement signed by Roosevelt and Churchill at Quebec in August 1943, the United States and Great Britain would share information needed for the construction of an atomic bomb at the earliest moment, but the British would not obtain "any post-war advantages of an industrial or commercial character" without American consent. The agreement also specified that neither country would communicate any information about the project "to third parties except by mutual consent."[103]

While Roosevelt was willing to exchange information about the atomic bomb with the British, however, he was not prepared to share any knowledge about secret weapons with the Russians. Although the president hoped that it would be possible to maintain friendly relations with the Soviet Union after the war, his misgivings about Russian intentions prompted him to hedge his bets. When Secretary of War Stimson learned in December 1942 that Great Britain and the Soviet Union had agreed three months earlier to exchange information about their weapons, he warned Roosevelt that the understanding might endanger the confidentiality of any information about the atomic bomb that the United States furnished Great Britain. The president indicated that he was not worried because the Anglo-Soviet agreement did not obligate the British to disclose any atomic secrets to the Russians. But Roosevelt agreed with Stimson that it would be unwise for the United States to enter into a similar pact with the Soviet Union.[104]

President Roosevelt showed greater concern when Niels Bohr, an eminent scientist who had escaped from Nazi-occupied Denmark, began advocating the international control of atomic energy. Hoping to prevent a postwar nuclear arms race that would threaten the world with destruction, Bohr proposed to Roosevelt and Churchill during the spring and summer of 1944 that they should inform Stalin before the war ended about their attempts to build an atomic bomb. But Roosevelt and Churchill wanted to maintain an Anglo-American nuclear monopoly. Thus, they agreed on 10 June that the United States and Great Britain would cooperate both during and after the war in seeking to control the raw materials required for manufacturing nuclear weapons. Then in an *aide-mémoire* signed on 19 September, Roosevelt and Churchill explicitly rejected the suggestion that Stalin should be told that they were trying to construct an atomic bomb. "The matter should continue to be regarded as of the utmost secrecy," they agreed. "Inquiries should be made regarding the activities of Professor Bohr and steps taken to ensure that he is responsible for no leakage of information particularly to the Russians."[105]

Vannevar Bush, the director of the Office of Scientific Research and Development, and James B. Conant, the chairman of the National Defense Research Committee, soon came to suspect that Roosevelt had made a commitment to perpetuate the exclusive Anglo-American partnership with respect to atomic energy. Realizing that the president did not look to them for diplomatic advice, they decided to approach the secretary of war, and on 25 September 1944 Stimson agreed that Bush and Conant should draft a proposal for a postwar atomic energy policy. In a memorandum prepared for Stimson five days later, they pointed out that any nation with good technical and scientific resources could build an atomic bomb in three or four years. Bush and Conant warned that, if the United States and Great Britain attempted to develop nuclear weapons in complete secrecy after the war, the Soviet Union would undoubtedly proceed along the same lines. Hoping to avoid a nuclear arms race that might culminate in a devastating conflict, they recommended the free interchange of all scientific information about atomic weapons at the end of the war.[106]

Stimson gradually began toying with the idea of telling the Russians about the atomic bomb project if they first showed a willingness to cooperate in other areas. When Roosevelt mentioned to him on 31 December 1944 that the Soviets were trying to dominate countries in Eastern Europe, Stimson informed the president that the head of the U.S. military mission in Moscow had recommended that the United States should insist upon a quid pro quo from the Soviet Union for any assistance that did not contribute to winning the war. Then Stimson said he knew that the Russians were spying on American work on atomic weapons but that he did not think they had obtained any useful information. While he was "troubled about the possible effects" of not saying anything about that work to the Russians, Stimson told Roosevelt, he believed it was "essential not to take them into our confidence until we were sure to get a real quid pro quo from our frankness." Stimson said that he had "no illusions as to the possibility of keeping permanently such a secret" but that he did not think "it was yet time to share it with Russia." The president expressed his agreement.[107]

But Stimson was disturbed when Vannevar Bush seemed ready to open discussions with the Soviet Union concerning the postwar control of atomic weapons. "Bush is so delighted at the news which came this morning of the agreement at Yalta that he is anxious to be very chivalrous to the Russians on this subject," Stimson observed on 13 February 1945. "But I am still inclined to tread softly and to hold off conferences on the subject until we have some much more tangible 'fruits of repentance' from the Russians as a quid pro quo for such a communication to them."[108] During a conversation with Stimson two days later, Bush proposed the creation of an international pool for the postwar exchange of all scientific research that could be used for military purposes. Stimson agreed that this would be a good way to prevent the development of secret weapons after the war, but he thought it would be inadvisable to put such a plan into full force until the United States had gotten all it could from the Soviet Union in return for information about the atomic bomb program. After Stimson agreed that it might be good to make a start with one kind of scientific research, Bush suggested that bacteriological research would probably be the most practical one to try.[109]

As work on the atomic bomb came closer to completion, however, Stimson knew that American leaders would soon have to make a fundamental choice in connection with the postwar control of nuclear weapons. "We are up against some very big decisions," he noted on 5 March 1945. "The time is approaching when we can no longer avoid them."[110] Stimson went to the White House ten days later to brief the president on his options with respect to the future control of the atomic bomb. "I went over with him the two schools of thought that exist," Stimson recorded in his diary, "one of them being the secret close-in attempted control of the project by those who control it now, and the other being the international control." He emphasized that the issue should be settled before the atomic bomb was used. Although Roosevelt indicated that he agreed with Stimson, the president did nothing to settle this pressing question before his death.[111]

On 25 April 1945, just two weeks after Roosevelt died, Stimson went to the White House to warn President Truman about the possibility of a nuclear arms race and to suggest the need for international cooperation to control atomic energy after the war. "Within four months," he informed Truman, "we shall in all probability have completed the most terrible weapon ever known in human history, one bomb of which can destroy a whole city." Although the Soviet Union was probably the only nation other than the United States that could produce an atomic bomb in the next few years, Stimson explained, it was highly likely that smaller countries would eventually be able to construct such a weapon in secret and use it suddenly to devastate an unsuspecting nation of much greater size and power. Unless a system of international control with thoroughgoing rights of inspection could be devised, he warned, modern civilization might be completely destroyed by atomic warfare. "On the other hand," Stimson concluded, "if the problem of the proper use of this weapon can be solved, we would have the opportunity to bring the world into a pattern in which the peace of the world and our civilization can be saved."[112]

After obtaining authorization from Truman a week later, Stimson set up the Interim Committee to make recommendations concerning atomic energy until Congress established a permanent commission to regulate its development and use after the war. Stimson selected the following individuals to serve as official members of the small committee that would operate under his chairmanship: James F. Byrnes, the personal representative of the president; Under Secretary of the Navy Ralph A. Bard; Assistant Secretary of State William L. Clayton; Vannevar Bush; James B. Conant; and Karl T. Compton, the president of Massachusetts Institute of Technology. In addition, he appointed the Scientific Panel to provide the committee with technical advice. The panel consisted of the following scientists who were directing research on the atomic bomb project: J. Robert Oppenheimer, Earnest O. Lawrence, Arthur H. Compton, and Enrico Fermi.[113] Shortly after convening the Interim Committee for the first time on 9 May, Stimson decided to relieve himself from all routine duties in the War Department and focus his attention on the subject of atomic energy.[114]

During a meeting on 31 May, the Interim Committee discussed the postwar implications of atomic energy with the members of the Scientific Panel. Stimson opened the meeting by stating that atomic energy must be employed in the future to ensure peace rather than to destroy civilization. When he referred to the need for the free interchange of scientific information and an effective system of inspection, Oppenheimer suggested that the United States should broach the subject with the Russians in a tentative fashion without giving them any details about the American research program. But Byrnes objected to offering the Soviet Union any information, even in the most general terms, about the atomic bomb. There was general agreement when Byrnes argued that "the most desirable program would be to push ahead as fast as possible in production and research to make certain that we stay ahead and at the same time make every effort to better our political relations with Russia." During a conversation six days later, Stimson and Truman talked about bringing the Soviet Union into the atomic partnership, after using the bomb to defeat Japan, if the Russians agreed to modify their territorial ambitions.[115]

But the Scientific Panel soon persuaded the Interim Committee that the Russians should be notified before the atomic bomb was dropped on Japan. During a meeting on 21 June, the committee discussed the need for an effective international mechanism for controlling atomic energy. The members unanimously agreed that there would be considerable advantage, if a suitable opportunity arose during the forthcoming Big Three conference at Potsdam, "in having the President advise the Russians that we were working on this weapon with every prospect of success and that we expected to use it against Japan." They thought that the president might also say that he hoped this matter could be discussed after the war for the purpose of ensuring that atomic energy would be used to help preserve world peace. "Not to give them this prior information at the time of the 'Big Three' Conference and within a few weeks thereafter to use the weapon," they reasoned, "might well make it impossible ever to enlist Russian cooperation in the set-up of future international controls over this new power." Truman concurred. During a discussion with Stalin at Potsdam a month later, Truman casually mentioned that the United States had a new weapon of unusual destructive force, and the Russian leader replied that he hoped it would be used against the Japanese.[116]

When Japan agreed to surrender on 14 August 1945 shortly after atomic bombs had devastated Hiroshima and Nagasaki, U.S. leaders held conflicting opinions about how nuclear weapons should be handled in the future. Secretary of War Stimson, while away on vacation, immediately began work on a paper calling for the president to approach Stalin about the need for international cooperation to prevent an arms race. But his aides soon reported that Byrnes, who had recently been named secretary of state, thought that it would be very difficult to do anything on the international level to control atomic energy. Believing that the Russians could not be trusted to keep their promises, Byrnes argued that the United States should continue its atomic research program in full force to stay ahead in the race for nuclear supremacy. Stimson returned to Washington on 4 September just as Byrnes was about to depart for a meeting in London with the British and Russian foreign ministers. After a brief conversation between the two secretaries, Stimson concluded that Byrnes "wished to have the implied threat of the bomb in his pocket during the conference."[117]

In a memorandum that he handed President Truman on

12 September, Stimson recommended that the United States should approach the Russians with a proposal to make an agreement limiting the use of the atomic bomb as an instrument of war and encouraging the development of nuclear energy for industrial and humanitarian purposes. Stimson acknowledged that a free interchange of scientific information might result in the Russians getting into the production of atomic bombs a little sooner than otherwise. But he argued that an attempt to maintain the Anglo-American monopoly would have far worse consequences. "For if we fail to approach them now and merely continue to negotiate with them, having this weapon rather ostentatiously on our hip, their suspicions and their distrust of our purposes and motives will increase," he warned the president. "Such a condition will almost certainly stimulate feverish activity on the part of the Soviets toward the development of this bomb in what will in effect be a secret armament race of a rather desperate character."[118]

Truman agreed with Stimson. The president gave a general indication of his ideas about atomic power on 18 September when he raised the subject at a cabinet meeting. Although technical information about methods of manufacturing atomic bombs should remain secret, he asserted, the United States should be willing to exchange theoretical knowledge concerning atomic energy.[119] Truman decided that the next cabinet meeting, to be held five days later, would be devoted entirely to a discussion of the issue. While Stimson and several others at the meeting advocated a free interchange of scientific information, Forrestal and a few others argued against sharing any information about nuclear power with the Russians. Forrestal suggested that the United States should exercise a trusteeship over the atomic bomb and use it on behalf of the United Nations.[120] In a message to Congress on 3 October, Truman articulated his own position. "The hope of civilization," he declared, "lies in international arrangements looking, if possible, to the renunciation of the use and development of the atomic bomb, and directing and encouraging the use of atomic energy and all future scientific information toward peaceful and humanitarian ends."[121]

President Truman discussed the subject a month later with British prime minister Clement Attlee and Canadian prime minister Mackenzie King. In a public announcement on 15 November 1945, the three leaders stated that their countries were prepared to share, on a reciprocal basis with other nations, detailed information concerning the industrial application of atomic energy as soon as effective safeguards against its use for destructive purposes could be devised. Thus, they proposed the establishment of a United Nations atomic energy commission that would make recommendations for the elimination of all weapons of mass destruction and for the creation of a worldwide system of inspection to prevent the secret production of such weapons.[122] But it eventually became clear that the Russians would not allow representatives from the United Nations to survey their raw materials or to inspect their industrial facilities. And when negotiations for the international control of atomic energy ultimately broke down, the United States and the Soviet Union became locked in a frightening race for nuclear supremacy.

While the postwar planners in Washington agreed on the need to maintain a powerful American military establishment to deter aggression and to protect the basic interests of the United States, they had engaged in two key debates that revealed their fundamental economic and strategic aims. First, President Roosevelt and his State Department advisers resisted the proposals of U.S. military leaders for the annexation of the Pacific islands taken from Japan. Their efforts eventually led to an arrangement that gave the United States exclusive control of these strategic outposts without provoking a territorial scramble that could have undermined their campaign to build a new international economic order devoted to the doctrine of equal opportunity. Second, President Truman agreed with Secretary of War Stimson on the need for collaboration among the great powers to develop atomic energy for commercial rather than military ends. His desire to work out an international accord that would prevent a nuclear arms race with the Russians grew out of long-standing American plans to create a new system of world security with the United States shouldering the major burden for policing the Western Hemisphere and the Far East while Great Britain and the Soviet Union assumed primary responsibility for keeping Germany from disturbing the peace in Europe.

NINE | REINTEGRATING GERMANY

The State Department, with firm backing from the War Department, aimed to transform Germany from an aggressive country into a peaceful member of the international community. Beyond their basic determination to prevent Germany from once again threatening the security of the world, U.S. diplomats looked forward to the industrial rehabilitation of Germany as an integral part of their plan to promote the economic reconstruction of Europe and the restoration of international trade. But President Roosevelt, along with Treasury Department officials, feared that the Germans might start a third world war if they were allowed to regain their industrial power. The predisposition of the president to keep Germany weak coincided with his intention to collaborate with Russia in policing the postwar world. Although they shared his desire to cooperate with the Soviet Union, however, State Department officials hoped that a strong and friendly Germany would serve as a counterweight if the Russians someday attempted to dominate Europe. Acting upon their advice after Roosevelt died, President Truman worked to reintegrate as much of Germany as possible into a liberal capitalist world system.

Several members of the Advisory Committee on Postwar Foreign Policy, from the very beginning of their deliberations about Germany, expressed serious misgivings about Russian ambitions. During a meeting of the Subcommittee on Political Problems on 11 April 1942, Isaiah Bowman suggested that the Soviet Union might try to establish a communist government in Germany. Norman H. Davis replied that he did not think this would happen "if Allied troops were actually inside Germany at the critical time because they would suppress uprisings." Assuming that the weeks immediately following the Nazi surrender would be the most critical period, James C. Dunn reasoned that "it would be necessary to occupy Germany as fast as possible to stop the process of deterioration." But Green H. Hackworth worried that, even if American and British soldiers could be rapidly deployed to prevent radical uprisings in western Germany, communist rebels might seize power in eastern Germany. "If a revolution does occur," he asked, "would not the Soviets attempt to gain control not only in the east, but attempt also to communize all the situation?" In a less pessimistic vein, Sumner Welles said that he had not seen any recent indications that Stalin wished to establish a communist regime in Germany.[1]

But Isaiah Bowman and Norman Davis, two key postwar planners with close ties to Secretary of State Cordell Hull, feared that the Russians might endeavor to extend their influence into other parts of Europe even if they made no effort to promote communism in Germany. When the political subcommittee met on 18 April 1942, Bowman argued against the dismemberment of Germany because a counterpoise to the Soviet Union might be necessary sometime after the war ended. "We would have nothing by which to oppose Russia if we proceeded to fragment Germany," he declared, "since the only effective future check on Russia would be a strong central European unit." Davis concurred. "We might in the future some day have to beg Germany on our knees to help us against Russia," he asserted, "and for that reason as well as others we must deal fairly with Germany in order not to give her any grievance." Davis said that Germany should be disarmed but not dismembered. "Our objective," he concluded, "is that Germany should be strong enough to be satisfied but not strong enough to be offensive."[2]

Bowman did not believe that it would be necessary either to dismember or to deindustrialize Germany to diminish its capacity to wage war. In a letter to a colleague on the political subcommittee on 5 May 1942, Bowman argued that it would be possible to render Germany powerless to make trouble without drastically reducing its "industrial strength." He suggested that once Germany was disarmed it would only be necessary to establish strict controls over the coal- and steel-producing areas of the Ruhr and Saar in the west and Silesia in the east.[3] During a political subcommittee discussion on 20 June, Bowman reiterated his argument that the imposition of tight controls over small areas vital to the production of arms would be sufficient to prevent Germany from starting another war. He added that any attempt to dismember the country would only invite some future Hitler to make national reunification his rallying cry. If the separate parts of a divided Germany tried to reunite, Bowman predicted, the American people would not be willing to fight to keep them apart.[4]

The members of the Subcommittee on Security Problems, working under the chairmanship of Norman Davis, quickly came to the same conclusion. But while they doubted that the American people would be willing to go to war to keep Germany dismembered, Davis and his colleagues believed that public opinion in the United States would support whatever military action might be required to keep Germany disarmed. They thought the only practicable method of preventing Germany from becoming a renewed threat to world peace would be to create an effective international security organization that would inspect basic industries in that nation and take immediate military steps if it started rearming.[5] In summarizing their views on 7 November 1942, Davis advanced three arguments against the partition of Germany. First, the American people would not support military measures that would be needed to prevent German reunification. Second, dismemberment would be unnecessary if international controls were effective in preventing German rearmament. Third, the Soviet Union would insist on policing one or two sections of a divided Germany, and this would have the undesirable consequence of "extending Russian control too far to the west."[6]

Furthermore, the members of the various subcommittees on postwar foreign policy feared that dismemberment of Germany would delay the economic reconstruction of Europe. Realizing that Germany had traditionally played an important commercial role on the European continent, they hoped it would once again exchange large quantities of industrial products for raw materials and food supplies from neighboring countries. Thus, the Subcommittee on Economic Reconstruction warned that any division of Germany would necessarily reduce its efficiency as a highly integrated unit of production.[7] The Subcommittee on Territorial Problems, chaired by Isaiah Bowman, likewise concluded that partition would impair the prosperity of Germany and thereby impede the economic recovery of the rest of Europe.[8] Reasoning in a similar fashion, Norman Davis and his associates on the security subcommittee opposed the deindustrialization as well as the dismemberment of Germany. While advocating "the control of key industries of potential military importance throughout the Reich," they warned that "the destruction of any industries for security reasons would retard European economic reconstruction."[9]

In addition to their desire to render Germany incapable of future aggression without hindering the postwar rehabilitation of Europe, the security subcommittee members wanted to prevent a repetition of what had happened after World War I when the Nazis claimed that their country had not been defeated on the battlefield but rather "stabbed in the back" by its political leaders, who had arranged the armistice. Thus, they drafted a surrender formula designed to convince the German people that their country had lost World War II. "On the assumption that the victory of the United Nations will be conclusive," the security subcommittee recommended on 21 May 1942, "unconditional surrender, rather than an armistice, should be sought from the principal enemy states." Norman Davis reported these views to President Roosevelt, and shortly before departing for the Casablanca Conference, Roosevelt told the Joint Chiefs of Staff that he intended to advance unconditional surrender as a basic Allied war aim.[10] After discussing the idea with Churchill at Casablanca, Roosevelt announced the principle at a press conference on 24 January 1943, when he called for the "unconditional surrender" of Germany and its Axis partners.[11]

Although he agreed with his State Department advisors that Germany must surrender absolutely, President Roosevelt did not share their views with respect to the question of dismemberment. The president revealed his ideas during a conversation at the White House on 14 March 1943 with Harry Hopkins and British foreign secretary Anthony Eden. After noting that it would be necessary to get a meeting of the minds with regard to the issue of partition, Eden said that from earlier conferences he had held with Russian leaders, he was sure that Stalin had a deep-seated distrust of the Germans and would insist that Germany be broken up into a number of states after the war. The president said in reply that he thought they should encourage any separatist movement that might spring up within Germany. When Hopkins asked what should be done if no separatist movement arose, both Roosevelt and Eden agreed that in any case Germany would have to be divided into several independent states. "The Prussians," they concluded, "cannot be permitted to dominate all Germany."[12]

In a follow-up conversation two days later, Under Secretary of State Welles discussed the future of Germany with Eden and Lord Halifax, the British ambassador in Washington. Welles maintained close ties with President Roosevelt, and he was the only ranking State Department official who remained convinced that nothing short of partition would end the German menace. When Eden indicated that his own thoughts were turning toward dismemberment, Welles said that it seemed clear to him that "the urge of militaristic Pan-Germanism was so potent a force as to make any united Germany a very dangerous factor in the world."[13] On the same day that Welles met with the two British diplomats, Hopkins called on Soviet ambassador Maxim Litvinov in an effort to learn about Russian war aims. After outlining what he believed Soviet territorial demands would be with respect to Europe, Litvinov said that he was sure Russia would like to see Germany dismembered. "Certainly Prussia should be cut off from the rest of Germany," he explained, "and probably two or three other additional states created."[14]

During a conversation in the White House the next day, Hopkins talked with Roosevelt and Hull about how Germany should be treated during the first six months after the war ended. Hopkins pointed out that the United States did not have an understanding with the British and the Russians concerning which Allied armies would be where in Germany and what kind of administration should be developed in the occupied country. "Unless we acted promptly and surely," he warned, "one of two things would happen—either Germany will go Communist or an out and out anarchic state would set in." To prevent either one from happening, Hopkins said that he thought the State Department should first work out an agreement with the British and then discuss their plan for handling Germany with the Russians. The president agreed that this procedure should be followed. "It will, obviously, be a much simpler matter if the British and American armies are heavily involved in France or Germany at the time of the collapse," Hopkins observed, "but we should work out a plan in case Germany collapses before we get to France."[15]

Although President Roosevelt and his State Department advisers hoped to conclude an agreement for the tripartite military occupation of Germany, they feared the establishment of Russian hegemony throughout Europe if only Soviet troops were present when Germany surrendered. Roosevelt therefore instructed the War Department to make contingency plans for the immediate dispatch of American and British troops to Germany in the event of a sudden collapse of Nazi military operations against the Russians.[16] In response to questions from the War Department, Charles E. Bohlen, a Soviet expert in the State Department, prepared a memorandum explaining how he and his colleagues viewed the situation. "It would certainly not be in the interest of the United States or of world peace in general if the Soviet Union completely overran and controlled Germany," Bohlen wrote on 24 June 1943, "since that would automatically mean the complete domination of the European continent by one power which could not fail to produce at least a potential danger to the non-European nations of the world." But, Bohlen noted, "this does not mean that we should oppose the *participation* of the Soviet Union in any United Nations occupation of German territory."[17]

American suspicions about the postwar aims of the Soviet Union increased a month later when the Russians organized the Free Germany Committee, comprised of captured Nazi soldiers and communist refugees who had fled from the Third Reich. In a radio broadcast on 20 July 1943, the committee urged the German people to get rid of Hitler and establish "a real national German Government with a strong democratic order."[18] Adm. William H. Standley, the U.S. ambassador in Moscow, was not greatly worried about the formation of the committee. He reported to the State Department that the Free German Committee had been created for the purpose of sowing the seeds of defeatism behind Nazi lines. But some State Department officials feared that the Russians might be planning to use the committee not simply for propaganda purposes during the war but also to establish Soviet control over Germany after the war.[19]

Amid escalating concerns about Russian intentions, American and British military experts drafted Plan RANKIN at the direction of the Anglo-American Combined Chiefs of Staff. The plan called for the rapid dispatch of American and British combat forces to the European continent if German military resistance either substantially weakened or completely collapsed. American and British leaders considered the contingency plan when they met in August 1943 at the first Quebec Conference. During a discussion at Quebec with Prime Minister Churchill and the Combined Chiefs of Staff, President Roosevelt indicated that he thought American and British troops should be "ready to get to Berlin as soon as the Russians did." The Combined Chiefs promptly approved RANKIN in principle and agreed that the emergency plan should be continuously reviewed as events unfolded in Europe.[20]

Growing apprehensions about Soviet ambitions likewise influenced the development of State Department planning for postwar Germany. In a document prepared on 23 September 1943, the Interdivisional Country Committee on Germany advocated the establishment of a broadly based democratic government to replace the Nazi regime. Assuming that the survival of such a government would require a tolerable living standard for the German people, the committee recommended that the United States sponsor a program aimed at promoting the economic recovery of Germany. The committee further recommended that the United States and Great Britain announce their support for the development of democracy in Germany after the war. "The recent appearance of a democratic German program under tacit Russian patronage," the committee warned, "might serve to give the Communists control of the democratic movement, and therefore establish a Russian hegemony in Germany, unless Anglo-American support encourages the moderates to participate and make the movement genuinely democratic."[21]

Hoping to prevent the spread of communism in Europe, Isaiah Bowman argued that the United States and Great Britain should reach an agreement with the Soviet Union in regard to the future of Germany. "If Russia arrives in Berlin in advance of Great Britain and the United States," he warned, "Russia will probably wish to make all Germany available to the new Moscow-sponsored German movement against Hitler." Thus, Bowman advocated a prior agreement with the Soviet Union concerning the terms of military occupation and the procedures for creating a democratic government in Germany. "If we act in opposition to Russia," he reasoned, "she can put arms into the hands of Germans, arrange an alliance, insist on a unitary Germany, and start the usual purge of Nazis and all other anti-Bolshevik elements." Bowman worried that, if the Americans and British failed to reach a firm understanding on Germany with the Soviets, the result would be the establishment of "Bolshevism throughout the length and breadth of Europe."[22]

Shortly before departing for the Foreign Ministers' Conference in Moscow, where he hoped to lay the groundwork for an agreement on Germany, Secretary of State Hull took several of his aides to the White House for a meeting with the president. Roosevelt stated categorically during their discussion, held on 5 October 1943, that he favored the partition of Germany into three or more states, completely sovereign but joined by a network of common services with respect to communications, transportation, and customs. When the assembled State Department officials argued that partition would have many undesirable consequences and that a customs union among independent German states would either prove unworkable or become a powerful instrument for their reunification, Roosevelt said that he thought they were inclined to exaggerate the problems that might result from dismemberment. Later in the discussion, however, the president remarked that the whole transition period would have to be one of trial and error. "It may well happen," he admitted, "that in practice we shall discover that partition, undertaken immediately after the war, may have to be abandoned."[23]

After the Moscow Conference opened on 19 October 1943, Hull handed the British and Russian foreign ministers a document setting forth ideas that might serve as the basis for a tripartite agreement on the postwar treatment of Germany. The U.S. proposal called for Germany's unconditional surrender, its occupation by Allied troops, the demobilization of its forces, the destruction of its armaments, the dissolution of the Nazi regime, and the establishment of a broadly based democratic government in Berlin.[24] During a detailed discussion of the proposal, Eden said that his government would encourage any separatist tendencies that might arise within Germany but that it was divided in its opinion on the desirability of dismembering that nation by forcible means. Hull likewise admitted that there were divergent views on the subject of dismemberment in the United States. Vyacheslav Molotov, the Russian foreign minister, indicated that there was a strong disposition in the Soviet Union in favor of partition but that his government felt it had to pay attention to American and British attitudes. After remarking that the Soviet Union would approve all measures that would render Germany harmless in the future, Molotov said that the U.S. proposal should be regarded as a minimum and not a maximum program.[25]

The Foreign Ministers' Conference gave President Roosevelt reason to believe that it would be possible to conclude an agreement for dealing with Germany on the basis of three-way responsibility. During a conversation with the Joint Chiefs of Staff on 19 November 1943 while en route to meet with Churchill and Stalin at Teheran, Roosevelt said that the Soviet government would offer no objection to the partition of Germany after the war. The president suggested that the Allied zones of military occupation would provide a logical basis for breaking up Germany into three different states. He indicated that American troops should occupy the northwestern part of Germany, while British and Russian forces occupied respectively the southern and eastern portions of Germany. Although he thought that Stalin would approve such an arrangement, Roosevelt believed that there would be a race for Berlin in the event of a sudden collapse of Germany resistance. "We may," he told the Joint Chiefs, "have to put the United States divisions into Berlin as soon as possible."[26]

The Big Three considered the question of German dismemberment when they met for the first time at Teheran. During a discussion on 1 December 1943, Roosevelt asked whether or not Germany should be split up, and Stalin promptly replied that he favored partition. Then Roosevelt proposed that Germany should be divided into five self-governing states and that three regions—the Kiel Canal/Hamburg area and the Ruhr and Saar basins—should be placed under some form of international control. As an alternative plan, Churchill suggested that Prussia should be separated from the rest of the Reich and that various southern provinces should be detached from Germany and made part of a Danubian confederation. Stalin was unenthusiastic about either proposal, but he indicated a preference for the plan that the president had advanced. Commenting that there would always be a strong urge on the part of the Germans to unite, Stalin said he thought that the whole purpose of any international security organization should be to prevent their unification by employing force if necessary. The discussion ended with an agreement that the European Advisory Commission, a tripartite body that had been established by the Moscow Conference, should study the issue of German dismemberment.[27]

Unaware that the Big Three had tentatively endorsed the principle of partition at Teheran, State Department officials began drafting plans for the extraction of reparations from a united Germany. They believed that Germany should be required to make reparation payments in the form of year-to-year deliveries of industrial products that would be used to speed the economic reconstruction of the rest of Europe. The Interdivisional Committee on Reparations thought that the industrial output of postwar Germany should be sufficient not only to provide the German people with a minimum standard of living but also to help rebuild the devastated economies of their neighbors. "The period over which reparation is to be paid," the committee argued on 14 December 1943, "should be fixed with a view to the impracticability of imposing heavy obligations on future generations." After the period of reparation payments ended, the committee hoped Germany would resume its traditional commercial role as a major importer of raw materials and exporter of industrial goods.[28]

State Department officials believed that the reintegration of Germany into a liberal international trading system would contribute to the preservation of world peace as well as to the restoration of European prosperity. In a memorandum prepared for his colleagues in the Division of European Affairs on 3 September 1943, John D. Hickerson argued that Germany should be permitted to develop a flourishing overseas trade after the war. "It seems to me most important," he explained, "that the German people receive a convincing demonstration that they can have a high standard of living, higher than perhaps they have ever had before, without any necessity of threatening their neighbors."[29] Along with their desire to give the German people the opportunity to enjoy prosperity by engaging in peaceful commerce, State Department officials also wanted to make Germany dependent upon foreign trade and thereby more vulnerable to a naval blockade and less able to wage a long war in the future. The Interdivisional Committee on Germany therefore concluded on 17 December 1943 that after the cessation of hostilities, Germany should reoccupy its "former position of prosperous dependence upon overseas markets and resources."[30]

As the State Department proceeded to draw up plans for the economic treatment of Germany, the British placed a proposal for the military occupation of Germany before the European Advisory Commission. The British plan, submitted on 14 January 1944, called for the establishment of three occupation zones in postwar Germany, with the Russians in the east, the Americans in the southwest, and the British in the northwest. Although Berlin was to lie deep inside the Soviet zone, it would be jointly occupied by American, British, and Russian troops. The Soviets quickly indicated that they approved the British proposal, but Roosevelt insisted that U.S. forces should occupy the northwestern zone. The president feared that American troops might be called upon to put down a revolution in France if they were assigned responsibility for policing southwestern Germany. After several months of argument, however, Roosevelt and Churchill finally resolved the issue: The United States would occupy southwestern Germany, but American forces would have access to ports in northwestern Germany so they could be evacuated without having to go through France.[31]

Long before Roosevelt and Churchill reached this agreement with respect to the allocation of occupation zones, the State and War Departments had commenced developing plans for the military administration of Germany. The State Department advocated the establishment of an Allied Control Council that would have authority over all three occupation zones in Germany. If a strong central ruling body in Berlin could agree on the administrative policies that the zonal military commanders would carry out, it would be possible to limit Russian influence and avoid German dismemberment. But the War Department wanted to ensure that the U.S. Army would be responsible for the execution of policies within the American zone. If the Allied military commanders had ultimate authority for implementing policies in their respective zones in Germany, it would be possible to minimize civilian interference with military government.[32]

Despite these differences concerning who would execute policies in Germany, the War Department approved a short-range military occupation program that was consistent with the long-range economic goals of the State Department. The Anglo-American Combined Chiefs of Staff issued a directive on 28 April 1944 for the establishment of military government in Germany prior to the defeat or surrender of Nazi forces. After explaining that the U.S. and British military commanders would hold supreme authority in areas occupied by their troops, the directive instructed them to destroy the Nazi regime and to restore normal living conditions among the civilian population as soon as possible. The American and British military commanders were to see that the systems of production and distribution of food were maintained in order to prevent disease and unrest in Germany. They were also to instruct German authorities to restore utilities to full working order and to maintain coal mines in full operation so far as transportation facilities would permit.[33]

While the Combined Chiefs of Staff were making preparations for the establishment of Allied military control in Germany, State Department officials continued to worry that Stalin intended to set up a communist regime in eastern Germany. They also feared that Stalin would insist upon the dismemberment of Germany and the destruction of its heavy industries in order to prevent the Germans from ever again being in a position to threaten the peace of Europe. When Under Secretary of State Edward R. Stettinius and several of his aides were in London discussing postwar questions with British diplomats in April 1944, they found that their counterparts in the Foreign Office were convinced that the Russians would be very tough in their attitude toward Germany after the termination of hostilities. "They feel," Stettinius reported to Secretary of State Hull, "that any argument that a stable peaceful Europe requires a prosperous stable Germany will fall on decidedly deaf Russian ears."[34]

But the State Department believed that Germany should be allowed to regain its industrial strength after its armaments were destroyed so that it would be able to contribute to the economic reconstruction of Europe and the expansion of world trade. During a meeting of the Executive Committee on Economic Foreign Policy on 9 June 1944, State Department representatives submitted two papers on postwar Germany. One document outlined the general objectives of U.S. economic policy toward Germany, while the other focused on the specific issue of reparations. After explaining that he and his State Department colleagues wanted to prohibit the manufacture of armaments but not restrict the development of heavy industry, Leroy D. Stinebower emphasized that "the documents envisage the return of Germany to a status of full equality in the family of nations." Assistant Secretary of State Dean G. Acheson noted that the economic control of Germany, as proposed in the two papers, would not serve as a substitute for a general system of world security. But he argued that such control would help prevent Germany "from attempting to rebuild a war economy and from causing trouble in Europe as it might otherwise be in a position to do."[35]

With Acheson serving as chairman, the Executive Committee on Economic Foreign Policy approved on 4 August 1945 a broad statement outlining American objectives concerning postwar Germany. The committee explained that U.S. economic policies toward Germany should buttress, but not replace, the security measures that would be primarily responsible for maintaining peace. "On the one hand, they are intended to provide necessary safeguards against resumption by Germany of its prewar policies of economic preparation for war. On the other hand, they are intended to create conditions under which Germany will contribute to the reconstruction of Europe and the development of a peaceful and expanding world economy." While advocating the prohibition of discriminatory trade practices and the elimination of German economic domination in Europe, the committee opposed the destruction of German industrial plants that were manufacturing implements of war if they could be converted to produce civilian goods for peacetime use.[36]

The executive committee emphasized that U.S. policy with respect to reparations should conform to the long-range objective of integrating Germany into an interdependent world economy. "The reparation program must be designed so as to make the maximum contribution to the rehabilitation of the countries injured by German aggression, while at the same time avoiding or minimizing possible harm in other directions." Besides arguing that reparation payments should be made predominantly, though not exclusively, in the form of scheduled deliveries of goods and services to claimant nations, the committee asserted that reparation obligations should be heavy, though not crushing, so that Germany could make a substantial contribution to the economic reconstruction of Europe. "The time period should be short (preferably five years but in no event more than ten) in order not to delay unduly a return to normal world trade and finance, and not to prejudice the establishment and maintenance of democratic government in Germany."[37]

Secretary of the Treasury Henry Morgenthau learned about these and other plans for postwar Germany during a trip to Europe with Harry Dexter White, his chief economic and financial adviser. White had attended the meetings of the Executive Committee on Economic Foreign Policy, and while aboard an airplane en route to London, he told Morgenthau about the State Department proposals for the economic treatment of Germany. Shortly after their arrival in England, Morgenthau found out that civil-affairs planners working under Gen. Dwight D. Eisenhower had produced the *Handbook for Military Government of Germany,* which called for the conversion of industrial plants from the manufacture of war materials to the production of consumer goods. Both the army handbook and the State Department recommendations seemed to Morgenthau to be too soft on Germany. While meeting with several officers from the U.S. embassy in London on 12 August 1944, Morgenthau argued that the only sure way to prevent Germany from starting another war would be to destroy its industrial facilities and turn it into an agricultural country.[38]

During a discussion at the British Foreign Office a few days later, Anthony Eden informed Morgenthau and White that the Big Three had made a tentative decision at Teheran to dismember Germany after the war. But the American and British representatives on the European Advisory Commission acknowledged during the course of the conversation that their technical staffs were preparing economic memoranda based upon the assumption that Germany would remain united. When the British representative argued that Germany could not produce reparations if it were fragmented, Morgenthau and Eden retorted that reparations should not be the main consideration in formulating a policy for postwar Germany. Then Eden warned that the Russians might pursue an independent policy toward Germany if the Americans and British opposed partition. After noting that some people hoped to have a powerful Germany as a bulwark against a possible threat from the Soviet Union, Eden said that he believed there would be greater danger from a strong Germany than from a strong Russia.[39]

Secretary Morgenthau decided to discuss the issue of dismemberment with President Roosevelt and Secretary of State Hull. On 18 August 1944, a day after his return to Washington, Morgenthau told Hull that nobody had made a study about the future of Germany along the lines that the Big Three had considered at Teheran. Hull said that he had never seen the minutes of the Teheran Conference, but Morgenthau received the impression that "if Hull got a directive on the dismemberment of Germany he would go to town."[40] The next day Morgenthau went to the White House to talk with Roosevelt. Morgenthau started the conversation by saying that Britain was broke, and the president seemed to be very concerned about it. Then the Treasury secretary raised the German question. When Morgenthau reiterated what he had said to Hull, the president indicated that he wanted to be harsh. "We have got to be tough with Germany and I mean the German people, not just the Nazis," Roosevelt declared. "You either have to castrate the German people or you have got to treat them in such a manner so they can't just go on reproducing people who want to continue the way they have in the past."[41]

Encouraged by his conversation with the president, Morgenthau decided that he should try to obtain support from Secretary of War Henry L. Stimson for a hard policy toward Germany. Morgenthau made an appointment to have lunch with Stimson on 23 August in his office in the War Department. During their discussion, Stimson said that he thought it would be necessary for the United States, Great Britain, and the Soviet Union to police Germany for at least twenty years or as long as the present generation of Germans remained in power. Stimson also indicated that he was very much interested in a proposal that had been made by Jean Monnet of the French Committee on National Liberation. Monnet believed that the Ruhr and the Saar should be placed under international control but that Germans should be permitted to continue working in the coal mines and steel factories of these regions. Hoping to convince Stimson that more-extreme measures would be needed to keep the Germans from waging another war, Morgenthau suggested "the possibility of removing all industry from Germany and simply reducing them to an agricultural population of small land owners."[42]

Realizing that Morgenthau had no responsibility in the foreign policy field, Stimson did not at first take his ideas very seriously. But he did want to impress upon the president the importance of making wise decisions with respect to Germany. During a luncheon at the White House on 25 August, Stimson warned Roosevelt that a policy aimed at dismembering and deindustrializing Germany "would starve her excess population of thirty million people." He then raised the possibility of placing the Ruhr and the Saar under some kind of international control as a way of preventing Germany from disturbing the peace again. Finally, Stimson suggested that, since Roosevelt could not himself do the studies necessary for making sound decisions, he ought to appoint a cabinet committee to prepare a plan for the treatment of Germany. Roosevelt complied. At a cabinet meeting immediately following this discussion, the president announced that he would appoint Hull, Stimson, and Morgenthau to a committee that would advise him on Germany. Roosevelt decided shortly thereafter that Hopkins should serve as his personal representative on the committee.[43]

After that meeting ended, Morgenthau sought to persuade the president that the army plans for the occupation of Germany were far too mild. He immediately sent Roosevelt a memorandum pointing out that the *Handbook for Military Government* called for the gradual rehabilitation of peacetime industry in Germany and the provision of sufficient food to furnish the German people a diet of two thousand calories per day.[44] In an angry note to Stimson the next day, Roosevelt demanded that the handbook be discarded. "It gives the impression that Germany is to be restored just as much as the Netherlands or Belgium," he complained. "It is of the utmost importance that every person in Germany should realize that this time Germany is a defeated nation." If the German people had to be fed at U.S. Army soup kitchens to keep body and soul together, Roosevelt suggested, it would be an experience they would never forget. The president asserted that too many people held the mistaken view that only the Nazi leaders, not the citizenry, were responsible for the war. "The German people as a whole," he concluded, "must have it driven home to them that the whole nation has been engaged in a lawless conspiracy against the decencies of modern civilization."[45]

On 31 August, Morgenthau ordered White and his aides in the Treasury Department to prepare as fast as possible studies based upon the assumption that the Ruhr and the Saar would be put completely out of business. He wanted them to consider how this would help Britain and Belgium and to estimate how long it would take until those two countries and Russia could produce enough coal and steel to take care of the customers that Germany used to supply.[46] The next day White sent Morgenthau a memorandum setting forth general principles for a post-surrender program for Germany. The document recommended that several areas of Germany should be given to other countries, that the Ruhr and the Kiel Canal should be turned into an international zone, and that the rest of the country should be divided into two independent states. "Your suggestion that the industry in the Ruhr and Saar Valley might be completely eliminated and the population moved elsewhere has not yet been incorporated," White informed Morgenthau, "inasmuch as we have not yet figured out what to do with the population there."[47]

While having an afternoon tea with Roosevelt and his wife on 2 September, Morgenthau gave the president the hastily drafted Treasury Department memorandum on Germany. Morgenthau said that, in his opinion, it did not go far enough in reducing the ability of the Germans to produce armaments for another war. "I would like to see the Ruhr completely dismantled, and the machinery given to those countries that might need it," he explained. "I realize this would put 18 or 20 million people out of work, but if we make an international zone out of it, it is just time before Germany will attempt an Anschluss." Morgenthau also argued that deindustrializing the Ruhr would have "a tremendous effect on England and Belgium, and ought to guarantee their prosperity for the next 20 years because their principle competition for their coal and steel came from the Ruhr." During the course of their conversation, Roosevelt told Morgenthau that the Germans should not be allowed to march or wear uniforms after the war in order to drive home the point that they had been defeated.[48]

At a morning discussion in the Treasury Department on 4 September, Morgenthau announced that the president especially liked the idea that by destroying the industries in the Ruhr, the United States could help put Britain back on its feet. White retorted that he and his aides were troubled about what to do with the four million Germans who would be thrown out of work and unable to support their families. But Morgenthau said he did not know any other way to stop Germany from starting another war than to shut down the Ruhr completely. "I don't care what happens to the population," he declared. "I would take every mine, every mill and factory, and wreck it." Morgenthau reiterated that his basic aim was to keep Germany from waging future wars and that he was not going to worry if millions of people were forced to move out of the Ruhr to find employment in some other part of the country. "We didn't put millions of people through gas chambers," he said in defense of his position. "They have asked for it." Morgenthau emphasized that American engineers should be sent to the Ruhr to strip its machinery, flood its mines, dynamite its factories, and thereby turn it into an area of "ghost towns."[49]

During another meeting in the Treasury Department that afternoon, White reported that he and his aides were reworking their memorandum on Germany in light of the instructions they had received from Morgenthau. White explained that the document would state very definitely that everything in the Ruhr should be moved or destroyed except homes and farms. But he warned that some of his assistants thought that there would be a terrific coal shortage in Europe for at least a year after the war ended and that it might be wise to permit the mines in the Ruhr to produce coal. Despite this plea for caution, Morgenthau insisted upon a complete shutdown of industrial production in the Ruhr. "Listen," he exclaimed, "you people aren't going to be able to budge me." After noting that coal provided the basis for chemical and steel production, Morgenthau repeated his main point. "I want to make Germany so impotent," he declared, "that she cannot forge the tools of war—another World War."[50]

But the State Department continued to oppose either the enforced dismemberment or the deindustrialization of Germany. "During the period of reparation the German people should be permitted to retain enough of their production to maintain a minimum prescribed standard of living," the Post-War Programs Committee explained in a report sent to Secretary of State Hull on 1 September. "Ultimately, Germany should be assimilated into the world economy without discrimination other than that necessary for security controls."[51] Realizing that President Roosevelt wanted to be hard on the German people, however, State Department officials drafted a punitive-sounding memorandum on Germany. Their suggested program advocated demilitarization and denazification while advising that no decision should be taken on the issue of partition. They argued that U.S. economic policy should be aimed at the achievement of three primary objectives: "(1) the standard of living of the German population shall be held down to subsistence levels; (2) German economic position of power in Europe must be eliminated; (3) German economic capacity must be converted in such manner that it will be so dependent upon imports and exports that Germany cannot by its own devices reconvert to war production."[52]

When the cabinet committee on Germany met in his office on 5 September, Hull presented the State Department paper and stressed the need for a tough policy. "We may have to sacrifice a little of our trade," he said, "in order to make the Germans suffer." As the discussion developed, Morgenthau argued that the Saar and the Ruhr should be stripped of all existing industries, while Hopkins said that he wanted to prohibit the manufacture of steel in these areas. But Stimson came out very emphatically against any program aimed at turning Germany into a barren farm country. "Well," he concluded, "I think that we can't solve the German problem except through Christianity and kindness."[53] After the meeting ended, Morgenthau asked Hopkins to arrange for the cabinet committee to go to the White House the next afternoon so that the president could hear how Stimson felt in his own words. "If I get a chance, I am going to tip off the Boss because I think he might blow right up in Stimson's face," Hopkins assured Morgenthau. "That would settle it, you know."[54]

After returning to the War Department, Stimson spent the rest of the day preparing a memorandum for the president. Stimson wrote that he was utterly opposed to the proposition that the great industrial centers of the Ruhr and the Saar, with their important deposits of coal and ore, should be totally transformed into an agricultural area. "The production of these materials from this region could not be sealed up and obliterated," he warned, "without manifestly causing a great dislocation to the trade upon which Europe has lived." Stimson also noted that as a result of the industrial activity in the Ruhr and the Saar, the German population had grown by about thirty million more people than had ever been supported by agricultural production alone. "I cannot conceive of turning such a gift of nature into a dust heap," he declared. "Nor can I agree that it should be one of our purposes to hold the German population 'to a subsistence level' if this means the edge of poverty." Such methods of economic oppression, Stimson concluded, would tend to breed war rather than prevent war.[55]

When the cabinet committee assembled at the White House on 6 September, Stimson pointed out that the Treasury Department was now calling for the complete deindustrialization of the Ruhr. He argued that the region's resources should be used for the economic reconstruction of Europe before dangerous social convulsions rocked the continent. After

Stimson finished talking, Roosevelt said that Great Britain would be in sore financial straits after the war, and he thought the raw materials of the Ruhr might be used to supply the British steel industry. Hopkins then said that he believed that all steelmaking in the Ruhr should be prohibited, and Morgenthau argued that the Ruhr steel mills should be dismantled without delay. But Hull gave Morgenthau no support, and Stimson felt that the meeting went off better than he had expected.[56]

Stimson learned the following morning that Morgenthau had persuaded the president to confer once again with the cabinet committee on Germany. At lunch an hour later, Stimson and Assistant Secretary of War John J. McCloy talked with Jean Monnet about his proposal to place the Ruhr and Saar areas under an international trusteeship in order to preserve their resources for the reconstruction of Europe. Stimson and Monnet agreed that Russia must be included as a trustee to maintain confidence among the three major powers, but McCloy wanted to exclude the Soviet Union. Hoping to gain a powerful ally in the battle against Morgenthau, Stimson invited Supreme Court justice Felix Frankfurter to come to his home for dinner that evening. Frankfurter responded with astonishment and disdain when Stimson explained that Morgenthau wanted to deindustrialize the Ruhr and shoot the Nazi leaders without giving them a fair trial. The justice immediately telephoned Hamilton Fish Armstrong, the influential editor of *Foreign Affairs*, to enlist his support against Morgenthau. During a conversation with Isaiah Bowman the next morning, Stimson was pleased to find that he agreed that the assets of the Ruhr should be placed under the trusteeship of the United States, Great Britain, and the Soviet Union.[57]

Discouraged because he feared that Roosevelt was moving toward the Stimson position, Morgenthau called upon Hull on 8 September to discuss what should be done to Germany. After explaining that he was too exhausted to accompany the president to the forthcoming Anglo-American conference in Quebec, Hull indicated that he did not want Roosevelt to take up the issue of partition or to discuss the economic future of Germany there. Despite his feeling that Hull was holding back his real thoughts, Morgenthau suggested that they should try to get the president to decide on a statement that would clarify his position regarding Germany. But Morgenthau did not tell Hull that his aides in the Treasury Department had prepared a briefing book for Roosevelt to take to the Quebec Conference.[58] In an effort to sell the president on the need for a harsh peace settlement, the book argued that a reduction in German industrial capacity would not only remove the danger of a third world war but would also enable Great Britain to recapture foreign markets that had been lost to Germany. Although British coal mines had passed their peak of productivity, it asserted that British coal production could be expanded to meet the needs of European countries formerly served by mines in the Ruhr.[59]

When he met with the cabinet committee on 9 September, Roosevelt said he would ask Morgenthau to come to Quebec if the British wanted to discuss their financial situation. Realizing that neither Roosevelt nor Morgenthau had much training in economics, Stimson distributed a memorandum that reiterated his main argument that the resources of the Ruhr must be preserved for the benefit of the entire European continent. It also advocated fair trials for Nazi leaders to make a record of German war crimes and the Allied effort to prevent their recurrence.[60] When Hopkins raised the question of partition, Roosevelt said he would go along with the idea of trusteeship for the Ruhr, the Saar, and the Kiel Canal, but he wanted the rest of Germany divided into three parts. Hull had very little to say, but Stimson stressed the importance of maintaining friendly relations with Russia. While looking through the briefing book that Morgenthau had presented, the president read aloud a headline claiming that Europe did not need a strong industrial Germany. "That is the first time I have seen anybody say that," he remarked. "All the economists disagree, but I agree with that." After arrogantly dismissing the view that Stimson had articulated, Roosevelt said that he believed Germany should be turned back into "an agricultural country."[61]

When the second Quebec Conference began on 11 September, it soon became clear that Churchill was not particularly concerned about Germany but that he was tremendously interested in obtaining lend-lease aid during the period between the end of hostilities in Europe and the defeat of Japan.[62] Roosevelt asked Morgenthau to come to Quebec on the second day of the meeting to help persuade the British to back his plan for deindustrializing Germany. At dinner on 13 September, Roosevelt asked Morgenthau to explain his proposal for dealing with the Ruhr to Churchill and Lord Cherwell, a close adviser to the prime minister. Churchill responded to the Treasury Department program with contempt, and he unleashed a flood of foul language against Morgenthau. After noting that another war could be prevented simply by prohibiting the production of arms in Germany, the prime minister said that he did not believe that Great Britain would benefit very much even if it inherited the German steel business. Lord Cherwell attempted to change the subject during a conversation with Morgenthau later that evening, but when Cherwell said he hoped they would soon have a talk about lend-lease assistance, Morgenthau replied that he would be glad to do so but only after they had had a discussion about Germany.[63]

Churchill quickly took the bait. During a discussion the next morning, he indicated his support for a program designed to deindustrialize Germany. Roosevelt and Morgenthau were pleased. Then Churchill said that the British hoped to continue receiving lend-lease materials after Germany surrendered so that they could begin rebuilding their export trade, and the president replied that he thought this would be proper. The prime minister expressed his profound gratitude the following day, 15 September, when Roosevelt signed an agreement to provide lend-lease aid to Great Britain until Japan capitulated. Churchill then dictated a document that became the final version of the Morgenthau Plan. According to his formulation, the metallurgical, chemical, and electrical industries in the Ruhr and the Saar would be closed down, and Germany would be converted "into a country primarily agricultural and pastoral in character." Foreign Secretary Eden, who had just arrived in Quebec, immediately registered his strong objection. "You can't do this," he told Churchill. "We have a lot of things in the works in London which are quite different." But Churchill had made up his mind. After warning Eden not to rush home to line up the war cabinet against him, Churchill joined with Roosevelt in initialing the memorandum on Germany.[64]

The Morgenthau Plan generated diametrically opposed reactions within the Roosevelt administration. While conferring with Morgenthau in Quebec, the president indicated that he hoped the plan to deindustrialize the Ruhr and the Saar would convince Stalin that the United States and Great Britain had no desire to rebuild Germany as a future counterweight against the Soviet Union. Morgenthau was jubilant, and when he returned to Washington told his aides that Quebec marked the highpoint in his long career in the Treasury Department. "I think it comes very rarely in a person's lifetime," he stated with great satisfaction, "that you can participate in a thing like this which, if carried through, will go a long way toward assuring the peace for many years."[65] But Stimson and Hull were horrified when they learned that Roosevelt had endorsed the Morgenthau Plan. "If ultimately carried out," Stimson predicted, "it as sure as fate will lay the seeds for another war in the next generation."[66] Besides his concerns about the effects on Germany, Hull was angry because Morgenthau had intruded into the affairs of the State Department and because Roosevelt had promised to continue lend-lease shipments to Great Britain without extracting a commitment from Churchill that his country would adopt a liberal commercial policy after the war.[67]

The president quickly began to backtrack under a barrage of criticism after the Morgenthau Plan had been leaked to the press.[68] During a conversation with Under Secretary of State Stettinius on 26 September, Hopkins acknowledged that Roosevelt had made a great blunder in discussing Germany at Quebec without having Hull at his side.[69] The next day Roosevelt called Stimson on the telephone to say that he did not intend to make Germany a purely agricultural country and that his underlying motive was to help the British regain their export trade so they could avoid bankruptcy after the war.[70] He gave the same explanation of his position in a memorandum sent to Hull two days later.[71] While lunching with Stimson at the White House on 3 October, Roosevelt said that Morgenthau had "pulled a boner." The president told Stimson once again that he had no intention of turning Germany into an agrarian state but that he wanted to save a portion of the resources of the Ruhr for the benefit of British industry. Then Stimson produced a copy of the Quebec memorandum. When Stimson read the sentences calling for the elimination of the basic industries in the Ruhr and the Saar and for the conversion of Germany into a pastoral country, the embarrassed president said that he had no idea how he could have initialed such a document.[72]

Nevertheless, while backing away from the Morgenthau Plan, Roosevelt sought to keep his options open with respect to the future of Germany. Thus, he approved a directive that had been drafted by representatives of the State, War, and Treasury Departments on 22 September regarding military government in Germany during the immediate postsurrender period. This document was punitively worded but filled with loopholes. While General Eisenhower was to take no steps to promote the economic rehabilitation of Germany, he was to assure the production of goods and services essential for the prevention of disease and disorder.[73] The State Department hoped to get Roosevelt to approve a memorandum, dated 29 September, recommending the destruction of only those German factories that could not be converted to civilian production and the imposition of reforms that would make Germany dependent upon world markets. But the president refused to be pinned down to any long-range program for the economic treatment of Germany. "I dislike making detailed plans," he wrote Hull on 20 October, "for a country which we do not yet occupy."[74]

After Hull entered the hospital for a long period of convalescence, Stettinius made a concerted effort to get Roosevelt to approve the State Department program for the economic treatment of Germany. The president admitted during a conversation with Stettinius on 10 November that he should not have used the word "agrarian" when discussing postwar Germany at Quebec.[75] The next day Stettinius sent Roosevelt a memorandum arguing that the Russians would oppose the Morgenthau Plan because "sweeping deindustrialization" would prevent Germany from making large reparation payments in the form of manufactured goods needed for the reconstruction and development of the Soviet Union.[76] But the president did not want to commit himself to support the State Department position on Germany. "There are many questions that must be left for future determination," he told Stettinius on 15 November, "since we have no way of knowing what we shall find in Germany."[77] Vacillating a week later, Roosevelt informed Stettinius that the State Department memorandum was basically in accord with his views but that he thought some of the wording could be a little clearer and wished to redraft the document himself.[78]

On 22 November, Stettinius sent the president another memorandum summarizing the State Department position. In it he advocated the conversion of the German economy to the production of civilian products needed for the maintenance of a minimum standard of living in Germany and for the payment of reparations to promote the reconstruction of the rest of Europe. "In the long run," he concluded, "we should look forward to a German economy geared into a liberal world economy on the basis of efficient specialization."[79] In a follow-up memorandum a week later, just prior to his appointment as secretary of state, Stettinius informed the president that British officials were in basic agreement with these views.[80] But Roosevelt still would not fully embrace the State Department position on Germany. "We should let her come back industrially to meet her own needs," he wrote Stettinius on 4 December, "but not to do any exporting" until "we know better how things are going to work out."[81] In a conversation with Stettinius three weeks later, Roosevelt said that he had not yet completed all his ideas with regard to the economic treatment of Germany but that he realized "the agrarian thing was absurd."[82]

President Roosevelt was actually leaning more toward the views of Bernard M. Baruch, an old friend and financial adviser, than those of either the State Department or the Treasury. During a meeting with top State Department officials on 3 January 1945, Baruch argued that Germany must never be allowed to recover industrially to such a degree that it could again be a menace to world peace. He advocated the imposition of long-term economic controls that would severely restrict German exports and thereby enable the United States and Great Britain to obtain vast new markets overseas. Baruch emphasized that he was particularly eager to help England by eliminating German competition in foreign markets. If the British would modernize their industries, he reasoned, they would be able to gain more by adopting liberal commercial policies than by employing discriminatory trade practices. After asserting that the Allies should be as stone hearted as necessary to prevent the Germans from starting another war, Baruch said that he would try to sell British leaders on the idea of modernizing their industries and taking over the export business that formally belonged to Germany.[83]

But Morgenthau continued to advocate his more drastic plan for turning Germany into a predominantly agrarian country. During a meeting with Secretary of State Stettinius and his top aides on 17 January 1945, Morgenthau argued that U.S. policy should aim at making Germany economically weak in order to accomplish two central objectives: "(1) to make Germany incapable of further aggression, and (2) to assure the Soviet Union that we do not look to Germany as a buffer and possible future ally against her." Then he charged that those who opposed his program were motivated largely by anti-Russian attitudes. When Stettinius replied that the State Department was thoroughly in accord with his goal of rendering Germany incapable of waging war, Morgenthau asserted that the State Department proposals for destroying the German armament and aircraft industries would not be adequate to achieve the desired result. When State Department officials explained that they wanted to impose economic controls that had the best chance of sustained enforcement, Morgenthau questioned whether their recommendations were "based on a genuine desire to make Germany incapable of further aggression."[84]

But while State Department officials did hope to cooperate with the Soviet Union in keeping Germany disarmed, they continued to harbor fears that the Russians might try to dominate Germany. Their apprehensions grew on the eve of the Yalta Conference as Soviet troops swept westward to the Oder River, only forty miles from Berlin, after Anglo-American forces had been pushed back during the Battle of the Bulge. Since neither the U.S. nor British government had formally approved the protocol worked out by the European Advisory Commission on zones of occupation in Germany, American diplomats worried that the Russians might soon cross their zone and then say that because no formal agreement existed, they would not restrict themselves to their area.

Stettinius discussed the urgency of the situation with Eden on 1 February 1945, and U.S. and British military leaders immediately approved the protocol on occupation zones. During a discussion with State Department officials three days later, Roosevelt said that he agreed on the importance of obtaining Russian approval of the protocol but that he thought the final tripartite agreement on the occupation should be left until the issue of a French zone had been settled.[85]

During their meetings in Yalta between 4 and 11 February, the Big Three discussed several issues concerning the postwar treatment of Germany. They quickly agreed that France should be given an occupation zone taken from those areas allotted to the United States and Great Britain. After considerable debate, they also agreed that France should be represented on the Allied Control Council to be headquartered in Berlin. But the Big Three could not decide if Germany should be divided into multiple states. While Stalin pressed for a commitment to partition Germany, Churchill recommended that the subject should be left for later consideration. Roosevelt sided with Churchill. In the end the Big Three could only agree that they would reserve the right to dismember Germany if they deemed it necessary for the future peace and security of the world. They accordingly decided to establish a special committee that would do nothing except study the procedure that might be used in postwar partitioning. By the time Germany surrendered on 8 May, it had become evident that none of the great powers wanted to dismember the defeated nation.[86]

During their deliberations at Yalta, the Big Three also wrestled with the reparations question. The Russians proposed that the Allies should obtain reparations from Germany in two ways: by dismantling its industrial establishments and removing 80 percent of the heavy equipment; and by demanding annual deliveries of goods produced in German factories and mines. In addition, they suggested that the total amount of reparations should be fixed at $20 billion and that the share going to the Soviet Union should not be less than $10 billion. But Churchill argued that it would be impossible to extract such a large sum without causing starvation in Germany. Recalling that huge American loans had financed German reparation payments after the last war, Roosevelt asserted that the United States would not repeat that mistake. The president then said that the Soviet Union should obtain reparations in the form of material and labor needed for postwar reconstruction, though not to the extent that Germany would become a financial burden on other countries. Although he believed the Russian proposal was relatively moderate,

Roosevelt would not commit himself to support a specific reparations figure. Thus, he simply agreed that the Allied Reparations Commission, to be set up in Moscow, "should take in its initial studies as a basis for discussion" the Soviet proposal.[87]

After Roosevelt asked Stettinius to assume responsibility for implementing the Yalta decisions, the State Department prepared a general directive on U.S. policy toward Germany. The document not only recommended that the Allied Control Council should have paramount authority throughout Germany but also proposed that the German people should produce enough industrial goods to maintain a minimum standard of living and to make substantial reparation payments. Although the president approved the general policy statement on 14 March, both Stimson and Morgenthau registered strong objections the next day when they were given an opportunity to examine the text. Stimson disliked the directive because it gave the Allied Control Council authority over the individual military commanders in their separate occupation zones. Morgenthau protested against the paper because it opened the way for the economic rehabilitation of Germany. When Morgenthau complained to the president on 20 March, Roosevelt told his old friend that he did not remember signing the directive and that it would have to be revised.[88]

Roosevelt met with State and War Department officials two days later to discuss the directive without any Treasury representative present. After acknowledging that he had made a mistake at Quebec, the president blamed Churchill for using the word "pastoral" in connection with Germany. He indicated that the German armaments industry should be destroyed but that factories making civilian goods for domestic consumption should not be eliminated. So long as the Germans used their industries to satisfy their own internal needs, Roosevelt said that he would let them manufacture locomotives, machine tools, and many other such products. "I want to have German industry maintained to the fullest extent necessary to maintain the Germans so that we don't have the burden of taking care of them," he explained. "I think that means a very substantial degree of preservation of the German industry, but I am very leery of their exports."[89] After the meeting ended, State and War Department officials drafted another document that Treasury officials agreed to support since its recommendations for dealing with Germany were subject to varying interpretations. The president approved the new directive on 24 March, even though it differed very little from the policy statement he had canceled only four days earlier.[90]

After President Roosevelt died on 12 April 1945, the State and War

Departments joined forces in a final battle to bury the Morgenthau Plan. They were pleased to find that President Truman had no desire to prevent either the revival of German industrial strength or the reintegration of Germany into a liberal world trading system. During a conversation with the new president on 16 May, Stimson warned that it would be a grave mistake to prohibit the restoration of German industry because there were approximately thirty million more people living in Germany than could be supported by agriculture alone. "Deprive her permanently of her weapons, her General Staff, and perhaps her entire army," he advised. "But do not deprive her of the means of building up ultimately a contented Germany interested in following non-militaristic methods of civilization."[91] Agreeing that it would be unwise to impose punitive measures that might drive the Germans to embark upon a course of conquest to satisfy their economic needs, Truman made it clear that he was strongly opposed to the Treasury Department proposal to convert Germany into an agrarian nation.[92]

His desire to discard the Morgenthau Plan was reinforced by growing fears that a coal shortage during the next winter might provoke widespread disturbances and communist upheavals in Western Europe. After State Department officials warned him that adequate quantities of coal for the region could not be obtained from any source other than Germany, Truman decided on 24 June to send Churchill a message explaining the urgency of the situation. "From all the reports which reach me," he cabled, "I believe that without immediate concentration on the production of German coal we will have turmoil and unrest in the very areas of Western Europe on which the whole stability of the continent depends." Truman indicated that he intended to direct General Eisenhower to take all steps necessary in his occupation zone in Germany to increase coal production and to make the maximum quantities available for export to other European nations. He asked Churchill to send a similar directive to the military commander in the British occupation zone, which included the Ruhr, and on the same day decided to ask French leaders to instruct their zonal commander to take vigorous action in the Saar to increase the production of coal for export.[93]

But American policymakers realized that it would not be possible for Germany to export large amounts of coal to countries in Western Europe unless the value of reparation shipments to Russia were far below the $10 billion level that Stalin had requested at Yalta. When the Allied Reparations Commission began meeting in Moscow in June 1945, therefore, the Soviet representatives encountered stiff U.S. resistance as they renewed their demand for $10 billion in reparations from Germany. Edwin W. Pauley, the head of the American delegation, insisted that the United States would not agree to any specific reparations figure until more was known about the German economy. Determined that the United States would not once again finance reparation shipments from Germany, Pauley argued that the first charge placed on German exports should be levied to pay for essential imports. But the Russians countered that Germany should pay reparations to the countries it had damaged during the war before using money received from exports to pay for imports. By early July 1945, the reparations commission had reached an impasse.[94]

President Truman and his State Department advisers wanted to stimulate German coal production and limit reparation transfers without arousing Russian apprehensions that the Western powers aimed to rearm Germany in order to contain the Soviet Union. On the one hand, their determination to prevent communist upheavals and to promote economic recovery in Western Europe led them to shelve earlier proposals to separate the Ruhr from the rest of Germany and place it under international supervision. They worried that Ruhr industries would be destroyed if the Russians were allowed to participate in any scheme for the international control of the region.[95] On the other hand, their desire to convince Stalin that he had no reason to fear an attack from the West prompted them to consider the possibility of concluding a formal treaty that would commit all the major powers to use force to assure the permanent demilitarization of Germany. James F. Byrnes, the newly appointed secretary of state, told his colleagues on 4 July that he thought such a treaty would "do much to counteract the argument so frequently used by Stalin that the most important factor in Russian foreign relations is security."[96]

As the great powers made preparations for their final wartime conference, to be held at Potsdam during July 1945, President Truman looked primarily to Secretary of State Byrnes and secondarily to Secretary of War Stimson for advice on how to handle the crucial German question. Morgenthau realized that his plan to deindustrialize Germany was dead after Truman turned down his request to participate in the conference. The isolated Treasury secretary resigned in protest, and the president accepted his resignation without hesitation. When Truman and Byrnes arrived at Potsdam, they were determined to prevent the Soviet Union from collecting reparations from the U.S. and British occupation zones until German mines had produced enough coal to meet the urgent needs of Western Europe. Truman and Byrnes hoped that the Russians would eventually agree to support the application of the first-charge principle throughout Germany and that the whole country could then be treated as a single economic unit.[97]

As the negotiations at Potsdam got underway, the Americans and Russians sought to resolve their differences with respect to Germany. Secretary of State Byrnes firmly rejected a Russian proposal to internationalize the Ruhr and place its industries under the direct control of the four occupying powers. Byrnes also rebuffed Soviet demands for a fixed amount of reparation payments from Germany. After several days of debate, Byrnes proposed that each occupying power should satisfy their claims against Germany by extracting reparations from their own zone. He persuaded the Russians to agree to his proposal by offering them a chance to obtain at least some reparations from the western zones. According to the final protocol of the conference, the Soviet Union would receive from the Anglo-American zones 10 percent of the industrial equipment that would not be needed to sustain a peacetime economy in Germany and another 15 percent of such material in exchange for an equivalent value of food, coal, or other commodities from the Russian zone. The U.S. and British military commanders would have the ultimate authority in determining how much industrial equipment would be available for reparation deliveries.[98]

From the outset of their deliberations, the postwar planners in the State Department had wanted Germany to remain united, to regain its industrial strength, and to resume its role as a peaceful and prosperous member of the international community. They hoped that Germany would not only contribute to the economic reconstruction of Europe and the restoration of world trade but also would serve as a counterweight against any expansion of Soviet influence on the European continent. Although President Roosevelt committed himself to the dismemberment and deindustrialization of Germany, he quickly backtracked in the face of powerful opposition from both the State and War Departments. The architects of globalism at State emerged triumphant over Morgenthau when President Truman endorsed their plans for postwar Germany. Despite their desire to see the entire nation reintegrated into a liberal capitalist world system, however, the reparations deal concluded at Potsdam paved the way for the eventual division of Germany into two states.

TEN | STABILIZING EAST ASIA

American postwar planners began drafting blueprints for the establishment of a liberal capitalist order in East Asia shortly after the Japanese attack on Pearl Harbor. First and foremost, U.S. policymakers were determined to prevent Japan from once again disturbing the peace in the Pacific. Thus, they aimed to disarm Japan, to liquidate its overseas empire, and to occupy its home islands until the Japanese organized a representative government with peaceful aspirations. Then Japan would eventually be readmitted into the family of nations and allowed to trade on an equal basis with the rest of the world. Secondly, American leaders hoped that China would emerge from the war as a stable, united, and democratic country devoted to the doctrine of equal commercial opportunity. Thus, they intended to promote industrial development in China and to support the Nationalist government in Chungking. Although officials in Washington feared that China would plunge into a civil war that the Communist forces would ultimately win, they continued to hope that China would become a vast market for American products and an important military power to help police the Far East.

As State Department officials began planning for the postwar world, their ideas about Japan ran parallel to their thoughts about Germany. They assumed that it would be necessary to disarm the two Axis powers and to establish an international security system that would prevent either one from starting another war. Realizing that both aggressor nations lacked an adequate natural-resource base to sustain their dense urban populations, State Department planners concluded that Japan as well as Germany should be allowed to export manufactured goods in order to obtain foreign exchange needed to pay for essential imports of food and raw materials. In a memorandum prepared on 20 February 1942, Joseph M. Jones of the Division of Special Research argued that the Japanese must be permitted to solve their economic problems by engaging in peaceful commerce so that they would not feel compelled to embark upon a renewed program of military conquest. "Unless provision is made in this manner for Japan's fundamental economic needs, and an outlet thus provided for the energies and enterprise of the Japanese people," he warned, "there can be no enduring basis for peace in the Far East regardless of the system of general security which may be established."[1]

Hugh Borton, a member of the Division of Political Studies and a former professor of Japanese history at Columbia University, agreed that Japan must be reintegrated into a liberal capitalist world system. Rather than imposing surrender terms that would lead to the impoverishment of its people and sow the seeds for another war in the Pacific, Borton asserted on 27 September 1943, the Allied powers should give Japan a chance to maintain a decent standard of living and to develop a healthy political structure. He noted that during the 1920s, a civilian regime in Japan had sought to achieve domestic prosperity by advocating peaceful overseas commercial expansion. Borton thought that, after the Japanese program of territorial conquest had met with complete defeat, civilian leaders in Tokyo would be eager to guide their nation along a peaceful course as they had done before militarists took control. In a memorandum prepared on 6 October 1943, Borton specifically mentioned several prewar leaders, with close ties to the Throne, who might once again head a civilian regime that would place effective checks on the power of the military. "The institution of the Emperor is likely to be one of the more stable elements of postwar Japan," he concluded. "As such, it may be a valuable factor in the establishment of a stable and moderate postwar government."[2]

Joseph C. Grew, who had served as U.S. ambassador in Tokyo for ten years prior to the Pearl Harbor attack, had set forth similar views a week earlier in a memorandum for Stanley K. Hornbeck, the State Department political advisor on Far Eastern affairs. "When, through defeat in war and postwar measures, the Japanese military caste and cult have been rendered powerless," he wrote Hornbeck, "elements will be found in Japan who will welcome and who will cooperate in the building of a new and nonmilitary national structure, so long as they are not denied hope for the future." Grew argued that the institution of the Throne, as distinct from the rule of the current emperor, should be preserved in order to prevent chaos. "I believe," he declared, "that as a symbol it can be made to serve as a cornerstone for healthy and peaceful internal growth as it did for the erstwhile cult of militarism." But Grew warned that not even the wisest and most temperate political treatment of Japan could be expected to yield desirable results "if economic disabilities of a severe character are to be imposed on her."[3]

While agreeing that Japan should have access to raw materials and commodity markets around the world, the members of the Advisory Committee on Postwar Foreign Policy believed that its overseas empire must be dismantled in order to safeguard the future peace of the Pacific. During a meeting of the Subcommittee on Political Problems on 1 August 1942, Under Secretary of State Sumner Welles asserted that "Japan should not start off the new era with territories obtained through its aggressive action." His colleagues quickly agreed that Japan should be deprived of Formosa, Korea, and the mandated islands in the Pacific. Some were inclined to let the Japanese keep Okinawa and the Kurile Islands. But no one dissented when Stanley Hornbeck suggested that the southern part of Sakhalin, which Japan had acquired in 1905 as a result of a war with Russia, should be transferred to the Soviet Union.[4] In a study prepared for the Council on Foreign Relations on 29 November 1943, Hanson W. Baldwin articulated the prevailing American view toward Japan. "She must be totally and completely disarmed," he emphasized. "And those territories outside the main Japanese islands which she has acquired by force in the course of decades of aggression—territories which have added greatly to her military strength—must be amputated from the Japanese Empire."[5]

President Roosevelt had come to the same conclusion. During a conversation with British foreign secretary Anthony Eden on 27 March 1943, Roosevelt said that Korea and the Japanese mandates in the Pacific should be placed under the trusteeship of the United Nations. He added that Manchuria and Formosa should be returned to China, while southern Sakhalin should be given back to Russia.[6] These ideas became the basis of the Cairo Declaration, issued by Roosevelt, Churchill, and Chiang Kai-shek on 1 December 1943 with the full approval of Stalin. The statement asserted that "Japan shall be stripped of all the islands in the Pacific which she has seized or occupied since the beginning of the First World War in 1914, and that all the territories Japan has stolen from the Chinese, such as Manchuria, Formosa and the Pescadores, shall be restored to the Republic of China." The statement also promised that Japan would be "expelled from all other territories which she has taken by violence and greed." Although the declaration did not specifically mention southern Sakhalin or the Kuriles, it did pledge that "in due course Korea shall become free and independent."[7]

After the Cairo Declaration made it clear that the Japanese would be confined to their home islands following the Allied victory, the State Department proceeded to develop plans to keep Japan from once again menacing the peace of the Pacific. The Interdivisional Area Committee on the Far East prepared several papers on the future of Japan for the Post-War Programs Committee. In a memorandum completed on 13 March

1944, the Area Committee on the Far East recommended that the military occupation of the home islands should be predicated upon three basic principles. First, Japan should be occupied and administered by those Allied military forces, including Asian units, that had taken part in the fighting in the Pacific. Second, although the occupation forces were to be multinational, Japan should not be divided into distinct zones that would be administered separately by different national contingents. Third, while Allied troops should help shoulder the burden of occupying Japan, Americans should play the predominant role in administering the country.[8]

To help the State Department decide what should be done with regard to the emperor, Hugh Borton and Earle Dickover of the Far East area committee drafted two opposing papers on the subject. Dickover argued in his memorandum that the retention and use of the emperor for the purpose of administering Japan would contribute to the perpetuation of an undemocratic institution. Since peace in the Pacific could best be assured by creating a truly democratic Japan, Dickover reasoned, the Allies should work toward the eventual destruction of the imperial system. But in his memorandum, Borton recommended that the emperor should be permitted to delegate administrative duties to subordinate officials who would be willing to serve directly under the supervision of Allied civil affairs officers. Borton added that the emperor should be placed under protective custody but that Allied military authorities should cease using him as a political instrument if a substantial movement developed in Japan for the abolition of the imperial system.[9] Although the Post-War Programs Committee approved the Borton paper with slight modifications on 9 May 1944, the issue of whether or not the emperor system should be retained on a permanent basis remained open.[10]

That same day the Far East area committee approved a document, also drafted by Hugh Borton, that looked forward to the reintegration of Japan into an interdependent world economy. Borton argued that the Japanese people would be ready to turn to new leaders after they realized that their military leaders had led them to destruction and disgrace. "There exists a fairly substantial body of moderate political influence," he asserted, "which has been rigidly suppressed and silenced since 1931 but which it is believed can be encouraged and made the nucleus of a liberal movement." Prominent among those who Borton thought might provide moderate leadership in postwar Japan were the statesmen who had been proponents of peace during the 1920s and the businessmen who had based their prosperity on world trade rather than upon an exclusive sphere of economic influence in East Asia.[11] His conclusion that Japan should be permitted to share "in the world economy on a reasonable basis" restated a fundamental view that the Post-War Programs Committee had recently adopted.[12]

American policymakers believed that it would be vitally important for Japan to trade with other countries after the war. "During the 250 years that the Japanese remained in seclusion, the population of their country remained stationary at about 30,000,000 for the reason that the country could not support a larger population on the basis of an agricultural economy," Joseph Grew explained on 27 January 1945 in a letter written shortly after he became under secretary of state. "When commercial relations were established with other countries in 1858, new industries were established, and by processing to a large extent the goods produced in other countries and not obtainable in Japan, industrial employment could be provided for an increasing number of people, so that today the population is over 70,000,000." Then Grew put his finger on the crux of the problem. "The country does not provide sufficient food to feed that many people," he wrote, "and without foreign trade it would be impossible for millions of people to have any form of livelihood."[13] During a discussion with Secretary of War Henry L. Stimson twelve days later, Grew warned that half the population would starve unless Japan was permitted to engage in international trade. Stimson agreed. After comparing the potential for agricultural production in Germany and Japan, Stimson concluded that "Japan's situation is much worse and more acute."[14]

While they envisioned postwar Japan as a demilitarized country stripped of its empire but free to trade with others, President Roosevelt and his State Department advisers were determined to build up China to be the principal stabilizing factor in the Far East. Cordell Hull later recalled that, while serving as secretary of state during most of the war, he had never faltered in his belief that the United States should do everything possible to assist China to become strong and stable. "It was obvious to me that Japan would disappear as a great Oriental power for a long time to come," Hull explained. "Therefore, the only major strictly Oriental power would be China. The United States, Britain, and Russia were also Pacific powers, but the greater interests of each were elsewhere. Consequently, if there was ever to be stability in the Far East, it had to be assured with China at the center of any arrangement that was made."[15] During a conversation at the White House on 29 May 1942 with Soviet foreign minister Vyacheslav Molotov, Roosevelt expressed his hope that China would emerge from the war as one of the four great powers that would act as "the policemen of the world."[16] Molotov informed Roosevelt a few days later that Stalin was in full accord with his ideas about establishing a postwar security system with "the participation of at least Great Britain, the United States, the Soviet Union, and possibly China."[17]

President Roosevelt reiterated his hope that China would assume the responsibilities of a great power when Anthony Eden came to Washington to discuss postwar issues. During a conference at the White House on 22 March 1943, Roosevelt told the British foreign secretary that he thought "China might become a very useful power in the Far East to help police Japan" and that he wanted "to strengthen China in every possible way." But Eden said that he doubted "if China could stabilize herself" and that he thought it might have "to go through a revolution after the war." The president was not pleased. While talking with Eden five days later about the need for a postwar security organization, Roosevelt said that "the real decisions should be made by the United States, Great Britain, Russia, and China" because for many years to come, these four powers would have "to police the world." Then the president told his British guest that "China, in any serious conflict of policy with Russia, would undoubtedly line up on our side."[18]

But President Roosevelt did not, of course, mention to Eden that he had good reason to believe China would support the United States in any conflict with Great Britain concerning the colonial question in Asia. Shortly after the Japanese attack on Pearl Harbor, Roosevelt had privately urged Prime Minister Churchill that the British should take immediate steps to permit the peaceful evolution of self-government in India, and in February 1942 Generalissimo Chiang Kai-shek had delivered a public address calling upon Great Britain to grant India "real political power" without undue delay. Roosevelt and his State Department advisers soon began formulating plans to place various dependent territories under some form of international trusteeship until they were prepared for independent nationhood. Churchill feared that the Chinese would provide strong backing for U.S. efforts to decolonize Asia. Writing to Eden in October 1942, Churchill warned that after the war China would vote on the side of the United States "in any attempt to liquidate the British Overseas Empire."[19]

President Roosevelt soon began to realize that he would have a hard time getting Churchill to treat China as a great power. During the Anglo-American conference held at Quebec in August 1943, the British prime minister referred to the Chinese as "pigtails" on numerous occasions after

Roosevelt had suggested that China should be brought within the circle of great powers. Churchill did this so frequently and so scornfully that the president finally appealed to Eden. "Anthony," he admonished, "you must get Winston to understand that in 25 years China will be powerful and will sweep us out of the East unless we begin now to treat her as an equal and win her permanent friendship."[20] In a letter that he sent a few months later to Adm. Louis Mountbatten, the Supreme Allied Commander in Southeast Asia, Roosevelt reiterated his belief in the importance of having friendly relations with 425 million Chinese after the war. "They will be very useful twenty-five or fifty years hence," he wrote the British admiral, "even though China cannot contribute much military or naval support for the moment."[21]

President Roosevelt and Secretary of State Hull sought Russian as well as British support for their plan to include China among the great powers that would police the postwar world. In October 1943 Hull reported from the Moscow Foreign Ministers' Conference that Eden and Molotov had agreed to allow a Chinese representative to join them in signing a declaration that the four major powers would establish an international security organization to preserve world peace. Roosevelt was elated.[22] He soon departed for the Teheran Conference with the hope that Stalin would approve his "Four Policemen" concept. During a private discussion at Teheran on 29 November 1943, however, Stalin told Roosevelt that he did not believe China would be very strong when the war ended. He also expressed the opinion that the small nations of Europe would be resentful if China played a prominent role in postwar security arrangements. But the president refused to abandon his position. Although he realized the weakness of China at the present time, Roosevelt explained, he was thinking far into the future. "China was a nation of 400 million people," he emphasized, "and it was better to have them as friends rather than as a potential source of trouble."[23]

President Roosevelt and his State Department advisers did not want anything to jeopardize the maintenance of friendly relations with China after the war. Viewing the British possession of Hong Kong as a symbol of the old system of Western imperialism that should be ended, Roosevelt hoped that Churchill would agree to return the territory to China and that Chiang Kai-shek, the head of the Nationalist government in Chungking, would make Hong Kong a free port open to the commerce of all nations. But Churchill specifically mentioned Hong Kong when he declared during a meeting in Teheran on 29 November 1943 that nothing would be taken away from Britain without a war.[24] While Roosevelt encountered this stiff resistance to his plan for Hong Kong, the State Department succeeded in persuading Congress to repeal the law that prohibited Chinese immigration. The new act, passed on 17 December 1943, would permit only 105 Chinese immigrants to enter the United States each year. Yet American leaders believed that even this small step away from an exclusionary policy that prevented any Chinese immigrants from entering the United States would make it easier to maintain friendly relations with China.[25]

Government officials and business spokesmen in the United States wanted to have good relations with postwar China for economic as well as strategic reasons. If their dreams about the future of the Far East were to come true, China would become not only an important military ally of the United States but also a huge market for American products. An article published in *Fortune* magazine in May 1941 looked forward to the investment of American capital after the war both to promote industrial development in China and to persuade its government to adopt liberal commercial principles. "With a population of more than 400 million China is the biggest single potential market in the world," the writer declared. "The main point to insist upon, in our dealings with China, is that she does not carry state control to the point of closing her markets to competition."[26] Policymakers in Washington concurred. Eager to help a wartime ally and to prepare the ground for a lucrative postwar commercial relationship, the United States decided to loan China a half-billion dollars. The loan agreement, signed on 21 March 1942, committed the two nations to conduct "mutually advantageous economic and financial relations" after the war.[27]

But American statesmen and businessmen had reason to worry that the reactionary Chiang Kai-shek regime might pursue a rigid policy of economic nationalism in the postwar era. During the spring of 1943, Chiang published two books, *China's Destiny* and *China's Economic Theory,* which expressed antiforeign and even anticapitalist sentiments. The U.S. embassy in Chungking immediately translated the volumes and dispatched summaries of their contents to Washington. State Department officials feared that Chiang intended to close the doors of China to American trade and investment.[28] Their apprehension grew when Ambassador Clarence E. Gauss warned Secretary Hull on 9 December 1943 that "in discussions for the formulation of plans for a new and powerful China the tendency is distinctly toward a closed economy designed solely for Chinese benefit and definitely away from those liberal principles" that were needed to lay the

foundation for a "mutually beneficial world economy." Gauss strongly recommended that "we should without further delay quietly put China on
notice as to our expectations before she adopts policies which for reasons
of oriental face she may not later be willing to alter."[29]

Wishing to foster close economic relations with China, President
Roosevelt sent Donald M. Nelson, the chairman of the War Production
Board and the former vice president of Sears, on a special mission to China.
He instructed Nelson not only to help organize Chinese war production
but also to study what kind of financial assistance would be needed to promote Chinese industrial development after the defeat of Japan.[30] Stopping
in Moscow on his way to Chungking, Nelson explained to Molotov on
31 August 1944 that Roosevelt believed that industry should be built up in
China so that nation could eventually "take care of its own civilian requirements and those in other areas formerly supplied by Japan."[31] Nelson proceeded to China with that objective in mind. In his final report to the
president on 20 December 1944, Nelson emphasized that China had the
capacity and the desire to develop industrially with economic aid from the
United States. "If that aid is realistically planned, and if financial arrangements are put on a sound business basis, China should soon after the war
begin to replace Japan as the leading industrial nation of the Orient," he
predicted. "In that event, a market of enormous size should progressively
open up for American export industries."[32]

Many government officials and military officers shared his desire to
turn China into a vast postwar market for American products. In an
address delivered on 17 March 1945, Foreign Economic Administrator
Leo T. Crowely argued the United States should help China develop its
great industrial potential. "An almost untapped market for our goods," he
declared, "lies on the other side of the world."[33] It would be important to
have good relations with China after the war, Congressman Walter H. Judd
of Minnesota explained, because in order to defeat the Axis powers, the
United States was producing far more goods than the American people
could purchase. "A free Orient," he asserted, "will become a huge market."[34] Adm. Milton Miles, the head of the U.S. Naval Intelligence unit in
China, agreed. Miles told his staff on 29 May 1945 that the United States
must be prepared to defeat Great Britain in a postwar contest for commercial supremacy in China, a country that he believed would be the largest
market in the world. "It is our job to look at the commercial field we will
have to protect," he exclaimed. "Our biggest competitor will be England."[35]

Seeking to outmaneuver their British rivals, several large American corporations had already established the China-America Council of Commerce and Industry. Its founding members included Coca-Cola, General Electric, Standard Vacuum Oil, International Harvester, and the Chase National Bank. "The British have always profited by a successful organization of their foreign trade," the prospectus for the council proclaimed in October 1943. "If this advantage is to be neutralized, similar steps must be taken by American business."[36] The council and other American business associations hoped that the Chungking government would provide a solid legal basis for the expansion of foreign trade and private investment in China. In a joint memorandum presented to a Chinese representative in Washington on 23 January 1945, the National Foreign Trade Council and the China-America Council urged that American banks should be permitted to operate as freely as possible in China, that Chinese regulations concerning foreign corporations should be simplified, that patent and copyright laws should be passed in China, and that Chinese tariffs should be reduced as much as possible.[37]

Determined to ensure the best possible opportunities for American business interests in China, the State Department had already begun drafting a comprehensive Sino-American treaty of friendship, commerce, and navigation. But Ambassador Gauss continued to warn that many Chinese officials looked forward to the establishment a state-controlled and ultra-nationalistic economy after the war. Worried that China might adopt protectionist and discriminatory commercial policies, the State Department decided to send John Sumner to Chungking to investigate Chinese plans for postwar economic reconstruction. Sumner left on 18 October 1944 on an assignment scheduled to last for at least six months. In a cable explaining the mission to the U.S. embassy in Chungking, Under Secretary of State Edward R. Stettinius emphasized that he and his colleagues hoped that Chinese reconstruction plans would be "in harmony with our general postwar economic objectives, including an increase in the interchange of goods and services under non-discriminatory conditions."[38]

The State Department soon learned, however, that the Chinese government was contemplating the release of a statement that would commit it to engage in discriminatory commercial practices. In a message sent on 23 November 1944, Stettinius instructed George Atcheson, the U.S. chargé d'affaires in Chungking, to dissuade the Nationalist government from issuing any statement that would make it more difficult to consummate a Sino-American trade agreement.[39] Atcheson promptly reminded Chinese authorities that the United States attached great importance to the principle of equal commercial opportunity. After receiving assurances that China's postwar commercial policies would be predicated upon the principles of reciprocity and equality, the State Department directed Atcheson on 27 March 1945 to present a draft trade agreement to serve as a basis for negotiations.[40] State Department officials wanted to lay the foundation for a rapid expansion of American trade and investment in China, but they were unable to conclude a commercial treaty with the Chinese government before the war ended.[41]

American policymakers also met with frustration in their effort to get China to make a significant contribution to the defeat of Japan. A month after the attack on Pearl Harbor, the War Department decided to send Gen. Joseph W. Stilwell to China to serve as chief of staff under Chiang Kai-shek. "Vinegar Joe" was a no nonsense soldier who had learned the Chinese language while serving as the U.S. military attaché in Peking before the war began. American military leaders hoped that Stilwell would be able to turn the Chinese army into an effective fighting machine that could reopen a land route to speed the flow of lend-lease supplies across Burma and then begin driving Japanese forces out of China. When Stilwell arrived in Chungking in March 1942, however, he found that the generalissimo had different ideas. His regime depended upon the support of warlords who dominated various regions of China and landlords who exploited peasants throughout the country. To maintain their allegiance, Chiang rewarded loyal military commanders with money and equipment even if they were incompetent. The generalissimo opposed any American reform proposals that threatened to undermine his control over the Chinese army. He also resisted all American military plans that would prevent him from hoarding his troops for use against the Communists in a postwar struggle to control China.[42]

Chiang wanted to employ American airpower rather than Chinese manpower in attacks against the Japanese. In a letter to Stilwell on 29 June 1942, the generalissimo demanded that the United States create a five-hundred-plane air force in China. He drew encouragement a few months later when Gen. Claire L. Chennault, the head of the American Volunteer Air Group in China, boasted that with a well-supplied air force he could cause the downfall of Japan within a year. But Stilwell opposed an air offensive against the Japanese before Chinese troops were prepared to protect American air bases from being overrun by Japanese ground forces, and he argued that U.S. military aid should be withheld from China until Chiang permitted him to reorganize the Chinese army. Secretary of War Stimson and Army Chief of Staff George C. Marshall agreed with Stilwell. Without demanding anything from Chiang in return, however, President Roosevelt decided in March 1943 that a five-hundred-plane air force under the command of Chennault should be established in China. Roosevelt feared that a quid pro quo approach to Chiang might precipitate a political collapse in Chungking and prompt China to withdraw from the war.[43]

While they continued to hope that Chinese troops would eventually launch a major ground offensive against the Japanese, U.S. policymakers became increasingly attracted to the idea that Russian soldiers might destroy the Japanese army in China. Secretary of State Hull was delighted when Stalin promised during a discussion in Moscow on 30 October 1943 that the Soviet Union would join the war against Japan after the Allies defeated Hitler.[44] While talking a month later with President Roosevelt in Teheran, Stalin repeated this pledge. He also mentioned that the Soviet Union lacked an ice-free port in the Far East and seemed pleased when Roosevelt suggested that the warm-water port of Dairen in Manchuria should be open to the commerce of all nations. Soon after his return to Washington, the president told the Pacific War Council that Stalin had indicated that Russia wanted southern Sakhalin and all the Kurile Islands but that he had agreed that the Manchurian railroads should become the property of the Chinese government.[45]

After receiving assurances that Russia would participate in the Far Eastern war, President Roosevelt began taking a sterner approach to Chiang Kai-shek. The president was not inclined to respond favorably when on 8 December 1943 Chiang demanded a billion-dollar loan from the United States. The next day Ambassador Gauss sent Roosevelt a telegram arguing that such a loan could not be justified on either financial or political grounds. The Chinese government had adequate dollar reserves to pay for imports, Gauss explained, and there was "no reason to fear that China might seek a separate peace."[46] In a message to Chungking on 5 January 1944, the president turned down the Chinese demand for economic assistance. Chiang was stung. A few months later, Roosevelt threatened Chiang with a cutoff in military aid unless he agreed to send Chinese troops into action in Burma. The quid pro quo approach worked. Chiang promptly ordered Chinese forces to move into Burma, and they eventually cleared the way for the construction of a road for trucks to carry supplies into China.[47]

President Roosevelt also sought to prod the generalissimo to compose his differences with the Chinese Communists headquartered in Yenan. On 2 February 1944, Harry Hopkins gave Roosevelt a memorandum written by John P. Davies, a foreign-service officer who advised Stilwell on political matters. Davies urged that the United States should send a group of military and political observers to Yenan to obtain accurate information about the strength of the Communist armies in North China and to assess the possibility of North China and Manchuria developing into a separate Chinese state and becoming a Russian satellite. "Chiang's blockade of the Communists and their consequent isolation are forcing them toward dependence upon Russia," Davies argued. "An American observers' mission would break this isolation, reduce the tendency toward dependence upon Russia and, at the same time, serve to check Chiang's desire to attempt [the] liquidation of the Communists by civil war."[48] Roosevelt promptly asked permission to dispatch an American team to visit Yenan, but Chiang rejected his request.[49]

Despite this rebuff, Roosevelt decided in early March 1944 to send Vice Pres. Henry A. Wallace on a special mission to China to induce Chiang to establish harmonious relations with both the Chinese Communists and the Soviet Union. Roosevelt and his State Department advisers did not want the United States and the Soviet Union to become embroiled on opposite sides in a Chinese civil war. Nor did they want to see a communist regime, under Russian domination, emerge in North China or Manchuria. On 18 May, Wallace called on Isaiah Bowman in the State Department to discuss his forthcoming trip. Bowman told the vice president that, if Chiang did not move fast and come to an understanding with the Chinese Communists, Russia might take control of Manchuria after entering the war against Japan. During a meeting at the White House later that day, Roosevelt instructed Wallace to tell Chiang that he would be happy to serve as an arbiter between the rival factions in China. Roosevelt also asked Wallace to warn the generalissimo that Manchuria might be lost to the Russians if he did not settle his differences with the Chinese Communists.[50]

During his brief stay in Chungking, 20–24 June 1944, Wallace had several long talks with the generalissimo. The vice president warned Chiang again and again that he must not leave pending any question that might lead to a war between China and the Soviet Union. Acting upon instructions from the president, Wallace sought permission for U.S. military observers to proceed to North China to gather information about the Chinese Communists. Chiang agreed on the need to avoid a conflict with the Soviet Union, and he requested American help in arranging a conference with the Russians. But the generalissimo maintained a hostile attitude toward the Chinese Communists. Although he reluctantly agreed to allow

Americans to visit North China, Chiang insisted that the Chinese Communists could not be trusted to carry out any commitment they made. He indicated his eagerness to have a closer understanding with Roosevelt and suggested that the president send a personal representative to Chungking to work with him on both military and political matters.[51]

Although willing to recommend that the president send a personal representative to Chungking, Wallace did not believe that Chiang had either the intelligence or the political strength to run postwar China. "Discussion between Government and Communist representatives is taking place in Chungking but the Generalissimo's attitude toward the problem is so imbued with prejudice that I perceive little prospect of a satisfactory long-term settlement," Wallace cabled Roosevelt on 28 June. "The political situation is unstable and tense with rising lack of confidence in the Generalissimo and his reactionary entourage."[52] In his final report submitted to the president two weeks later, Wallace admitted that at present there seemed to be no other alternative than to continue giving Chiang support because no one else appeared to have sufficient strength to take over the government in Chungking. But he advised that U.S. policy should be flexible enough to work with any Chinese leader or group that might emerge and offer greater promise than the generalissimo. "Chiang, at best, is a short-term investment," Wallace concluded. "The leaders of post-war China will be brought forward by evolution or revolution, and it now seems more likely the latter."[53]

President Roosevelt and his State Department advisers had become increasingly worried about the possibility of a political collapse in China. On 18 May 1944, shortly after the Japanese army launched a major offensive in East China, the president told his cabinet that he was "apprehensive for the first time as to China holding together for the duration of the war."[54] His fears grew as Japanese ground forces advanced against very little Chinese resistance. Roosevelt told a group of postwar planners in the State Department on 15 June that they would be faced with a difficult situation "if there should be a political upheaval in China in the near future."[55] In a memorandum sent to Secretary of State Hull a day later, Stanley Hornbeck urged the immediate dispatch of U.S. military aid to bolster Chiang Kai-shek politically and to prevent China from becoming a willing satellite of the Soviet Union. "Should Chiang cease to be China's leader, it is impossible to say who or what might succeed him," Hornbeck warned. "There would almost certainly be, however, a weakening of China's military effort—already weak—and a tendency in

Chinese political circles to move toward the left and to become suscep-
tible to influence from Moscow."[56]

Roosevelt and his military advisers became alarmed when, as Stilwell
had foreseen, Japanese troops began overrunning exposed U.S. air bases
that the disorganized Chinese army could not protect. In a memorandum
presented to the president on 4 July, the Joint Chiefs of Staff pointed out
that Chiang's ground forces were impotent and that Chennault's air force
could do little more than slightly delay the Japanese advances in East China.
The Joint Chiefs recommended that the time had come to press the generalissimo to place Stilwell in command of all Chinese armed forces.[57] In
a cable sent to Chiang two days later, Roosevelt stated that drastic measures needed to be taken immediately to stem the Japanese offensive. The
president urged Chiang to give Stilwell "the power to coordinate all the
Allied military resources in China, including the Communist forces." The
message, which had been drafted in the War Department, concluded with
the blunt observation that "air power alone cannot stop a determined
enemy."[58]

Chiang opted to play for time. In a cable answering Roosevelt on
July 8, the generalissimo claimed that he agreed in principle with his proposal but there would be misunderstanding and confusion if Stilwell were
given absolute command of Chinese troops without a period of preparation. He added that he wished the president would dispatch a personal
envoy to Chungking. In his reply to the generalissimo five days later,
Roosevelt indicated that he was searching for someone with farsighted
political vision to send to China and that he hoped Chiang would prepare the way for Stilwell to assume command of all Chinese military
forces.[59] The president decided a month later to appoint Patrick J. Hurley
as his personal representative in Chungking after Secretary of War
Stimson and General Marshall had suggested that he would be able to
ameliorate relations between Stilwell and Chiang. "Hurley is extremely
pleasant and diplomatic in his manner," Stimson wrote in his diary, "and
will offset Stilwell's acidness."[60]

When Roosevelt insisted that Stilwell be placed in command of all
Chinese forces without further delay, however, Chiang responded on 24
September by demanding that Stilwell be recalled instead.[61] The general
promptly warned Washington that Chiang had no intention of making
further efforts to prosecute the war, of instituting any democratic reforms,
or of forming a united front with the Communists.[62] But after briefly studying the situation in Chungking, Hurley reported to Roosevelt on 11 October

that he had to choose between Stilwell and Chiang, and the generalissimo offered a better basis for cooperation with the United States than any other Chinese leader.[63] "My opinion is that if you sustain Stilwell in this controversy you will lose Chiang Kai-shek and possibly you will lose China with him," Hurley cabled Roosevelt two days later. "I respectfully recommend that you relieve General Stilwell and appoint another American general to command all the land and air forces in China."[64] The president decided on 18 October to recall Stilwell. A few days later, he selected Gen. Albert C. Wedemeyer to serve as the new chief of staff under Chiang but not to command any Chinese forces.[65]

American policymakers hoped that the Russians would attack the Japanese army in China but do nothing to undermine the Nationalists. During a conversation with Ambassador Harriman in June 1944, Stalin had agreed that the generalissimo must be supported because he was the only man who could hold China together.[66] Molotov furthermore assured Hurley, who had stopped in Moscow on his way to Chungking in September 1944, that the Soviet Union was not supporting the Chinese Communists.[67] American leaders also wanted assurance that the Russians would assume the burden of fighting the Japanese forces in Manchuria and China. While talking with Stimson on 13 October, Roosevelt agreed that the United States should use seapower and airpower to defeat Japan and that American troops should not be deployed in major ground operations on the Chinese mainland.[68] Stalin told Harriman two days later that, if stocks could be built up now, the Russian army would be ready for action in China two or three months after the collapse of Germany. But he indicated for the first time that certain political matters would have to be taken into consideration before Russia entered the war against Japan.[69]

Ambassador Harriman left for Washington shortly thereafter to confer with the president. During a conversation at the White House on 10 November, Harriman explained that the Russians planned to launch a military campaign across the Mongolian Desert with the objective of splitting the Japanese forces in Manchuria and China. "If the Russians go in," Roosevelt asked, "will they ever go out?" While discussing the same subject in the White House a week later, Harriman told Roosevelt that he thought Stalin was eager to have a settlement between the generalissimo and the Chinese Communists so that when he started his offensive against the Japanese the Communists would protect his right flank. Harriman believed that Stalin would cooperate in bringing pressure on the Chinese Communists to accept any reasonable deal that Chiang might offer prior to the opening of the Russian campaign. But if a settlement was not reached before the Russians got into China and Manchuria, he reasoned, they would back the Communists and Chiang would be in a difficult situation.[70]

Hurley had been working hard to promote the peaceful unification of all political and military groups in China under the leadership of Chiang Kai-shek. On 7 November, he flew to Yenan in hopes of persuading Communist leaders to pledge their support to the Nationalist regime headed by Chiang and his Kuomintang party. But Mao Tse-tung made it clear that the Communist party must be allowed to share power on an equal basis with the Kuomintang. Hurley thereupon proposed the establishment of a new coalition government to rule China. Eager to participate, the Communists dispatched Chou En-lai to Chungking to begin negotiations with the Nationalists. But the discussions reached an impasse when Kuomintang spokesmen demanded that the Communists give Chiang control of their armed forces in return for only token political representation in the central government. On 8 December, a disappointed Chou returned to Yenan after breaking off talks with the Nationalists.[71]

During a conversation in Moscow a week later, Ambassador Harriman asked Stalin to explain the meaning of his earlier remark that certain political questions would have to be addressed before Russia entered the war against Japan. Stalin replied that the Russians wanted to lease Port Arthur and Dairen and the surrounding area on the Liaotung peninsula. Stalin also said that the Russians wished to lease the Chinese Eastern Railway, but he assured Harriman that they did not intend to interfere with the sovereignty of China in Manchuria. After adding that southern Sakhalin and the Kurile Islands should be returned to Russia, Stalin indicated that the status quo should be maintained in Outer Mongolia, a polite way of saying that it should remain nominally independent but under Soviet domination.[72] In his report to the president on 15 December, Harriman noted that Stalin had made no comment regarding the negotiations that had been suspended in Chungking. "If no agreement is made before the Soviets attack the Japanese," Harriman warned, "it must be assumed that the Soviets will back the Communists in the north and turn over to them the administration of the Chinese territory liberated by the Red Army."[73]

But Hurley, who had just replaced Gauss as U.S. ambassador in Chungking, had nothing encouraging to report about the political situation in China. In a telegram to the State Department on 24 December, he pointed out that the gap between Chiang and the Communists was wide and deep. The Communists wanted a coalition government with one-third Communist, one-third Kuomintang, and one-third minority party representation, he explained, but Chiang was unwilling to entertain any proposal that threatened the continuation of Kuomintang rule in China. Hurley noted that Chiang found himself in a difficult dilemma. "A coalition would mean the end of conservative Kuomintang dominance and open the way for the more virile and popular Communists to extend their influence to the point perhaps of controlling the government," he observed. "Failure to settle with the Communists, who are daily growing stronger, would invite danger of an eventual overthrow of the Kuomintang." Yet Hurley continued to hope that Chiang would "rise above party selfishness and anti-Communist prejudice to lead a coalition government which might bring new life to the war effort and assure unity after hostilities."[74]

During the ensuing week, cables from both Ambassador Hurley and General Wedemeyer gave policymakers in Washington additional cause for concern. The two Americans in Chungking claimed that the British, French, and Dutch were endeavoring to keep China weak and divided because they feared that a strong and united China would be detrimental to their position in Asia.[75] Referring to these reports during a meeting with Secretary of State Stettinius on 2 January 1945, President Roosevelt said it seemed that the British, in particular, were working to undermine U.S. plans with regard to China. "Our policy," he declared, "was based on the belief that despite the temporary weakness of China and the possibility of revolutions and civil war, 450,000,000 Chinese would someday become united and modernized and would be the most important factor in the whole Far East."[76] After making the same point two weeks later during a conversation with the British colonial secretary, Roosevelt reiterated his hope that Hong Kong would be returned to China and that Chiang "or his successor" would convert it into a free port open to all nations on equal terms.[77]

The State Department likewise remained hopeful that China, with or without Chiang, would become the principal stabilizing factor in Asia. In a memorandum prepared for the guidance of the War Department on 29 January 1945, the State Department pointed out that the long-range policy of the U.S. government was to assist in the development of a united and progressive China that would be "capable of contributing to security and prosperity in the Far East." Chiang appeared to be the only available leader who might achieve the short-term goal of mobilizing all the human and material resources of China for the war against Japan, the

State Department noted, but it did not necessarily follow that China would ultimately be unified under the generalissimo. "With regard to our long-term objective," the State Department explained, "it is our purpose to maintain a degree of flexibility which would permit cooperation with any leadership in China that would offer the greatest likelihood of fostering a united, democratic, and friendly China."[78]

Roosevelt and Stalin discussed Far Eastern affairs when they met a week later at Yalta. During a conversation on 8 February 1945, the president told Stalin that he hoped it would be possible to defeat Japan by an intensive bombing campaign and thus save American lives. He indicated that the United States would not invade the Japanese home islands unless it became absolutely necessary. After talking with Stalin about the political conditions under which the Soviet Union would enter the war against Japan, Roosevelt said that Wedemeyer and Hurley were making some progress in bringing the Chinese Communists together with the Chungking government. But the president remarked that Kuomintang leaders were less cooperative than the Communists. For his part, Stalin said that he did not understand why Chiang Kai-shek and the Communists did not get together because they should maintain a united front against the Japanese. He thought that for this purpose Chiang should assume leadership.[79]

In a secret protocol signed at Yalta on 11 February, it was agreed that the Soviet Union would join the Allies in the war against Japan under the following conditions: the status quo in Outer Mongolia would be preserved; the southern part of Sakhalin would be returned to Russia; Port Arthur would be leased as a naval base to the Soviet Union; the commercial port of Dairen would be internationalized; the Chinese Eastern and South Manchurian Railroads would be operated by a joint Sino-Soviet company; China would retain full sovereignty in Manchuria, but the preeminent interests of the Soviet Union with respect to Dairen and the two major Manchurian railroads would be safeguarded; and the Kurile Islands would be ceded to the Soviet Union. While the United States offered to take steps to get Chiang Kai-shek to accept these terms, the Soviet Union expressed its readiness to conclude a pact of friendship and alliance with the Chungking government for the purpose of liberating China from Japanese bondage. But Stalin did not give Roosevelt any written assurance that Russia would help Chiang maintain his authority in China after the war.[80]

Yet Roosevelt continued to hope that China would emerge from the war as a strong and united country under the leadership of the generalissimo. During a conversation in Washington on 24 March, the president instructed Hurley to stop in London and Moscow on his return trip to Chungking to obtain British and Russian support for U.S. policy toward China.[81] Roosevelt died while Hurley was carrying out his assignments. In a message sent to the State Department on 14 April, Hurley reported that both Churchill and Eden had agreed to support American efforts to foster the unification of all Chinese military forces and the establishment of a free, united, and democratic government in China. But Churchill branded the long-range U.S. policy toward China as "the great American illusion," and he declared that "Hong Kong will be eliminated from the British Empire only over my dead body." When Hurley warned that Russia might make demands with respect to North China if the British continued to hold Hong Kong in violation of the principles of the Atlantic Charter, Churchill replied that Great Britain was not bound by the principles of the Atlantic Charter.[82]

In a message from Moscow the next day, Hurley reported that Stalin had stated that he would support U.S. policy regarding the unification of all military forces in China and the establishment of a free, united, and democratic government in Chungking under the leadership of Chiang Kai-shek.[83] But Harriman, who had taken part in these talks, gave a less optimistic report when he returned to Washington a few days later to confer with President Truman and his State Department advisers. "If Chiang does not make a deal with the Communists before the Russians occupy Manchuria and North China," Harriman warned State Department officials on 21 April, "they are certainly going to establish a Soviet-dominated Communist regime in these areas and then there will be a completely divided China."[84] George F. Kennan, the U.S. chargé d'affaires in Moscow, also predicted that the Russians would attempt to dominate Manchuria and North China. "Stalin is prepared to accept the principle of unification of Chinese armed forces and the principle of a united China," Kennan cabled Harriman on 23 April, "since he knows that these conditions are feasible only on terms acceptable to the Chinese Communists."[85]

The State Department responded to these forecasts by searching for ways to check the spread of Russian influence in Asia. In a memorandum for Secretary of War Stimson on 12 May, Under Secretary of State Grew explained that he and his colleagues believed it would be desirable to obtain several political commitments from the Soviet Union before the U.S. government asked the Chinese to accept the Yalta agreements regarding the Far East. The State Department hoped that the Russians would agree to use their influence with the Chinese Communists to bring about the unification of China under the Nationalist government. It also hoped that the Russians would agree that Manchuria should be returned to China and that Korea should be placed under international trusteeship. After outlining these desires, Grew posed the following two questions: "Is the entry of the Soviet Union into the Pacific War at the earliest possible moment of such vital interest to the United States as to preclude any attempt by the United States Government to obtain Soviet agreements to certain desirable political objectives in the Far East prior to such entry? Should the Yalta decision in regard to Soviet political desires in the Far East be reconsidered or carried into effect in whole or in part?"[86]

But Stimson did not think that these questions should be answered until scientists working on the secret Manhattan Project had produced an atomic bomb for the United States. During a meeting with Grew and Secretary of the Navy James V. Forrestal on 15 May, Stimson argued that the United States was not yet ready to get into a quarrel with Russia over Far Eastern issues. "It seems a terrible thing," he cautioned, "to gamble with such big stakes in diplomacy without having your master card in your hand."[87] After consulting with his colleagues in the War Department over the next several days, Stimson sent Grew a formal memorandum containing the following points: Russian entry into the war against Japan would almost certainly shorten the war and thus save American lives, but Soviet military decisions would be based upon Russian interests with little regard to any political action taken by the United States; and while it would be desirable to obtain Soviet political commitments on Far Eastern matters, the concessions made at Yalta were generally within the power of Russia to obtain regardless of any U.S. military action short of war.[88]

President Truman and his State Department advisers decided not to seek a revision of the Yalta agreements but to have Harry Hopkins ask Stalin to clarify his position with respect to the Far East. During a conversation with Hopkins and Harriman on 28 May, Stalin indicated that Russia would enter the war against Japan in August if by that time China had agreed to the Yalta proposals. Stalin made a categorical statement that he would do everything he could to promote the unification of China under the leadership of Chiang Kai-shek. He added that Chiang should remain in power after the war because no Communist leader, or anyone else, was strong enough to unify the country. After declaring that he had no territorial claims against China, Stalin told Hopkins that he would allow representatives of the generalissimo to enter Manchuria with Soviet troops so they could set up a civil administration in liberated areas. Stalin agreed that all countries should have an equal opportunity to trade in China and that Korea should be placed under international trusteeship. But he made it clear that the Russians expected to share in the military occupation of Japan and wanted an Allied agreement concerning occupation zones.[89]

President Truman, encouraged by what Stalin had said about China and plans to fight the Japanese, decided to seek Chinese acceptance of the secret Yalta agreements. During a conversation in the White House on 9 June, Truman informed T. V. Soong, the Chinese foreign minister, about the Yalta agreements, telling him that Stalin wanted to see him in Moscow no later than 1 July to discuss Soviet desires. The president made it clear that the U.S. government would support the commitments Roosevelt had made at Yalta.[90] During a follow-up discussion on 14 June, Truman gave Soong a detailed account of the assurances that Hopkins had received from Stalin concerning Russian support for the restoration of Chinese sovereignty in Manchuria and the unification of China under Chiang. Then the president said that his "chief interest now was to see the Soviet Union participate in the Far Eastern war in sufficient time to be of help in shortening the war and thus save American and Chinese lives."[91]

When Soong arrived in Moscow on 30 June to begin negotiations, however, Stalin made demands that extended far beyond the specific provisions in the Yalta protocol. Besides insisting that China recognize the independence of Outer Mongolia, Stalin advocated the establishment of a Russian military zone in a large area on the Liaotung peninsula. He also demanded that the port of Dairen be placed under joint Sino-Soviet control and that Russia should have exclusive ownership of the Chinese Eastern and South Manchurian Railroads. On 10 July, Stalin accepted a Chinese compromise proposal that the status of Outer Mongolia should be determined by a plebiscite after the war. But the talks reached an impasse when Stalin insisted that a majority of the directors of the two Manchurian railroads should be Russian and that the military zone under Soviet control should include Dairen as well as Port Arthur.[92] During these negotiations, Harriman repeatedly urged Soong to make realistic concessions in an effort to reach an agreement with Stalin before Soviet troops entered Manchuria.[93] But Harriman also constantly pressed Soong not to give Russia any special privileges that would prevent other nations from enjoying equal commercial opportunities in Manchuria.[94]

Policymakers in Washington hoped not only to keep the Russians from closing the doors of Manchuria against American exports but also to induce the Japanese to surrender before U.S. troops began invading their home islands. From a military viewpoint, they thought the Japanese might surrender if the Soviet Union attacked Manchuria or the United States dropped atomic bombs on Japan.[95] From a diplomatic perspective, they believed that the Japanese might sue for peace if the United States clarified the meaning of "unconditional surrender" as it would be applied to Japan. "If the Japanese people were assured that the Emperor would be retained," Grew told his State Department colleagues on 28 May, "surrender might be possible and tens of thousands of American lives might be saved."[96] During a conversation in the White House on the same day, Grew warned President Truman that unless he issued a statement that the Japanese would be permitted to determine their future political structure, they might continue fighting to the last man.[97]

President Truman and his top military advisers agreed that the United States should issue a proclamation designed to induce the Japanese to surrender without fighting to the finish.[98] But during a meeting with Grew and the Joint Chiefs of Staff on 18 June, Truman said that he did not believe that any statement should be released until it could be discussed at the forthcoming Big Three conference in Potsdam.[99] When Grew, Stimson, and Forrestal discussed the subject a week later, they decided to ask their aides to draft a declaration that the Allied nations might release at the meeting.[100] The tentative statement, delivered to the president on 2 July, promised that the Japanese people would be allowed to participate in the world economic system and to establish a representative government that might take the form of a constitutional monarchy under the present dynasty.[101] In a supporting memorandum submitted to Truman at the same time, Stimson indicated that he thought Japan had "enough liberal leaders (although now submerged by the terrorists) to be depended upon for her reconstruction as a responsible member of the family of nations."[102]

The Potsdam Declaration, issued by the United States, Great Britain, and China on 26 July, called upon Japan to proclaim an unconditional surrender in order to avoid prompt and utter destruction. The joint statement did not contain any reference to the future status of the emperor because President Truman and Secretary of State James F. Byrnes feared that there would be serious political repercussions in the United States if the Japanese refused to surrender even after they had been assured that the imperial system could be retained. But the proclamation did leave the way open for the preservation of the Throne by indicating that the

Allied occupation forces would be withdrawn from Japan after a peacefully inclined government had been established "in accordance with the freely expressed will of the Japanese people." The declaration also promised that the Japanese would be permitted to maintain industries that would enable them to sustain their economy but not to rearm for war, to have access to raw materials but not to control them, and to participate in world trade relations.[103]

During the Potsdam Conference, both Stimson and Harriman voiced strong fears that the Russians intended to monopolize the trade of Manchuria in direct violation of the Open Door policy. They urged Truman and Byrnes to oppose any Soviet claims for exclusive commercial rights in Manchuria. During a meeting on 17 July, Truman asked Stalin how his proposal for Dairen would affect U.S. economic interests. Stalin replied that Dairen would be a free port open to all nations. At dinner that evening, Truman told Stimson that he thought that he had clinched the Open Door in Manchuria. But Stimson was not so sure. He pointed out that a free port in Manchuria would be useless if the Russians could shut out American exports because they controlled the Chinese Eastern Railway. When Truman repeated the next day that he was confident about sustaining the Open Door policy, Stimson responded by emphasizing "the importance of going over the matter detail by detail so as to be sure that there would be no misunderstanding over the meaning of the general expressions."[104]

Although President Truman had gone to Potsdam intent on securing Russian entry into the war, glowing reports about the atomic bomb test in New Mexico suggested that the war could be ended without either an American invasion of Japan or a Soviet invasion of Manchuria. Truman told Stimson on 23 July that he was eager to know if General Marshall thought "we needed the Russians in the war or whether we could get along without them." The next day Stimson informed the president that Marshall believed that "now with our new weapon we would not need the assistance of the Russians to conquer Japan."[105] Truman and Byrnes hoped that the Japanese could be induced to surrender as a result of atomic-bomb attacks before the Soviets were in a position to close the doors of Manchuria against American commerce. During a conversation with Forrestal on 28 July, Byrnes said that he was "most anxious to get the Japanese affair over with before the Russians got in" and pressed their claims regarding Dairen and Port Arthur.[106] "Japs will fold up before Russia comes in," Truman predicted. "I am sure they will when Manhattan appears over their homeland."[107]

When Sino-Soviet negotiations resumed in Moscow, Truman and Byrnes tried to prevent the Russians from extracting concessions that might adversely affect U.S. economic interests in Manchuria. On 6 August, the day Hiroshima was destroyed by an atomic bomb, Byrnes instructed Harriman to tell Stalin that "we believe that Soong has already met the Yalta requirements" and to indicate that "we would be opposed, because of our interest in the Open Door Policy, to the inclusion of the port of Dairen in the Soviet military zone." Byrnes also directed Harriman to request that Stalin publish a statement, upon the conclusion of an agreement between Russia and China, reaffirming the verbal assurances that he had previously given to support the Open Door policy in Manchuria.[108] On 8 August, the day Russia declared war on Japan, Stalin promised Harriman that he would "guarantee full freedom of trade in the port of Dairen." But when Harriman promptly reported this conversation to Truman, he expressed doubt that Dairen could be "a truly free port under Soviet management with security control by Soviet secret police."[109]

American concern shifted to Japan when word arrived in Washington on 10 August, a day after Nagasaki had been destroyed by an atomic blast, that the Japanese were ready to accept the surrender terms enumerated in the Potsdam Declaration with the understanding that they did not prejudice the prerogatives of the emperor.[110] Hoping to bring the war to a quick conclusion before the Russians advanced toward Japan and demanded a voice in ruling the defeated nation, Stimson argued that the emperor should be retained under U.S. command and supervision so that his authority could be used to get Japanese forces to stop fighting at once.[111] Truman asked Byrnes to draft a reply that the Allies could send to Japan. After preparing an answer asserting that the authority of the emperor would be subordinate to the supreme commander of the Allied powers, Byrnes explained that he had used the term "Supreme Commander" rather than "Supreme Command" in order to make it "quite clear that the United States would run this particular business and avoid a situation of composite responsibility such as had plagued us in Germany."[112] The message was sent with Allied approval on 11 August, and Japan agreed to surrender three days later.

American policymakers also helped bring the Sino-Soviet negotiations in Moscow to a satisfactory conclusion. In a cable to Harriman on

11 August, Byrnes suggested that Soong should insist that Soviet military authority in Dairen must not be exercised in time of peace. Byrnes furthermore authorized Harriman to support Soong in resisting Soviet demands for joint ownership of the port facilities.[113] The next day Harriman informed Molotov that the United States would not support the Russian proposal regarding Dairen because a joint ownership of the port facilities would adversely affect U.S. interests in China.[114] The Sino-Soviet Treaty of Friendship and Alliance, signed on 14 August, provided that Dairen would be a free port under Chinese control and that Soviet military authority there would be exercised only in time of war. The treaty included a Russian pledge to refrain from interfering in the internal affairs of China and to give moral and military aid solely to the Nationalist government.[115] "Soong is very grateful for our support," Harriman cabled Truman and Byrnes, "and is convinced that he would have had to concede to all Stalin's demands unless we had taken an active part in the negotiations."[116]

Soong and Chiang Kai-shek were equally grateful for U.S. efforts to help the Nationalists reestablish their authority in Japanese-occupied areas of China and to prevent the Communists from acquiring Japanese weapons. In a telegram sent to Chungking on 10 August, the Joint Chiefs of Staff instructed General Wedemeyer to assist in the rapid transport of Nationalist troops to key areas in China to accept the surrender of Japanese forces. Wedemeyer and his staff promptly drew up plans for U.S. ships and planes to carry Chiang's soldiers to strategic points throughout the country. Fearing that the Communists would attempt to secure the surrender of Japanese troops and obtain their arms, U.S. policymakers drafted General Order Number One to be issued by Emperor Hirohito under the authority of Gen. Douglas MacArthur, supreme commander for the Allied powers. This document, which was transmitted to the Allied governments on 15 August, directed Japanese forces in China to lay down their arms and surrender to Chiang or his representatives only.[117]

General Order Number One, by stipulating that MacArthur would accept the surrender of enemy forces in the Japanese home islands, was designed to put the United States in a position to exercise a controlling voice in the military occupation of Japan. But in a message to Truman on 16 August, Stalin proposed that Soviet troops should be allowed to receive the surrender of Japanese forces in the northern half of Hokkaido Island. Truman responded two days later by informing Stalin that MacArthur would accept the surrender of enemy forces in every part of

Japan proper but that he would employ token forces provided by the Allied powers, including Russia, in the temporary occupation of as much of Japan as he considered necessary.[118] During the ensuing months, the Russians pressed for a larger role in the occupation of Japan. William D. Leahy, the chief of staff to the president, opposed any Soviet participation because he thought that conditions in Japan were ideal for the propagation of communism.[119] In the end, Truman agreed to establish a Far Eastern commission and an Allied council that could advise MacArthur but could not interfere with his authority to carry out policy directives that he received from the U.S. government.[120]

American policymakers remained determined to reintegrate Japan into a liberal capitalist world system. Truman promptly approved a document, endorsed by the State-War-Navy Coordinating Committee on 27 August, that outlined the initial U.S. policy for postwar Japan. According to this paper, Japan would be completely disarmed and demilitarized, the large industrial and banking combinations that had buttressed its war machine would be dissolved, its people would be encouraged to embrace individual freedoms and to establish democratic organizations, and the nation would be permitted eventually to resume normal trade relations with the rest of the world.[121] Truman also quickly approved a report on reparations, drafted by Edwin W. Pauley on 18 December, that aimed at promoting economic development in China and other East Asian countries without pauperizing Japan. While recommending that neighboring countries should receive reparations in the form of heavy industrial equipment, Pauley advised that Japan should be left with the ability to export manufactured goods and thereby obtain foreign exchange needed to pay for essential imports to meet the peacetime requirements of its dense population.[122]

While hoping to make Japan a peaceful member of the international community, U.S. policymakers sought to implement their plans for postwar China. They looked forward to the emergence of a strong and stable China, under the leadership of Chiang Kai-shek, that would not only help police the Far East but also provide a large market for American products. They continued to support Chiang even though he remained firm in his refusal to create a coalition government in which the Communists would have more than token representation. But when a full-scale civil war eventually erupted in China, Truman and his foreign policy advisers decided not to intervene. They did not want U.S. troops to be drawn into a ground war against millions of Communist soldiers on the Asian mainland.

American leaders altered their policy toward the Far East as it became clear that the Communists would emerge triumphant. Rather than carrying out their plans to dissolve the large Japanese business combinations and to extract reparations from the Japanese in the form of heavy machinery, they began promoting the development of Japan as the industrial center of East Asia. They hoped Japan would assume the role that had been envisioned for China and thus provide the United States with an important economic and strategic partner to help counter the spread of Russian influence in the Far East.

ELEVEN | RESTRAINING THE RUSSIANS IN EASTERN EUROPE

Policymakers in Washington hoped to dissuade the Russians from using their power to establish an exclusive sphere of influence in Eastern Europe after the defeat of Germany. If the U.S. government indicated a willingness to help keep Germany disarmed and to offer the Soviet Union loans for postwar reconstruction, the Russians might permit the people of Eastern Europe to choose their own political leaders in free elections and to engage in unrestricted economic relations with Western Europe and the United States. But if the Russians decided to impose puppet governments in the countries along their western frontier in an effort to protect themselves against future military attacks, the American people might refuse to support plans for the creation of a general system of international security. President Roosevelt and Secretary of State Cordell Hull moved cautiously as they sought to achieve their basic objectives in Eastern Europe. First, they attempted to avoid dealing with difficult territorial questions until the final peace settlement. Second, they tried to build a feeling of trust among the Big Three in hopes that after the war the Soviets would adopt a good-neighbor policy toward the countries along their western border.

But the Russians sought to extract a commitment from Great Britain to recognize as Soviet territory several areas they had taken since the outbreak of the war in Europe. During talks in Moscow in December 1941, Stalin pressed Foreign Secretary Anthony Eden to agree that the Baltic states of Estonia, Latvia, and Lithuania, along with portions of Finland and Rumania, should be kept within the Soviet Union. This demand provoked a debate among British leaders. In the Atlantic Charter issued just four months earlier, Prime Minister Churchill had joined with President Roosevelt in declaring a "desire to see no territorial changes that do not accord with the freely expressed wishes of the peoples concerned" and in promising to "respect the right of all peoples to choose the form of government under which they will live." Churchill did not want to abandon these principles in order to satisfy Russian ambitions, and he agreed with Roosevelt that frontier issues should not be settled until the war ended. But Eden argued that from a practical standpoint it would be good to have an agreement that defined Soviet boundaries while the Red Army remained on the defensive against the German Wehrmacht.[1]

The State Department feared that the British would try to obtain U.S. approval for a territorial deal that would be included in an Anglo-Soviet treaty of alliance. In a memorandum sent to President Roosevelt on 4 February 1942, Secretary Hull warned that disastrous consequences might ensue if Great Britain started bargaining with the Soviet Union about frontiers. Not only would the war effort against the Axis be weakened if the Allies began scrambling to acquire territory at the expense of each other, but the Western powers also would find it harder to restrain the Russians if the tide of battle on the eastern front ever turned against Germany. "If the British Government, with the tacit or expressed approval of this Government, should abandon the principle of no territorial commitments prior to the peace conference," Hull emphasized, "it would be placed in a difficult position to resist additional Soviet demands relating to frontiers, territory, or to spheres of influence which would almost certainly follow whenever the Soviet Government would find itself in a favorable bargaining position."[2]

Worried that the British would soon endorse Russian territorial claims, Assistant Secretary of State Adolf A. Berle hoped that it might be possible to work out an arrangement that would satisfy the security interests of the Soviet Union without violating the principles of the Atlantic Charter. Berle noted in his diary on 5 February that the smaller countries in Eastern Europe would inevitably come under the military domination of either Russia or Germany. "I see no reason why we should object to their being within the orbit of Russia, provided we were assured that the U.S.S.R. would not use this power to subvert the governments and set up a regime of terror and cruelty," he explained. "There should be some basis of adjustment whereby the safety and international interest of the U.S.S.R. will be assured without their claiming to dictate the method of life, cultural development and type of civilization to be enjoyed by these countries." Berle thought that perhaps Stalin could be persuaded to act like a good neighbor in Eastern Europe if he were told that the United States had been able to protect its legitimate military and economic interests in the Western Hemisphere while "at the same time leaving nations as weak as Costa Rica or Honduras with the feeling that they are entirely free and entirely safe."[3]

President Roosevelt decided that he should try to steer the Russians and British away from concluding a wartime treaty containing territorial clauses. In a message to Stalin on 2 March 1942, Roosevelt indicated that he could not subscribe to any treaty dealing with frontiers until the war had been won but that the United States would be willing to support all legitimate postwar arrangements necessary to assure the security of the Soviet Union. But Stalin continued to press the British for a territorial agreement, and the rapidly deteriorating military situation in the Far East prompted Churchill to change his position.[4] "The increasing gravity of the war has led me to feel that the principles of the Atlantic Charter ought not to be construed so as to deny Russia the frontiers she occupied when Germany attacked her," Churchill cabled Roosevelt on 7 March. "I hope therefore that you will be able to give us a free hand to sign the treaty which Stalin desires as soon as possible."[5]

But Roosevelt thought it would be better to open a second military front against Germany than to approve Russian acquisitions in Eastern Europe. In a message to Churchill on 9 March, Roosevelt stated that he was becoming more and more interested in the establishment of a new European front, sometime during the coming summer, that would compel the Germans to divert many divisions away from the Russian front.[6] American military leaders had already concluded that, for strategic reasons, it was essential it keep the Soviet Union in the war.[7] Working under the direction of Gen. Dwight D. Eisenhower, army planners quickly developed a grand strategy to ensure the defeat of Germany by opening a second front in France. The plan called for the build-up of Anglo-American forces on the British Isles and then for the dispatch of a large number of ground troops across the English Channel in the spring of 1943. The plan also provided for a smaller emergency operation that could be launched in September 1942 if an early invasion of France seemed necessary to prevent a Russian military collapse.[8]

After Roosevelt approved this grand strategy on 1 April 1942, he asked Harry Hopkins and Army Chief of Staff George C. Marshall to go to London to present the plan to British leaders. Then the president sent Churchill a cable expressing his hope that Great Britain would support the American proposal for a second front in France and that the Russians would greet the plan with enthusiasm. After arriving with Marshall in London on 8 April, Hopkins informed Churchill that "the United States was ready to take great risks to relieve the Russian front." He also told Eden in a follow-up conversation that Roosevelt did not want Great Britain and the Soviet Union to sign a treaty that included territorial provisions. "I impressed upon Eden as strongly as I could," Hopkins noted before he and Marshall departed from London, "the President's belief that our main proposal here should take the heat off Russia's diplomatic demands upon England." In other words, Roosevelt hoped that the Russians would be willing to drop their frontier claims until the war ended if the United States and Great Britain promised to open a second front in Europe as soon as possible.[9]

Roosevelt wanted Soviet foreign minister Vyacheslav Molotov to come to Washington to discuss the American military proposal before he traveled to London to negotiate a treaty with the British. But Stalin ordered Molotov to go first to Great Britain and then proceed to the United States.[10] After Molotov arrived in London on 20 May 1942, the British decided that his territorial demands were too extensive, and Eden asked Molotov to accept a British proposal for a security pact that omitted any reference to borders. John G. Winant, the U.S. ambassador in London, tried to influence Molotov during a private talk on 24 May in the Russian embassy. Winant not only emphasized that both Roosevelt and Hull were definitely opposed to an Anglo-Soviet treaty that included an agreement on frontiers but also explained that the United States was interested in opening a second front against Germany. Two days later, after Stalin gave his permission, Molotov joined with the British in signing a military treaty that made no mention of boundaries.[11]

The Russians were eager to obtain a commitment regarding the formation of a new military front in the near future. When Molotov arrived in Washington on 29 May, he told President Roosevelt that Stalin hoped the United States and Great Britain would land enough combat troops on the European continent to draw forty German divisions away from the Russian front. The next day the president authorized Molotov to tell Stalin that he expected to establish a second front before the year ended. Roosevelt also approved a public statement, released on 11 June after the completion of his conversations with Molotov, that a "full understanding was reached with regard to the urgent tasks of creating a second front in Europe in 1942." But the British argued steadfastly against a subsequent American proposal for a limited cross-channel invasion of France that year, and contrary to the wishes of his own military advisers, Roosevelt ultimately agreed to an alternative plan for a combined Anglo-American offensive in North Africa. When Churchill flew to Moscow on 12 August to explain the decision, Stalin expressed disappointment that there would be no second front in Europe during 1942, but he did show enthusiasm for the projected North African operation.[12]

Worried about Russian territorial ambitions, the Advisory Committee on Postwar Foreign Policy had already begun drafting plans for the establishment of an East European federation. The Subcommittee on Political Problems, chaired by Under Secretary of State Sumner Welles, expressed general support on 30 May 1942 for the principle that all Eastern European states should be included in a regional association. Welles suggested that two arguments could be used to persuade Stalin to allow the Baltic states to join an East European union: first, the federation would act as a buffer that would protect Russia from Germany if the proposed international security organization broke down; and second, it would serve as a large market for Soviet products.[13] During a meeting of the political subcommittee four weeks later, Welles explained that the purpose for creating an East European union was to foster peace by preventing the great powers from dominating the small states in Eastern Europe and by making the people of the region as prosperous as possible. "The best way to achieve this," he concluded, "was by creating a buffer, not subservient to Germany, the Soviet Union, or to Great Britain."[14]

Assistant Secretary of State Berle played a major role in formulating plans for an East European federation. During a meeting of the Subcommittee on Territorial Problems on 27 June 1942, Berle said that he thought the Soviets wanted to extend their border to the crest of the Carpathian Mountains so they could control the small Balkan countries. "If Russia were able to thrust a salient across to Czechoslovakia," he warned, "she would be able to divide these countries in such a way as to make impossible any East European Union."[15] Upon reconsidering the issue several months later, the subcommittee unanimously recommended that the Soviet frontier should not be permitted to reach the Carpathians.[16] The Subcommittee on Political Problems likewise responded favorably when Berle argued on 22 August 1942 that the proposed East European federation would require four principal economic agencies: a central power authority; a transportation and communications administration; a development corporation that could request financial assistance from the projected United Nations; and a central bank that could maintain a unified currency system.[17] In addition, the subcommittee decided a few months later that the regional association should have a political council that would be responsible for administering a unified customs service.[18]

The Polish émigré government, set up in London shortly after the beginning of World War II, was also developing schemes for the creation of an East European federation. At the Versailles Peace Conference in 1919, a commission headed by Lord Curzon of Great Britain had used ethnographic maps to establish a boundary, the so-called Curzon Line, between Poland and the Soviet Union. But the Poles invaded Russia, which was mired in a civil war, shortly thereafter, and the resulting Treaty of Riga in 1921 pushed the Polish-Soviet frontier 150 miles east of the Curzon Line. The Soviets never forgot that Ukrainians and Russians made up more than half of the population of the area the Poles had annexed, and in 1939 they joined with the Germans in attacking Poland and partitioning the country along a line that corresponded roughly to the one Lord Curzon had drawn twenty years earlier. After Germany invaded the Soviet Union in 1941, however, the Polish government-in-exile in London hoped not only to regain the territory the Red Army had recently taken but also to bring the small nations of Eastern Europe into a federation that would bar future Russian expansion.[19]

Meanwhile, as the London Poles were preparing to protect their interests in postwar Europe, President Roosevelt and Foreign Secretary Eden had a private dinner on 14 March 1943 at the White House during which they discussed the territorial demands that the Russians would most likely make at the peace conference. Eden predicted that Stalin would insist that the Baltic states be absorbed into the Soviet Union for security reasons and would claim that, in a plebiscite held in 1939, these countries had expressed their desire to join the Soviet Union. After indicating that he thought many people in the United States and Great Britain would be upset if the Soviet Union annexed those countries, Roosevelt said he realized that they would be occupied by Russian troops when Germany surrendered and that nobody would be able to force out the Red Army. Then the president suggested a solution to the problem: the Russians should refrain from taking the Baltic states without holding a new plebiscite, and in the meantime the Soviet Union should have close economic and military arrangements with these countries. But Eden believed that Stalin would refuse to hold another plebiscite and would insist upon the immediate incorporation of the Baltic states into the Soviet Union.[20]

As for the future of Poland, Eden told Roosevelt that the Poles would create more problems than the Russians. Eden did not think that Soviet demands for territory would go beyond the Curzon Line, and he believed Stalin wanted a strong Poland, provided the right kind of people were running the country. But the foreign secretary warned that the Polish exiles in London had very large ambitions based upon the unrealistic belief that their country would be more powerful after the war than either Russia or Germany. They not only wanted to obtain East Prussia, he explained, but they also hoped that the prewar boundaries of Poland would be restored. Although the president agreed with Eden that the Poles should get East Prussia, he said that the big powers would have to determine the postwar boundaries of Poland and that he did not intend to go to the peace conference to bargain with the small countries. "As far as Poland is concerned," Roosevelt concluded, "the important thing is to set it up in a way that will help maintain the peace of the world."[21]

But American and British leaders soon had reason to worry about Russian aims regarding Poland. On 13 April 1943, the Germans announced that they had just discovered in the Katyn Forest near Smolensk a mass grave containing the remains of ten thousand Polish officers who had been executed by the Russians three years earlier. When the London Poles asked the International Red Cross to investigate the report, Stalin condemned them for having acted on German propaganda before giving him a chance to comment. Then Moscow radio suddenly announced on 26 April that the Soviet Union had severed all diplomatic relations with the Polish government in London. Two days later, the Union of Polish Patriots, a group of Polish communists recently organized in the Soviet Union with help from Russian officials, issued a declaration that denounced the Polish government-in-exile. Churchill promptly warned Stalin that neither Great Britain nor the United States would recognize a second Polish government set up by the Soviet government on Russian soil.[22]

Despite their agreement concerning Poland, American and British leaders did not see eye to eye with respect to the Balkans. The British made repeated proposals during Anglo-American military conferences in May and August 1943 for joint operations in the eastern Mediterranean to protect their economic and strategic interests in the Balkans. But President Roosevelt and the Joint Chiefs of Staff remained firm in their conviction that the United States and Great Britain should concentrate on the logistical buildup in England for a direct cross-channel invasion in hopes of defeating Germany as soon as possible.[23] "The British Foreign Office does not want the Balkans to come under Russian influence," Roosevelt observed during a meeting with the Joint Chiefs on 10 August 1943. "Britain wants to get to the Balkans first." But the president said he did not believe the Russians aimed to take over the Balkan countries after the war and thought it would be "unwise to plan military strategy based upon a gamble as to political results."[24]

Informed by the War Department that American and British forces could not successfully oppose the Red Army in Eastern Europe, postwar planners in the State Department hoped to devise a formula that would protect Russian security interests in Poland, the Baltics, and the Balkans without undermining the principles of the Atlantic Charter. "It must be our task to try to get an understanding if we possibly can," Adolf Berle noted in his diary on 1 September 1943, "provided that in doing so we make no sacrifice of principle."[25] The Russian specialists in the State Department agreed. In a memorandum completed on 23 September 1943, Charles E. Bohlen and several other Russian experts suggested that it might be possible to reconcile Soviet demands for security and American desires for self-government and unrestricted trade in Eastern Europe. "If a basis for long-term collaboration between the U.S.S.R. and the western powers should be established under which the former's greater interest and political influence in the East European region was recognized," the group reasoned, "the Soviet leaders might feel that they could safely tolerate the existence of comparatively free economic relations between the western powers and the East European states." Furthermore, the group believed, a majority of the people in Eastern Europe could probably be persuaded to accept "a solution under which the U.S.S.R. would exercise solely a preponderant strategic interest in the area," while they would be "free to conduct their domestic affairs without interference."[26]

When the Moscow Conference of Foreign Ministers began three weeks later, Secretary of State Hull concentrated most of his energy on obtaining a commitment from the four major powers to establish a postwar system of international security. He did not want to get bogged down in any debate about specific issues that might undercut his efforts to promote the general principle of international collaboration for the maintenance of world peace.[27] When Foreign Secretary Eden stated that he would like to see the restoration of normal diplomatic relations between the Soviet Union and Poland, Hull said that he wished the two neighbors would compose their differences but that he did not want to discuss the causes of their dispute.[28] Hull was relieved that the difficult question regarding the Polish-Soviet border did not come up at the conference. He hoped that, if relations among the great powers gradually deepened into feelings of mutual trust, it might eventually be possible to persuade the Russians to treat neighboring countries in Eastern Europe the same way the United States treated small nations in Latin America.[29]

During the Moscow Conference, Foreign Minister Molotov gave some indication of Russian aims with respect to Eastern Europe. He made it clear that Russian leaders regarded the Polish government-in-exile as hostile and therefore completely unacceptable to the Soviet government. Officials in the Kremlin would not recognize any Polish authority that was unfriendly to Russia, Molotov said, but they were willing to have a strong independent Poland with whatever social and political system the Poles wanted. He also explained that the Russians were opposed to the establishment of any kind of East European federation and that they were especially determined to prevent a restoration of the old "cordon sanitaire" that had been directed against the Soviet Union. Although Molotov indicated that Russian leaders would take unilateral action to make sure that the countries in Eastern Europe maintained satisfactory relations with the Soviet Union, Ambassador W. Averell Harriman reported from Moscow that he thought "that this rigid attitude may well be tempered in proportion to their increasing confidence in their relations with the British and ourselves in the establishment of over-all world security."[30]

During a conversation with Stalin at the Teheran Conference on 1 December 1943, President Roosevelt expressed his hope that Eastern European problems could be solved without hurting his chances for reelection in the coming year. There were between six and seven million people of Polish extraction in the United States, Roosevelt explained, and he did not want to lose their vote. Aware that Churchill had suggested to Stalin that Poland should be given German territory in the west in compensation for land it would lose to Russia in the east, Roosevelt said that he would like to see Polish borders moved westward, but for political reasons he "could not publicly take part in any such arrangement at the present time." Turning to a related problem, the president noted that there were a number of people of Lithuanian, Latvian, and Estonian origin also in the United States. Roosevelt said he had no intention of going to war to prevent Russia from taking the Baltic states, but from the standpoint of domestic public opinion, he hoped that Stalin would allow a referendum to determine if the people in those countries wished to join the Soviet Union.[31]

A few days after Soviet troops crossed into Poland on 5 January 1944, Foreign Minister Molotov handed Ambassador Harriman a statement that he hoped would evoke a favorable reaction from President Roosevelt. Harriman reported to Roosevelt and Hull that the Russians seemed to be ready to deal with the Polish government in London provided it eliminated its extreme anti-Soviet elements and accepted the Curzon Line as a basis for negotiating a boundary settlement with the Soviet Union.[32] In a telegram to Hull on 21 January, Harriman explained that the Russians feared that the landowners and military officers in the Polish émigré government were irrevocably hostile to the Soviet Union and that they might conspire with Germany against Russia after the war. "It is my belief that, provided of course it is well disposed toward the Soviet Union, the Russians are sincere in their willingness to have a strong and independent Poland emerge," he added. "Apparently they feel that the vast majority of the Polish population are so disposed, particularly the peasants and workers, and would elect a democratic government friendly to the Soviet Union if given a chance to express their political views."[33]

But President Roosevelt and Secretary of State Hull feared that the Soviet position with respect to Poland would imperil the principle of international cooperation that had been set forth at the conferences in Moscow and Teheran. "American public opinion will not understand the approach of the Soviet Government in its present insistence on an almost complete reconstitution of the Polish Government-in-exile with persons of its own choosing as an essential prerequisite to any direct discussion of mutual problems," Hull cabled Harriman on 25 January. "It is of vital importance that the Soviet Government be made to understand that the faith of the people of the United States in the workability of any international security organization in which Russia is a full and cooperating member depends upon the willingness of the Soviet Government to seek to attain its ends by free and frank discussions with a Polish Government that is not hand-picked."[34] But when Harriman told Stalin a week later that the president hoped some way might be found for the Russians to settle their differences with the Poles, Stalin replied that he did not believe this could be done as long as certain persons who were antagonistic to the Soviet Union remained in the Polish government.[35]

After discussing the problem with Hull, the president decided on 7 February to make a direct appeal to Stalin. "I fully appreciate your desire to deal only with a Polish Government in which you can repose confidence and which can be counted upon to establish permanent friendly relations with the Soviet Union," Roosevelt cabled Stalin, "but it is my earnest hope that while this problem remains unsolved neither party shall by hasty word or unilateral act transform this special question into one adversely affecting the larger issues of future international collaboration." If Churchill could persuade Stanislaus Mikolajczyk, the prime minister of the Polish government-in-exile, to accept the Curzon Line as a basis for negotiating a boundary settlement, Roosevelt asked, would it not be possible for Stalin to "leave it to the Polish Prime Minister himself to make such changes in his Government as may be necessary without any evidence of pressure or dictation from a foreign country?"[36] In his reply to Roosevelt on 16 February, however, Stalin complained that the Polish government in London continued to reject the Curzon Line as the basis for a border settlement and that most of its members were pro-fascist imperialists who did not want friendly relations with the Soviet Union.[37]

Nevertheless, the postwar planners in the State Department remained hopeful that Stalin would be satisfied with a regional arrangement that protected Russian security interests in Eastern Europe and yet permitted the small countries in the area to elect their own leaders and to trade with the rest of the world. At a meeting of the Subcommittee on Problems of European Organization on 4 February 1944, Adolf Berle suggested that it would not be in the interest of the United States to oppose the establishment of a Russian "Monroe Doctrine" in Eastern Europe. Charles Bohlen agreed.[38] During a discussion in the same subcommittee a month later, Bohlen said that he did "not believe that the consummation of the Soviet Union's minimum program (a system of treaties with the Eastern European states, under which the sovereignty and independence of the latter would not be impaired) would constitute a threat to American interests."[39] James C. Dunn, the political adviser on European affairs, expressed the prevailing view in the State Department when he told his colleagues on 8 March that they should not attempt "to deny or offset legitimate Soviet interests" in Eastern Europe but that they should try to keep the countries in the area from "complete dependence on the Soviet Union."[40]

Ambassador Harriman advocated U.S. economic aid for the postwar reconstruction of Eastern Europe to prevent the region from falling under total Russian domination. In a telegram to the State Department on 20 February 1944, Harriman pointed out that the small countries in Eastern Europe and the Balkans would be on the verge of economic collapse by the end of the war. "Irrespective of any design on the part of the Soviet Government," he warned, "in the absence of assistance from any other quarter, there will be a natural gravitational pull on the peoples of those areas toward the Soviet Union."[41] In a follow-up telegram three weeks later, Harriman asserted that "economic assistance is one of the most effective weapons at our disposal to avoid the development of a Soviet sphere of influence over Eastern Europe and the Balkans."[42] He thought that the countries in these areas would "look to Moscow for security" but that U.S. financial aid could "help keep them from following the Communist philosophy."[43] While meeting in Washington with a group of top State Department officials on 10 May, Harriman reiterated his argument for a long-term program of economic aid for Eastern Europe. He reasoned that in most of the countries in the region, "the sense of individual liberty is developed to a point where they will not wish to adopt Communism unless driven to it by economic disaster."[44]

The British, in the meantime, hoped to protect their economic and strategic interests from the spread of communism by joining with the Russians in a wartime arrangement that would divide the Balkans into areas of responsibility. In a conversation with the Russian ambassador in London on 5 May 1944, Eden suggested that during the war, the Soviet Union should manage the situation in Rumania, while Great Britain should have a controlling influence in Greece. The Russian ambassador told Eden two weeks later that his government liked the idea, but before giving any final assurance in the matter, it wanted to know if the United States would approve such an arrangement.[45] In a cable to Washington on 31 May, Churchill asked Roosevelt to give his blessing to the British proposal. "We do not of course wish to carve up the Balkans into spheres of influence," he assured the president, "and in agreeing to the arrangement we should make it clear that it applied only to war conditions and did not affect the rights and responsibilities which each of the three great powers will have to exercise at the peace settlement and afterwards in regard to the whole of Europe."[46]

President Roosevelt and his State Department advisers, however, feared that the proposed agreement might develop into a permanent sphere-of-influence arrangement that would not only run counter to the principles of equal commercial opportunity and national self-determination but also sow the seeds for another war in Europe.[47] In a message drafted in the State Department and sent to Churchill on 10 June, Roosevelt indicated that he and his advisors were unwilling to approve the proposed arrangement because they believed it would strengthen the natural tendency for military decisions to extend into the political and economic fields. "In our opinion," he admonished, "this would certainly result in the persistence of differences between you and the Soviets and in the division of the Balkan region into spheres of influence despite the declared intention to limit the arrangement to military matters."[48] Yet two days later, in response to a plea from Churchill while Hull was away from Washington, the president agreed that the proposed arrangement should be given a trial for three months and then reviewed by the three major powers. "We must be careful to make it clear," he warned Churchill, "that we are not establishing any postwar spheres of influence."[49]

But the Russians were given pause when they learned from Eden that his government had proposed a trial period of three months to overcome American opposition to the plan. On 1 July, the Soviet embassy in Washington sent the State Department an *aide-mémoire* asking for American views regarding the matter. The State Department responded to the Soviet inquiry two weeks later in a message approved by the president. After explaining that the United States had consented to a three-month trial for overriding military considerations, the message expressed apprehension that the agreement would lead to the division of the Balkans into spheres of influence and thereby work against "the establishment and effective functioning of a broader system of general security in which all countries would have their part."[50] The Russians subsequently decided to back away from the proposal for a division of responsibilities in the Balkans, and the British soon began making plans to dispatch troops to Athens to prevent a communist-led coup when German forces withdrew from Greece.[51]

Although British and American leaders differed in their attitudes toward the Balkans, they were in agreement on the need to prevent the Polish-Soviet dispute from undermining their efforts to cultivate a spirit of solidarity among the three major powers. Ambassador Harriman believed that Stalin was basically correct in his conviction that the Polish government in London was dominated by Gen. Kasimierz Sosnkowski and military officers who regarded a war against Russia as inevitable.[52] "Your Polish friends are the chief ones who are creating difficulties between us and the Soviets at the moment," Harriman wrote Lord Beaverbrook on 5 April 1944. "Can't you do something about them?"[53] While en route to Washington a month later, Harriman stopped in London to discuss the Polish issue with British officials. He explained to Churchill that Prime Minister Mikolajczyk and other leaders from Polish democratic parties were not unacceptable to the Russians, but Stalin was convinced that the Poles in London were "under the domination of Sosnkowski and the military men who saw in the future only war with the Soviet Union."[54]

President Roosevelt and his State Department advisers continued to hope that the Polish-Soviet controversy could be resolved. In a memorandum prepared on 16 May, Charles Bohlen suggested that when the Red Army reached Warsaw, the Russians might be willing to return the cities of Lwow and Vilna to Poland and to permit the establishment of a coalition government that included some members of the Polish government-in-exile.[55] During a meeting in the White House the next day,

Roosevelt instructed Harriman that upon his return to Moscow he should give Stalin the following message: the president could not take an active interest in the Polish question until his campaign for reelection was over; the Curzon Line with some modifications seemed to him a reasonable basis for a settlement, though he did not know what should be done about Lwow; Mikolajczyk would be coming to Washington in the near future, but the Polish prime minister had agreed not to make any public speeches while in the United States; and the president would tell Mikolajczyk that "he must get rid of Sosnkowski and one or two others who are uncooperative in attempts to reach a settlement."[56]

President Roosevelt did what he said he would do when Mikolajczyk arrived in Washington. During a conversation with the prime minister on 7 June 1944, Roosevelt indicated that he thought it would be very important for Mikolajczyk to go to Moscow to confer with Stalin and Molotov. "The Poles must recognize the fact," he asserted, "that they would have to make certain definite changes in their leadership in order to create a working arrangement with the Russians." The president added that he hoped the Poles would not be stubborn about this point. When Mikolajczyk asked if he thought the Russians aimed to dominate neighboring countries in Eastern Europe, Roosevelt answered that he believed "they would wish to cooperate with the other United Nations in having strong, independent adjoining states friendly to them." The president reiterated these points during another discussion with Mikolajczyk five days later. After stating that he was convinced the Russians wanted a strong and independent Poland, Roosevelt said that he thought it would be a pretty good exchange if the Poles obtained East Prussia and Silesia even though they had to give up a little territory elsewhere.[57]

While Mikolajczyk was in Washington, Ambassador Harriman reported from Moscow that he had just had his first friendly talk with Stalin about the Polish problem. "I got the feeling," Harriman cabled Roosevelt, "that he saw a solution in the making which would be acceptable all around."[58] After completing his discussions with the Polish prime minister, Roosevelt cabled Stalin on 17 June that he had gained the impression that Mikolajczyk was a very sincere and reasonable man who was "fully cognizant that the whole future of Poland depends upon the establishment of genuinely good relations with the Soviet Union." Roosevelt added that the prime minister would not hesitate to go to Moscow to discuss Polish-Soviet affairs if Stalin would welcome him.[59] In his reply to the president, Stalin expressed no interest in receiving Mikolajczyk. But Harriman predicted on 21 July that Poles with close ties to the Soviet government would invite Mikolajczyk and certain other Polish leaders in Britain, Russia, and the United States to come to Poland to form a new government. Harriman concluded that the Russians would make sure that the members of the new Polish government desired friendly relations with the Soviet Union but that they would not interfere with religious practices or dictate the character of the economic system in Poland.[60]

When news arrived in London that the Polish Committee of National Liberation had been formed on 21 July in Lublin, a city in eastern Poland, the British immediately asked Stalin if he would see the Polish prime minister. Stalin replied that he would not refuse to receive Mikolajczyk but that it would be better if the prime minister of the émigré government were to address himself to the Polish Committee of National Liberation. Stalin explained that this committee would administer Polish territory liberated by the Red Army. "It is possible," he suggested, "that, in due course, it will serve as a nucleus for the formation of a provisional Polish government." Churchill persuaded Mikolajczyk to depart for Moscow at once. Then in a cable to Stalin on 27 July, Churchill wrote that he believed that "Poles who are friendly to Russia should join with Poles who are friendly to Great Britain and the United States in order to establish a strong, free, independent Poland." Stalin promptly responded that he thought a good start had been made toward the unification of Polish groups by the creation of the Committee of National Liberation and that he was prepared to help the Poles reach an agreement among themselves.[61]

Mikolajczyk arrived in Moscow on 30 July just as the Polish underground army was about to start an uprising against German forces in Warsaw in an effort to take over the city before Russian troops appeared. During their first conversation in the Kremlin on 3 August, Stalin told Mikolajczyk that if he reached an agreement with the Polish Committee of National Liberation, the Soviet Union might be willing to make some concessions with respect to the eastern border of Poland. When Mikolajczyk said he was ready to negotiate, Stalin said he would ask the committee in Lublin to send representatives to Moscow to begin talks as soon as possible. But Mikolajczyk refused to join the Lublin Poles in the establishment of a new Polish government when he found that they were only willing to assign four of the eighteen cabinet posts to independent parties.[62] But after Stalin assured him during their final discussion on 9 August that he did not intend to communize Poland and that Russian planes would drop arms to assist the underground forces in Warsaw,

Mikolajczyk left for London in hopes of working out a plan for the creation of a provisional government that would unite all Polish factions until free elections could be held.[63]

But the Russians made little effort to help the Polish underground forces, and President Roosevelt subsequently decided that U.S. planes should fly from France, drop supplies over Warsaw, and then land in the Soviet Union. Yet when Ambassador Harriman presented the plan in Moscow on 14 August, he was told that the Soviet government regarded the Warsaw uprising as a "purely adventuristic affair" and would not approve the proposal.[64] "For the first time since coming to Moscow," Harriman cabled Roosevelt, "I am gravely concerned by the attitude of the Soviet Government" because its position seemed to be based upon "ruthless political considerations."[65] In another cable to Washington, Harriman indicated that he agreed with British leaders that "there is little hope for a Polish settlement if Stalin reverses his promise to Mikolajczyk to aid the Poles in Warsaw."[66] Roosevelt and Hull shared these concerns. On 20 August, Roosevelt joined with Churchill in urging Stalin to drop munitions to the Polish insurgents or to help U.S. planes do so.[67] But when Stalin refused to budge, Roosevelt decided not to press the matter.[68]

Hoping to deter the Soviet Union from becoming a "world bully," Harriman began to advocate a quid-pro-quo policy toward the Russians. "I am disappointed but not discouraged," he cabled Hopkins on 9 September. "Our problem is to strengthen the hand of those around Stalin who want to play the game along our lines and to show Stalin that he is being led into difficulties by the advice of the counselors of a tough policy."[69] His argument that the Russians would accede to reasonable American demands received support a day later when the Soviet Union agreed to act jointly with Great Britain and the United States in airlifting supplies to the Poles in Warsaw.[70] "I believe that it is their intention to have a positive sphere of influence over their western neighbors and the Balkan countries," Harriman cabled Hull on 20 September. "It is my conviction that only by our taking a definite interest in the solution of the problems of each individual country as they arise can we eventually come to an understanding with the USSR on the question of non-interference in the internal affairs of other countries."[71]

As the Red Army continued pushing into Eastern Europe, Churchill and Eden decided to go to Moscow not only to help settle the Polish dispute but also to protect British interests in the Balkans. But the State Department feared that a bilateral meeting between the British and the Russians would result in either a first-class row or the division of Europe into exclusive spheres of influence.[72] After Hopkins briefed the president about these dangers on 4 October 1944, Roosevelt immediately sent Stalin a telegram indicating that he regarded the forthcoming talks in Moscow as preliminary to a meeting of the Big Three. "There is literally no question, political or military, in which the United States is not interested," he informed Stalin. "I am convinced that the three of us, and only the three of us, can find the solution to the still unsolved questions." Roosevelt added that he would like Harriman to be present as an observer at the Anglo-Soviet conversations in Moscow but that the ambassador would not be in a position to commit the U.S. government with respect to the important matters that would be discussed.[73] In an accompanying message to Harriman, the president emphasized that he and Hull must have "complete freedom of action" when the conference ended.[74]

Upon his arrival in Moscow, Churchill gave Harriman a rough idea about what he and Eden would propose to Stalin and Molotov. "On matters in the Balkans," Harriman cabled Roosevelt on 10 October, "Churchill and Eden will try to work out some sort of spheres of influence with the Russians."[75] But in a telegram to Roosevelt later that day, Harriman was happy to report that Stalin had opposed a phrase implying the creation of spheres of influence. The president replied that he hoped practicable steps would be taken "to insure against the Balkans getting into an international war in the future." After wrangling over the relative responsibility the British and Russians would have in each country, Eden and Molotov eventually reached an agreement: Great Britain would have predominance in Greece; the Soviet Union would have predominance in Rumania, Bulgaria, and Hungary; and the two powers would have equal influence in Yugoslavia.[76] "It is absolutely necessary we should try to get a common mind about the Balkans, so that we may prevent civil war breaking out in several countries," Churchill cabled Roosevelt on 11 October. "Nothing will be settled except preliminary agreements between Britain and Russia, subject to further discussion and melting-down with you."[77]

Churchill and Stalin had invited both Mikolajczyk and representatives from the Polish Committee of National Liberation to come to Moscow to settle their differences. If discussions between the Poles failed to produce an agreement, Harriman reported to Roosevelt on 12 October, the British and Russians would attempt to force an equitable solution upon them.[78] In conversations over the next several days, Churchill and Stalin exerted pressure on Mikolajczyk to accept the Curzon Line, with small adjustments, as the boundary between Poland and Russia. Mikolajczyk said that he could not agree to their demands. But in response to threats from

Churchill, he finally promised to urge his colleagues in London to accept the Curzon Line with Lwow on the Russian side of the border. Talks concerning the composition of a new Polish government were also inconclusive. Stalin made it plain that the Lublin Poles must have a majority of the cabinet posts, while Churchill argued that unless the London Poles had at least half of the cabinet positions, the Western world would not believe that an independent Polish government had been established. Churchill could only hope that a settlement would be reached after the London and Lublin Poles returned home and consulted with their colleagues.[79]

American diplomats, in the meantime, had been discussing how the United States could integrate Poland and the other countries of Eastern Europe into a liberal capitalist world system. In a memorandum prepared for the top-level State Department Policy Committee on 26 September 1944, Adolf Berle observed that a Russian "sphere of influence" in Eastern Europe "operated in somewhat the same fashion as we have operated the good neighbor policy in Mexico and the Caribbean area would be no threat to anyone." But he argued that the United States should oppose the establishment of "closed" systems with trade or travel restrictions placed on American citizens but "not applicable to those of the greatest power in the region."[80] Pessimists like Lincoln MacVeagh, the U.S. ambassador to the Greek government-in-exile, feared that the decision not to send Western troops to the Balkans would mean the "elimination or suppression of the classes possessed of western trade affiliations" throughout Eastern Europe and the "virtual if not nominal annexation to the Soviet Union of imperial domain of some hundred million souls."[81] But optimists like Ambassador Harriman remained hopeful that the United States could use its financial resources to prevent Eastern Europe from falling under complete Russian domination.[82]

On 31 October 1944, a week after Harriman had expressed his views while attending a policy committee meeting, Under Secretary of State Edward R. Stettinius sent President Roosevelt a memorandum outlining American interests in promoting the economic reconstruction of Poland. "Postwar Poland will be under strong Russian influence," the State Department memorandum explained. But U.S. aid in Polish reconstruction would help bring about economic conditions that would enable the Poles to adopt a liberal policy of "equal opportunity in trade, investment, and access to sources of information."[83] On 8 November, Stettinius sent Roosevelt a broader State Department position paper based upon the memorandum that Berle had drafted for the policy committee. The paper emphasized that it was in the interest of the United States to promote in Eastern Europe, as elsewhere, not only "the right of peoples to choose and maintain for themselves without outside interference the type of political, social, and economic systems they desire" but also the principle of equal opportunity with respect to "commerce, transit, and trade" as well as phil-anthropic, educational, and news-gathering activities.[84]

President Roosevelt and his State Department advisors, however, feared that it would be difficult to implement these plans if the Russians began the process of establishing puppet regimes in Eastern Europe by rec-ognizing the Polish Committee of National Liberation as the only legal government of Poland.[85] Their apprehensions grew when Mikolajczyk resigned as prime minister of the Polish government-in-exile on 24 November and Poles who had rejected his program for reconciliation formed an anti-Soviet cabinet in London. In a message to Moscow on 16 December, Roosevelt asked Stalin to refrain from recognizing the Lublin committee as the government of Poland before the troublesome Polish question could be discussed at the next Big Three conference.[86] But Stalin replied that there was no reason to support the Polish émigré government because it lacked popular backing in Poland and its underground forces were attacking Soviet troops fighting to liberate the country.[87] Although Roosevelt asked Stalin again on 30 December to hold the question of recog-nition in abeyance until they had an opportunity to discuss the matter, the Soviet Union announced the next day that it would recognize the Lublin committee as the provisional government of Poland.[88]

American policymakers worried that Stalin aimed to set up puppet governments throughout Eastern Europe. In a cable to the State Depart-ment on 10 January 1945, Ambassador Harriman warned that the Russians were employing various means at their disposal in Eastern Europe "to assure the establishment of regimes which, while maintaining an outward appearance of independence and of popular support, actually depend for their existence on groups responsive to all suggestions emanating from the Kremlin."[89] George F. Kennan, the counselor at the U.S. embassy in Moscow, believed that the United States should agree with the Soviet Union to "divide Europe frankly into spheres of influence" by making a deal that would "keep ourselves out of the Russian sphere and keep the Russians out of ours."[90] But President Roosevelt was not willing to write off Eastern Europe. Since the United States was in no position to force things to an issue there, Roosevelt told a group of Senate leaders on 11 January, "the only practicable course was to use what influence we had to ameliorate the situation." Roosevelt said that he still believed that eventually "much could be done by readjustment" if the Russians could be brought into a United Nations security organization.[91]

The president and his State Department advisers hoped to use U.S. financial aid to dissuade the Russians from establishing a closed sphere in Eastern Europe. On 6 January 1945, Harriman informed Secretary of State Stettinius that Molotov had proposed that the United States extend a $6 billion reconstruction credit to the Soviet Union. "At the appropriate time," Harriman advised Stettinius, "the Russians should be given to understand that our willingness to cooperate whole-heartedly with them in their vast reconstruction problems will depend upon their behavior in international matters."[92] During a meeting with Stettinius on 10 January, Roosevelt said that he did not want to discuss any postwar credit proposal with the Russians until after the forthcoming Big Three conference at Yalta. "I think it's very important," Stettinius declared, "that we hold this back and don't give them any promise of finance until we get what we want."[93] Assistant Secretary of State William L. Clayton agreed. "From a tactical point of view," he advised Stettinius on 20 January, "it would seem harmful for us to offer such a large credit at this time and thus lose what appears to be the only concrete bargaining lever for use in connection with the many other political and economic problems which will arise between our two countries."[94] A week later, the State Department authorized the embassy in Moscow to inform the Soviet government that the United States could not provide long-term credits for postwar reconstruction until Congress enacted the necessary legislation.[95]

In preparation for the Yalta Conference, the State Department drafted proposals for both a European high commission and a joint declaration on policy toward liberated areas. Together, the purpose of the proposals was to promote the establishment of popular governments in Eastern Europe and to help solve pressing economic problems in the region pending the formation of the United Nations. Encouraged by their belief that free elections in Eastern Europe would produce liberal regimes that would be acceptable to the Russians, State Department officials hoped that a high commission and a joint declaration would reassure the American people that the projected world organization would not underwrite a new era of territorial and political aggrandizement. But President Roosevelt had misgivings about the effectiveness of a European high commission, and he decided that only the proposal for a joint declaration should be advanced at Yalta.[96] On 10 February, after the wording was changed to emphasize consultation rather than enforcement, the Big Three adopted the Declaration on Liberated Europe, which stated that their governments would jointly assist in the organization of "interim governmental authorities broadly representative of all democratic elements in the population and pledged to the earliest possible establishment through free elections of governments responsive to the will of the people."[97]

Despite their disagreement regarding the proposal for a European high commission, there was no difference of opinion between Roosevelt and the State Department with respect to Poland. During a meeting with Eden on 1 February at Malta, Secretary of State Stettinius said that there would be a public uproar if the United States and Great Britain recognized the Lublin government. The British foreign secretary concurred when Stettinius argued that there should be a new Polish government that included Mikolajczyk and other leaders representing all segments of the political spectrum. "Failure to reach a satisfactory solution of this question," Stettinius warned, "would greatly disturb public opinion in America especially among the Catholics and might prejudice the whole question of American participation in the postwar world organization." He said that Roosevelt and Churchill should explain the importance of this matter during their discussions with Stalin at Yalta. On 4 February, when Stettinius briefed the president about his conversations with Eden, Roosevelt agreed that the Lublin government should not be recognized.[98]

During the Yalta Conference, the Big Three wrestled with the Polish question. They agreed that the eastern frontier of Poland should follow the Curzon Line with minor deviations and that the western frontier should be determined at the final peace settlement. After considerable discussion, they also reached an agreement regarding its provisional government. Stalin believed that the Lublin regime should merely be enlarged by adding a few eminent Poles from inside and outside the country. Taking a different position, Roosevelt and Churchill advocated the creation of an entirely new interim government comprising all factions and committed to free elections in the near future. The final compromise formula, approved on 10 February, stated that the provisional government currently functioning in Poland should be "reorganized on a broader democratic basis" and that the new interim government would be "pledged to the holding of free and unfettered elections as soon as possible." Although Stalin estimated that those elections could be held in about one month, he rejected an American proposal calling for international supervision to guarantee their fairness.[99]

As they departed from Yalta, the president and his State Department advisers hoped the people of Eastern Europe would be permitted to choose their own political leaders and engage in unrestricted economic relations with the rest of the world. But the Russians soon demanded the installation of a communist government in Rumania, and they rejected American requests for tripartite consultations as envisaged in the Declaration on Liberated Europe.[100] The Russians also refused to allow representatives of American oil companies to go into Rumania. At a cabinet meeting on 2 March, Roosevelt said that he was thinking about offering the Soviet Union some warships "as a *quid pro quo* in persuading Russia to let down the bars for American businessmen to enter Rumania."[101] The president also wanted Great Britain to open the doors of Greece to American trade and investment. In a cable to Churchill on 21 March, Roosevelt suggested the dispatch of a special mission, comprised of U.S., British, and Soviet representatives, to promote economic development in Greece. When Churchill objected to an economic mission that included the Russians, the president replied that he might send Donald M. Nelson, who had returned from a similar assignment in China, to make a survey of Greek financial needs and commercial possibilities.[102]

But the Polish question had become the focal point of Anglo-American concern. In early March 1945 a tripartite commission made up of Harriman, Clark Kerr (who was serving as the British ambassador in Russia), and Molotov began meeting in Moscow to determine which Poles should be invited for consultations to form a new government. But Molotov would agree to invite only those Poles, either from Poland or London, who were on a list submitted by the Lublin government, which had moved to Warsaw.[103] Stating that he regarded the Polish question as a test case of Russian willingness to carry out the Yalta agreements, Churchill proposed on 8 March that both he and Roosevelt send Stalin messages taking a tough stand on Poland. But Roosevelt and his State Department advisers wanted to avoid a confrontation with Stalin, and they hoped that Harriman and Kerr would be able to settle their differences with Molotov. "I feel," the president replied to Churchill on 11 March, "that our personal intervention would best be withheld until every other possibility of bringing the Soviet Government into line has been exhausted."[104]

American policymakers decided to make a direct appeal to Stalin, however, after Harriman reported on 25 March that Molotov insisted that only those Poles who were acceptable to the provisional government in Warsaw should be invited to Moscow and that the present Warsaw regime should serve as the basis for the formation of a new Polish government.[105] "I must make it quite plain to you that any such solution which would result in a thinly disguised continuance of the present Warsaw regime would be unacceptable and would cause the people of the United States to regard the Yalta agreement as having failed," Roosevelt warned Stalin on 1 April. "It is equally apparent that for the same reason the Warsaw Government cannot under the agreement claim the right to select or reject what Poles are to be brought to Moscow by the commission for consultation." The president emphasized that it was the task of the tripartite commission in Moscow to decide which Polish leaders should be invited to begin the process of creating a new government. "I wish I could convey to you," he concluded, "how important it is for the successful development of our program of international collaboration that this Polish question be settled fairly and speedily."[106]

American policymakers hoped that the message would produce satisfactory results. But in a cable to the State Department on 3 April, Harriman reported that Molotov had firmly rejected his proposal to invite Mikolajczyk for consultations and that the negotiations in Moscow were near a breaking point. "I still believe that there is a chance at least that the Soviet Government may yield," he observed, but only "if they are confronted with a definite and firm position on our part."[107] Since the Russians had shown little willingness to implement the Yalta decisions on Poland, Harriman advised a day later, the United States should be cautious in making commitments on reparations for the Soviet Union.[108] Roosevelt promptly instructed Isador Lubin, the head of the U.S. delegation on the Allied Reparations Commission, to refer any proposals to him when discussions began in Moscow.[109] After receiving a very unsatisfactory message from Stalin on 7 April, the president and his State Department advisers tried to dissuade Churchill from making a rash public statement that would undermine their plans for postwar cooperation with the Soviet Union.[110] This was the situation when Roosevelt suddenly died five days later.

Pres. Harry S. Truman immediately turned to the State Department for advice on the principal international problems facing the country. On 13 April 1945, his first day in the White House, Truman received briefings from Stettinius and Bohlen about the Polish issue and the deterioration in U.S. relations with the Soviet Union. Truman quickly indicated that he was prepared to take a firm stand against the Russians.[111] In a memorandum prepared for him later that day, the State Department reported that Soviet authorities were sabotaging American efforts to implement the Yalta agreement on Poland and were violating the Declaration on Liberated

Europe by taking unilateral political action in the Balkans. Truman promptly decided that he and Churchill should send Stalin a joint message rejecting the Russian claim that the Warsaw government had the right to determine which Polish leaders should be invited to Moscow for consultations and suggesting a list of men who might be invited to begin talks for forming a new government.[112]

Ambassador Harriman delivered their message to Stalin and then hurried back to Washington to give his views on U.S. relations with the Soviet Union. During a meeting with top State Department officials on 20 April, Harriman said that the Russians had undoubtedly regarded American generosity as a sign of weakness but that now they were greatly disturbed by the determination of the United States to maintain its position with regard to Poland. He also said it was obvious that Stalin had come to realize that it would be difficult to dominate that nation if the Yalta decisions were carried out. "It seemed evident that Mikolajczyk and the other old leaders would be welcomed by the majority of the Poles," he explained, "and thus the Lublin group would be weakened." Harriman concluded that the United States should try to prevent the Soviet Union from establishing puppet governments in Eastern Europe because the urge for security would propel the Russians to extend their influence as far as possible. "The Soviet Union," he warned, "once it had control of bordering areas, would attempt to penetrate the next adjacent countries."[113]

When he left the State Department meeting, Harriman went directly to the White House to prepare Truman for discussions with Foreign Minister Molotov, who had accepted an invitation to come to Washington. Harriman told the president that the Russians had "two policies which they thought they could successfully pursue at the same time—one, the policy of cooperation with the United States and Great Britain, and the other, the extension of Soviet control over neighboring states through unilateral action." Harriman said he did not believe the Russians wished to break with the United States. "Since they needed our help in order to reduce the burden of reconstruction," he reasoned, "we had nothing to lose by standing firm on issues that were of real importance to us." Truman replied that he intended to be firm in dealing with the Soviets because he thought they "needed us more than we needed them." When Harriman observed that some concessions would have to be made in the give and take of negotiations, the president said he realized that "we could not, of course, expect to get 100 percent of what we wanted," but he believed that on important matters "we should be able to get 85 percent." Unless the Polish question could be settled in a satisfactory manner, he noted, the Senate would not ratify a treaty permitting U.S. participation in a world security organization.[114]

After several talks with State Department officials during the next two days, Truman met with his chief diplomatic and military advisers on 23 April to review the Polish problem.[115] Secretary of State Stettinius began the discussion by explaining that it was now clear that the Russians intended to force the United States and Great Britain to recognize the provisional government in Warsaw even though it was not representative of the Polish people. After declaring that he thought "our agreements with the Soviet Union so far had been a one way street," Truman asked the others for their views. Secretary of War Henry L. Stimson urged caution because he did not think the Russians would yield on Poland, but Secretary of the Navy James V. Forrestal said that since it was evident the Soviets aimed to dominate Eastern Europe, "we had better have a showdown with them now than later." Although Gen. George C. Marshall warned that a break with the Russians might have serious consequences with regard to the war against Japan, Gen. John R. Deane, the head of the U.S. military mission in Moscow, said he thought the Soviet Union would enter the war in the Pacific as soon as possible regardless of what happened in other fields. The president concluded that from a military viewpoint there was no reason why he should not stand up to the Russians.[116]

During his meeting with Molotov later that day, Truman emphasized that the United States would not agree to the formation of a Polish government that was not representative of all democratic elements. Then he suggested that unless the American people were satisfied with the solution to the Polish problem, Congress would not pass legislation that would permit him to furnish the Soviet Union economic assistance for postwar reconstruction. After he asked Molotov to give Stalin a message stating that the Yalta decision could only be implemented if a group of genuinely representative Polish leaders were invited to Moscow for consultation, Truman bluntly told the Soviet foreign minister that an agreement had been reached on Poland and that he wanted Stalin to carry it out in accordance with his word. The president ended his conversation with Molotov by saying that he desired friendly relations with the Soviet Union but only "on the basis of mutual observation of agreements and not on the basis of a one way street."[117]

When Stalin refused to change his position on Poland, the president demonstrated his desire for continued Big Three collaboration by sending

Harry Hopkins on a special mission to Moscow. During his discussions with Stalin between 26 May and 6 June 1945, Hopkins emphasized that without the support of public opinion, Truman could not carry forward the Roosevelt policy of cooperation with Russia. He explained that the Polish issue had become "a symbol of our ability to work out problems with the Soviet Union" and that the American people were disturbed because the Russians had taken unilateral action. After stating that it was in "Russia's vital interest that Poland should be both strong and friendly" so it would never again serve as a corridor for German attacks on the Soviet Union, Stalin assured Hopkins that he did not intend to "interfere in Poland's internal affairs." Stalin proposed that members of the present Warsaw regime should retain a majority of the posts in a new Polish government, and he eventually agreed with Hopkins on a list of Poles who would be invited to Moscow for consultation.[118]

Those who received invitations to Moscow promptly established a new Polish government, with communists holding most of the key positions. In a cable to the State Department on 28 June, Harriman reported that Mikolajczyk, who had been named deputy prime minister in the new regime in Warsaw, hoped that Poland would be able to enjoy "a reasonable degree of freedom and independence" even though he realized it would have to "follow the lead of Moscow" on security matters. "There is a fair chance that things will work out satisfactorily from our standpoint," Harriman surmised, "if we continue to take a sympathetic interest in Polish affairs and are reasonably generous in our economic relations."[119] State Department officials shared his wish that the Poles would hold free elections and adopt a liberal commercial policy if the U.S. government provided financial assistance for their nation's reconstruction. During the Potsdam Conference, which began two weeks after the Americans and British recognized the new government in Warsaw on 5 July, Polish leaders promised to hold free elections and expressed great enthusiasm for close economic relations with the United States.[120]

Plans to provide financial aid to Poland were part of a broader American campaign to reintegrate Eastern Europe into a liberal capitalist international order. During a conversation with Stimson on 16 May 1945, Truman said he hoped the agricultural areas of Eastern Europe could be linked to the industrial centers of Western Europe by the free flow of trade along the Rhine and Danube Rivers. State Department officials agreed that the countries of Eastern Europe should be permitted to exchange their foodstuffs and raw materials for industrial goods made in Western Europe and the United States. During the Big Three meeting at Potsdam, Truman proposed that the inland waterways of Europe should be open to unrestricted navigation all the way from the North Sea to the Black Sea. The president also proposed that the puppet governments the Russians had installed in Rumania and Bulgaria should be reorganized along democratic lines as called for in the Declaration on Liberated Europe. Although the Soviet delegation at Potsdam did not accept either proposal, President Truman and his State Department advisers remained confident that they would be able to persuade Stalin to go along with their plans for Eastern Europe.[121]

Their optimism was based primarily upon the knowledge that the Russians wanted U.S. financial aid for postwar reconstruction. "We should not grant large irrevocable credits to Russia without retaining to ourselves the power to restrict or reduce them as we may see fit," Harriman advised a day before Roosevelt died. "We should at all times make it plain that our cooperation is dependent upon a reciprocal cooperative attitude in other matters on the part of the Soviet Government."[122] During a meeting in the State Department on 21 April 1945, Harriman agreed with Clayton that the Russian desire for American credits was "the greatest element in our leverage," and he suggested making a one-year arrangement that could be expanded or terminated as conditions warranted.[123] Truman subsequently approved a State Department proposal to offer the Soviet Union a $1 billion Export-Import Bank loan if political conditions were favorable. On 9 August, Harriman informed Soviet officials that the United States was ready to consider a request for financial aid. The Russians asked the Export-Import Bank for a $1 billion dollar loan three weeks later, but they eventually learned that their request would not be approved unless they relaxed their controls over Eastern Europe.[124]

Secretary of State James F. Byrnes thought that the Russians could satisfy their strategic interests while permitting free elections and unrestricted trade in Eastern Europe. But during the Foreign Ministers' Conference, which began in London on 11 September 1945, Molotov remained unwilling to reorganize the Rumanian and Bulgarian governments along democratic lines. Yet Byrnes did not give up hope that he could reach an accommodation with the Russians. In a public speech directed at the Kremlin on 31 October, he acknowledged that the Soviet Union had legitimate security interests in Eastern Europe, although he made it clear that the United States would oppose the establishment of an exclusive Russian sphere of influence in that region. Byrnes subsequently proposed that the foreign ministers should meet in Moscow, where he would have a chance to talk directly with Stalin. Byrnes arrived in the Soviet capital on

14 December eager to break the deadlock over the Balkans. When Stalin indicated that he would accept token changes in the existing governments in Rumania and Bulgaria, Byrnes felt that he had obtained a meaningful concession.[125]

But President Truman decided it was time to draw the line against the further spread of Soviet influence in Eastern Europe and elsewhere. On 5 January 1946, he read a report that the Russians were using local communist parties to establish economic and political domination over the Balkans. "To concede a limited Soviet sphere of influence at the present time," the report warned, "would be to invite its extension in the future."[126] In a letter to Byrnes later that day, Truman stated that he would not grant recognition to Rumania and Bulgaria until their governments were "radically changed." The president charged that the Soviets were stirring up a rebellion in Iran and preparing an invasion of Turkey for the purpose of seizing the straits linking the Black Sea to the Mediterranean. "Unless Russia is faced with an iron fist and strong language," he declared, "another war is in the making." Truman insisted that American interests throughout Europe, the Middle East, and Asia must be protected from the continued expansion of Russian influence. "I do not think we should play compromise any longer," he concluded. "I'm tired of babying the Soviets."[127]

President Truman, like President Roosevelt and the postwar planners in the State Department, had hoped that it would be possible to collaborate with the Soviet Union in establishing a peaceful and prosperous international order. Furthermore, along with Roosevelt and the top State Department officials, Truman had planned on using U.S. financial resources to reintegrate Eastern Europe into a liberal capitalist world system. American policymakers had believed from the beginning of their deliberations that they might be able to persuade the Soviets to treat the small countries along their western border in much the same way that the United States behaved toward its small neighbors in the Western Hemisphere. But it became increasingly clear after Roosevelt died that Stalin had no intention of permitting the people of Eastern Europe to choose their own political leaders in free elections or to engage in unrestricted economic relations with Western Europe and the United States. When Truman found that he could not dissuade the Russians from creating an exclusive sphere of Soviet influence in Eastern Europe to protect themselves against future military attacks, he decided that the United States should embark upon a policy of containment to prevent the spread of communism into other parts of the world.

CONCLUSION | THE POSTWAR ERA

President Roosevelt and his State Department advisers formulated comprehensive plans for the inauguration of a new era of peace and prosperity after the defeat of the Axis powers. In the first place, they aimed to use American financial resources to help establish a liberal capitalist world system. Their economic program called for the reduction of trade barriers and the elimination of commercial discriminations, the industrial reconstruction of Germany and the other countries in Western Europe, the reintegration of Japan and the smaller nations of Eastern Europe into a multilateral trading network, the decolonization of Asia and Africa, the modernization of China, and the development of the petroleum reserves in the Middle East. In the second place, they intended to use U.S. military power to help construct an effective system of international security. Their strategic agenda called for the disarmament of Germany and Japan, the collaboration of the four major powers in policing the planet in the years immediately following the cessation of hostilities, and the creation of a general security organization able to deter or defeat any country with aggressive designs.

Policymakers in the United States perceived an intimate connection between the economic and strategic aspects of their plans for the postwar world. On the one hand, President Roosevelt and his State Department advisers reasoned that countries would be less likely to embark upon programs of territorial conquest if their economic needs could be satisfied within a framework of peaceful commerce. They realized that the restoration of liberal commercial practices would not be sufficient to prevent the outbreak of any military conflicts in the future. But they did believe that it would be difficult for the projected international security organization to preserve the peace unless commercial restrictions were relaxed around the globe. On the other hand, civilian officials and military leaders in Washington agreed that the United States must be prepared not only to repel an attack against its shores but also to protect its economic interests overseas. Thus, they advocated the institution of a system of universal military training in the United States and the acquisition of a far-flung network of naval and air bases so that American military power could be projected throughout the world.

The architects of globalism in the State Department maintained close relations with President Roosevelt as they drafted their blueprints for a new world order. Adolf Berle, Isaiah Bowman, Norman Davis, Cordell Hull, Edward Stettinius, Myron Taylor, and Sumner Welles all had direct access to the president, and they kept him fully informed about the work of the various postwar planning committees. Hoping to see how things unfolded before committing himself to a definite course of action, Roosevelt sometimes refused to be pinned down by his State Department advisers. But he ultimately endorsed their position with respect to the most important postwar issues, such as the debate about the economic treatment of Germany or the controversy over the Japanese possessions in the Pacific. Agreeing with the State Department that the Japanese mandates should be placed under some form of international trusteeship, Roosevelt turned a deaf ear to War and Navy Department arguments for U.S. ownership of these islands. Although he did approve the Morgenthau Plan to deindustrialize Germany, Roosevelt quickly backtracked when he realized that the Treasury Department proposal would undermine State Department efforts to promote the economic reconstruction of Europe.

The foreign policy of the United States did not undergo any fundamental change when Roosevelt died and Truman moved into the White House. From the very outset of his administration, President Truman made it clear that he intended to implement the postwar plans that had been formulated in the State Department and approved by Roosevelt. The new president immediately turned to the State Department for advice about crucial issues concerning Great Britain and the Soviet Union. Although Truman decided that James F. Byrnes should replace Stettinius as secretary of state, the basic ideas that had been institutionalized in the State Department continued to guide the conduct of U.S. diplomacy. Byrnes and his aides knew that their hopes for international collaboration to deter aggression would be dashed if the Russians used their military power to establish Soviet hegemony in Eastern Europe. They also understood that their program to expand world trade could not be carried out if the British refused to abandon their restrictive commercial practices.

During the long military ordeal that had begun when Germany invaded Poland in September 1939, Great Britain developed a serious balance of payments problem as its industries shifted to the production of military goods and its export trade declined by 70 percent. The lend-lease program enabled the British to obtain essential supplies from the United States despite their shortage of foreign exchange. In addition, the British were able to purchase vital materials from India, Egypt, and other countries in the sterling area by using blocked funds that could not be converted into dollars to pay for goods or services from the United States. Policymakers in Washington believed that most of these blocked sterling balances (like the debits in the lend-lease accounts) should be written off and that the rest should be unfrozen. "The barriers and discriminations against American trade in the sterling area are due basically to the shortage of dollars and the consequent blocking of sterling," a State Department official explained on 11 May 1945. "The success of any international postwar program for reducing trade barriers and removing discriminations will depend on finding some means of unblocking these funds."[1]

President Truman and his State Department advisers were prepared to offer the British a generous financial-aid package after the termination of the lend-lease program if the United Kingdom would adopt a liberal commercial policy. They hoped that a large American loan would make it possible for Great Britain to acquire foodstuffs and machinery from the United States in the immediate postwar years before its industries could be turned back to the production of civilian goods and its export trade could be restored to prewar levels. Acting upon instructions from President Truman in August 1945, Assistant Secretary of State William L. Clayton held informal talks about postwar economic problems with British officials in London. "I have indicated," Clayton reported to Secretary of State Byrnes, "that it will be necessary for us to come to a broad understanding as to postwar trading methods and policy before we can ask the Congress for any large scale financial aid for the British."[2] When formal economic negotiations between the United States and Great Britain commenced in Washington on 11 September 1945, Clayton and Secretary of the Treasury Fred M. Vinson headed the American delegation.

Realizing that the British were already cutting their imports from the United States to the bone and channeling their trade into the sterling area, Clayton believed that the Anglo-American economic talks would determine the pattern of international commerce for the next fifty years. "If the discussions fail," he warned his colleagues in the State Department on 9 October 1945, "world trade will go back to a bilateral autarkic bargaining basis involving the formation of economic blocs and the recurrence of trade warfare."[3] In a letter a month later to Robert E. Wood, the chairman of the board of Sears, Clayton noted that the vast majority of

Americans did not understand why it was vitally important for the their government to extend a reasonable credit to Great Britain. "If we make the loan," he wrote, "one of the principal purposes will be to enable the British people to open up their commerce to the United States and all other countries instead of confining it to the British Empire as they would largely be compelled to do if they were not able to obtain the necessary assistance to get their trade back on a multilateral basis."[4]

The Anglo-American financial agreement was signed on 6 December 1945 after Great Britain promised to cooperate with the United States in establishing a multilateral trading network based upon the principle of equal commercial opportunity. The U.S. government agreed to provide the United Kingdom with a $3.75 billion credit to be repaid over a fifty-year period at an effective interest rate of only 1.63 percent. In return, the British agreed to make sterling proceeds from current transactions fully convertible into any monetary unit within a year after the accord went into effect. The British also indicated that they would completely write off or gradually unfreeze the sterling funds that had accumulated in blocked accounts. Finally, the British pledged that they would quickly remove any discriminatory import restrictions or exchange controls that they had imposed against American commerce. President Truman and his State Department advisers were pleased. They believed that the low-interest American loan would enable the United Kingdom to dispense with discriminatory commercial practices after a much shorter transition period than the Bretton Woods accord had envisaged.[5]

Assistant Secretary Clayton and his associates in the State Department promptly began a vigorous campaign to win congressional support for the Anglo-American financial agreement. "Now that World War II is over, there are only two economic courses open to the countries of the world," Clayton declared in a public speech delivered on 15 February 1946. "They can continue on a nationalistic bilateral barter system, patterned along the lines developed so intensively by Nazi Germany, or they can go back to the multilateral basis where every country is free to trade with every other country with a minimum of restrictions and discriminations." Rather than standing aside and permitting the planet to be divided into closed economic blocs that would breed poverty and war, Clayton argued, the United States must take the lead in building an open system of multilateral trade that would generate prosperity and peace around the globe. "With the help of Britain, leader of the greatest international trading area in the world, there is strong reason to believe that we can be successful in charting the right course," he concluded. "Without her help we can hardly hope to succeed."[6]

Although Congress approved the Anglo-American financial agreement on 15 July 1946, it soon became apparent that Great Britain and the industrial countries in Western Europe would need something more than low-interest loans from the United States in order to recover from the devastating effects of the war. The British faced a serious balance-of-payments crisis in 1947, when they attempted to carry out their commitment to make sterling convertible into other monetary units, and many of their trading partners rushed to exchange sterling for dollars. American policymakers quickly decided that the British and their neighbors on the European continent would require free grants so they could modernize their industries, expand their export trade, and earn dollars needed to purchase goods and services from the United States. After Congress appropriated funds for the Marshall Plan in 1948, Great Britain and the war-torn countries of Western Europe began receiving U.S. economic aid in the form of grants that never had to be repaid. But the State Department officials who drafted the Marshall Plan did extract promises from these countries to adhere to liberal commercial principles.

President Truman and his State Department advisers had intended to use U.S. financial aid as a tool not only to promote economic cooperation with Great Britain but also to foster strategic collaboration with the Soviet Union. As World War II drew to a close in August 1945, they remained hopeful that the Soviets would seek to protect their western borders from any future attacks by working with the other great powers to build a strong international security organization rather than by taking unilateral steps to establish an exclusive sphere of influence in Eastern Europe. Policymakers in the United States believed that Stalin could satisfy his legitimate security aspirations without subjecting the small countries in Eastern Europe to his political and commercial domination. If Stalin demonstrated that he was willing to rely upon the United Nations to keep Russia secure and to permit the people of Eastern Europe to elect their own political leaders and engage in unrestricted trade with the rest of the world, American officials were ready to offer the Soviet Union a $1 billion Export-Import Bank loan that could be used to buy reconstruction equipment from the United States.

State Department officials continued to regard their Good Neighbor policy toward Latin America as a model for the Soviet Union to emulate in Eastern Europe. In a memorandum prepared on 18 October 1945,

Charles E. Bohlen argued that the present relationship between the United States and the Latin American republics provided an excellent precedent for the way great powers could exercise their legitimate prerogatives with respect to smaller countries in close geographical proximity. "We would," he explained, "oppose and even forbid the conclusion of military and political alliances between a Latin American state and a European or Asiatic power. We do not on the other hand attempt to prevent normal trade, cultural exchange, and other normal international intercourse."[7] In a speech directed at the Kremlin two weeks later, Secretary of State Byrnes expressed his hope that the Russians would follow the American example and act like good neighbors toward the small countries along their western frontier. "The policy of the good neighbor," Byrnes declared, "is not an exclusive arrangement. The best neighbors do not deny their neighbors the right to be friends with others."[8]

But it soon became clear that Stalin would not allow unrestricted trade and free elections in Eastern Europe. He decided that it would be safer to bring the countries occupied by the Red Army under his complete domination rather than to depend solely upon the United Nations to protect the Soviet Union from any future aggression. Fearful that democratic governments in Eastern Europe would not be friendly toward the Soviet Union, the Russians installed puppet regimes that could be counted on to keep the entire region under their economic and strategic control. President Truman and his State Department advisers were chagrined. But they did not challenge the establishment of Russian hegemony in Eastern Europe because the United States did not have vital interests in the area. Instead, as their efforts to dissuade the Russians from closing the doors of Eastern Europe met with continued frustration, U.S. policymakers decided to use their financial resources and military strength to prevent the further spread of Soviet influence and to contain the cancer of communism.

The ensuing confrontation between the United States and the Soviet Union shattered American plans for the establishment of an effective system of international security. As Americans and Russians became increasingly hostile toward each other, they divided Germany into two different states representing the opposing ideologies of capitalism and communism. The countries of Western Europe, worried about the possibility of an invasion from the Soviet Union, joined with the United States in creating the North Atlantic Treaty Organization. As part of their endeavor to deter the

Russians from making any aggressive moves on the European continent, U.S. policymakers decided to rearm West Germany. They also decided, after China fell into the communist orbit, to rearm Japan and help build that former Axis power into a capitalist bastion in East Asia. In the meantime, despite their membership in the United Nations and their commitment to work together for the preservation of world peace, the United States and the Soviet Union became locked in a nuclear arms race that provoked growing fears of worldwide destruction.

The architects of globalism in the United States were far more successful in laying the foundations for the establishment of a liberal capitalist world system. Their efforts during World War II paved the way for the General Agreement on Tariffs and Trade, the North American Free Trade Agreement, and the World Trade Organization. From the beginning of their deliberations, the postwar planners in the State Department hoped that an expansion of international commerce would lead to a long period of world peace. But they were prepared to employ military force, if necessary, to keep foreign markets open for American products and thereby assure the survival of free enterprise in the United States. After World War II ended, U.S. policymakers waged limited wars in Korea and Vietnam to prevent the countries of Southeast Asia from being drawn into the communist bloc. They also fought a regional war in the Persian Gulf so that the United States and its trading partners would continue to have access to low-priced oil from the Middle East. Finally, they authorized the Central Intelligence Agency to conduct covert operations to safeguard American trade and investment in various countries such as Guatemala, Chile, and Nicaragua.

President Roosevelt and the postwar planners in the State Department would have been dismayed had they been able to read many of the stories that appeared on the front page of newspapers during the last half of the twentieth century. Despite their efforts to bring about the gradual decolonization of Asia and Africa, the actual transition to independent nationhood often involved revolutionary upheavals that jeopardized U.S. economic and strategic interests. Furthermore, despite their search for a peaceful solution to the Palestine question, violent clashes between Arabs and Jews threatened to disrupt the flow of oil from the Middle East. Worse yet, despite their desire for friendly relations with the Russians, the United States and the Soviet Union became enemies in a cold war that polarized the international community for almost fifty years. Roosevelt and his postwar advisers would have been disappointed to learn that the two superpowers became bitter rivals for decades after the defeat of Germany and Japan. But they would have been relieved to find that the Soviet-American confrontation did not culminate in a third world war. Moreover, they would have been pleased to learn that the United States, though plagued by recurrent bouts of recession, did enjoy the fruits of prosperity throughout most of the postwar era.

NOTES

ABBREVIATIONS

CFR   Council on Foreign Relations
FDRL   Franklin D. Roosevelt Library, Hyde Park, N.Y.
FRUS   *Foreign Relations of the United States*
HBSBL   Harvard Business School, Baker Library, Boston, Mass.
HCHL   Herbert C. Hoover Library, West Branch, Iowa
HSTL   Harry S. Truman Library, Independence, Mo.
HUHL   Harvard University, Houghton Library, Cambridge, Mass.
JFDPC   John F. Doyle Private Collection, Naperville, Ill.
JHUSCL   Johns Hopkins University, Special Collections Library,
              Baltimore, Md.
LC   Library of Congress, Washington, D.C.
NA   National Archives, Washington, D.C.
PUML   Princeton University, Mudd Library, Princeton, N.J.
RG   Record Group
UVAL   University of Virginia, Alderman Library, Charlottesville
WSHS   Wisconsin State Historical Society, Madison
YUSL   Yale University, Sterling Library, New Haven, Conn.

1. POSTWAR PLANNING BEFORE PEARL HARBOR

1. Harley A. Notter, *Postwar Foreign Policy Preparation, 1939–1945* (Washington: Government Printing Office, 1949), 19; Laurence H. Shoup and William Minter, *Imperial Brain Trust: The Council on Foreign Relations and United States Foreign Policy* (New York: Monthly Review Press, 1971), 118–25. From early 1940 until the end of the war, the Council on Foreign Relations transmitted 682 memoranda to the State Department. Serially titled Studies of American Interests in the War and the Peace, they were financed by grants from the Rockefeller Foundation.

2. Maurice Cowling, *The Impact of Hitler: British Politics and British Policy, 1933–1940* (Chicago: University of Chicago Press, 1975), 355–60. See also Joseph Kennedy to Franklin D. Roosevelt and Cordell Hull, 8 Nov. 1939, 740.0019 E. W. 1939/133, RG 59, NA; William C. Bullitt to Roosevelt, 4 Oct. 1939, S. F., Box 2, Franklin D. Roosevelt Papers; and Bullitt to Roosevelt, 11 Dec. 1939, S. F., Box 43, Roosevelt Papers, FDRL.

3. William R. Davis to Franklin D. Roosevelt, 11 Oct. 1939, Box 3, Robert E. Wood Papers, HCHL; Beatrice B. Berle and Travis B. Jacobs, eds., *Navigating the Rapids, 1918–1971: From the Papers of Adolf A. Berle* (New York: Harcourt Brace Jovanovich, 1973), 256–66; J. Pierrepont Moffat Diary, 7 Oct. 1939, J. Pierrepont Moffat Papers, HUHL; Moffat to Leland Harrison, 14 Nov. 1939, Moffat Papers; George S. Messersmith to Cordell Hull, 8 Oct. 1939, Cordell Hull Papers, LC.

4. Joseph E. Davies to Cordell Hull, 15 Oct. 1939, 740.0011 E. W. 1939/1035, RG 59, NA. See also John C. Wiley to Arthur Bliss Lane, 27 Nov. 1939, Box 8, John C. Wiley Papers, FDRL.

5. Berle and Jacobs, *Navigating the Rapids,* 254. See also J. Pierrepont Moffat to John C. Wiley, 31 Oct. 1939, Wiley Papers; and Moffat to Owen Norem, 18 Nov. 1939, Moffat Papers.

6. Fred L. Israel, ed., *The War Diary of Breckinridge Long* (Lincoln: University of Nebraska Press, 1966), 1 (see also 66).

7. Herbert Feis to Henry L. Stimson, 16 Oct. 1939, Henry L. Stimson Papers, ser. 1, Box 132, YUSL.

8. Breckinridge Long Diary, 6 Dec. 1939, Breckinridge Long Papers, LC.

9. Elliot Roosevelt, ed., *F.D.R.: His Personal Letters, 1925–1945,* 2 vols. (New York: Duel, Sloan, and Pearce, 1950), 2:967–68.

10. William L. Langer and S. Everett Gleason, *The Challenge to Isolation,* 2 vols. (New York: Harper and Row, 1952), 1:222–29; Robert Dallek, *Franklin D. Roosevelt and American Foreign Policy, 1932–1945* (New York: Oxford University Press, 1979), 201; Joseph Lash, *Roosevelt and Churchill: The Partnership that Saved the West, 1939–1941* (New York: W. W. Norton, 1976), 64–65, 87; Harold Ickes, *The Secret Diary of Harold L. Ickes,* vol. 3, *The Lowering Clouds, 1939–1941* (New York: Simon and Schuster, 1954), 37, 182.

11. Israel, *War Diary of Breckinridge Long,* 24.

12. R. Walton Moore to Francis B. Sayre, 28 Feb. 1940, Box 25, R. Walton Moore Papers, FDRL.

13. Moffat Diary, 1 Sept. 1939. See also Moffat Diary, 8 Dec. 1939; Joseph E. Davies to Cordell Hull, 15 Oct. 1939, 740.0011 E. W./1035, RG 59, NA; John Cudahy to Missy Le Hand, 17 Nov. 1939, S. F., Box 56, Roosevelt Papers; and Alexander C. Kirk to Herbert Feis, 12 Feb. 1940, Box 20, Herbert Feis Papers, LC.

14. Alvin H. Hansen, memorandum, "Alternative Outcomes of the War," 28 June 1940, Studies of American Interests in the War and the Peace, CFR.

15. *Fortune,* Jan. 1940, 72–73.

16. Ibid., Apr. 1940, 96. See also *Barron's,* 13 May 1940, 10; and *Magazine of Wall Street,* 15 June 1940, 272.

17. Cordell Hull, *The Memoirs of Cordell Hull,* 2 vols. (New York: Macmillan, 1948), 1:748–49. See also ibid., 734–35; and Joseph Kennedy to Hull, 28 Nov. 1939, 640.11 E. W. 1939/1, RG 59, NA.

18. Moffat Diary, 24 Jan. 1940.

19. Ibid., 2 Feb. 1940.

20. Leo Pasvolsky to Cordell Hull, 12 Mar. 1940, 600.0031 World Program/386 1/2, RG 59, NA.

21. Israel, *War Diary of Breckinridge Long,* 43.

22. *Vital Speeches,* 15 Jan. 1940, 195.

23. Business Advisory Council, "Report on the Reciprocal Trade Agreements Program," 12 Jan. 1940, Box 109, Harry L. Hopkins Papers, FDRL. See also Edgar W. Smith to Cordell Hull, 5 Jan. 1940, 611.0031/4599, RG 59, NA.

24. U.S. Congress, Senate, *Extension of the Reciprocal Trade Agreements Act: Hearings before the Committee on Finance,* 76th Cong., 3d sess., 1940, 12.

25. *Foreign Affairs,* Jan. 1940, 330; Israel, *War Diary of Breckinridge Long,* 38; *Commercial and Financial Chronicle,* 6 Jan. 1940, 46.

26. *Commercial and Financial Chronicle,* 20 Jan. 1940, 363. See also Henry A. Wallace to Dan Wallace, 16 Jan. 1940, Henry A. Wallace Papers, University of Iowa, reel 21.

27. Cordell Hull to Edward A. O'Neal, 26 Jan. 1940, Hull Papers.

28. Berle and Jacobs, *Navigating the Rapids,* 301. See also Francis B. Sayre to R. Walton Moore, 21 May 1940, Box 19, Moore Papers.

29. *Commercial and Financial Chronicle,* 13 Apr. 1940, 2346.

30. Ibid., 25 May 1940, 3295.

31. *Proceedings of the Export Managers' Club of New York,* 26 Mar. 1940, 3–11.

32. *Commercial and Financial Chronicle,* 13 Jan. 1940, 158.

33. Russell C. Leffingwell to Thomas W. Lamont, 4 Apr. 1940, Box 103, Thomas W. Lamont Papers, HBSBL. See also Leffingwell to Lamont, 11 Sept. 1940, ibid.

34. Russell C. Leffingwell to Thomas W. Lamont, 21 Nov. 1939, Box 103, Lamont Papers.

35. Thomas W. Lamont to Julian S. Huxley, 2 Jan. 1940, Box 99, ibid.

36. Thomas W. Lamont to Jan C. Smuts, 16 Feb. 1940, Box 131, ibid. See also Lamont to Quincy Wright, 29 Dec. 1939, Box 20; Lamont to Walter T. Layton, 10 Jan. 1940, Box 102; and Lamont to Julian S. Huxley 2 Jan. 1940, Box 99, ibid.

37. Henry A. Wallace to Franklin D. Roosevelt, 30 Mar. 1940, S. F., Box 73, Roosevelt Papers. See also Wallace to Roosevelt, 1 Apr. 1940, ibid.

38. Sumner Welles to Cordell Hull, 18 Dec. 1939, 740.00119 E. W. 1939/200 1/2, RG 59, NA.

39. Notter, *Postwar Foreign Policy Preparation,* 20–22. See also Hull, *Memoirs,* 2:1626–27.

40. Hugh R. Wilson Jr., *A Career Diplomat: The Third Chapter, The Third Reich* (New York: Vantage, 1960), 95. See also Long Diary, 13 Jan. 1940.

41. Berle and Jacobs, *Navigating the Rapids,* 284. See also ibid., 281.

42. Adolf A. Berle, "Organization of Peace," 3 Jan. 1940, Box 54, Adolf A. Berle Papers, FDRL. This memo was discussed at a meeting of the political subcommittee on 17 Jan. 1940. See also Hugh R. Wilson, memorandum, "World Order," 22 Jan. 1940, Box 15, Moore Papers; and Breckinridge Long, "Considerations of Political and Economic Nature," 31 Jan. 1940, Box 199, Long Papers.

43. Notter, *Postwar Foreign Policy Preparation,* 456–57.

44. Leo Pasvolsky, "The Basis of an International Economic Program in Connection with a Possible Conference of Neutrals," 29 Jan. 1940, Box 1, Leo Pasvolsky Papers, LC.

45. Leo Pasvolsky to Cordell Hull, 29 Jan. 1940, ibid.

46. Hull, *Memoirs,* 2:1628.

47. Notter, *Postwar Foreign Policy Preparation,* 457.

48. Leo Pasvolsky, "Suggestions for a Possible Formula in Conversations with the Treasury," 8 Mar. 1940; and Pasvolsky to Cordell Hull, 18 Mar. 1940, Box 1, Pasvolsky Papers.

49. Myron C. Taylor to Franklin D. Roosevelt, 27 Feb. 1940, Box 10, Myron C. Taylor Papers, FDRL. See also Berle and Jacobs, *Navigating the Rapids,* 279.

50. James D. Mooney to Franklin D. Roosevelt, 12 Mar. 1940, 740.0011 E. W. 1939/1824, RG 59, NA.

51. Sumner Welles, *The Time for Decision* (New York: Harper and Brothers, 1944), 74, 83–86, 103–7.

52. Langer and Gleason, *Challenge to Isolation,* 1:365–70.

53. Sumner Welles, The Peace Settlement, n. d., Franklin D. Roosevelt Papers, S. F., Box 9.

54. Sumner Welles, "Which Is the More Practical—A Co-operative or an Enforced Peace Settlement?" n.d.; and "Methods for Securing a Co-operative Peace," n.d., S. F., Box 9, Roosevelt Papers.

55. Welles, "Which Is the More Practical"; and "Methods for Securing a Co-operative Peace."

56. Welles, "Which Is the More Practical"; and "Methods for Securing a Co-operative Peace."

57. Hugh R. Wilson Diary, 8 Mar. 1940, Hugh R. Wilson Papers, HCHL.

58. Julian Wadleigh, "An Analysis of the Replies to the Proposal for Consultation on Post-War Reconstruction," 23 May 1940, Box 108, Harley A. Notter File, RG 59, NA; Hull, *Memoirs*, 1:735.

59. Economic Subcommittee, memorandum, "America's Post-War Policy," 2 Apr. 1940, Box 108, Notter File.

60. Wilson Diary, 16 Apr. 1940.

61. Hugh R. Wilson, memoranda, 1, 7 May 1940, Box 54, Berle Papers.

62. Wilson Diary, 20 May 1940.

63. Henry A. Wallace Diary, 12 Apr. 1940, Wallace Papers, University of Iowa.

64. Hull, *Memoirs*, 1:777–84.

65. Wallace Diary, 17 May 1940.

66. Ibid., 18 May 1940.

67. Israel, *War Diary of Breckinridge Long,* 98.

68. Bernard M. Baruch to Joseph E. Davies, 31 May 1940; Baruch to Franklin D. Roosevelt, 4 June 1940; and Baruch to Sheridan Downey, 14 June 1940, Bernard M. Baruch Papers, PUML; W. Averell Harriman, "Remarks before the Greater Omaha Association," 1 June 1940, Box 302, Hopkins Papers; Lewis W. Douglas to Carl Hayden, 5 June 1940, Box 261, Lewis W. Douglas Papers, Special Collections Library, University of Arizona.

69. *Bankers' Magazine,* June 1940, 509. See also *Bankers' Magazine,* July 1940, 65; and Aug. 1940, 156; and *Magazine of Wall Street,* 15 June 1940, 271; and 29 June 1940, 381.

70. *Business Week,* 22 June 1940, 42. See also *Commercial and Financial Chronicle,* 27 July 1940, 489; *Barron's,* 5 Aug. 1940, 3; *Annalist,* 15 Aug. 1940, 202; and *Magazine of Wall Street,* 24 Aug. 1940, 562.

71. Adolf A. Berle Diary, 25 May 1940, Berle Papers. See also Hugh R. Wilson, memorandum, "Meeting of the Advisory Committee on Problems of Foreign Relations," 31 May 1940, Box 1, Wilson Papers; and Wallace Diary, 1, 3, 6 June 1940.

72. "Summary of the First Meeting of the Interdepartmental Group to Consider Post-War Problems and Policies," 27 May 1940, Box 1, Wilson Papers.

73. Franklin D. Roosevelt to Henry Morgenthau, 15 June 1940, Morgenthau Diaries, FDRL, 273:49–53.

74. Wallace Diary, 19 June 1940; memorandum, "Interdepartmental

Conference," 19 June 1940, Morgenthau Diaries, 274:118–30; Wallace to Harry L. Hopkins, 26 June 1940, Box 301, Hopkins Papers.

75. Sumner Welles, Henry Morgenthau, Henry A. Wallace, and Harry L. Hopkins to Franklin D. Roosevelt, 20 June 1940, Morgenthau Diaries, 274:232–35.

76. Memorandum of White House conference, 27 June 1940, ibid., 276:177. See also Franklin D. Roosevelt to Bernard M. Baruch, 22 June 1940, Baruch Papers.

77. *Official Report of the Twenty-Seventh National Foreign Trade Convention*, 1940, 346–47.

78. Eugene Thomas to Harry C. Hawkins, 9 July 1940, 600.1115 N. F. T. C./517, RG 59, NA.

79. Patrick J. Hearden, *Roosevelt Confronts Hitler: America's Entry into WWII* (Dekalb: Northern Illinois University Press, 1987), 173–76.

80. Ibid., 177–81.

81. Ibid., 189–92.

82. Ibid., 192–97.

83. *Business Week*, 8 Feb. 1941, 64; 1 Mar. 1941, 64; 5 Apr. 1941, 68; and 3 May 1941, 72; *Bankers' Magazine*, Sept. 1941, 207–11; *Fortune*, May 1941, 54–55; July 1941, 53; and Nov. 1941, 19.

84. *Annals of the American Academy of Political and Social Science*, July 1941, 50. See also *Proceedings of the Export Managers' Club of New York*, 25 Mar. 1941, 22–30; and Thomas W. Lamont to Jan C. Smuts, 20 June 1941, Box 131, Lamont Papers.

85. Warren F. Kimball, *The Juggler: Franklin Roosevelt as Wartime Statesman* (Princeton: Princeton University Press, 1991), 49–52; Moffat Diary, 31 Mar. 1941; Berle Diary, 15 Apr. 1941; Morgenthau Diaries, 28 Apr. 1941, 392:86; John H. Fuqua to Dean G. Acheson, 12 May 1941, 611.4131/2556, RG 59, NA.

86. Morgenthau Diaries, 4 June 1941, 404:272–73. See also memorandum for the president, 9 June 1941, Box 307, Hopkins Papers.

87. Lloyd C. Gardner, *Economic Aspects of New Deal Diplomacy* (Madison: University of Wisconsin Press, 1964), 276–77; Christopher Thorne, *Allies of a Kind: The United States, Britain, and the War against Japan, 1941–1945* (New York: Oxford University Press, 1978), 104; Randall B. Woods, *A Changing of the Guard: Anglo-American Relations, 1941–1946* (Chapel Hill: University of North Carolina Press, 1990), 33–55; Kimball, *The Juggler*, 51–52.

88. Moffat Diary, 14 July 1941. See also Bernard M. Baruch to Franklin D. Roosevelt, 9 July 1941; and Roosevelt to Baruch, 11 July 1941, S. F., Box 117, Roosevelt Papers.

89. Berle Diary, 17 July 1941.

90. Memorandum, "Conversation between Dean G. Acheson and John Maynard Keynes," 28 July 1941, S. F., Box 16, Roosevelt Papers. See also Keynes to Acheson, 29 July 1941, Box 2, Leo Pasvolsky File, RG 59, NA.

91. Harry C. Hawkins to Dean G. Acheson, Sumner Welles, and Cordell Hull, 4 Aug. 1941, Box 1, John D. Hickerson File, RG 59, NA. See also Hawkins to Acheson, 1 Aug. 1941, Box 2, Pasvolsky File.

92. Sumner Welles, memorandum, "Conversation at Sea," 11 Aug. 1941, Box 14, Hickerson File, RG 59. See also memorandum, "Conversation between Welles and Alexander Cadogan," 9 Aug. 1941, ibid.

93. Welles, "Conversation at Sea," 11 Aug. 1941. See also Moffat Diary, 20 Aug. 1941; and William L. Langer and S. Everett Gleason, *The Undeclared War, 1940–1941* (New York: Harper and Brothers, 1953), 681–84.

94. Cordell Hull to American Embassy in London, 25 Aug. 1941, 740.0011 E. W. 1939/14454, RG 59, NA. See also Langer and Gleason, *The Undeclared War,* 688–89.

95. Moffat Diary, 24, 25 Sept. 1941; memorandum, "Conversation between Dean G. Acheson and Lord Halifax," 3 Oct. 1941, Box 2, Pasvolsky File; Harry C. Hawkins to Acheson, 10 Oct. 1941, Box 14, Notter File; and John D. Hickerson to Moffat, 15 Oct. 1941, Reel 5, Matthews-Hickerson File, RG 59, NA.

96. Dean G. Acheson to Cordell Hull, 28 Oct. 1941, Box 2, Pasvolsky File. See also Hull to Franklin D. Roosevelt, 19 Nov. 1941, S. F., Box 16, Roosevelt Papers.

97. Memorandum, "Conversation between Dean G. Acheson, Herbert Feis, and Lord Halifax," 2 Dec. 1941, Box 14, Notter File, RG 59.

98. Loy W. Henderson to Adolf A. Berle, 15 July 1941, *FRUS,* 1940, 1:390. See also Langer and Gleason, *Challenge to Isolation,* 2:644–46.

99. Laurence A. Steinhardt to Cordell Hull, 28 Oct. 1940, *FRUS,* 1940, 1:623. For an excellent discussion of the British negotiations with Russia, see Lloyd C. Gardner, *Spheres of Influence: The Great Powers Partition Europe, from Munich to Yalta* (Chicago: Ivan R. Dee, 1993), 75–90.

100. Langer and Gleason, *The Undeclared War,* 529.

101. Lash, *Roosevelt and Churchill,* 366.

102. Langer and Gleason, *The Undeclared War,* 535–36.

103. Adolf A. Berle to Franklin D. Roosevelt, 8 July 1941, Box 54, Berle Papers. See also Berle to Harry Hopkins, 7 July 1941; and Berle to Sumner Welles, 7 July 1941, ibid.; and John D. Hickerson to Berle, 21 July 1941, Box 1, Hickerson File, RG 59.

104. Robert E. Sherwood, *Roosevelt and Hopkins: An Intimate History*

(New York: Harper and Brothers, 1948), 311; Gardner, *Spheres of Influence*, 95–96.

105. Franklin D. Roosevelt to Winston Churchill, 14 July 1941, S. F., Box 52, Roosevelt Papers.

106. Memorandum, "Conversation in the Office of Adolf A. Berle to Consider Eastern European Questions," 1 Aug. 1941, 740.00/2148 2/10, RG 59, NA; Berle to Cordell Hull, 4 Aug. 1941, Box 58, Berle Papers. See also memorandum, "Conversation between Berle and Ralph C. S. Stevenson," 25 Sept. 1941, 840.50/248, RG 59, NA.

107. Memorandum, "Conversation between Sumner Welles and Alexander Cadogan," 9 Aug. 1941, Box 14, Hickerson File, RG 59. See also Welles to Franklin D. Roosevelt, 21 Oct. 1941, S. F., Box 1, Roosevelt Papers.

108. Cordell Hull to John G. Winant, 5 Dec. 1941, S. F., Box 68, Roosevelt Papers. See also William C. Bullitt to Roosevelt, 5 Dec. 1941, S. F., Box 1124, ibid.; and W. Averell Harriman, "Notes on a Conversation with Stafford Cripps," 3 Oct. 1941, Box 160, W. Averell Harriman Papers, LC.

109. John G. Winant to Cordell Hull, 19 Dec. 1941, S. F., Box 1; and State Department memorandum, 4 Feb. 1942, S. F., Box 68, Roosevelt Papers; Gardner, *Spheres of Influence*, 100–114.

110. Welles, "Conversation at Sea," 11 Aug. 1941.

111. Langer and Gleason, *The Undeclared War*, 685–88.

112. Michael S. Sherry, *Preparing for the Next War: American Plans for Postwar Defense, 1941–1945* (New Haven: Yale University Press, 1977), 1–66.

113. William Diebold Jr., "Economic War Aims: General Considerations as of 1 April 1941," 17 Apr. 1941; Diebold, "The Economic Organization of the Peace in the Far East," 20 June 1941; Diebold, "Economic War Aims: Main Lines of Approach, Preliminary Statement," 22 June 1941; and no author, "Scope of the New Trade Agreements," 3 Sept. 1941, Studies of American Interest in the War and the Peace, CFR.

114. Walter R. Sharp, "Basic American Interests," preliminary draft, 10 July 1941; Sharp, "Institutional Arrangements for Post-War American-British Cooperation," preliminary draft, 17 Sept. 1941; Arthur Sweetser, "Approaches to Postwar International Organization," preliminary draft, 17 Sept. 1941; and Grayson Kirk, "The Atlantic Charter and Postwar Security," 4 Dec., 1941, ibid.

115. Notter, *Postwar Foreign Policy Preparation*, 41–56. See also Harley A. Notter to C. Easton Rothwell, 30 Aug. 1941; and Notter to Leo Pasvolsky, 13 Oct. 1941, Box 8, Notter File.

116. Harley A. Notter to Leo Pasvolsky, 24 Sept. 1941, Box 8, Notter File.

117. Harry Dexter White to Henry Morgenthau, 7 July 1941, Harry Dexter White Papers, PUML; White to Morgenthau, 9 July 1941,

Morgenthau Diaries, 419:300; Berle and Jacobs, *Navigating the Rapids,* 377–78.

118. Moffat Diary, 24 Sept. 1941. See also James C. Dunn to Cordell Hull, 2 Oct. 1941, 611.0031/5162, RG 59, NA; and Moffat Diary, 1–4 Dec. 1941.

119. Hull, *Memoirs,* 2:1631–33; Notter, *Postwar Foreign Policy Preparation,* 59–65; Shoup and Minter, *Imperial Brain Trust,* 148–53.

2. OPENING THE WORLD

1. Russell C. Leffingwell to Thomas W. Lamont, 18 May 1943, Box 103, Thomas W. Lamont Papers, HBSBL. See also Leffingwell to Lamont, 3 Mar. 1943; and Leffingwell to R. G. W., 28 Sept. 1942, ibid.

2. Randall B. Woods, *A Changing of the Guard: Anglo-American Relations, 1941–1945* (Chapel Hill: University of North Carolina Press, 1990), 188–211. See also Berle and Jacobs, *Navigating the Rapids,* 152–61, 170–72; and Oliver Zunz, *Why the American Century?* (Chicago: University of Chicago Press, 1998), 88–90.

3. Georg M. Schild, "Bretton Woods and Dumbarton Oaks: American Postwar Planning in the Summer of 1944" (Ph.D. diss., University of Maryland, 1993), 199–203.

4. William A. Williams, *The Tragedy of American Diplomacy* (New York: Dell, 1972), 234–36. For similar statements made by William L. Clayton before he entered the State Department, see Frederick J. Dobney, ed., *Selected Papers of Will Clayton* (Baltimore: Johns Hopkins University Press, 1971), 71–101.

5. Harley A. Notter, *Postwar Foreign Policy Preparation, 1939–1945* (Washington: Government Printing Office, 1949), 622–24.

6. Leo Pasvolsky to Cordell Hull, 12 Dec. 1941, Box 2, Leo Pasvolsky File, RG 59, NA.

7. State Department memorandum, "Negotiations between the United States and Great Britain for the Mutual-Aid Agreement with Particular Reference to Article VII," Box 13, Harley A. Notter File, RG 59, NA. See also Hull, *Memoirs,* 2:1152–53.

8. "Negotiations between the United States and Great Britain for the Mutual-Aid Agreement with Particular Reference to Article VII."

9. Warren F. Kimball, ed., *Churchill and Roosevelt: The Complete Correspondence,* 3 vols. (Princeton: Princeton University Press, 1984), 1:344–45.

10. Ibid., 1:349–51.

11. Ibid., 1:356–58.

12. E. F. Penrose, memorandum, enclosed in Harry C. Hawkins to Leo Pasvolsky and Dean Acheson, 21 Apr. 1942, Box 2, Pasvolsky File.

13. Memorandum, "Conversation between J. Pierrepont Moffat and Dana Wilgress," 1 Oct. 1942, Box 3, ibid.

14. E. F. Penrose, "Some Confidential Notes on Questions Relating to Article VII of the Mutual Aid Agreement," 19 Dec. 1942, Franklin D. Roosevelt Papers, S. F., Box 175, FDRL.

15. Subcommittee on Political Problems, minutes, 12 Dec. 1942, Box 55, Notter File, RG 59.

16. Israel, *War Diary of Breckinridge Long*, 307–8; Hull, *Memoirs*, 2:1211–12.

17. Thomas W. Lamont, memorandum, "Talk with Congressman Joe Martin," 11 May 1943, Box 209, Lamont Papers; and John Franklin Carter to Franklin D. Roosevelt, 9 June 1943, P.F., Box 70, Roosevelt Papers.

18. Franklin D. Roosevelt to Thomas W. Lamont, 10 June 1943, Box 127; and Cordell Hull to Lamont, 10 July 1943, Box 209, Lamont Papers.

19. Notter, *Postwar Foreign Policy Preparation*, 190–93.

20. Edward R. Stettinius to Cordell Hull, 20 Oct. 1943, Reel 24, Cordell Hull Papers, LC.

21. John M. Leddy, memorandum, "Post-War Commercial Policy," 16 Feb. 1944, Box 13, Notter File, RG 59.

22. "Tentative Views of the State Department Postwar Programs Committee," 6 Mar. 1944, Box 88A, RG 353, NA.

23. Edward R. Stettinius, calendar notes, 15 Feb. 1944, Edward R. Stettinius Papers, Box 239, UVAL.

24. Thomas M. Campbell and George C. Herring, eds., *The Diaries of Edward R. Stettinius Jr., 1943–1946* (New York: Franklin Watts, 1975), 55–68.

25. "Tentative Views of the Economic Subcommittee," 20 Feb.–21 Aug. 1942, Box 32, Notter File, RG 59. See also memorandum, "Conversation between Adolf A. Berle and British Officials," 10 Sept. 1942, Box 3, Pasvolsky File, RG 59.

26. Edward R. Stettinius, "Report on Conversations in London," 7–29 Apr. 1944, Box 29, Notter File, RG 59.

27. Edward R. Stettinius to Cordell Hull, 27 June 1944, Reel 11, Matthews-Hickerson File, RG 59, NA.

28. Campbell and Herring, *Diaries of Edward R. Stettinius*, 92–94. See also memorandum, "Telephone Conversation between Stettinius and Leo Pasvolsky," 19 July 1944, Box 241, Stettinius Papers.

29. Memorandum, "Credits for Great Britain," enclosed in Cordell Hull to Franklin D. Roosevelt, 8 Sept. 1944, Box 332, Harry L. Hopkins Papers, FDRL.

30. "Record of a Conversation at Quebec between Franklin D.

Roosevelt and Winston Churchill," 14 Sept. 1944, Presidential Diaries of Henry Morgenthau, Reel 2, Henry Morgenthau Papers, FDRL.

31. Memorandum, "Meeting in Hull's Office," 20 Sept. 1944, Henry Morgenthau Diaries, Morgenthau Papers, 773:5; Israel, *War Diary of Breckinridge Long,* 382–83.

32. Cordell Hull to Franklin D. Roosevelt, 17 Sept. 1944, Box 332, Hopkins Papers.

33. Cordell Hull to Franklin D. Roosevelt, 30 Sept. 1944, S. F., Box 94, Roosevelt Papers. See also Hull to Roosevelt, 2 Oct. 1944, Reel 12, Matthews-Hickerson File.

34. Memorandum, "Conversation Regarding British Phase II Discussions," 20 Oct. 1944, Box 5, Clayton-Thorp File, HSTL.

35. John D. Hickerson to Edward R. Stettinius, 2 Nov. 1944, Reel 18, Matthews-Hickerson File. See also Henry L. Stimson Diary, 19 Nov. 1944, Henry L. Stimson Papers, YUSL.

36. Campbell and Herring, *Diaries of Edward R. Stettinius,* 174–76.

37. State Department Policy Committee document, 4 Nov. 1944, Box 137, Notter File, RG 59. See also Policy Committee, minutes, 8 Nov. 1944, Box 138, ibid.; and untitled document, 22 Dec. 1944, Box 88E, Secretary's Staff Committee Papers, RG 353, NA.

38. Edward R. Stettinius to Gen. Bedell Smith, 28 Nov. 1944, Box 398, Stettinius Papers.

39. Harry L. Hopkins to Franklin D. Roosevelt, 28 Nov. 1944, S. F., Box 91, Roosevelt Papers.

40. Kimball, *Churchill and Roosevelt,* 3:530–31.

41. Ibid., 3:535–36.

42. Woods, *Changing of the Guard,* 220–25.

43. Executive Committee on Economic Foreign Policy, minutes, 14 July, 9 Oct. 1944, 10 July 1945, Box 776, RG 169, NA; "Policy Decisions of the ECEFP," 15 Sept. 1945, Box 32, Notter File, RG 59.

44. "Methods and Procedures for the Expansion of International Trade," 5 Mar. 1945, Box 88E, Secretary's Staff Committee Papers, RG 353.

45. Memorandum, "Meeting between State Department Officials and Leo T. Crowley," 31 Aug. 1945, Leo T. Crowley Papers, JFDPC.

46. Dean G. Acheson to Harry S. Truman, 7 Sept. 1945, Box 59, RG 353.

47. William L. Clayton to St. John Garwood, 10 Oct. 1945, Box 1, William L. Clayton Papers, HSTL. For a similar statement that Clayton made in a public speech on 21 May 1945, see Dobney, *Selected Papers of Will Clayton,* 135.

48. Woods, *Changing of the Guard,* 212–18.

49. Berle and Jacobs, *Navigating the Rapids,* 482.

50. Adolf A. Berle to Cordell Hull, 11 Mar. 1943, Box 54, Adolf A. Berle Papers, FDRL.

51. Adolf A. Berle to Cordell Hull, 30 Apr. 1943, ibid. See also Berle to Hull, 18 Aug. 1943, Box 55, ibid.

52. Memorandum, "Conversation on Aviation Policy," 11 Nov. 1943, Box 215, ibid. See also Adolf A. Berle Diary, 18 Feb. 1943, ibid.; Adm. Arthur J. Hepburn to the Secretary of the Navy, 21 July 1943, Box 196, Records of the General Board, RG 80, NA; and Pacific War Council, minutes, 11 Aug. 1943, Box 168, Map Room, Roosevelt Papers.

53. Memorandum, "Conversation on Aviation Policy," 11 Nov. 1943. See also Berle Diary, 18 Feb. 1943; Hepburn to the Secretary of the Navy, 21 July 1943; and Pacific War Council, minutes, 11 Aug. 1943.

54. Cordell Hull to Franklin D. Roosevelt, 29 Nov. 1943, Box 17, Map Room, Roosevelt Papers.

55. Berle Diary, 22 Feb. 1944. See also Berle to Cordell Hull, 9 July 1943, Box 55, Berle Papers.

56. Livingston Satterwaite, letter, 22 Feb. 1944, enclosed in John D. Hickerson, memorandum, 2 Mar. 1944, Reel 11, Matthews-Hickerson File, RG 59. See also Satterwaite to Joe D. Walstrom, 18 Jan. 1944, ibid.

57. Berle and Jacobs, *Navigating the Rapids,* 284–87.

58. Memorandum, "First Conference on Post-War Civil Aviation with the Russian Group," 29 May 1944, Box 216, Berle Papers.

59. Berle Diary, 13 May 1944.

60. Ibid., 10, 23 June 1944.

61. Adolf A. Berle to Cordell Hull, 30 May 1944, Box 59, Berle Papers. See also Berle, memorandum, "Projected Time Schedule for Preliminary Aviation Conferences," 17 Feb. 1944, Reel 11, Matthews-Hickerson File, RG 59; and Edward R. Stettinius to Cordell Hull, 4 Aug. 1944, Box 731, Stettinius Papers.

62. Berle and Jacobs, *Navigating the Rapids,* 488–90. See also Loy W. Henderson to Adolf A. Berle, 30 July 1943, Box 3, Charles E. Bohlen File, RG 59, NA.

63. Adolf A. Berle to Cordell Hull, 2 Aug. 1944, Box 59, Berle Papers. See also L. Welch Pague to Berle, 3 Aug. 1944, Harry L. Hopkins Papers, Box 336; and Edward R. Stettinius to Hull, 2 Aug. 1944, Stettinius Papers, Box 731.

64. Adolf A. Berle, memorandum, 16 Sept. 1944, Box 216, Berle Papers.

65. Notter, *Postwar Foreign Policy Preparation,* 356.

66. Adolf A. Berle to Franklin D. Roosevelt, 7 Dec. 1944, Box 60, Berle Papers; Berle Diary, 6 Dec. 1944.

67. Berle and Jacobs, *Navigating the Rapids,* 500–505. See also Jordan

Schwartz, *Liberal: Adolf A. Berle and the Vision of an American Era* (New York: Free Press, 1977), 229–47; and Thomas J. McCormick and Walter LaFeber, eds., *Behind the Throne: Servants of Power to Imperial Presidents* (Madison: University of Wisconsin Press, 1993), 155–62.

68. Kimball, *Churchill and Roosevelt,* 3:402–43. See also Berle and Jacobs, *Navigating the Rapids,* 505–6; and Adolf A. Berle to Franklin D. Roosevelt, 29 Nov. 1944, Box 20, Map Room, Roosevelt Papers.

69. Berle and Jacobs, *Navigating the Rapids,* 507–10.

70. Adolf A. Berle to Secretary of State, 2 Dec. 1944, Box 216, Berle Papers.

71. Kimball, *Churchill and Roosevelt,* 3:519–20, 543–44, 566–67. See Joseph C. Grew to Franklin D. Roosevelt, 30 Jan. 1945, Box 32, Map Room, Roosevelt Papers.

72. Memorandum, "Conversation about Aviation Problems," 5 June 1945, "Conversations," vol. 7, Joseph C. Grew Papers, HUHL.

73. Joe D. Walstrom, memorandum for the files, 7 Sept. 1945, Box 1, Clayton-Thorp File.

74. Fred L. Block, *The Origins of International Economic Disorder: A Study of United States International Monetary Policy from World War II to the Present* (Berkeley: University of California Press, 1977), 22–30.

75. Schild, "Bretton Woods and Dumbarton Oaks," 212–20.

76. Block, *Origins of International Economic Disorder,* 43–46.

77. Schild, "Bretton Woods and Dumbarton Oaks," 227.

78. Alvin H. Hansen to Harry Dexter White, 28 Sept. 1942, Box 19, Notter File, RG 59.

79. Schild, "Bretton Woods and Dumbarton Oaks," 223.

80. Ibid., 272–77.

81. Ibid., 292–99.

82. Ibid., 300–301.

83. Block, *Origins of International Economic Disorder,* 50–55.

84. Thomas W. Lamont to Gilbert Murray, 10 June 1943, Box 114, Lamont Papers.

85. Thomas W. Lamont to Leland Stowe, 2 May 1944, Box 131, ibid.

86. W. Randolph Burgess to Henry Morgenthau, 22 June 1944, Morgenthau Diaries, 746:139 NN–139 RR.

87. Memorandum, "Conversation between Winthrop W. Aldrich and Treasury Department Officials," 25 Aug. 1944, ibid., 766:25–29.

88. "Conversation at the Treasury Department," 20 Sept. 1944, ibid., 773:32.

89. Memorandum, "Meeting between W. Randolph Burgess and Treasury Department officials," 4 Jan. 1945, ibid., 807:151–56.

90. Schild, "Bretton Woods and Dumbarton Oaks," 268.

91. Thomas W. Lamont to Arthur H. Sulzerger, 16 Feb. 1944, Box 121, Lamont Papers.

92. Schild, "Bretton Woods and Dumbarton Oaks," 416–21.

93. H. G. Nicholas, ed., *Washington Dispatches, 1941–45: Weekly Political Reports from the British Embassy* (Chicago: University of Chicago Press, 1981), 557.

3. RECONSTRUCTING EUROPE

1. Leroy D. Stinebower, memorandum, "Surplus Commodities Arrangements," 5 June 1941, Box 5, Dean G. Acheson File, RG 59, NA.

2. Dean G. Acheson to Frederick Leith-Ross, 22 July 1941, Box 2, Leo Pasvolsky File, RG 59, NA.

3. Adolf A. Berle to Franklin D. Roosevelt, 9 July 1941, S. F., Box 7, Franklin D. Roosevelt Papers, FDRL.

4. Adolf A. Berle Diary, 25 Sept. 1941, Adolf A. Berle Papers, FDRL.

5. Harley A. Notter, *Postwar Foreign Policy Preparation, 1939–1945* (Washington: Government Printing Office, 1949), 54–55, 86–87; John G. Winant to Cordell Hull, 3 Oct. 1941, Box 54, Berle Papers.

6. Notter, *Postwar Foreign Policy Preparation*, 83, 87–91; Berle and Jacobs, *Navigating the Rapids*, 405.

7. Subcommittee on International Organization, minutes, 7 Aug. 1942, Box 85, Harley A. Notter File, RG 59, NA.

8. Memorandum, "Conversation between Myron C. Taylor and Antonio Salizar," 2 Oct. 1942, S. F., Box 71, Roosevelt Papers; John J. McCloy to Harry L. Hopkins, 3 Nov. 1943, Box 329, Harry L. Hopkins Papers, FDRL.

9. Notter, *Postwar Foreign Policy Preparation*, 137, 203.

10. Subcommittee on Economic Reconstruction, minutes, 12 June 1942, Box 80, Notter File, RG 59.

11. Notter, *Postwar Foreign Policy Preparation*, 203–6.

12. Subcommittee on Security Problems, minutes, 23 Oct. 1942, Box 76, Notter File, RG 59.

13. Notter, *Postwar Foreign Policy Preparation*, 641–44.

14. Subcommittee on Economic Policy, minutes, 6 Mar. 1942, Box 80, Notter File, RG 59.

15. Leo T. Crowley, "Address Delivered before the Commerce and Industry Association of New York," 17 Jan. 1944, Leo T. Crowley Papers, JFDPC.

16. Leo T. Crowley, "Address Delivered before the Son's of St. Patrick in Scranton, Pennsylvania," 17 Mar. 1945, Crowley Papers.

17. Charles Bunn to Leo Pasvolsky, 14 Mar. 1942, Box 2, Pasvolsky File.

18. Henry L. Stimson Diary, 22, 27 Dec. 1944, Henry L. Stimson Papers, YUSL.

19. Subcommittee on Security Problems, minutes, 5 Dec. 1942, Box 76, Notter File, RG 59.

20. Leo T. Crowley to Arthur H. Vandenberg, 22 Aug. 1945, Crowley Papers. See also Randall B. Woods, *A Changing of the Guard: Anglo-American Relations, 1941–1946* (Chapel Hill: University of North Carolina Press, 1990), 159.

21. Edward R. Stettinius to Cordell Hull, 20 Jan. 1944, Box 218, Edward R. Stettinius Papers, UVAL.

22. State Department, document on postwar reconstruction, 17 Feb. 1944, S. F., Box 175, Roosevelt Papers.

23. Meeting notes, 26 May 1944, Box 45, Executive Committee on Economic Foreign Policy Records, RG 353, NA; Dean G. Acheson to Franklin D. Roosevelt, 2 June 1944, Box 772, RG 169, NA. See also John D. Hickerson to Theodore Achilles, 22 June 1944, Reel 2, Matthews-Hickerson File, RG 59, NA.

24. Edward R. Stettinius to Franklin D. Roosevelt, 31 Oct. 1944, S. F., Box 66, Roosevelt Papers.

25. Henry Morgenthau to Franklin D. Roosevelt, 2 May 1944, S. F., Box 62, ibid.

26. Franklin D. Roosevelt to Henry Morgenthau, 3 May 1944, ibid.

27. Grace Tully to Franklin D. Roosevelt, 6 June 1944, ibid.

28. Cordell Hull and Henry Morgenthau to Franklin D. Roosevelt, n.d., ibid. See also Jesse H. Jones, memorandum, "Netherlands Loan Application," 24 Aug. 1943, Box 31, Jesse H. Jones Papers, LC.

29. Franklin D. Roosevelt to Jesse H. Jones, 4 Sept. 1944, S. F., Box 62, Roosevelt Papers.

30. Treasury Department Group Discussion, 8 Sept. 1944, Henry Morgenthau Diaries, 770:138–39, Henry Morgenthau Papers, FDRL.

31. Franklin D. Roosevelt to Leo T. Crowley, 9 Sept. 1944, Box 794, RG 169.

32. Daniel W. Bell to Henry Morgenthau, 14 Sept. 1944, Reel 2, Presidential Diaries of Morgenthau, Morgenthau Papers; memorandum, "Meeting of Cordell Hull, Henry L. Stimson, and Henry Morgenthau," 20 Sept. 1944, Morgenthau Diaries, 773:4–8.

33. Bell to Morgenthau, 14 Sept. 1944; "Meeting of Cordell Hull, Henry L. Stimson, and Henry Morgenthau," 20 Sept. 1944.

34. Stimson Diary, 13 Oct. 1944; Daniel W. Bell, "Notes on Cabinet Meeting," 13 Oct. 1944, Morgenthau Diaries, 782:18. See also memorandum,

"Conversation between Stimson and Morgenthau," 26 Oct. 1944, ibid., 787:2.

35. Leo T. Crowley to Bernard M. Baruch, 13 Feb. 1945, Box 794, RG 169. See also "Notes on Executive Policy Committee Meeting," 16 Feb. 1945, Box 795; and Executive Policy Committee, minutes, 1 Mar. 1945, Box 773, ibid.

36. Leo T. Crowley, memorandum, n.d., Crowley Papers; Oscar Cox to Franklin D. Roosevelt, 4 Apr. 1945, Box 794, RG 169.

37. Subcommittee on Political Problems document, 29 Apr. 1942, Box 56, Notter File, RG 59.

38. Financial and Economic Group, memorandum, "American Interests in the Economic Unification of Europe with Respect to Trade Barriers," 14 Sept. 1942, Studies of American Interest in the War and the Peace, CFR.

39. Subcommittee on Economic Policy, "Post-War Economic Unification of Europe," 19 Nov. 1942, Box 81, Notter File, RG 59.

40. Berle and Jacobs, *Navigating the Rapids,* 426–27. See also Adolf A. Berle, "Draft Minutes of the Economic Subcommittee," 5 Jan. 1943, Box 65, Berle Papers.

41. Notter, *Postwar Foreign Policy Preparation,* 143–45.

42. Subcommittee on Economic Policy, "How Much of a Desire for the Unification of Europe Has Been Expressed by European Leaders and What Plans Have Been Proposed by Them?" 4 June 1943, Box 81, Notter File, RG 59.

43. Subcommittee on Economic Policy, "A Continental European Organization," 17 June 1943, ibid.

44. Division of Economic Studies, "Economic Unification of All Continental Europe West of Russia," 13 July 1943, Box 82, ibid.

45. Division of Economic Studies, "Potentialities and Problems of Economic Collaboration among European Countries," 8 July 1943, ibid.

46. Division of Economic Studies, "How Would a European Full Customs Union Affect the Long-Run Economic Interests of the United States?" 17 Sept. 1943, ibid.

47. Subcommittee on Economic Policy, memorandum, "The Interest of the United States in European Inland Transportation and Proposed Methods of Implementing Them," 3 Jan. 1944, Box 83, ibid.

48. Notter, *Postwar Foreign Policy Preparation,* 180, 243, 263.

49. Ibid., 50–52.

50. Carter Goodrich, "Probable Demands of Labor in the Peace Settlement," 8 Dec. 1942, Studies of American Interest in the War and the Peace, CFR.

51. Notter, *Postwar Foreign Policy Preparation*, 185, 239–40, 360–61.

52. Edward R. Stettinius to Franklin D. Roosevelt, 30 Mar. 1945, Box 59, RG 59.

53. Subcommittee on Economic Policy, "Germany's Place in the World Economy in Relation to the Problem of Maintaining Peace," 28 Mar. 1943, Box 81, Notter File, RG 59.

54. Percy W. Bidwell, "Economic Aspects of Postwar Treatment of Germany," 27 May 1944, Studies of American Interest in the War and the Peace, CFR.

55. "Policy Decisions of the Executive Committee on Economic Foreign Policy," 4 Aug. 1944, Box 32, Notter File, RG 59. See also "Tentative Views of the State Department Interdivisional Committee on Reparations," 14 Dec. 1943, Box 88 A, RG 353, NA.

56. Leo Pasvolsky to Cordell Hull, 1 Sept. 1944, Box 145, Notter File, RG 59.

57. Berle Diary, 12 May 1943. See also William D. Leahy Diary, 14 Apr. 1943, WSHS.

58. Stimson Diary, 1 June 1943.

59. Kimball, *Churchill and Roosevelt*, 2:366, 369, 380–81.

60. Ibid., 2:456.

61. Hull, *Memoirs*, 2:1552–53. See also "Minutes of a Meeting between Franklin D. Roosevelt and the Joint Chiefs of Staff," 15 Nov. 1943, Box 29, Map Room, Roosevelt Papers.

62. Kimball, *Churchill and Roosevelt*, 2:723.

63. Robert D. Murphy, *Diplomat among Warriors* (New York: Doubleday, 1964), 229.

64. Kimball, *Churchill and Roosevelt*, 3:176–77, 188–89.

65. Hull, *Memoirs*, 2:1565–69.

66. Kimball, *Churchill and Roosevelt*, 3:533–34.

67. Hull, *Memoirs*, 2:1160.

68. H. Freeman Matthews to Ray Atherton, 11 Sept. 1942, Reel 9, Matthews-Hickerson File, RG 59.

69. Isaiah Bowman, "Notes of Steering Committee Meeting," 22 Jan. 1943, Box 7, Ser. 14, Isaiah Bowman Papers, JHUSCL; H. Freeman Matthews to Ray Atherton, 10 Mar. 1943, Reel 9, Matthews-Hickerson File; memorandum, "Conversation among Cordell Hull and Anthony Eden and Lord Halifax," 22 Mar. 1943, 740.00119 E W 1939/1370, RG 59, NA.

70. Cordell Hull to Franklin D. Roosevelt, 10 May 1943, Box 65, Cordell Hull Papers, LC.

71. Kimball, *Churchill and Roosevelt*, 2:208–11, 235–37; Leahy Diary,

11 June 1943; Stimson Diary, 17 June 1943; Berle and Jacobs, *Navigating the Rapids,* 437.

72. Franklin D. Roosevelt to Dwight D. Eisenhower, 17 June 1943, Box 30, Map Room, Roosevelt Papers.

73. Kimball, *Churchill and Roosevelt,* 2:254–56.

74. Ibid., 2:257–58, 261–62, 310–11, 333–36.

75. Hull, *Memoirs,* 2:1225–26, 1232–33, 1241–42. See also H. Freeman Matthews to Ray Atherton, 25 June 1943, Reel 9, Matthews-Hickerson File, RG 59.

76. H. Freeman Matthews, memorandum, "The Stettinius Mission to London," 6 May 1944, Reel 13, Matthews-Hickerson File, RG 59. See also Edward R. Stettinius to Cordell Hull, 13 Apr. 1944, Box 250, Stettinius Papers; and Stimson Diary, 8, 14 June 1944.

77. Kimball, *Churchill and Roosevelt,* 3:128–30, 136–38, 145–47; Stimson Diary, 17 May 1944; Franklin D. Roosevelt to George C. Marshall, 2 June 1944, S. F., Box 4, Roosevelt Papers; Roosevelt to Marshall, 14 June 1944, Box 12, Map Room, Roosevelt Papers.

78. W. Averell Harriman to Franklin D. Roosevelt, 29 May 1944, Reel 8, Map Room, Roosevelt Papers.

79. Hull *Memoirs,* 2:1432–35; Julian G. Hurtsfield, *America and the French Nation, 1939–1945* (Chapel Hill: University of North Carolina Press, 1986), 207–24.

80. Simon L. Millner, memorandum for the Foreign Economic Administration, 9 Oct. 1944, S. F., Box 42, Roosevelt Papers. See also V. Frank Coe, memorandum for Henry Morgenthau, 15 Mar. 1945, Morgenthau Diaries, 828:274.

81. Edward R. Stettinius to Franklin D. Roosevelt, 28 Dec. 1944, Box 231, Stettinius Papers.

82. Jefferson Caffery to Edward R. Stettinius, 12 Dec. 1944, S. F., Box 95, Roosevelt Papers.

83. Maxwell M. Hamilton to Edward R. Stettinius and Franklin D. Roosevelt, 22 Oct. 1943, Reel 24, Hull Papers. See also H. Freeman Matthews to Stettinius, 15 Nov 1943, Reel 9, Matthews-Hickerson File, RG 59.

84. Donald M. Nelson to Franklin D. Roosevelt, memorandum on Nelson interview with Stalin on 15 Oct. 1943, 6 Nov. 1943, S. F., Box 68, Roosevelt Papers. See also Nelson to Roosevelt, memorandum on Nelson interview with Molotov on 12 Oct. 1943, 6 Nov. 1943, ibid.

85. Hull, *Memoirs,* 2:1303.

86. John L. Gaddis, *The United States and the Origins of the Cold War, 1941–1947* (New York: Columbia University Press, 1972), 177.

87. Memorandum, "Conference at Teheran," 28 Dec. 1943, Box 28, Map Room, Roosevelt Papers.

88. Gaddis, *The United States and the Origins of the Cold War,* 177–78. See also Herbert Feis, *Churchill, Roosevelt, Stalin: The War They Waged and the Peace They Sought* (Princeton: Princeton University Press, 1957), 642–43.

89. W. Averell Harriman to Cordell Hull and Edward R. Stettinius, 9 Jan. 1944, Box 335, Hopkins Papers. See also Harriman to Hopkins, 7 Jan. 1944, ibid.

90. Harriman to Hull and Stettinius, 9 Jan. 1944.

91. Gaddis, *The United States and the Origins of the Cold War,* 180; Feis, *Churchill, Roosevelt, Stalin,* 643–44.

92. W. Averell Harriman to Harry L. Hopkins, 9 Feb. 1944, Box 13, Map Room, Roosevelt Papers.

93. Ibid.

94. W. Averell Harriman to Harry L. Hopkins, 13 Feb. 1944, ibid.

95. Henry D. White to Henry Morgenthau, 7 Mar. 1944, Morgenthau Diaries, 707:59–62. See also an unsent Treasury Department memorandum for the president, 16 May 1944, ibid., 732:97–99.

96. W. Averell Harriman to State Department, 27 June 1944, Box 173, W. Averell Harriman Papers, LC.

97. Gaddis, *The United States and the Origins of the Cold War,* 185–88.

98. George F. Kennan to W. Averell Harriman, 3 Dec. 1944, Box 175, Harriman Papers.

99. W. Averell Harriman to Edward R. Stettinius, 6 Jan. 1945, Box 176, ibid. See also Stettinius to Franklin D. Roosevelt, 8 Jan. 1945, S. F., Box 91, Roosevelt Papers; and Minutes of the Committee of Three, 9 Jan. 1945, RG 59, NA.

100. Morgenthau Diaries, 808:294–315. See also ibid., 806:168; and Leahy Diary, 10 Jan. 1945.

101. W. Averell Harriman to State Department, 4 Apr. 1945, Box 178, Harriman Papers.

102. Edward R. Stettinius to Harry S. Truman, 16 Apr. 1945, S. F., Box 120, Harry S. Truman Papers, HSTL.

103. Leo T. Crowley to Harry S. Truman, 30 Apr. 1945, Crowley Papers. See also Executive Committee on Economic Foreign Policy, minutes, 1 June 1945, Box 776, RG 169, NA.

104. Henry L. Stimson to Harry S. Truman, 16 May 1945, S. F., Box 157, Truman Papers. See also John M. Blum, ed., *The Price of Vision: The Diary of Henry A. Wallace, 1942–1946* (Boston: Houghton Mifflin, 1973), 443.

105. Harry S. Truman to Harold L. Ickes, 21 May 1945, Box 15, Henry L. Stimson Safe File, RG 107, NA.

106. Harry S. Truman, *The Memoirs of Harry S. Truman*, 2 vols. (New York: DaCapo Press, 1955–56), 1:17, 45, 308, 465.

107. Harold D. Smith Diary, 26 Apr. 1945, HSTL. See also Truman, *Memoirs*, 1:46, 98.

108. Leo T. Crowley to Fred M. Vinson, 6 June 1945, Box 794, RG 169, NA. See also Crowley to William L. Clayton, 7 June 1945, ibid.

109. Leo T. Crowley to Harry S. Truman, 6 July 1945, Box 794, RG 169.

110. Truman, *Memoirs*, 1:233–34; Gaddis, *The United States and the Origins of the Cold War*, 222–23.

111. Leo T. Crowley to Harry S. Truman, memorandum, 13 Aug. 1945 (approved by Truman, 17 Aug. 1945), Crowley Papers.

4. DECOLONIZING ASIA AND AFRICA

1. William R. Louis, *Imperialism at Bay: The United States and the Decolonization of the British Empire, 1941–1945* (New York: Oxford University Press, 1978), 121–33, 154–55.

2. Breckinridge Long to Sumner Welles, 25 Feb. 1942, in *FRUS*, 1942, 1:606–7. See also Christopher Thorne, *Allies of a Kind: The United States, Britain, and the War against Japan, 1941–1945* (New York: Oxford University Press, 1978), 240–41.

3. Kimball, *Churchill and Roosevelt*, 1:400–404.

4. Thorne, *Allies of a Kind*, 234–36, 242.

5. Kimball, *Churchill and Roosevelt*, 1:444–49. See also Sherwood, *Roosevelt and Hopkins*, 529–31.

6. Thorne, *Allies of a Kind*, 243–44.

7. Capt. John L. McCrea, "Notes on Pacific War Council Meeting," 12 Aug. 1942, Box 168, Map Room, Franklin D. Roosevelt Papers, FDRL.

8. Hull, *Memoirs*, 2:1486–90.

9. Louis, *Imperialism at Bay*, 198–200.

10. Thorne, *Allies of a Kind*, 246–47.

11. Cordell Hull to William Phillips, 18 Nov. 1942, Reel 22, Cordell Hull Papers, LC.

12. Subcommittee on Political Problems, minutes, 12 Dec. 1942, Box 55, Harley A. Notter File, RG 59, NA.

13. William Phillips to Franklin D. Roosevelt, 3 Mar. 1943, in *FRUS*, 1943, 4:205–7.

14. William Phillips to Franklin D. Roosevelt, 19 Apr. 1943, Box 29, William Phillips Papers, HUHL.

15. William Phillips Diary, 14, 22 May 1943, Phillips Papers.

16. Memorandum, "Conversation between Isaiah Bowman and

Winston Churchill," 15 Apr. 1944, Box 1, Ser. 15, Isaiah Bowman Papers, JHUSCL.

17. "Extension of Immigration and Naturalization Privileges to the People of India," 24 Jan. 1945, Box 88 E, Secretary's Staff Committee Records, RG 353, NA. See also Policy Committee, minutes, 13 Mar. 1945, Box 138, Notter File, RG 59.

18. Joseph C. Grew to William Phillips, 6 Mar. 1945, "Letters," vol. 122, Joseph C. Grew Papers, HUHL; Edward R. Stettinius Diary, 18 Mar.–7 Apr. 1945, Box 29, Notter File, RG 59.

19. Joseph C. Grew to Harry S. Truman, 9 June 1945, S. F., Box 180, Harry S. Truman Papers, HSTL. See also memorandum, "Conversation between Grew and Anthony Eden," 16 May 1945, "Conversations," vol. 7, Grew Papers.

20. Harry S. Truman to Richard B. Russell, 2 Nov. 1945, S. F., Box 130, Truman Papers.

21. Prof. S. H. Cross, memorandum, "Conversation at the White House," 1 June 1942, Reel 22, Hull Papers.

22. Capt. John L. McCrea, "Notes on a Pacific War Council Meeting," 15 Sept. 1942, Box 168, Map Room, Roosevelt Papers. See also Blum, *Price of Vision*, 135.

23. Cordell Hull to William Phillips, 18 Nov. 1942, Reel 22, Hull Papers.

24. Subcommittee on Political Problems, minutes, 1 Aug. 1942, Box 55, Notter File, RG 59.

25. Subcommittee on Political Problems, minutes, 8 Aug. 1942, ibid.

26. "Tentative Views of the Subcommittee on Political Problems," 8 Aug. 1942, Box 56, ibid. See also Walter R. Sharp, "Dependent Areas and the Postwar World," 3 Aug. 1942, Studies of American Interest in the War and the Peace, CFR.

27. Subcommittee on Political Problems, minutes, 15 Aug. 1942, Box 55, Notter File, RG 59.

28. Louis, *Imperialism at Bay*, 169.

29. Ibid., 170–73.

30. Subcommittee on International Organization, minutes, 25 Sept. 1942, Box 85, Notter File, RG 59.

31. Subcommittee on International Organization, minutes, 2 Oct. 1942, ibid.

32. Louis, *Imperialism at Bay*, 183–84.

33. Subcommittee on Political Problems, minutes, 14 Nov. 1942, Box 55, Notter File, RG 59.

34. Louis, *Imperialism at Bay*, 177–79.

35. Cordell Hull to Franklin D. Roosevelt, 17 Nov. 1942, Box 62, Hull Papers. See also Hull to Sumner Welles, 14 Nov. 1942, Box 66, ibid.

36. Thorne, *Allies of a Kind*, 22–224; Louis, *Imperialism at Bay*, 187–97, 211–24.

37. Harley A. Notter, *Postwar Foreign Policy Preparation, 1939–1945* (Washington: Government Printing Office, 1949), 470–72. See also Leo Pasvolsky to Cordell Hull, 9 Mar. 1943, Box 7, Leo Pasvolsky Papers, LC; and Subcommittee on Political Problems, minutes, 10 Apr. 1943, Box 55 Notter File, RG 59.

38. Louis, *Imperialism at Bay*, 243–58; Thorne, *Allies of a Kind*, 342.

39. Hull, *Memoirs*, 2:1234–38, 1304–5; memorandum, "Meeting at the White House," 5 Oct. 1943, Box 54, Notter File, RG 59. See also Leo Pasvolsky to Cordell Hull, 18 Aug. 1943, Box 7, Pasvolsky Papers.

40. Isaiah Bowman, memorandum, 29 Oct. 1943, Box 2, Ser. 14, Bowman Papers. See also Gary R. Hess, *The United States' Emergence as a Southeast Asian Power, 1940–1950* (New York: Columbia University Press, 1987), 74–76.

41. Rupert Emerson, "The Future Status of Indochina as an Example of Postwar Colonial Relationships," 16 Nov. 1943, Studies of American Interest in the War and the Peace, CFR. See also "Inventory of Policy Recommendations Formulated in State Department Committees," 29 Dec. 1943, Box 365, Edward R. Stettinius Papers, UVAL.

42. Hess, *The United States' Emergence as a Southeast Asian Power*, 70–73. See also "Minutes of a Meeting between Franklin D. Roosevelt and the Joint Chiefs of Staff," 15 Nov. 1943, Box 195, RG 218, NA.

43. Pacific War Council, minutes, 9 Dec. 1942, Box 168, Map Room, Roosevelt Papers.

44. Meeting at the White House, minutes, 7 Jan. 1943, Box 29, ibid.

45. Hess, *The United States' Emergence as a Southeast Asian Power*, 72.

46. Louis, *Imperialism at Bay*, 235–36.

47. *FRUS: Conferences at Washington and Quebec*, 1943, 726.

48. Lt. Col. Chester Hammond, "Notes on Pacific War Council Meeting," 21 July 1943, Box 168, Map Room, Roosevelt Papers.

49. Franklin D. Roosevelt to Cordell Hull, 4 Aug. 1943, Box 171, ibid.

50. Cordell Hull to Franklin D. Roosevelt, 10 Aug. 1943, ibid.

51. Louis, *Imperialism at Bay*, 279–82.

52. *FRUS: Conferences at Cairo and Teheran*, 1943, 485, 554.

53. Hess, *The United States' Emergence as a Southeast Asian Power*, 89–91.

54. Hull, *Memoirs*, 2:1597.

55. RAdm. Wilson Brown, "Notes on Pacific War Council Meeting," 12 Jan. 1944, Box 168, Map Room, Roosevelt Papers.

56. Franklin D. Roosevelt to Cordell Hull, 24 Jan. 1944, S. F., Box 62,

Roosevelt Papers. See also RAdm. Wilson Brown, "Notes on Pacific War Council Meeting," 3 Feb. 1943, Box 168, Map Room, Roosevelt Papers; and W. Averell Harriman, "Notes on a Conversation with the President in Marrakech," 24 Jan. 1943, Box 163, W. Averell Harriman Papers, LC.

57. Franklin D. Roosevelt to Cordell Hull, 8 Feb. 1944, S. F., Box 62, Roosevelt Papers.

58. Hess, *The United States' Emergence as a Southeast Asian Power,* 93.

59. Edward R. Stettinius to James C. Dunn, 25 Feb. 1944, Box 216, Stettinius Papers. See also Stettinius, calendar notes, 22 Feb. 1944, Box 239, ibid.

60. Louis Hector, "Diary of the London Mission," 17 Mar. 1944, Box 1, Ser. 15, Bowman Papers.

61. Louis, *Imperialism at Bay,* 40.

62. Thorne, *Allies of a Kind,* 465–66.

63. Hess, *The United States' Emergence as a Southeast Asian Power,* 92.

64. Thorne, *Allies of a Kind,* 219, 346–47, 460–62; and Hess, *The United States' Emergence as a Southeast Asian Power,* 111–18.

65. John Davies, "Memorandum Advocating a Coordinated Attack on Japan's Inner Zone," 16 Jan. 1944, Box 334, Harry L. Hopkins Papers, FDRL.

66. Kimball, *Churchill and Roosevelt,* 2:751–56.

67. Thorne, *Allies of a Kind,* 409–18.

68. Louis, *Imperialism at Bay,* 356–57.

69. Isaiah Bowman, "Notes on a Conversation with Franklin D. Roosevelt," 17 Mar. 1944, Box 6, Ser. 14, Bowman Papers.

70. Isaiah Bowman, memorandum, 23 Mar. 1944, Box 1, Ser. 15, ibid.

71. Memorandum, "Conversation between Isaiah Bowman and Winston Churchill," 15 Apr. 1944, ibid.

72. Memorandum, "Conversation between Isaiah Bowman and Oliver Stanley," 18 Apr. 1944, ibid.

73. Louis, *Imperialism at Bay,* 332–33.

74. Ibid., 360–65. See also "Summary of a Meeting of the Post-War Programs Committee," 3 Mar. 1944, 740.00119/3–344, RG 59, NA; and Jacob Viner, "The United States and the Colonial Problem," 24 June 1944, Studies of American Interest in the War and the Peace, CFR.

75. Notter, *Postwar Foreign Policy Preparation,* 254, 276, 295–96, 606–7.

76. Hess, *The United States' Emergence as a Southeast Asian Power,* 99–101. See also Joseph W. Ballantine to Cordell Hull, 10 Mar. 1944, 740.00119 PW/37, RG 59, NA.

77. State Department memorandum for the president, 8 Sept. 1944, Box 1, Clayton-Thorp File, HSTL. This memorandum had been approved by the European, the Near Eastern and African, and the Far Eastern Offices.

78. Hess, *The United States' Emergence as a Southeast Asian Power*, 106, 126–30.

79. Edward R. Stettinius to Franklin D. Roosevelt, 11 Dec. 1944; and Stettinius to Roosevelt, 27 Dec. 1944, S. F., Box 55, Roosevelt Papers.

80. Edward R. Stettinius, calendar notes, 2 Jan. 1945, Box 243, Stettinius Papers. See also Franklin D. Roosevelt to Stettinius, 1 Jan. 1945, S. F., Box 55, Roosevelt Papers.

81. Memorandum, "Telephone Conversation between Lord Halifax and Edward R. Stettinius," 4 Jan. 1945, Box 243, Stettinius Papers. See also Minutes of the Committee of Three, 9 Jan. 1945, RG 59; and Hess, *The United States' Emergence as a Southeast Asian Power*, 131–32.

82. Minutes of the Committee of Three, 2 Jan. 1945, RG 59; Edward R. Stettinius to James C. Dunn, 4 Jan. 1945, Box 220, Stettinius Papers.

83. Edward R. Stettinius to Franklin D. Roosevelt, 12 Jan. 1945, 740.0011 PW/1–1245, RG 59, NA.

84. Edward R. Stettinius, calendar notes, 27 Sept. 1944, Box 242, Stettinius Papers. See also Stettinius, calendar notes, 29 July 1944, Box 241, ibid.

85. *FRUS: Conferences at Malta and Yalta*, 1945, 57.

86. Memorandum, "Telephone Conversation between Edward R. Stettinius and John Foster Dulles," 27 Nov. 1944, Box 243, Stettinius Papers.

87. Louis, *Imperialism at Bay*, 333.

88. Memorandum, "Conversation between Oliver Stanley and State Department Officials," 18 Jan. 1945, Box 8, Pasvolsky Papers. See also memorandum, "Conversation between Stanley and Franklin D. Roosevelt," 16 Jan. 1945, Reel 18, Matthews-Hickerson File, RG 59, NA.

89. Hess, *The United States' Emergence as a Southeast Asian Power*, 135–36.

90. Louis, *Imperialism at Bay*, 458–60.

91. William A. Williams et al., eds., *America in Vietnam: A Documentary History* (New York: W. W. Norton, 1985), 61.

92. Gareth Porter, ed., *Vietnam: The Definitive Documentation of Human Decisions*, 2 vols. (New York: Coleman Enterprises, 1979), 1:11. See also Edward R. Stettinius, calendar notes, 15, 16 Mar. 1945, Box 244, Stettinius Papers.

93. Thorne, *Allies of a Kind*, 632–33; Hess, *The United States' Emergence as a Southeast Asian Power*, 147–53.

94. Louis, *Imperialism at Bay*, 475–96.

95. Ibid., 115–17, 512–73.

96. Ibid.

5. DEVELOPING THE MIDDLE EAST

1. Herbert Feis, *Three International Episodes: Seen from E. A.* (New York: W. W. Norton, 1946), 93–109.

2. David S. Painter, *The Political Economy of United States Foreign Oil Policy, 1941–1954* (Baltimore: Johns Hopkins University Press, 1986), 11–16.

3. Ralph K. Davies to Harold L. Ickes, 18 Oct. 1941, S. F., Box 12, Franklin D. Roosevelt Papers, FDRL. See also Walton C. Ferris to Max W. Thornburg, 24 Nov. 1941, Box 1, Records of the Petroleum Division, RG 59, NA.

4. Painter, *Political Economy of United States Foreign Oil Policy*, 32–34.

5. W. L. Parker, memorandum, 9 Feb. 1943, Box 19, Records of the Petroleum Division, RG 59.

6. Hull, *Memoirs*, 2:1512. See also Daniel Yergin, *The Prize: The Epic Quest for Oil, Money, and Power* (New York: Simon and Schuster, 1991), 393–96.

7. Philip W. Bonsal to Herbert Feis, 1 Mar. 1943; Harry C. Hawkins to Feis, 4 Mar. 1943; and Committee on International Petroleum Policy, minutes, 5, 9 Mar. 1943, Box 1, Records of the Petroleum Division, RG 59.

8. Committee on International Petroleum Policy, report for Cordell Hull, 22 Mar. 1943, ibid.

9. Painter, *Political Economy of United States Foreign Oil Policy*, 39.

10. Joint Chiefs of Staff, minutes, 8 June 1943, Box 194, RG 218, NA.

11. William D. Leahy to Franklin D. Roosevelt, 8 June 1943, Box 1, Records of the Petroleum Division, RG 59.

12. Memorandum, "Conversation between Adolf A. Berle and Franklin D. Roosevelt," 10 June 1943, Adolf A. Berle Diary, Adolf A. Berle Papers, FDRL.

13. William D. Leahy to Cordell Hull, 11 June 1943, Box 1, Records of the Petroleum Division, RG 59.

14. Henry L. Stimson Diary, 4 June 1943, Henry L. Stimson Papers, YUSL.

15. Ibid., 8 June 1943.

16. Ibid., 9 June 1943.

17. Ibid., 10, 11 June 1943; Herbert Feis to Cordell Hull, 11 June 1943, Box 1, Records of the Petroleum Division, RG 59.

18. Feis to Hull, 11 June 1943.

19. Herbert Feis to Philip W. Bonsal, 15 June 1943, Box 1, Records of the Petroleum Division, RG 59.

20. Hull, *Memoirs*, 2:1518–20. See also Stimson Diary, 15 June 1943; and Joint Chiefs of Staff, minutes, 15 June 1943, Box 194, RG 218.

21. Hull, *Memoirs*, 2:1518–20; Feis, *Three International Episodes*, 110–33.

22. Painter, *Political Economy of United States Foreign Oil Policy*, 45–47.

23. Patrick J. Hurley to Franklin D. Roosevelt, 9 June 1943, S. F., Box 68, Roosevelt Papers.

24. Cordell Hull to Harold L. Ickes, 13 Nov. 1943, Box 5, Leo Pasvolsky File, RG 59, NA.

25. Cordell Hull to William D. Leahy, 15 Dec. 1943, ibid.

26. Painter, *Political Economy of United States Foreign Oil Policy*, 52–54. See also memorandum, "State Department Position on the Petroleum Reserves Corporation," n.d., Box 1, Records of the Petroleum Division, RG 59; and Ralph K. Davies, memorandum, "Conversation with Harold L. Ickes," 31 Jan. 1944, Box 15, Ralph K. Davies Papers, HSTL.

27. Painter, *Political Economy of United States Foreign Oil Policy*, 56–59, 201–2. See also John A. Loftus to Francis O. Wilcox, 17 Nov. 1945, Box 1, Records of the Petroleum Division, RG 59; and Nicholas, *Washington Dispatches*, 318–19, 328–29.

28. Isaiah Bowman to Myron C. Taylor, 18 June 1943, Box 7, Ser. 14, Isaiah Bowman Papers, JHUSCL.

29. Special Committee on Petroleum, minutes, 28 Sept. 1943, Box 28, Records of the Petroleum Division, RG 59. See also Wallace Murray to Edward R. Stettinius, 6 Nov. 1943, Box 219, Edward R. Stettinius Papers, UVAL; and Murray to Stettinius and Cordell Hull, 24 Nov. 1943, Box 3, Records of the Petroleum Division, RG 59.

30. James C. Sappington, memorandum, 1 Dec. 1943, Box 3, ibid.

31. Ibid. See also John A. Loftus, memorandum, "Background Information on the Anglo-American Oil Agreement," 15 Nov. 1944, Box 8, ibid.

32. Hull, *Memoirs*, 2:1521–23.

33. "Notes on a Meeting between Franklin D. Roosevelt and Edward R. Stettinius," 18 Feb. 1944, Box 239, Stettinius Papers. See also Stettinius to John G. Winant, 29 Feb. 1944, S. F., Box 91, Roosevelt Papers.

34. Kimball, *Churchill and Roosevelt*, 2:733–34, 744–45.

35. Ibid., 2:754–55, 3:13–14, 16–17, 26–27.

36. "Objectives of United States Petroleum Policy," n.d. (approved by the Post-War Programs Committee in early Apr. 1944), Box 6, Records of the Petroleum Division, RG 59. See also Charles Rayner, memorandum, "Foreign Petroleum Policy of the United States," 3 Apr. 1944, Box 1, ibid.; and a document on American foreign petroleum policy, discussed by the Post-War Programs Committee on 3 Mar. 1944, 740.00119/3–344, RG 59.

37. Painter, *Political Economy of United States Foreign Oil Policy*, 59–60;

Harley A. Notter, *Postwar Foreign Policy Preparation: 1939–1945*
(Washington: Government Printing Office, 1949), 238–39.

38. Plenary Session 2, Anglo-American Petroleum Conversations, minutes, 27 July 1944, Box 3, Records of the Petroleum Division, RG 59. See also Edward R. Stettinius to Cordell Hull, 27 July 1944, Box 218, Stettinius Papers.

39. Plenary Session 3, Anglo-American Petroleum Conversations, minutes, 1 Aug. 1944, Box 3, Records of the Petroleum Division, RG 59.

40. Edward R. Stettinius to Cordell Hull, 15 Aug. 1944, Box 218, Stettinius Papers.

41. Hull, *Memoirs*, 2:1525–26.

42. Executive Committee on Economic Foreign Policy, minutes, 8 Sept. 1944, Box 776, RG 169, NA.

43. Painter, *Political Economy of United States Foreign Oil Policy*, 62–73, 202–3.

44. *Oil and Gas Journal*, 9 Dec. 1944, 3. For comments from petroleum industry sources, see *Oil and Gas Journal*, 19 Aug., 7, 14 Oct. 1944.

45. Harold L. Ickes to Franklin D. Roosevelt, 12 Mar. 1945, Box 232, Stettinius Papers.

46. Minutes, 16 Mar. 1945, Secretary's Staff Committee Records, RG 353, NA.

47. Edward R. Stettinius Diary, 18 Mar.–7 Apr. 1945, Box 29, Harley A. Notter File, RG 59, NA.

48. Painter, *Political Economy of United States Foreign Oil Policy*, 72–73.

49. Anglo-American Petroleum Agreement, 24 Sept. 1945, Box 4, Records of the Petroleum Division, RG 59; and *Oil and Gas Journal*, 15, 29 Sept. 1945.

50. State Department Policy Committee, minutes, 28 June 1944, Box 138, Notter File.

51. Robert Vitalis, "The 'New Deal' in Egypt: The Rise of Anglo-American Commercial Competition in World War II and the Fall of Neocolonialism," *Diplomatic History*, 20, no. 2 (spring 1996): 211–39; John D. Hickerson to H. Freeman Matthews and James C. Dunn, 9 Oct. 1944, Reel 2, Matthews-Hickerson File, RG 59, NA; Stettinius Diary, 15–23 Apr. 1945.

52. Cordell Hull to Franklin D. Roosevelt, 10 Aug. 1943, Box 171, Map Room, Roosevelt Papers. See also Lauchlin Currie to Roosevelt, 3 Sept. 1942, S. F., Box 2, Roosevelt Papers.

53. Cordell Hull to Franklin D. Roosevelt, 13 Sept. 1944, S. F., Box 40, Roosevelt Papers.

54. Hull, *Memoirs*, 2:1540–41; Gaddis Smith, *American Diplomacy during the Second World War, 1941–1945* (New York: Alfred A. Knopf, 1985),

105–6; William C. Bullitt to Franklin D. Roosevelt, 27 Dec. 1941, S. F., Box 72, Roosevelt Papers.

55. Hull, *Memoirs*, 2:1542–46; Kimball, *Churchill and Roosevelt*, 2:599–600.

56. Memorandum, "Conversation between Paul H. Alling and Francis Lacoste," 10 Mar. 1945, "Conversations," vol. 6, Joseph C. Grew Papers, HUHL. See also Stettinius Diary, 11–17 Mar. 1945.

57. Truman, *Memoirs*, 1:242–43.

58. Joseph C. Grew, *Turbulent Era: A Diplomatic Record of Forty Years, 1904–1945*, 2 vols. (Boston: Houghton Mifflin, 1952), 2:1515–17; Loy W. Henderson to H. H. Vaughan, 10 Nov. 1945, S. F., Box 118, Harry S. Truman Papers, HSTL.

59. William L. Langer and S. Everett Gleason, *The Undeclared War, 1940–1941* (New York: Harper and Brothers, 1953), 801–10.

60. Walton C. Ferris, memorandum of an earlier conversation in the office of Wallace Murray, 24 Mar. 1942, Box 2, Pasvolsky File. See also Israel, *War Diary of Breckinridge Long*, 246–47.

61. Hull, *Memoirs*, 2:1502–3.

62. Herbert Feis, *Churchill, Roosevelt, Stalin: The War They Waged and the Peace They Sought* (Princeton: Princeton University Press, 1957), 87–88.

63. Medi Heravi, *Iranian-American Diplomacy* (New York: Theo Caus' Sons, 1969), 60–61; Arthur C. Millspaugh, *Americans in Persia* (New York: DaCapo, 1976), 46–47.

64. Arthur C. Millspaugh to Franklin D. Roosevelt, 1 Dec. 1943, Box 332, Harry L. Hopkins Papers, FDRL.

65. Patrick J. Harley to Franklin D. Roosevelt, 13 May 1943, S. F., Box 153, Roosevelt Papers. See also William D. Leahy Diary, 4 Oct. 1943, WSHS.

66. Memorandum, "American Policy in Iran," enclosed in Cordell Hull to Franklin D. Roosevelt, 16 Aug. 1943, Box 329, Hopkins Papers.

67. James F. Byrnes to Franklin D. Roosevelt, 11 Nov. 1943, S. F., Box 147, Roosevelt Papers. See also Byrnes to Roosevelt, 15 Oct. 1943, ibid.

68. Hull, *Memoirs*, 2:1508–9.

69. Memorandum, "Conversation between Franklin D. Roosevelt and Edward R. Stettinius," 5 Nov. 1943, Box 238, Stettinius Papers.

70. Kimball, *Churchill and Roosevelt*, 3:3–4; Franklin D. Roosevelt to Edward R. Stettinius, 8 Dec. 1944, S. F., Box 68, Roosevelt Papers.

71. Hull, *Memoirs*, 2:1506–7.

72. Patrick J. Hurley to Franklin D. Roosevelt, 21 Dec. 1943, S. F., Box 3, Roosevelt Papers. See also Hurley to Roosevelt, 7 Nov. 1943, S. F., Box 153, ibid.

73. Franklin D. Roosevelt to Cordell Hull, 12 Jan. 1944, S. F. Box 55, Roosevelt Papers. See also Roosevelt to Patrick J. Hurley, 25 Mar. 1944, ibid.

74. Cordell Hull to Viscount Halifax, 20 June 1944, Box 91, ibid. See also Hull to Franklin D. Roosevelt, 1 July 1944, ibid.; and Adolf A. Berle to A. John Bittson, 7 June 1944, Box 29, Berle Papers.

75. Gabriel Kolko, *The Politics of War: The World and United States Foreign Policy, 1943–1945* (New York: Random House, 1968), 307–11. See also Hull, *Memoirs,* 2:1508–10.

76. Russell D. Buhite, *Decisions at Yalta: An Appraisal of Summit Diplomacy* (Wilmington, Del.: Scholarly Resources, 1986), 108–10. See also Kimball, *Churchill and Roosevelt,* 3:511–13.

77. Smith, *American Diplomacy during the Second World War,* 108–9.

78. Subcommittee on Political Problems, minutes, 29 Aug. 1942, Box 55, Notter File.

79. Subcommittee on Territorial Problems, minutes, 4 Sept., 2 Oct. 1942, Box 59, ibid.

80. Subcommittee on Political Problems, minutes, 5 Sept. 1942, Box 55, ibid.

81. Presidential Diaries of Henry Morgenthau, 3 Dec. 1942, Reel 2, Henry Morgenthau Papers, FDRL.

82. Harold B. Hoskins, "A Plan for Peace in the Near East," 20 Mar. 1943, Reel 22, Cordell Hull Papers, LC. For similar concerns that Zionist demands would provoke an increase in anti-Semitism in the United States after the war, see memorandum, "Conversation between Isaiah Bowman and Eleanor Roosevelt," 7 Jan. 1944, Box 6, Ser. 14, Bowman Papers; and memorandum, Wallace Murray to Cordell Hull, Edward R. Stettinius, and Breckinridge Long, 20 Jan. 1944, Box 200, Breckinridge Long Papers, LC.

83. Isaiah Bowman, "Notes on a Meeting of the Political Subcommittee," 27 Mar. 1943, Box 6, Ser. 14, Bowman Papers.

84. Subcommittee on Territorial Problems, minutes, 30 Apr. 1943, Box 59, Notter File.

85. Ibid., 28 May 1943.

86. Ibid., 11 June 1943. See also Adolf A. Berle to Emanuel Celler, 16 Aug., 6 Oct. 1943, Box 30; and Berle to Jacob Billikoph, 22 May 1944, Box 29, Berle Papers.

87. Isaiah Bowman to Franklin D. Roosevelt, 22 May 1943, Box 6, Ser. 14, Bowman Papers. Emphasis in the original.

88. State Department memorandum, 27 May 1943, S. F., Box 93, Roosevelt Papers. See also Patrick J. Hurley to Roosevelt, 5 May 1943, S. F., Box 153, ibid.

89. Hull, *Memoirs,* 2:1532–33.

90. Memorandum, "Conversation between Franklin D. Roosevelt and Col. Harold B. Hoskins," 27 Sept. 1943, Box 5, Ser. 14, Bowman Papers. See also Hoskins to Roosevelt, 27 Sept. 1943, S. F., Box 68, Roosevelt Papers.

91. "Conversation between Franklin D. Roosevelt and Col. Harold B. Hoskins," 27 Sept. 1943. See also Isaiah Bowman, memorandum, "Conversation with Franklin D. Roosevelt," 28 Oct. 1943, Box 5, Ser. 14, Bowman Papers.

92. Charles W. McCarthy to George C. Marshall, 5 Feb. 1944, Henry L. Stimson Safe File, Box 10, RG 107, NA. See also memorandum "Conversation between Breckinridge Long and Five Senators on the Subject of Arabian Oil and Palestine," 5 Feb. 1944, Box 200, Long Papers.

93. John J. McCloy to Henry L. Stimson, 6 Feb. 1944, Box 10, Stimson's Safe File. See also Stimson Diary, 14 Feb. 1944.

94. Henry L. Stimson to Tom Connally, 7 Feb. 1944; and John J. McCloy to Stimson, 8 Mar. 1944, ibid.

95. Memorandum, "Telephone Conversation between Wallace Murray and Edward R. Stettinius," 1 Mar. 1944, Box 239, Stettinius Papers. See also Stettinius, memorandum for the president, "Protest of Ibn Saud Regarding Palestine Resolutions," 4 Mar. 1944, Box 232, Stettinius Papers.

96. Hull, *Memoirs,* 2:1534–36.

97. Division of Near Eastern Affairs memorandum, 15 Mar. 1944, Box 19, Notter Files. See also Patrick J. Hurley to Franklin D. Roosevelt, 3 Feb. 1944, M. R., Box 12, Roosevelt Papers.

98. Hull, *Memoirs,* 2:1513–16.

99. State Department Policy Committee, minutes, 15 Nov. 1944, Box 138, Notter Files. See also Wallace Murray to Edward R. Stettinius, 1 Nov. 1944, Box 217, Stettinius Papers.

100. Edward R. Stettinius to Franklin D. Roosevelt, 13 Dec. 1944, S. F., Box 91, Roosevelt Papers. See also Stettinius to Roosevelt, 19 Dec. 1944, S. F., Box 68, ibid.

101. Edward R. Stettinius to Franklin D. Roosevelt, 22 Dec. 1944, S. F., Box 91, Roosevelt Papers. See also Stettinius to Wallace Murray, 23 Dec. 1944, Box 221, Stettinius Papers; Minutes of the Committee of Three, 27 Dec. 1944; 740.00119 Control (Germany)/12–2844, RG 59, NA; and Stettinius to Roosevelt, 8 Jan. 1945, S. F., Box 68, Roosevelt Papers.

102. Memorandum, "Conference with the President," 2 Jan. 1945, Box 4, Charles E. Bohlen File, RG 59, NA.

103. Edward R. Stettinius to Franklin D. Roosevelt, 9 Jan. 1945, S. F., Box 68, Roosevelt Papers. See also Stettinius to Roosevelt, 9 Jan. 1945, S. F., Box 91, ibid.

104. James M. Landis to Franklin D. Roosevelt, 17 Jan. 1945, Box 142, Roosevelt Papers. See also Edward R. Stettinius to Roosevelt, 4 Jan. 1945, Box 91, ibid.

105. Memorandum, "Conversation on the USS *Quincy* between Franklin D. Roosevelt and King Saud," 14 Feb. 1945, Box 337, Hopkins Papers; William D. Leahy, "Comments on the above Memorandum," n.d., Box 3, Samuel I. Rosenman Papers, HSTL. See also Buhite, *Decisions at Yalta*, 119–26.

106. Joseph C. Grew to Harry S. Truman, 11 May 1945, S. F., Box 184, Truman Papers.

107. Memorandum, "Conversation between James C. Dunn and Harold L. Ickes," 8 Jan. 1945; and Charles B. Rayner to Wallace Murray, 20 Jan. 1945, Box 6, Records of the Petroleum Division.

108. Ralph K. Davies, memorandum for the files, 6 Apr. 1945, Box 15, Ralph K. Davies Papers.

109. Joseph C. Grew to American Legation in Baghdad, 22 Mar. 1945, S. F., Box 64, Franklin D. Roosevelt Papers.

110. Edward R. Stettinius to Harry S. Truman, 18 Apr. 1945, S. F., Box 184, Truman Papers.

111. Joseph C. Grew to Harry S. Truman, 23 May 1945 (general objectives of the State Department memorandum approved in principle by Truman on 29 May 1945), Box 236, Stettinius Papers.

112. Joseph C. Grew to Harry S. Truman, 16 June 1945 (Truman approved the State Department recommendation on 26 June 1945), S. F., Box 184, Truman Papers. See also Grew to Truman, 26, 28 May 1945, ibid.

113. Memorandum, Gordon Merrian to Loy W. Henderson, 31 Aug. 1945 (attached to memorandum, Henderson to James F. Byrnes, 31 Aug. 1945), S. F., Box 184, Truman Papers. See also minutes, 9 July 1945, Secretary's Staff Committee Records.

114. Harry S. Truman to Clement Attlee, 18 Sept. 1945, S. F., Box 182, Truman Papers.

115. Informal record of a conversation, 19 Oct. 1945, Box 184, ibid.

116. Joseph H. Ball to Harry S. Truman, 19 Nov. 1945; and memorandum, Truman to Ball, 24 Nov. 1945 (filed but not sent), ibid.

117. Isaiah Bowman, "Comments on an Article in the *Baltimore Sun*," 13 Dec. 1947, Box 5, Ser. 9, Bowman Papers. See also Bowman, "Comments on an Article in the *New York Times*," 10 Jan. 1949, ibid.

6. PRESERVING WORLD PEACE

1. Advisory Committee on Postwar Foreign Policy, minutes, 2 May 1942, Reel 49, Cordell Hull Papers, LC.

2. Hull, *Memoirs,* 2:1635–38. See also Isaiah Bowman, "Notes on a Meeting of the Subcommittee on Political Problems," 27 June 1942, Box 6, Ser. 14, Isaiah Bowman Papers, JHUSCL.

3. Subcommittee on Political Problems, minutes, 14 Mar. 1942, Box 55, Harley A. Notter File, RG 59, NA.

4. Ibid., 28 Mar. 1942.

5. Subcommittee on Security Problems, minutes, 15 Apr. 1942, Box 76, ibid.

6. Ibid., 29 Apr. 1942. See also ibid., 13 Nov. 1942.

7. Ibid., 20 May 1942.

8. Franklin D. Roosevelt to Adolf A. Berle, 26 June 1941, Box 212, Adolf A. Berle Papers, FDRL.

9. *FRUS,* 1942, 3:573–74. See also memorandum, "Conversation among Franklin D. Roosevelt, Grace Tulley, and Samuel I. Rosenman," 13 Nov. 1942, S. F., Box 188; and Roosevelt to Jan Christian Smuts, 24 Nov.1942, S. F., Box 70, Franklin D. Roosevelt Papers, FDRL; and memorandum, "Meeting at the White House," 22 Feb. 1943, Box 8, Leo Pasvolsky Papers, LC.

10. *FRUS,* 1942, 3:580–81.

11. Subcommittee on Security Problems, minutes, 18 Sept. 1942, Box 76, Notter File. See also ibid., 5, 11 Dec. 1942.

12. Memorandum, "Conversation between Norman H. Davis and Isaiah Bowman," 2 Oct. 1942, Box 2, Ser. 14, Bowman Papers.

13. Subcommittee on Security Problems, minutes, 23 Oct. 1942, Box 76, Notter File.

14. Ibid., 30 Oct. 1942.

15. Ibid.

16. Ibid., 11 Dec. 1942.

17. Ibid., 18 Dec. 1942.

18. Ibid, 15 Jan. 1943.

19. Ibid. See also ibid., 15 Apr. 1942.

20. Ibid., 19 Feb. 1943. See also Joint Meeting of Subcommittees on Security Problems and International Organization, minutes, 16 Apr. 1943, Box 76, Notter File.

21. Subcommittee on Security Problems, minutes, 26 Feb. 1943, Box 76, Notter File. See also Armaments Group, memorandum, "The Disarmament of France," 12 Feb. 1943; and Political Group, memorandum, "Should Non-Axis Europe Be Permanently Disarmed?" 22 Mar. 1943, Studies of American Interests in the War and the Peace, CFR.

22. Subcommittee on Political Problems, minutes, 20 Feb. 1943, Box 55, Notter File.

23. Isaiah Bowman, memorandum on Russia, 6 Mar. 1943, Box 87, Sumner Welles Papers, FDRL. See also Welles to Cordell Hull, 9 Mar. 1943, Reel 22, Hull Papers; and Bowman, memorandum, 9 Mar. 1943, Box 7, Ser. 14, Bowman Papers.

24. Subcommittee on Security Problems, minutes, 12 Mar. 1943, Box 76, Notter File.

25. Ibid., 19 Mar. 1943. See also Isaiah Bowman, "Notes on Steering Committee Meeting," 26 Mar. 1943, Box 7, Ser. 14, Bowman Papers.

26. Subcommittee on Security Problems, minutes, 24 Mar. 1943, Box 76, Notter File.

27. Robert A. Divine, *Second Chance: The Triumph of Internationalism in America during World War II* (New York: Atheneum, 1967), 92–94; Nicholas, *Washington Dispatches,* 165–70.

28. Divine, *Second Chance,* 95–96; Nicholas, *Washington Dispatches,* 173, 182.

29. Harley A. Notter, *Postwar Foreign Policy Preparation, 1939–1945* (Washington: Government Printing Office, 1949), 108–10, 472–83. See also "Tentative Views of the Subcommittee on International Organization," 12 Mar. 1943, Box 193, Welles Papers.

30. Sherwood, *Roosevelt and Hopkins,* 717–18; Warren F. Kimball, *The Juggler: Franklin Roosevelt as Wartime Statesman* (Princeton: Princeton University Press, 1991), 86, 96. See also Isaiah Bowman, "Notes on the International Organization Subcommittee Meeting," 19 June 1943, Box 5, Ser. 14, Bowman Papers.

31. Hull, *Memoirs,* 2:1247–51; memorandum, "Conversation between Cordell Hull and Maxim Litvinov," 31 Mar. 1943, Box 82, Hull Papers.

32. Herbert Feis, *Churchill, Roosevelt, Stalin: The War They Waged and the Peace They Sought* (Princeton: Princeton University Press, 1957), 131–36; Elizabeth K. MacLean, "Joseph E. Davies and Soviet-American Relations, 1941–43," *Diplomatic History* 4 (winter 1980): 73–93; Kimball, *The Juggler,* 90–92.

33. Notter, *Postwar Foreign Policy Preparation,* 169–71.

34. Myron C. Taylor to Sumner Welles, 15 May 1943, Box 92, Welles Papers.

35. "Digest of Minutes of the Political Subcommittee," 22 May 1943, Box 54, Notter File.

36. Memorandum, "Conversation at the British Embassy," 22 May 1943, Box 7, Pasvolsky Papers. A copy of the memorandum, which Churchill sent to Roosevelt on 28 May 1943, is reprinted in Kimball, *Churchill and Roosevelt,* 2:221–27.

37. Subcommittee on Political Problems, minutes, 5 June 1943, Box 56,

Notter File. See also State Department memorandum for President Roosevelt, 11 Aug. 1943, Reel 11, Matthews-Hickerson File, RG 59, NA.

38. Isaiah Bowman, "Notes Concerning a Political Subcommittee Meeting," dictated on 12 June 1943, Box 5, Ser. 14, Bowman Papers.

39. Subcommittee on Political Problems, minutes, 19 June 1943, Box 56, Notter File. See also ibid., 12 June 1943.

40. W. Averell Harriman to Franklin D. Roosevelt, 5 July 1943, S. F., Box 49, Roosevelt Papers.

41. Myron C. Taylor, memorandum, 8 July 1943, , Box 52 Hull Papers.

42. Hull, *Memoirs*, 2:147.

43. Notter, *Postwar Foreign Policy Preparation*, 526–34.

44. Hull, *Memoirs*, 2:1646–47; Notter, *Postwar Foreign Policy Preparation*, 172.

45. Notter, *Postwar Foreign Policy Preparation*, 553.

46. Kimball, *Churchill and Roosevelt*, 2:385–86, 420–21, 432–34, 438–39, 448–49, 463–64, 485–86, 489–91, 523–26, 533, 545–47, 568–70, 576–79, 588–89, 597.

47. Lloyd C. Gardner, *Spheres of Influence: The Great Powers Partition Europe, from Munich to Yalta* (Chicago: Ivan R. Dee, 1993), 167–68.

48. Feis, *Churchill, Roosevelt, Stalin*, 215.

49. Hull, *Memoirs*, 2:1238–39.

50. Divine, *Second Chance*, 95–96, 110–13, 130–31, 141–46.

51. Hull, *Memoirs*, 2:1256–57.

52. Memorandum, "Conversation between Isaiah Bowman and Leo Pasvolsky," 7 Oct. 1943, Box 5, Ser. 14, Bowman Papers. See also memorandum, "Conversation between Bowman and Franklin D. Roosevelt," 28 Oct. 1943, ibid.; and William D. Leahy Diary, 5 Oct. 1943, WSHS.

53. Isaiah Bowman, memorandum, 7 Oct. 1943, Box 5, Ser. 14, Bowman Papers.

54. Hull, *Memoirs*, 2:1277–82, 1299–1301; Feis, *Churchill, Roosevelt, Stalin*, 207–11; Kimball, *The Juggler*, 95.

55. Hull, *Memoirs*, 2:1297, 1303; Gardner, *Spheres of Influence*, 168–69.

56. Cordell Hull to Franklin D. Roosevelt, 31 Oct. 1943, Box 16, Map Room, Roosevelt Papers. See also Gen. John R. Deane to Joint Chiefs of Staff, 26, 30, 31 Oct. 1943, Reel 17, Matthews-Hickerson File.

57. Harry L. Hopkins to John G. Winaut, 3 Nov. 1943, Box 336, Harry L. Hopkins Papers, FDRL. See also Edward R. Stettinius, memorandum for Ray Atherton and H. Freeman Matthews, 5 Nov. 1943, Box 217, Edward R. Stettinius Papers, UVAL.

58. W. Averell Harriman to Franklin D. Roosevelt, 5 Nov. 1943, Box 170, W. Averell Harriman Papers, LC.

59. Hull, *Memoirs*, 2:1313–15; Divine, *Second Chance*, 147–55; Nicholas, *Washington Dispatches*, 269–270, 272–73.

60. Sherwood, *Roosevelt and Hopkins*, 785–86; Feis, *Churchill, Roosevelt, Stalin*, 269–71.

61. Sherwood, *Roosevelt and Hopkins*, 776–99; Feis, *Churchill, Roosevelt, Stalin*, 237–79; Kimball, *The Juggler*, 91–92; Gardner, *Spheres of Influence*, 149, 174–76.

62. Notter, *Postwar Foreign Policy Preparation*, 172, 226–27, 246–51; Hull, *Memoirs*, 2:1249.

63. Notter, *Postwar Foreign Policy Preparation*, 576–81.

64. Myron C. Taylor, memorandum, "Enforcement of World Organization Council Decrees," 2 Jan. 1944, Reel 24, Hull Papers.

65. Ibid.

66. Leo Pasvolsky, "Notes on a Meeting at the White House," 3 Feb. 1944, Box 5, Pasvolsky Papers.

67. Isaiah Bowman, memorandum, "Meeting with President Roosevelt," 3 Feb. 1944, Box 6, Ser. 14, Bowman Papers; "Meeting of the Informal Political Agenda Group," 8 Feb. 1944, Box 54, Notter File.

68. Hull, *Memoirs*, 2:1645–51; Notter, *Postwar Foreign Policy Preparation*, 255–57, 581–82.

69. Memorandum, "Conversation between Cordell Hull and Charles W. Taussig," 8 Feb. 1944, Box 63, Hull Papers. See also memorandum, "Conversation between Hull and Andrei A. Gromyko," 20 Apr. 1944, 740.0019 EW 1939/2514, RG 59, NA.

70. W. Averell Harriman to Cordell Hull, 16 Mar. 1944, Box 172, Harriman Papers. See also Harriman to Franklin D. Roosevelt, 17 Mar. 1944; and Harriman to William L. Bett, 18 Mar. 1944, ibid.; and Harriman to Hull, 15 Mar. 1944, Box 171, ibid.

71. Cordell Hull to W. Averell Harriman, 18 Mar. 1944, Box 172, ibid.

72. H. Freeman Matthews, memorandum, "British Views on Russia," 9 May 1944, Reel 14, Matthews-Hickerson File. Edward R. Stettinius based his report to Cordell Hull on this memorandum.

73. William D. Leahy to Cordell Hull, 16 May 1944, Box 380, Records of the Joint Chiefs of Staff, RG 218, NA.

74. Campbell and Herring, *Diaries of Edward R. Stettinius*, 52–54, 59–60.

75. Ibid.

76. Hull, *Memoirs*, 2:1652; Notter, *Postwar Foreign Policy Preparation*, 582–91.

77. Hull, *Memoirs*, 2:1653, 1662–64, 1683.

78. Ibid., 2:1665.

79. Divine, *Second Chance*, 192, 196–97. See also Cordell Hull to Franklin D. Roosevelt, 4 May 1944; and Quincy Wright to Hull, 20 May 1944, Box 53, Hull Papers.

80. Hull, *Memoirs*, 2:1657–59.

81. Divine, *Second Chance*, 196–97.

82. Ibid., 198–203. See also Hull, *Memoirs*, 2:1669–70; and Notter, *Postwar Foreign Policy Preparation*, 267, 286–87.

83. Divine, *Second Chance*, 204–8.

84. Ibid., 208–12

85. W. Averell Harriman to Franklin D. Roosevelt, 12 June 1944, Reel 8, Map Room, Roosevelt Papers. See also memorandum, "Conversation between Harriman and Anthony Eden," 3 May 1944, Box 172, Harriman Papers.

86. Henry Morgenthau to Franklin D. Roosevelt, 23 July 1944, Box 19, Map Room, Roosevelt Papers. See also Harry Dexter White, memorandum, "Conference at the White House," 18 May 1944, Presidential Diaries of Henry Morgenthau, Reel 2, Henry Morgenthau Papers, Roosevelt Library.

7. ESTABLISHING THE UNITED NATIONS

1. Hull, *Memoirs*, 2:1671–72.

2. Ibid., 2:1672–73.

3. Harley A. Notter, *Postwar Foreign Policy Preparation, 1939–1945* (Washington: Government Printing Office, 1949), 282–84, 595–606.

4. Hull, *Memoirs*, 2:1674–76.

5. Ibid., 2:1686–89.

6. Ibid., 2:1689–93.

7. Notter, *Postwar Foreign Policy Preparation*, 290–303.

8. Edward R. Stettinius, Dumbarton Oaks Diary (draft), 20, 21 Aug. 1944, Box 241, Edward R. Stettinius Papers, UVAL.

9. Robert A. Divine, *Second Chance: The Triumph of Internationalism in America during World War II* (New York: Atheneum, 1967), 222.

10. Hull, *Memoirs*, 2:1696.

11. Divine, *Second Chance*, 223–24. See also Nicholas, *Washington Dispatches*, 413–16.

12. Georg M. Schild, "Bretton Woods and Dumbarton Oaks: American Postwar Planning in the Summer of 1944" (Ph.D. diss., University of Maryland, 1993), 336–44; Campbell and Herring, *Diaries of Edward R. Stettinius*, 116, 124, 126, 133; Hull, *Memoirs*, 2:1682, 1698.

13. Schild, "Bretton Woods and Dumbarton Oaks," 348–53; Hull, *Memoirs*, 2:1677.

14. Stettinius, Dumbarton Oaks Diary (draft), 24 Aug. 1944.

15. Schild, "Bretton Woods and Dumbarton Oaks," 361–62.

16. Campbell and Herring, *Diaries of Edward R. Stettinius*, 112.

17. Edward R. Stettinius, calendar notes, 28 Aug. 1944, Box 241, Stettinius Papers; Stettinius, Dumbarton Oaks Diary (draft), 28 Aug. 1944.

18. Campbell and Herring, *Diaries of Edward R. Stettinius*, 115–18.

19. Hull, *Memoirs*, 2:1679–84.

20. Campbell and Herring, *Diaries of Edward R. Stettinius*, 127–31.

21. Ibid., 133–36.

22. Schild, "Bretton Woods and Dumbarton Oaks," 375–79.

23. Memorandum, "Telephone Conversation between Edward R. Stettinius and Franklin D. Roosevelt," 17 Sept. 1944, Box 242, Stettinius Papers.

24. Edward R. Stettinius, calendar notes, 17 Sept. 1944, ibid.

25. "Transcript of a Report to the American Group by Edward R. Stettinius," 18 Sept. 1944, ibid. See also Campbell and Herring, *Diaries of Edward R. Stettinius*, 137–39; and "Record of a Telephone Conversation between Cordell Hull and Stettinius," 18 Sept. 1944, Box 242, Stettinius Papers.

26. Isaiah Bowman, memorandum to be attached to "Outline of Points Made at an Informal Group Meeting on 17 Sept. 1944," Box 1, Ser. 16, Isaiah Bowman Papers, JHUSCL; Schild, "Bretton Woods and Dumbarton Oaks," 380–81; Stettinius, Dumbarton Oaks Diary (draft), 19 Sept. 1944.

27. W. Averell Harriman to Cordell Hull, 19 Sept. 1944, Box 174, W. Averell Harriman Papers, LC. See also Hull to Harriman, 18 Sept. 1944, ibid.

28. W. Averell Harriman to Cordell Hull, 20 Sept. 1944, Box 174, Harriman Papers. See also Hull to Harriman, 25 Sept. 1944, ibid.

29. Hull, *Memoirs*, 2:1703–4.

30. Campbell and Herring, *Diaries of Edward R. Stettinius*, 142.

31. Bowman, memorandum to be attached to "Outline of Points"; Hull, *Memoirs*, 2:1705.

32. Memorandum, "Conversation between Edward R. Stettinius and Harry L. Hopkins," 26 Sept. 1944, Box 242, Stettinius Papers.

33. Campbell and Herring, *Diaries of Edward R. Stettinius*, 143–44. See also Edward R. Stettinius, calendar notes, 27 Sept. 1944, Box 242, Stettinius Papers; and Dumbarton Oaks Diary (draft), 27 Sept. 1944.

34. Notter, *Postwar Foreign Policy Preparation*, 328–38.

35. Joseph C. Grew to Endicott Peabody, 9 Oct. 1944, "Letters," vol. 119, Joseph C. Grew Papers, HUHL.

36. Divine, *Second Chance*, 238–39.

37. Nicholas, *Washington Dispatches*, 449–58.

38. Edward R. Stettinius, calendar notes, 21 Nov. 1944, Box 242, Stettinius Papers.

39. Hull, *Memoirs*, 2:1715–19.

40. Notter, *Postwar Foreign Policy Preparation*, 378–79; Divine, *Second Chance*, 245–47.

41. Notter, *Postwar Foreign Policy Preparation*, 380–81; Divine, *Second Chance*, 255.

42. Notter, *Postwar Foreign Policy Preparation*, 374–77, 657–58.

43. Ibid.

44. Memorandum, "Conversation at the White House," 15 Nov. 1944, Box 5, Leo Pasvolsky Papers, LC.

45. Kimball, *Churchill and Roosevelt*, 3:431–33.

46. Memorandum, "Conversation between W. Averell Harriman and Joseph V. Stalin," 14 Dec. 1944, Box 175, Harriman Papers.

47. Secretary's Staff Committee, "The Foreign Policy of the United States—A Summary Statement," 22 Dec. 1944, Box 88 E, Secretary's Staff Committee Records, RG 353, NA.

48. Herbert Feis, *Churchill, Roosevelt, Stalin: The War They Waged and the Peace They Sought* (Princeton: Princeton University Press, 1957), 552.

49. W. Averell Harriman to State Department, 28 Dec. 1944, Box 176, Harriman Papers.

50. Henry L. Stimson Diary, 31 Dec. 1944, Henry L. Stimson Papers, YUSL.

51. Campbell and Herring, *Diaries of Edward R. Stettinius*, 212–13.

52. Memorandum, "Conversation in the White House," 8 Jan. 1945, Box 5, Pasvolsky Papers. See also Pasvolsky, "The Problem of Voting in the Security Council," 9 Jan. 1945, Box 2, ibid.

53. Campbell and Herring, *Diaries of Edward R. Stettinius*, 213–14.

54. Llewellyn Woodward, *British Foreign Policy in the Second World War* (London: Her Majesty's Stationary Office, 1976), 5:173–74; Kimball, *Churchill and Roosevelt*, 3:431.

55. Campbell and Herring, *Diaries of Edward R. Stettinius*, 222–34. See also "Notes on a Discussion in Naples," 31 Jan. 1945; "Notes on a Conference in Malta," 1 Feb. 1945; and memorandum for the president, 2 Feb. 1945, Box 278, Stettinius Papers.

56. Campbell and Herring, *Diaries of Edward R. Stettinius*, 335–42. See also Edward R. Stettinius, calendar notes, 4 Feb. 1945, Box 278, Stettinius Papers.

57. Notter, *Postwar Foreign Policy Preparation*, 664–65; Campbell and

Herring, *Diaries of Edward R. Stettinius,* 242–45, James F. Byrnes, *Speaking Frankly* (New York: Harper and Brothers, 1947), 35–37.

58. Campbell and Herring, *Diaries of Edward R. Stettinius,* 246–48; Divine, *Second Chance,* 265–66.

59. Byrnes, *Speaking Frankly,* 40–42; Feis, *Churchill, Roosevelt, Stalin,* 554–55; Kimball, *Churchill and Roosevelt,* 3:531–33.

60. Divine, *Second Chance,* 267–70.

61. Notter, *Postwar Foreign Policy Preparation,* 398–407; Campbell and Herring, *Diaries of Edward R. Stettinius,* 260–84; Berle and Jacobs, *Navigating the Rapids,* 470–74.

62. Notter, *Postwar Foreign Policy Preparation,* 398–407; Campbell and Herring, *Diaries of Edward R. Stettinius,* 260–84; Berle and Jacobs, *Navigating the Rapids,* 470–74.

63. Notter, *Postwar Foreign Policy Preparation,* 398–407; Campbell and Herring, *Diaries of Edward R. Stettinius,* 260–84; Berle and Jacobs, *Navigating the Rapids,* 470–74.

64. Divine, *Second Chance,* 270–71.

65. Notter, *Postwar Foreign Policy Preparation,* 417–18.

66. "Notes of Conference of Secretary of State with Bipartisan Senate Committee," 15 Mar. 1945, Box 224, Stettinius Papers.

67. Divine, *Second Chance,* 273–75; Campbell and Herring, *Diaries of Edward R. Stettinius,* 297, 304–8.

68. Truman, *Memoirs,* 1:9, 11.

69. Notter, *Postwar Foreign Policy Preparation,* 434.

70. Truman, *Memoirs,* 1:26.

71. Campbell and Herring, *Diaries of Edward R. Stettinius,* 336, 340–45. See also Truman, *Memoirs,* 1:280–82.

72. Campbell and Herring, *Diaries of Edward R. Stettinius,* 349–52.

73. Ibid., 353–72. See also William D. Leahy to Henry L. Stimson and James V. Forrestal, 24 Apr. 1945, Box 33, William D. Leahy Records, RG 218, NA; memorandum, "Conversation in San Francisco," 9 May 1945, Box 179, Harriman Papers; and Stimson Diary, 26, 29 Apr., 2, 10, 11, 13 May 1945.

74. Campbell and Herring, *Diaries of Edward R. Stettinius,* 381–84.

75. Ibid., 385.

76. Truman, *Memoirs,* 1:287. See also Sherwood, *Roosevelt and Hopkins,* 910–12.

77. Edward R. Stettinius to Harry L. Hopkins, 9 June 1945, Box 180, Harriman Papers.

78. Truman, *Memoirs,* 1:289–93.

79. Nicholas, *Washington Dispatches,* 582–83, 591–92.

80. Divine, *Second Chance,* 299–315.

81. Ibid.

82. Isaiah Bowman, memorandum at Dumbarton Oaks, 13 Sept. 1944, Box 1, Ser. 16, Bowman Papers.

8. PROJECTING AMERICAN POWER

1. Samuel H. Cross, memorandum, "Conversation at the White House," 1 June 1942, Reel 22, Cordell Hull Papers, LC. See also Capt. John McCrea, "Notes on Meeting of the Pacific War Council," 23 May 1942, Box 168, Map Room, Franklin D. Roosevelt Papers, FDRL.

2. Subcommittee on Security Problems, minutes, 21 Aug. 1942, Box 76, Harley A. Notter File, RG 59, NA. See also William D. Leahy to Norman H. Davis, 15 Sept. 1942, Box 380, William D. Leahy Records, RG 218, NA; and "Postwar Security Arrangements in the Pacific Area," 11 Sept. 1942, Studies on American Interest in the War and the Peace, CFR.

3. William R. Louis, *Imperialism at Bay: The United States and the Decolonization of the British Empire, 1941–1945* (New York: Oxford University Press, 1978), 259–61. See also Adm. Wilson Brown, "Notes on Meeting of the Pacific War Council," 17 Feb. 1943, Box 168, Map Room, Roosevelt Papers.

4. Louis, *Imperialism at Bay,* 227–29. See also Adm. Wilson Brown, "Notes on Meeting of the Pacific War Council," 31 Mar. 1943, Box 168, Map Room, Roosevelt Papers; and Gen. H. H. Arnold to Harry L. Hopkins, 7 Aug. 1943, Box 336, Henry L. Hopkins Papers, FDRL.

5. Thomas C. Hart to Secretary of the Navy, 20 Mar. 1943, Box 196, Records of the General Board, RG 80, NA.

6. Thomas C. Hart to Secretary of the Navy, 27 Mar. 1943, ibid.

7. Louis, *Imperialism at Bay,* 262–67.

8. Franklin D. Roosevelt to Secretary of the Navy, 23 June 1943, S. F., Box 81, Roosevelt Papers. See also memorandum, "Conversation between Roosevelt and Adolf A. Berle," 10 June 1943, Box 215, Adolf A. Berle Papers, FDRL.

9. Memorandum, "Meeting in the White House," 5 Oct. 1943, Box 8, Leo Pasvolsky Papers, LC. See also Joint Chiefs of Staff, minutes, 15 Nov. 1943, Box 195, RG 218, NA.

10. Louis *Imperialism at Bay,* 271–72.

11. Minutes of a meeting between Franklin D. Roosevelt and the Joint Chiefs of Staff, 15 Nov. 1943, Box 29, Map Room, Roosevelt Papers. See also memorandum, "Meeting between Edward R. Stettinius and Roosevelt," 5 Nov. 1943, Box 238, Edward R. Stettinius Papers, UVAL.

12. Joint Chiefs of Staff, minutes, 19 Nov. 1943, Box 195.

13. Louis, *Imperialism at Bay*, 282–85.

14. Memorandum of a luncheon at Teheran, 30 Nov. 1943, Box 28, Map Room, Roosevelt Papers.

15. William D. Leahy to Franklin D. Roosevelt, 15 Nov. 1943, Box 19, William D. Leahy Records, RG 218, NA.

16. James C. Dunn to Edward R. Stettinius, 3 Aug. 1944, Box 219, Stettinius Papers. See also "Abstracts of Instructions," Isaiah Bowman Papers, Box 6, Ser. 14, JHUSCL; and memorandum, "Joint Post-War Committee," 7 June 1944, Box 209, RG 218.

17. Memorandum, "Meeting between Pres. Franklin D. Roosevelt and a State Department Group Preparing to Go to London," 17 Mar. 1944, Reel 14, Matthews-Hickerson File, RG 59, NA.

18. Cordell Hull to Franklin D. Roosevelt, 19 June 1944, S. F., Box 34, Roosevelt Papers.

19. Franklin D. Roosevelt to Jefferson Caffery, 21 June 1944, ibid.

20. Subcommittee on International Organization, minutes, 14 Aug. 1942, Box 85, Notter File.

21. Joint Chiefs of Staff memorandum on postwar military problems, n.d., Box 19, Leahy Records.

22. Sherwood, *Roosevelt and Hopkins*, 786. See also memorandum, "Conversation between W. Averell Harriman and Franklin D. Roosevelt," 2 Sept. 1943, Box 164, W. Averell Harriman Papers, LC.

23. Isaiah Bowman, memorandum, "Meeting with Franklin D. Roosevelt," 3 Feb. 1944, Box 6, Ser. 14, Bowman Papers. See also "Meeting of Informal Agenda Group," 8 Feb. 1944; and memorandum, "A Talk with Roosevelt," 11 Feb. 1944, Box 54, Notter File.

24. Franklin D. Roosevelt to John G. Winant, 9 Oct. 1944, Reel 9, Map Room, Roosevelt Papers.

25. Joint Chiefs of Staff, minutes, 19 Nov. 1943, Box 195.

26. Kimball, *Churchill and Roosevelt*, 2:708–9 (see also 766–67).

27. William D. Leahy to Franklin D. Roosevelt, 4 July 1944, Box 19, Leahy Records. See also Leahy to Roosevelt, 11 Jan. 1944, ibid.

28. Franklin D. Roosevelt to Joint Chiefs of Staff, 10 July 1944, Box 19, Leahy Records. See also Roosevelt to Adm. Wilson Brown, 14 Jan. 1944, ibid.; and Brown, "Notes on Meeting of the Pacific War Council," 12 Jan. 1944, Box 168, Map Room, Roosevelt Papers.

29. Adolf A. Berle Diary, 26 July 1944, Berle Papers.

30. Memorandum, "Conversation at the White House," 15 Nov. 1944, Box 5, Pasvolsky Papers. See also State Department Policy Committee, minutes, 20 Nov. 1944, Box 138, Notter File.

31. Campbell and Herring, *Diaries of Edward R. Stettinius,* 210–11. See also minutes, 24 Jan. 1944, Secretary's Staff Committee Records, RG 353, NA.

32. Henry L. Stimson to Edward R. Stettinius, 23 Jan. 1945, Box 13, Henry L. Stimson Safe File, RG 107, NA. Gen. Stanley D. Embick, a member of the Joint Strategic Survey Committee, strongly approved this memorandum. See Henry L. Stimson Diary, 23 Jan. 1944, Henry L. Stimson Papers, YUSL.

33. Minutes of the Committee of Three, 8 Feb. 1945, RG 59, NA.

34. Ibid., 20 Feb. 1945.

35. Louis, *Imperialism at Bay,* 476–85. See also Minutes of the Committee of Three, 3 Mar. 1945; and minutes, 19 Mar. 1945, Secretary's Staff Committee Records.

36. Stimson Diary, 29, 30 Mar., 2, 3, 7, 9 Apr. 1945; Walter Millis, ed., *The Forrestal Diaries* (New York: Viking, 1951), 37–38.

37. Harold L. Ickes to Franklin D. Roosevelt, 5 Apr. 1945, Box 232, Stettinius Papers.

38. Edward R. Stettinius to Franklin D. Roosevelt, 9 Apr. 1945, Box 23, Map Room, Roosevelt Papers. See also Edward R. Stettinius Diary, 18 Mar.–7 Apr. 1945, Box 29, Notter File; and minutes, 6 Apr. 1945, Secretary's Staff Committee Records.

39. Franklin D. Roosevelt to Edward R. Stettinius, 10 Apr. 1945, Box 23, Map Room, Roosevelt Papers. See also Stettinius Diary, 8–14 Apr. 1945; minutes, 10 Apr. 1945, Secretary's Staff Committee Records; and Louis, *Imperialism at Bay,* 491–94.

40. Edward R. Stettinius to James C. Dunn and Leo Pasvolsky, 16 Apr. 1945, Box 220, Stettinius Papers. See also Stettinius to Dunn and Pasvolsky, 14 Apr. 1945, ibid.

41. "Recommended Policy on Trusteeship," enclosed in memorandum for the president, 18 Apr. 1945, Box 232, Stettinius Papers.

42. Campbell and Herring, *Diaries of Edward R. Stettinius,* 320.

43. Stimson Diary, 18 Apr. 1945.

44. Ibid., 27 Sept. 1943. See also Joint Chiefs of Staff, minutes, 21 Dec. 1943, Box 195.

45. Gary R. Hess, *The United States' Emergence as a Southeast Asian Power, 1940–1950* (New York: Columbia University Press, 1987), 223–24.

46. Stimson Diary, 8 Feb. 1945. See also Minutes of the Committee of Three, 8 Feb. 1945.

47. Stimson Diary, 20 Feb. 1945.

48. Ibid., 21 Feb. 1945.

49. Ibid., 3 Mar. 1945. See also Minutes of the Committee of Three, 3

Mar. 1945; and Francis B. Sayre to Franklin D. Roosevelt, 7 Mar. 1945, Box 7, Francis B. Sayre Papers, LC.

50. Stimson Diary, 18 Apr. 1945.

51. Memorandum, "Meeting between Henry L. Stimson and Sergio Osmena," 18 Apr. 1945, Box 11, Stimson Safe File. See also Stimson to Edward R. Stettinius, 22 Apr. 1945, ibid.

52. Stimson Diary, 19 Apr. 1945.

53. Millard E. Tydings to Harry S. Truman, 25 Apr. 1945, S. F., Box 185, Harry S. Truman Papers, HSTL.

54. Henry L. Stimson to Harry S. Truman, 2 May 1945; Truman to Stimson, 4 May 1945, ibid. See also Stimson Diary 11 May 1945; and Stimson to Truman, 14 May 1945, Box 15, Stimson Safe File.

55. Truman, *Memoirs*, 1:276–77. See also Stimson Diary, 14 May 1945; and daily sheets, 14 May 1945, S. F., Box 82, Truman Papers.

56. Michael S. Sherry, *Preparing for the Next War: American Plans for Postwar Defense, 1941–1945* (New Haven: Yale University Press, 1977), 15–22.

57. Stimson Diary, 25 Apr. 1944.

58. Sherry, *Preparing for the Next War*, 196–98.

59. Millis, *Forrestal Diaries*, 45.

60. Sherry, *Preparing for the Next War*, 92.

61. Ibid., 15–35.

62. Earnest J. King to James V. Forrestal, 13 Feb. 1945, Box 90, James V. Forrestal Records, RG 80, NA.

63. Earnest J. King to James V. Forrestal, 3 Mar. 1945, Box 64, Records of the General Board. See also Forrestal to Franklin D. Roosevelt, 9 Apr. 1945; and Forrestal to Harry S. Truman, 29 June 1945, Box 123, Forrestal Records.

64. Sherry, *Preparing for the Next War*, 92, 196.

65. Ibid., 94–119.

66. Top Policy Group, minutes, 15 Jan. 1945, Box 1, NA, RG 80.

67. Stimson Diary, 12 Aug. 1943 (see also 10 May 1943).

68. Frank Knox to Arthur Krok, 31 Dec. 1943, Box 55, Frank Knox Records, RG 80, NA. See also Knox to David Lawrence, Walter Lippmann, et al. on 31 Dec. 1943; Knox to Lawrence, 4 Jan. 1944; and Knox to Mark Sullivan, 24 Jan. 1944, ibid.

69. James V. Forrestal to Henry L. Stimson, 13 Nov. 1944, Box 86, Forrestal Records.

70. Millis, *Forrestal Diaries*, 9.

71. Stimson Diary, 10 Nov. 1944.

72. Ibid. See also Millis, *Forrestal Diaries*, 15–16; Edward R. Stettinius,

calendar notes, 10 Nov. 1944, Box 242, Stettinius Papers; and memorandum, "Conversation between Harold D. Smith and Franklin D. Roosevelt," 16 Nov. 1944, Box 3, Harold D. Smith Papers, FDRL.

73. Stimson Diary, 17 Nov. 1944.

74. James V. Forrestal to Henry L. Stimson, 13 Nov. 1944; and Stimson to Forrestal, 24 Nov. 1944, Box 86, Forrestal Records. See also Top Policy Group, minutes, 11 Dec. 1944.

75. Henry L. Stimson to Edward R. Stettinius, 21 Dec. 1944; and Stettinius to Stimson, 28 Dec. 1944, Box 13, Stimson Safe File.

76. Joseph C. Grew to Godfrey Cabot, 6 Jan. 1945, "Letters," vol. 121, Joseph C. Grew Papers, HUHL. See also minutes, 30 Dec. 1944, Secretary's Staff Committee Records; and Stimson Diary, 29 Dec. 1944.

77. Stimson Diary, 31 Dec. 1944.

78. Henry L. Stimson to Harry S. Truman, 30 May 1945, Box 15, Stimson Safe File.

79. Henry L. Stimson to Franklin D. Roosevelt 12 Jan. 1945, S. F., Box 106, Roosevelt Papers. See also Stimson Diary, 2, 9, 10 Jan. 1945.

80. Minutes, 26 Apr. 1945, Secretary's Staff Committee Records. See also Stimson Diary, 4, 26 Apr. 1945.

81. Henry L. Stimson to Harry S. Truman, 30 May 1945, Box 15, Stimson Safe File.

82. Stimson Diary, 14 June 1945.

83. Grew, *Turbulent Era*, 2:1486–92.

84. Sherry, *Preparing for the Next War*, 78–90.

85. Memorandum, "Conversation between Joseph C. Grew and Harry S. Truman," 5 June 1945, "Conversations," vol. 7, Grew Papers; Samuel I. Rosenman, "Statement on Universal Military Training" (draft), 26 June 1945, Box 5, Samuel I. Rosenman Papers, HSTL.

86. Samuel I. Rosenman to James K. Vardaman, 21 June 1945, Box 5, Rosenman Papers. See also Rosenman to Harry S. Truman, 17 July 1945, ibid.

87. War Department proposal for a message to Congress from the president, 13 Sept. 1945, ibid. See also Rosenman to Harry S. Truman, 9 Oct. 1945; and Clark M. Clifford to Rosenman, 18 Oct. 1945, ibid.

88. Truman, *Memoirs*, 1:510–11.

89. Sherry, *Preparing for the Next War*, 211–25.

90. Memorandum, "Telephone Conversation between Edward R. Stettinius and Edward A. Tamm," 15 Feb. 1944, Box 239, Stettinius Papers.

91. Isador Lubin to Franklin D. Roosevelt, 25 Oct. 1944, Box 731, ibid.

92. Edward R. Stettinius to Franklin D. Roosevelt, 15 Dec. 1944, ibid.

93. Franklin D. Roosevelt to Edward R. Stettinius, 17 Jan. 1945, Box 733, ibid.

94. Memorandum, "Proposal for a Central Intelligence Agency," Box 15, Rose Conway File, Truman Papers.

95. Nicholas, *Washington Dispatches,* 518–19.

96. Millis, *Forrestal Diaries,* 37.

97. Franklin D. Roosevelt to William J. Donovan, 5 Apr. 1945, Box 731, Stettinius Papers.

98. Harold D. Smith Diary, 26 Apr. 1945, Smith Papers; Truman, *Memoirs,* 1:98–99.

99. William J. Donovan to Harry S. Truman, 25 Aug. 1945, Box 15, Rose Conway File, Truman Papers.

100. Minutes of the Committee of Three, 16 Oct. 1945; Millis, *Forrestal Diaries,* 101.

101. Sherry, *Preparing for the Next War,* 120–58.

102. Martin J. Sherwin, *A World Destroyed: The Atomic Bomb and the Grand Alliance* (New York: Random House, 1977), 36–38, 71–73, 79.

103. Ibid., 73–86.

104. Stimson Diary, 27 Dec. 1942 (see also 30 Dec. 1942).

105. Sherwin, *A World Destroyed,* 90–114.

106. Ibid., 114–30, 286–87.

107. Stimson Diary, 31 Dec. 1944. See also John R. Deane to George C. Marshall, 2 Dec. 1944; and Stimson to Franklin D. Roosevelt, 3 Jan. 1945, Box 170, Map Room, Roosevelt Papers.

108. Stimson Diary, 13 Feb. 1945.

109. Ibid., 15 Feb. 1945.

110. Ibid., 5 Mar. 1945.

111. Ibid., 15 Mar. 1945.

112. Ibid., 25 Apr. 1945.

113. Sherwin, *A World Destroyed,* 167–70.

114. Stimson Diary, 28 May 1945.

115. Sherwin, *A World Destroyed,* 193–94, 295–304. See also Henry L. Stimson, memorandum for talk with Harry S. Truman, 6 June 1945, Yale University Documents Regarding the Atomic Bomb, HSTL.

116. Sherwin, *A World Destroyed,* 214–16, 227, 304–6.

117. Stimson Diary, 12 Aug.–5 Sept. 1945; George L. Harrison, memorandum for the record, 18 Aug. 1945, Yale University Documents Regarding the Atomic Bomb.

118. Stimson Diary, 12 Sept. 1945 (see also 13, 17, 21 Sept. 1945).

119. Blum, *Price of Vision,* 481.

120. Ibid., 482–87; James V. Forrestal, memorandum on cabinet meeting, 21 Sept. 1945, S. F., Box 199, Truman Papers. See also Dean G. Acheson to Truman, 25 Sept. 1945, S. F., Box 199; Abe Fortas to Truman, 26 Sept. 1945, S. F., Box 199; Robert Patterson to Truman, 26 Sept. 1945, S. F., Box 112; and Forrestal to Truman, 1 Oct. 1945, S. F., Box 158, ibid.; and George L. Harrison, memorandum for the files, 25 Sept. 1945, Yale University Documents Regarding the Atomic Bomb.

121. Truman, *Memoirs*, 1:530–34.

122. Ibid., 542–44. See also Minutes of the Committee of Three, 16 Oct. 1945; William D. Leahy Diary, 17 Oct. 1945, WSHS; Leahy to Harry S. Truman, 23 Oct. 1945, Box 19, Leahy Records; Campbell and Herring, *Diaries of Edward R. Stettinius*, 438–39; and Millis, *Forrestal Diaries*, 102.

9. REINTEGRATING GERMANY

1. Subcommittee on Political Problems, minutes, 11 Apr. 1942, Box 55, Harley A. Notter File, RG 59, NA.

2. Ibid., 18 Apr. 1942. See also Adolf A. Berle Diary, 2 May 1942, Adolf A. Berle Papers, FDRL.

3. Isaiah Bowman to Hamilton Fish Armstrong, 5 May 1942, Box 3, Ser. 14, Isaiah Bowman Papers, JHUSCL. See also Hamilton Fish Armstrong, document for the Subcommittee on Political Problems, 30 Apr. 1942, Box 56, Notter File.

4. Subcommittee on Political Problems, minutes, 20 June 1942, Box 55, Notter File; Isaiah Bowman, "Remarks before the Subcommittee on Political Problems," 20 June 1942, Box 6, Ser. 14, Bowman Papers. See also Subcommittee on Territorial Problems, minutes, 10 July 1942, Box 59, Notter File.

5. Subcommittee on Security Problems, minutes, 3 July 1942, Box 76; and "Tentative Conclusions of the Security Subcommittee," 15 Apr.–31 July 1942, Box 56, Notter File.

6. Subcommittee on Political Problems, minutes, 7 Nov. 1942, Boxes 55, 56, ibid. See also two Armaments Group memoranda, "Controls over German War Potential," 14 Nov. 1942; and "Security Principles and Some Questions about the Peace Settlement," 22 Jan. 1943, Studies of American Interests in the War and the Peace, CFR.

7. Subcommittee on Political Problems, minutes, 7 Nov. 1942.

8. "Tentative Views of the Territorial Subcommittee" [7 Mar. 1942–5 Mar. 1943], Sumner Welles Papers, Box 193, FDRL.

9. "Tentative Views of the Security Subcommittee" [to 10 Mar. 1943], ibid.

10. Herbert Feis, *Churchill, Roosevelt, Stalin: The War They Waged and the Peace They Sought* (Princeton: Princeton University Press, 1957), 108–10. See also "Tentative Views of the Security Subcommittee" [to 10 Mar. 1943].

11. Robert Dallek, *Franklin D. Roosevelt and American Foreign Policy, 1932–1945* (New York: Oxford University Press, 1979), 373–75.

12. *FRUS*, 1943, 3:16–17.

13. Memorandum, "Conversation Involving Sumner Welles, Anthony Eden, and Lord Halifax," 16 Mar. 1943, 740.00119EW1939/1325, RG 59, NA.

14. Sherwood, *Roosevelt and Hopkins*, 713.

15. Ibid., 714–15.

16. Warren F. Kimball, *Swords or Ploughshares? The Morgenthau Plan for Defeated Nazi Germany, 1943–1946* (Philadelphia: J. B. Lippincott, 1976), 6.

17. Charles E. Bohlen, "Memorandum to Be Discussed Orally with Col. McCarthy," 24 June 1943, Box 3, Charles E. Bohlen File, RG 59, NA (emphasis in original).

18. Feis, *Churchill, Roosevelt, Stalin*, 219–20.

19. Gabriel Kolko, *The Politics of War: The World and United States Foreign Policy, 1943–1945* (New York: Random House, 1968), 318–19.

20. Maurice Matloff, *Strategic Planning for Coalition Warfare, 1943–1944* (Washington: Government Printing Office, 1959), 225–26.

21. Harley A. Notter, *Postwar Foreign Policy Preparation, 1939–1945* (Washington: Government Printing Office, 1949), 558–60.

22. Isaiah Bowman, "Supplement to His Letter of 27 Sept. 1943," Box 7, Ser. 14, Bowman Papers.

23. Leo Pasvolsky, memorandum, "Meeting at the White House," 5 Oct. 1943, Box 8, Leo Pasvolsky Papers, LC.

24. Hull, *Memoirs*, 2:1284–87.

25. *FRUS*, 1943, 1:631–32.

26. Joint Chiefs of Staff, minutes, 19 Nov. 1943, Box 195, RG 218, NA.

27. *FRUS: Conferences at Cairo and Teheran*, 1943, 600–604.

28. "Tentative Views of the State Department Interdivisional Committee on Reparations," 14 Dec. 1943, Box 88A, RG 353, NA. See also Bruce Kuklick, *American Policy and the Division of Germany: The Clash with Russia over Reparations* (Ithaca, N.Y.: Cornell University Press, 1972), 43–46.

29. John D. Hickerson to H. Freeman Matthews and James C. Dunn, 3 Sept. 1943, Reel 2, Matthews-Hickerson File, RG 59, NA.

30. Interdivisional Country Committee on Germany, paper on German war potential, 17 Dec. 1943, Box 114, Notter File. See also Subcommittee on

Territorial Problems, minutes, 9 Jan. 1943, Box 59, Notter File; Subcommittee on Economic Policy, "Germany's Place in the World Economy in Relation to the Problem of Maintaining Peace," 28 Mar. 1943, Box 81, Notter File; and Richard Eldridge, "Postwar Economic Control of Germany," 23 Sept. 1943, Box 117, Notter File.

31. John L. Gaddis, *The United States and the Origins of the Cold War, 1941–1947* (New York: Columbia University Press, 1972), 109–11; Kimball, *Swords or Ploughshares?* 20–21, 78–81; Joint Chiefs of Staff, minutes, 21 Feb. 1944, Box 195; Henry L. Stimson Diary, 31 July 1944, Henry L. Stimson Papers, YUSL; Edward R. Stettinius to Roosevelt, 2 Aug. 1944; and Roosevelt to Stettinius, 3 Aug. 1944, Box 19, Map Room, Franklin D. Roosevelt Papers, FDRL.

32. Kuklick, *American Policy and the Division of Germany*, 34–35; Gaddis, *The United States and the Origins of the Cold War*, 102–4.

33. Kimball, *Swords or Ploughshares?* 82–85.

34. Edward R. Stettinius, "Report on Conversations with British Officials in London," 7–29 Apr. 1944, Box 29, Notter File. See also Isaiah Bowman, memorandum, 19 Apr. 1944, Box 1, Ser. 15, Bowman Papers; and H. Freeman Matthews to James C. Dunn, 5 May 1944, Reel 9, Matthews-Hickerson File.

35. Executive Committee on Economic Foreign Policy, minutes, 9 June 1944, Box 776, RG 169, NA.

36. Executive Committee on Economic Foreign Policy, "General Objectives of United States Economic Policy with Respect to Germany," 14 Aug. 1944, Box 333, Harry L. Hopkins Papers, FDRL. See also Post-War Programs Committee, "The Treatment of Germany," 5 Aug. 1944, ibid.

37. Executive Committee on Economic Foreign Policy, "General Objectives of United States Economic Policy with Respect to Germany," 14 Aug. 1944. See also Kimball, *Swords or Ploughshares?* 90–91.

38. Gaddis, *The United States and the Origins of the Cold War*, 116–18.

39. Kimball, *Swords or Ploughshares?* 92–94.

40. Henry Morgenthau Diaries, 18 Aug. 1944, 763:202–5, Henry Morgenthau Papers, FDRL.

41. Presidential Diaries of Henry Morgenthau, 19 Aug. 1944, vol. 6. See also memorandum, "Conversation between Harry Dexter White and John Maynard Keynes," 20 Aug. 1944, 764:89–90; and memorandum, "Conversation between White and Gen. John Hilldring," 22 Aug. 1944, Morgenthau Diaries, 764:176–77.

42. Morgenthau Diaries, 23 Aug. 1944, vol. 765. See also Stimson Diary, 22, 23 Aug. 1944.

43. Stimson Diary, 25 Aug. 1944.

44. Kimball, *Swords or Ploughshares?* 98–100.

45. Memorandum, Franklin D. Roosevelt to Henry L. Stimson, 26 Aug. 1944, S. F., Box 104, Roosevelt Papers. Roosevelt sent copies of this memorandum to Hull and Morgenthau.

46. "Record of a Telephone Conversation between Henry Morgenthau and Harry D. White," 31 Aug. 1944, Morgenthau Diaries, 767:161–62.

47. Memorandum, Harry D. White to Henry Morgenthau, 1 Sept. 1944, Presidential Diaries of Morgenthau, vol. 6. White appended the suggested "Post-Surrender Program for Germany" document to this memorandum.

48. Memorandum, "Conversation with Franklin and Eleanor Roosevelt," 2 Sept. 1944, ibid.

49. Morgenthau Diaries, 4 Sept. 1944, 768:112–25.

50. Ibid., 768:134–45.

51. Leo Pasvolsky to Cordell Hull, 1 Sept. 1944, Box 145, Notter File. See also James W. Riddleberger, "American Policy for Treatment of Germany after Surrender," 1 Sept. 1944, 740.00119 Control (Germany)/9–144, RG 59, NA; Hull to Franklin D. Roosevelt, 2 Sept. 1944, S. F., Box 94, Roosevelt Papers; and Riddleberger, "Treatment of Germany," 4 Sept. 1944, 740.00119 Control (Germany)/9–444, RG 59, NA.

52. "Suggested Recommendations on Treatment of Germany from the Cabinet Committee for the President," 4 Sept. 1944, Box 5, Henry L. Stimson Safe File, RG 107, NA.

53. Morgenthau Diaries, 5 Sept. 1944, 769:9–17; Stimson Diary, 5 Sept. 1944; memorandum, "Telephone Conversation between Henry Morgenthau and John J. McCloy," 6 Sept. 1944, Morgenthau Diaries, 769:108–9.

54. "Record of a Telephone Conversation between Henry Morgenthau and Harry L. Hopkins," 5 Sept. 1944, Morgenthau Diaries, 769:1–8.

55. Stimson Diary, 5 Sept. 1944.

56. Ibid., 6 Sept. 1944; Morgenthau Diaries, 6 Sept. 1944, vol. 769.

57. Stimson Diary, 7, 8 Sept. 1944. See also memorandum, "Conversation between Henry L. Stimson and Isaiah Bowman," 8 Sept. 1944, Box 3, Ser. 14, Bowman Papers.

58. Morgenthau Diaries, 8 Sept. 1944, vol. 770.

59. *FRUS: Quebec Conference,* 1944, 131–40.

60. Stimson Diary, 9 Sept. 1944.

61. Morgenthau Diaries, 9 Sept. 1944, 771:41–44. See also Presidential Diaries of Morgenthau, 9 Sept. 1944, vol. 6.

62. Harry D. White, memorandum, "Meeting in Hull's Office,"

20 Sept. 1944, Morgenthau Diaries, 773:4–8; John J. McCloy, memorandum on the same meeting, appended to Stimson Diary, 20 Sept. 1944.

63. Harry D. White, memorandum for the files, 13 Sept. 1944, Presidential Diaries of Morgenthau, vol. 6. See also Stimson Diary, 20 Sept. 1944.

64. Presidential Diaries of Morgenthau, 14, 15 Sept. 1944, vol. 6; Morgenthau Diaries, 19 Sept. 1944, 772:208–12.

65. Morgenthau Diaries, 19 Sept. 1944, 772:208–12.

66. Stimson Diary, 16, 17 Sept. 1944. See also Henry L. Stimson to Franklin D. Roosevelt, 15 Sept. 1944, Box 5, Stimson Safe File.

67. Hull, *Memoirs*, 2:1612–16.

68. Nicholas, *Washington Dispatches*, 426, 436; Pierre Jay to Franklin D. Roosevelt, 26 Sept. 1944, Box 5, Stimson Safe File; Russell C. Leffingwell to Henry Morgenthau, 28 Nov. 1944, Morgenthau Diaries, 802:101–7.

69. Edward R. Stettinius, calendar notes, 26 Sept. 1944, Box 242, Edward R. Stettinius Papers, UVAL.

70. Stimson Diary, 27 Sept. 1944.

71. Franklin D. Roosevelt to Cordell Hull, 29 Sept. 1944, 740.00119 Control (Germany)/9–2944, RG 59, NA.

72. Stimson Diary, 3 Oct. 1944.

73. Kimball, *Swords or Ploughshares?* 130–34. See also Harry D. White, memorandum for the secretary's files, 20 Sept. 1944, Morgenthau Diaries, 773:4–8.

74. Hull, *Memoirs*, 2:1618–22. See also H. Freeman Matthews to John J. McCloy, 5 Oct. 1944, Reel 18, Matthews-Hickerson File; memorandum "Conversation in the State Department," 6 Oct. 1944, Box 721, Stettinius Papers; and Matthews to Robert D. Murphy, 14 Oct. 1944, Reel 13, Matthews-Hickerson File.

75. Edward R. Stettinius, calendar notes, 10 Nov. 1944, Box 242, Stettinius Papers.

76. Kuklick, *American Policy and the Division of Germany,* 60–61.

77. Memorandum, "Conversation at the White House," 15 Nov. 1944, Box 7, Pasvolsky Papers. See also Edward R. Stettinius to H. Freeman Matthews, 15 Nov. 1944, Box 216, Stettinius Papers.

78. Memorandum, "Meeting at the White House," 21 Nov. 1944, Box 243, Stettinius Papers.

79. Edward R. Stettinius to Franklin D. Roosevelt, 22 Nov. 1944, 740.00119 EW/11–2244, RG 59, NA.

80. Edward R. Stettinius to Franklin D. Roosevelt, 29 Nov. 1944, Reel 15, Matthews-Hickerson File.

81. Franklin D. Roosevelt to Edward R. Stettinius, 4 Dec. 1944, 740.00119 Control (Germany)/12/944, RG 59, NA.

82. Edward R. Stettinius, calendar notes, 22 Dec. 1944, Box 243, Stettinius Papers.

83. Minutes, 3 Jan. 1945, Secretary's Staff Committee Records, RG 353, NA. See also memorandum, "Conversation between Bernard M. Baruch and State Department Officials," 2 Dec. 1944, 740.00119 Control (Germany)/12–244, RG 59, NA; Stimson Diary, 11 Mar. 1945; Baruch to Franklin D. Roosevelt, 18 Mar. 1945, S. F., Box 117, Roosevelt Papers; and Kimball, *Churchill and Roosevelt,* 3:577, 601.

84. Memorandum, "Meeting between State and Treasury Department Officers," 17 Jan. 1945, Box 732, Stettinius Papers. See also memorandum, "Meeting between State and Treasury Department Officials," 19 Jan. 1945, 811:95–100; and Morgenthau, memorandum for the president, 10 Jan. 1944, Morgenthau Diaries, 808:297–99.

85. Campbell and Herring, *Diaries of Edward R. Stettinius,* 226–37.

86. Russell D. Buhite, *Decisions at Yalta: An Appraisal of Summit Diplomacy* (Wilmington, Del.: Scholarly Resources, 1986), 28–32. See also Feis, *Churchill, Roosevelt, Stalin,* 619–20.

87. Buhite, *Decisions at Yalta,* 33–37; Kimball, *Swords or Ploughshares?* 150–54; Gaddis, *The United States and the Origins of the Cold War,* 126–29; Kuklick, *American Policy and the Division of Germany,* 76–83. See also Minutes of the Committee of Three, 13 Mar. 1945, RG 59, NA.

88. Gaddis, *The United States and the Origins of the Cold War,* 129–30. See also minutes, 14, 16 Mar. 1945, Secretary's Staff Committee Records; William L. Clayton, memorandum, "Possible Cabinet Discussion on Germany," 16 Mar. 1945, Box 730, Stettinius Papers; memorandum, "Telephone Conversation Involving Edward R. Stettinius, James C. Dunn, and Joseph C. Grew," 22 Mar. 1945, "Conversations," vol. 6, Joseph C. Grew Papers, HUHL; Stimson Diary, 29 Mar. 1945; and Grew, memorandum for the president, 22 Mar. 1945, S. F., Box 142, Roosevelt Papers.

89. Memorandum, "Conference on the Treatment of Germany," 23 Mar. 1945, Morgenthau Diaries [9 Apr. 1945], 835:87–89; "Record of a Telephone Conversation between John J. McCloy and Henry Morgenthau," 22 Mar. 1945, ibid., 831:65.

90. Memorandum, "Telephone Conversation Involving Edward R. Stettinius, James C. Dunn, and Joseph C. Grew," 23 Mar. 1945, "Conversations," vol. 6, Grew Papers; minutes, 24 Mar. 1945, Secretary's Staff Committee Records; Stimson Diary, 29 Mar. 1945; Kimball, *Swords or Ploughshares?* 157–59.

91. Henry L. Stimson to Harry S. Truman, 16 May 1945, S. F., Box 157, Harry S. Truman Papers, HSTL. See also Kimball, *Swords or Ploughshares?* 160–65.

92. Truman, *Memoirs*, 1:235–37.

93. Ibid., 1:496–98. See also minutes, 20, 26 June 1945, Secretary's Staff Committee Records.

94. Kuklick, *American Policy and the Division of Germany*, 123–37; Carolyn W. Eisenberg, *Drawing the Line: The American Decision to Divide Germany* (Cambridge: Cambridge University Press, 1996), 87–89. See also memorandum, "Telephone Conversation between Edward R. Stettinius and Edwin W. Pauley," 29 Apr. 1945, Box 244, Stettinius Papers.

95. Melvyn Leffler, *A Preponderance of Power: National Security, the Truman Administration, and the Cold War* (Stanford: Stanford University Press, 1992), 64–67. See also Joint Chiefs of Staff to George C. Marshall, 27 June 1945, Box 11, Stimson Safe File; and Stimson Diary, 15 July 1945.

96. Minutes, 4 July 45, Secretary's Staff Committee Records. See also Oscar Cox to Harry S. Truman, 4 June 1945, S. F., Box 130, Truman Papers.

97. Kuklick, *American Policy and the Division of Germany*, 141–66. See also Truman, *Memoirs*, 1:327; and Stimson Diary, 3, 4 July 1945.

98. Kuklick, *American Policy and the Division of Germany*, 141–66; James F. Byrnes, *Speaking Frankly* (New York: Harper and Brothers, 1947), 82–87, 194–95.

10. STABILIZING EAST ASIA

1. Joseph M. Jones, "Statement of Major Post-War Problems in the Pacific Area," 20 Feb. 1942, Box 2, Leo Pasvolsky File, RG 59, NA. See also Subcommittee on Territorial Problems, minutes, 30 July 1943, Box 59, Harley A. Notter File, ibid.

2. Akire Iriye, *Power and Culture: The Japanese-American War, 1941–1945* (Cambridge: Harvard University Press, 1981), 149–51 (see also 58–59, 124–26).

3. Joseph C. Grew to Stanley K. Hornbeck, 30 Sept. 1943, "Letters," vol. 116, Joseph C. Grew Papers, HUHL. See also Grew to Paul Rowland, 9 July 1943, "Letters," vol. 117; Grew to Robert A. Fearey, 30 Nov. 1943, "Letters," vol. 115; and Grew to Adm. Harry E. Yarnell, 6 Jan. 1944, "Letters," vol. 120, ibid.

4. Iriye, *Power and Culture*, 60.

5. Hanson W. Baldwin, "Security Problems Vis á Vis Japan," 29 Nov. 1943, Studies of American Interests in the War and the Peace, CFR. See also George Fielding Eliot, "The Disarmament of Japan," 1 May 1944, ibid.

6. William R. Louis, *Imperialism at Bay: The United States and the Decolonization of the British Empire, 1941–1945* (New York: Oxford University Press, 1978), 227–28.

7. Herbert Feis, *Churchill, Roosevelt, Stalin: The War They Waged and the Peace They Sought* (Princeton: Princeton University Press, 1957), 252–54 (see also 280–86).

8. Iriye, *Power and Culture,* 202–4.

9. Ibid., 206–8.

10. Howard B. Schonberger, *Aftermath of War: Americans and the Remaking of Japan, 1945–1952* (Kent, Ohio: Kent State University Press, 1989), 27–28. See also Grew, *Turbulent Era,* 2:1408–15.

11. Iriye, *Power and Culture,* 209–10.

12. Harley A. Notter, *Postwar Foreign Policy Preparation, 1939–1945* (Washington: Government Printing Office, 1949), 591–92.

13. Joseph C. Grew to Mrs. Lester W. Harding, 27 Jan. 1945, "Letters," vol. 122, Grew Papers.

14. Minutes of the Committee of Three, 8 Feb. 1945, RG 59, NA. See also minutes, 23 Apr. 1945, Secretary's Staff Committee Records, RG 353, NA.

15. Hull, *Memoirs,* 2:1587.

16. *FRUS,* 1942, 3:573–74.

17. Ibid., 3:578–83.

18. Sherwood, *Roosevelt and Hopkins,* 716–18 (see also 706).

19. Christopher Thorne, *Allies of a Kind: The United States, Britain, and the War against Japan, 1941–1945* (New York: Oxford University Press, 1978), 184, 237–38.

20. Memorandum, "Conversation between Franklin D. Roosevelt and Isaiah Bowman," 28 Oct. 1943, Box 5, Ser. 14, Isaiah Bowman Papers, JHUSCL.

21. Franklin D. Roosevelt to Lord Louis Mountbatten, 8 Nov. 1943, S. F., Box 38, Franklin D. Roosevelt Papers, FDRL.

22. Hull, *Memoirs,* 2:1277–82, 1299–1302.

23. *FRUS: Conferences at Cairo and Teheran,* 1943, 532.

24. Louis, *Imperialism at Bay,* 7, 229, 280, 285.

25. Hull, *Memoirs,* 2:1583.

26. *Fortune,* May 1941, 69–120.

27. Gabriel Kolko, *The Politics of War: The World and United States Foreign Policy, 1943–1945* (New York: Random House, 1968), 226.

28. Ibid., 227.

29. Clarence E. Gauss to Franklin D. Roosevelt and Cordell Hull, 9 Dec. 1943, S. F., Box 38, Roosevelt Papers.

30. Franklin D. Roosevelt to Donald M. Nelson, 18 Aug. 1944, ibid.

31. Memorandum, "Conversation between Donald M. Nelson and V. M. Molotov," 31 Aug. 1944, Box 173, W. Averell Harriman Papers, LC. See also Harriman to State Department, 5 Sept. 1944, S. F., Box 92, Roosevelt Papers.

32. Donald M. Nelson to Franklin D. Roosevelt, 20 Dec. 1944, S. F., Box 38, Roosevelt Papers.

33. Leo T. Crowley, "Address in Scranton, Pennsylvania," 17 Mar. 1945, Leo T. Crowley Papers, JFDPC.

34. Thorne, *Allies of a Kind*, 402.

35. Ibid., 536–37. See also Edwin A. Locke to Harry S. Truman, 19 Dec. 1945, Box 3, William D. Leahy Records, RG 218, NA.

36. Thorne, *Allies of a Kind*, 313–14.

37. *FRUS*, 1945, 7:1206–7.

38. Edward R. Stettinius to Clarence E. Gauss, 3 Nov. 1944, *FRUS: China*, 1944, 1082–83.

39. Edward R. Stettinius to George Atcheson, 23 Nov. 1944, ibid., 1087–88.

40. George Atcheson to Secretary of State, 1 Mar. 1945, *FRUS*, 1945, 7:1337; Joseph C. Grew to Atcheson, 27 Mar. 1945, ibid., 7:1311–13.

41. State Department to George C. Marshall, 30 Nov. 1945, ibid., 7:1325.

42. Michael Schaller, *The U.S. Crusade in China, 1938–1945* (New York: Columbia University Press, 1979), 94–107, 125–26.

43. Tang Tsou, *America's Failure in China, 1941–1950* (Chicago: University of Chicago Press, 1963), 78–81, 107–9.

44. Hull, *Memoirs*, 2:1309–10.

45. Feis, *Churchill, Roosevelt, Stalin*, 225.

46. Clarence E. Gauss to Franklin D. Roosevelt and Cordell Hull, 9 Dec. 1943, S. F., Box 38, Roosevelt Papers.

47. Schaller, *U.S. Crusade in China*, 154–58.

48. John Davies to Harry L. Hopkins, 15 Jan. 1944, enclosed in Hopkins to Franklin D. Roosevelt, memorandum, 2 Feb. 1944, Reel 8, Map Room, Roosevelt Papers. See also Davies, memorandum, 24 June 1943, *FRUS*, 1943, 3:258–66; and Davies to Hopkins, 31 Dec. 1943, Box 334, Harry L. Hopkins Papers, FDRL.

49. Schaller, *U.S. Crusade in China*, 159.

50. Blum, *Price of Vision*, 332–33. See also memorandum, "Conversation between Isaiah Bowman and Henry Wallace," 18 May 1944, Box 2, Ser. 14, Bowman Papers; memorandum, "Conversation between W. Averell Harriman and Franklin D. Roosevelt," 17 May 1944, Box 172, Harriman Papers; and Harriman to Roosevelt, 11 June 1944, Reel 8, Map Room, Roosevelt Papers.

51. Blum, *Price of Vision,* 349–54. See also Franklin D. Roosevelt to Henry A. Wallace, 21 June 1944, Reel 9, Map Room, Roosevelt Papers.

52. Henry A. Wallace to Franklin D. Roosevelt, 28 June 1944, Box 2, Leahy Records.

53. Henry A. Wallace to Franklin D. Roosevelt, 10 July 1944, S. F., Box 190, Roosevelt Papers.

54. Edward R. Stettinius to Joseph C. Grew, 24 May 1944, Box 216, Edward R. Stettinius Papers, UVAL. See also State Department Policy Committee, minutes, 19 May 1944, Box 139, Notter File.

55. Edward R. Stettinius, calendar notes, 15 June 1944, Box 240, Stettinius Papers. See also Stettinius, calendar notes, 19, 21 June 1944, ibid.

56. Stanley K. Hornbeck to Cordell Hull and Edward R. Stettinius, 16 June 1944, Box 721, ibid. See also Hornbeck, memorandum on China, 1 July 1944, Box 193, Breckinridge Long Papers, LC; Hornbeck to Hull, 18 July 1944, Reel 49, Cordell Hull Papers, LC; and Hornbeck, memorandum on China, 15 Aug. 1944, Box 1, Ser. 16, Bowman Papers.

57. Joint Chiefs of Staff to Franklin D. Roosevelt, 4 July 1944, Reel 8, Map Room, Roosevelt Papers.

58. Franklin D. Roosevelt to Chiang Kai-shek, 6 July 1944, ibid. See also Henry L. Stimson Diary, 2 Aug. 1944, Henry L. Stimson Papers, YUSL.

59. Robert Dallek, *Franklin D. Roosevelt and American Foreign Policy, 1932–1945* (New York: Oxford University Press, 1979), 492.

60. Stimson Diary, 3 Aug. 1944. See also entry on 21 Aug. 1944.

61. Dallek, *Roosevelt and American Foreign Policy,* 494–97.

62. Joseph W. Stilwell to George C. Marshall, 26 Sept. 1944, Box 2, Leahy Records. See also Stilwell to Marshall, 10 Oct. 1944, ibid.

63. Patrick J. Hurley to Franklin D. Roosevelt, 11 Oct. 1944, Reel 8, Map Room, Roosevelt Papers.

64. Patrick J. Hurley to Franklin D. Roosevelt, 13 Oct. 1944, Reel 9, ibid.

65. Stimson Diary, 23 Oct. 1944 (see also 3, 4, 5, 16 Oct. 1944).

66. W. Averell Harriman to Franklin D. Roosevelt, 11 June 1944, Reel 8, Map Room, Roosevelt Papers.

67. Patrick J. Hurley to Franklin D. Roosevelt, 19 Oct. 1944, Reel 9, ibid.

68. Stimson Diary, 13 Oct. 1944. See also William D. Leahy Diary, 29 July 1944, WSHS.

69. W. Averell Harriman to Franklin D. Roosevelt, 15 Oct. 1944, Box 174, Harriman Papers. See also Feis, *Churchill, Roosevelt, Stalin,* 464–66.

70. Memorandum, "Conversations between W. Averell Harriman and Franklin D. Roosevelt," 21 Oct.–19 Nov. 1944, Box 175, Harriman Papers.

71. Schaller, *U.S. Crusade in China,* 191–98.

72. Memorandum, "Conversation between W. Averell Harriman and Marshal Stalin," 14 Dec. 1944, Box 175, Harriman Papers.

73. W. Averell Harriman to Franklin D. Roosevelt, 15 Dec. 1944, ibid.

74. Edward R. Stettinius to Franklin D. Roosevelt, 4 Jan. 1945, S. F., Box 38, Roosevelt Papers. See also Patrick J. Hurley to Roosevelt, 16 Nov. 1944, Reel 9, Map Room, Roosevelt Papers; Solomon Adler to Harry D. White, 27 Nov. 1944, Henry Morgenthau Diaries, 799:03, Henry Morgenthau Papers, FDRL; State Department Policy Committee, minutes, 27 Nov. 1944, Box 138, Notter File; and Stimson Diary, 13 Dec. 1944.

75. Patrick J. Hurley to Secretary of State, 24 Dec. 1944, S. F., Box 38, Roosevelt Papers; Albert C. Wedemeyer to Joint Chiefs of Staff, 29 Dec. 1944, Box 3, Leahy Records; Hurley to Roosevelt, 2 Jan. 1945, Reel 9, Map Room, Roosevelt Papers.

76. Memorandum, "Conversation at the White House," 2 Jan. 1945, Box 4, Charles E. Bohlen File, RG 59, NA.

77. Memorandum, "Conversation between Franklin D. Roosevelt and Oliver Stanley," 16 Jan. 1945, Reel 18, Matthews-Hickerson File, RG 59, NA.

78. State Department to War Department, 29 Jan. 1945, Box 3, Henry L. Stimson Safe File, RG, 107, NA.

79. *FRUS: Conferences at Malta and Yalta,* 1945, 766–71.

80. Ibid., 984.

81. Dallek, *Roosevelt and American Foreign Policy,* 523.

82. Patrick J. Hurley to Edward R. Stettinius, 14 Apr. 1945, Reel 18, Matthews-Hickerson File.

83. Tsou, *America's Failure in China,* 254.

84. Minutes, 21 Apr. 1945, Secretary's Staff Committee Records.

85. Joseph C. Grew to Harry S. Truman, 24 Apr. 1945, S. F., Box 159, Harry S. Truman Papers, HSTL.

86. Tsou, *America's Failure in China,* 256. See also Grew, *Turbulent Era,* 2:1455–57; Millis, *Forrestal Diaries,* 55–58; and Leahy Diary, 11 May 1945.

87. Stimson Diary, 15 May 1945 (see also 13, 14 May 1945). See also Minutes of the Committee of Three, 15 May 1945.

88. Grew, *Turbulent Era,* 2:1457–59.

89. Truman, *Memoirs,* 1:264–65.

90. Grew, *Turbulent Era,* 2:1465–66. See also Leahy Diary, 9 June 1945.

91. Grew, *Turbulent Era,* 2:1466–68. See also Harry S. Truman to Winston Churchill, 15 June 1945, Box 15, Leahy Records.

92. Tsou, *America's Failure in China,* 272–77.

93. W. Averell Harriman to Harry S. Truman, 1, 5, 9 July 1945, Box 180, Harriman Papers.

94. Memorandum, "Conversations between W. Averell Harriman and T. V. Soong," 12 July 1945, Box 181, ibid.

95. Stimson Diary, 10, 15 May, 19 June 1945.

96. Minutes, 28 May 1945, Secretary's Staff Committee Records.

97. Grew, *Turbulent Era*, 2:1428–31.

98. Ibid., 2:1434. See also Stimson Diary, 29 May 1945; minutes, 30 May 1945, Secretary's Staff Committee Records; and Millis, *Forrestal Diaries*, 66.

99. Grew, *Turbulent Era*, 2:1437. See also Stimson Diary, 19 June 1945; and Millis, *Forrestal Diaries*, 69–70.

100. Stimson Diary, 26 June 1945; Millis, *Forrestal Diaries*, 71–72.

101. Iriye, *Power and Culture*, 253–54.

102. Stimson Diary, 2 July 1945.

103. Iriye, *Power and Culture*, 254–63. See also Hull, *Memoirs*, 2:1593–94; and minutes, 7 July 1945, Secretary's Staff Committee Records.

104. Stimson Diary, 15, 17, 18 July 1945. See also W. Averell Harriman, memorandum on Yalta agreement affecting China, 18 July 1945, Box 181, Harriman Papers; and Tsou, *America's Failure in China*, 278–81.

105. Stimson Diary, 23, 24 July 1945.

106. Millis, *Forrestal Diaries*, 78. See also Barton J. Bernstein, "Roosevelt, Truman, and the Atomic Bomb, 1941–1945: A Reinterpretation," *Political Science Quarterly* (spring 1975): 23–62.

107. Walter LaFeber, *The Clash: U.S.-Japanese Relations throughout History* (New York: W. W. Norton, 1997), 246.

108. James F. Byrnes to W. Averell Harriman, 6 Aug. 1945, Box 181, Harriman Papers. See also Harriman to Byrnes, 28 July 1945, ibid.

109. W. Averell Harriman to Harry S. Truman, 8 Aug. 1945, Box 16, Leahy Records.

110. Truman, *Memoirs*, 1:427–37.

111. Stimson Diary, 10 Aug. 1945.

112. Millis, *Forrestal Diaries*, 82–85. See also James F. Byrnes, *Speaking Frankly* (New York: Harper and Brothers, 1947), 209–10; and Blum, *Price of Vision*, 473–74.

113. James F. Byrnes to W. Averell Harriman, 11 Aug. 1945, Box 181, Harriman Papers. See also Harriman to Byrnes, 11 Aug. 1945, ibid.

114. W. Averell Harriman to V. M. Molotov, 12 Aug. 1945, ibid.

115. Schaller, *U.S. Crusade in China*, 260.

116. W. Averell Harriman to Harry S. Truman and James F. Byrnes, 14 Aug. 1945, Box 181, Harriman Papers.

117. Tsou, *America's Failure in China*, 305–8; Schaller, *U.S. Crusade in China*, 262–65.

118. Truman, *Memoirs*, 1:440–44.

119. Leahy Diary, 24 Oct. 1945.

120. Byrnes, *Speaking Frankly*, 213–18.

121. "Initial Post-Surrender Policy for Japan," 27 Aug. 1945, Box 35, RG 218, NA.

122. Edwin W. Pauley, "Report on Reparations," 18 Dec. 1945, Box 7, Leahy Records; Harry S. Truman to James F. Byrnes, 21 Dec. 1945, ibid. See also "U.S. Reparations Policy for Japan" (preliminary statement), 31 Oct. 1945, Box 133, Truman Papers; and Pauley to Byrnes 27 Nov. 1945, ibid.

11. RESTRAINING THE RUSSIANS IN EASTERN EUROPE

1. Herbert Feis, *Churchill, Roosevelt, Stalin: The War They Waged and the Peace They Sought* (Princeton: Princeton University Press, 1957), 26–27, 58; Lloyd C. Gardner, *Spheres of Influence: The Great Powers Partition Europe, from Munich to Yalta* (Chicago: Ivan R. Dee, 1993), 112–21.

2. Hull, *Memoirs,* 2:1167–70.

3. Berle and Jacobs, *Navigating the Rapids,* 401–2. See also memorandum, "Conversation between Berle and Polish Ambassador Jan Ciechanowski," 24 Feb. 1942, Box 213, Adolf A. Berle Papers, FDRL; and Berle to Sumner Welles, 3 Apr. 1942, Box 73, ibid.

4. Hull, *Memoirs,* 2:1170–71; Feis, *Churchill, Roosevelt, Stalin,* 59; Gardner, *Spheres of Influence,* 125–29.

5. Kimball, *Roosevelt and Churchill,* 1:394.

6. Ibid., 1:398–99.

7. Henry L. Stimson Diary, 6 Mar. 1942, Henry L. Stimson Papers, YUSL.

8. Sherwood, *Roosevelt and Hopkins,* 518–20.

9. Ibid., 521, 525–26.

10. Kimball, *Churchill and Roosevelt,* 1:465–66, 470.

11. Hull, *Memoirs,* 2:1172–74; Gardner, *Spheres of Influence,* 134–38.

12. Sherwood, *Roosevelt and Hopkins,* 556–622.

13. Subcommittee on Political Problems, minutes, 30 May 1942, Boxes 55, 56, Harley A. Notter File, RG 59, NA.

14. Ibid., 27 June 1942.

15. Subcommittee on Territorial Problems, minutes, 27 June 1942, Box 59, Notter File. See also 6, 20 June 1942, ibid.

16. Subcommittee on Territorial Problems, minutes, 9 Oct. 1942, ibid. See also Harley A. Notter, *Postwar Foreign Policy Preparation* (Washington: Government Printing Office, 1949), 509–13.

17. Subcommittee on Political Problems, minutes, 22 Aug. 1942, Box 55, Notter File. See also Subcommittee on Territorial Problems, minutes, 14, 21 Aug. 1942, Box 59, ibid.

18. Subcommittee on Political Problems, minutes, 10 Oct. 1942, Box 56, ibid.

19. Gabriel Kolko, *The Politics of War: The World and United States Foreign Policy, 1943–1945* (New York: Random House, 1968), 99–102.

20. Sherwood, *Roosevelt and Hopkins,* 708–15. See also Blum, *Price of Vision,* 159–60.

21. Sherwood, *Roosevelt and Hopkins,* 708–15.

22. Hull, *Memoirs,* 2:1267–68; Kimball, *Churchill and Roosevelt,* 2:192–205.

23. Joint Chiefs of Staff to Franklin D. Roosevelt, 8 May 1943, S. F., Box 2, Franklin D. Roosevelt Papers, FDRL; Gen. H. H. Arnold to Harry L. Hopkins, 9 Apr. 1943, Box 329, Harry L. Hopkins Papers, FDRL; Stimson Diary, 17 May 1943; William D. Leahy Diary, 24 May 1943, WSHS.

24. Meeting between Franklin D. Roosevelt and the Joint Chiefs of Staff, minutes, 10 Aug. 1943, Box 194, RG 218, NA. See also Stimson Diary, 10 Aug. 1943.

25. Berle and Jacobs, *Navigating the Rapids,* 445. See also John D. Hickerson to Cordell Hull, 10 Aug. 1943, Reel 2, Matthews-Hickerson File, RG 59, NA.

26. Edward Mark, "Charles E. Bohlen and the Acceptable Limits of Soviet Hegemony in Eastern Europe: A Memorandum of 18 Oct. 1945," *Diplomatic History* 3 (spring 1979): 203–4.

27. Warren F. Kimball, *The Juggler: Franklin Roosevelt as Wartime Statesman* (Princeton: Princeton University Press, 1991), 95; Gardner, *Spheres of Influence,* 167–68.

28. Cordell Hull to Franklin D. Roosevelt and Edward R. Stettinius, 29 Oct. 1943, Reel 24, Cordell Hull Papers, LC.

29. Hull, *Memoirs,* 2:1466; Feis, *Churchill, Roosevelt, Stalin,* 237; Kimball, *The Juggler,* 107–25.

30. W. Averell Harriman to Franklin D. Roosevelt, 5 Nov. 1943, Box 170, W. Averell Harriman Papers, LC. See also Subcommittee on Problems of European Organization, minutes, 12 Nov. 1943, Box 84, Notter File; and Hull, *Memoirs,* 2:1298–99.

31. Memorandum, "Conversation at Teheran," 1 Dec. 1943, Box 28, Map Room, Roosevelt Papers. See also memorandum, "Conversation at Teheran," 28 Nov. 1943, ibid.; memorandum, "Conversation between Roosevelt and Isaiah Bowman," 28 Oct. 1943 Box 5, Ser. 14,, Isaiah Bowman Papers, JHUSCL; and Blum, *Price of Vision,* 284–85.

32. W. Averell Harriman to Franklin D. Roosevelt and Cordell Hull, 11 Jan. 1944, Box 171, Harriman Papers.

33. W. Averell Harriman to Cordell Hull, 21 Jan. 1944, ibid.

34. State Department to W. Averell Harriman, 25 Jan. 1944, ibid. See also Charles E. Bohlen to James C. Dunn, 2 Feb. 1944, Box 3, Charles E. Bohlen File, RG 59, NA.

35. Memorandum, "Conversation between W. Averell Harriman and Joseph Stalin," 2 Feb. 1944, Box 171, Harriman Papers. See also Harriman to Franklin D. Roosevelt and Cordell Hull, 3 Feb. 1944, ibid.

36. Kimball, *Churchill and Roosevelt*, 2:706–8. See also Cordell Hull to W. Averell Harriman, 9 Feb. 1944, Box 171, Harriman Papers; and Campbell and Herring, *Diaries of Edward R. Stettinius*, 27.

37. Joseph Stalin to Franklin D. Roosevelt, 16 Feb. 1944, Reel 7, Map Room, Roosevelt Papers. See also Stalin to Roosevelt, 3 Mar. 1944, ibid.; and Kimball, *Churchill and Roosevelt*, 2:762–65, 3:21.

38. Subcommittee on Problems of European Organization, minutes, 4 Feb. 1944, Box 84, Notter File.

39. Ibid., 3 Mar. 1944.

40. Edward Mark, "American Policy toward Eastern Europe and the Origins of the Cold War, 1941–1946: An Alternative Interpretation," *Journal of American History* 68 (Sept. 1981): 317.

41. "United States Participation in Economic Reconstruction in Eastern and Southeastern Europe," document prepared for the State Department Policy Committee, 6 Mar. 1944, Box 76, RG 353, NA.

42. W. Averell Harriman to State Department, 13 Mar. 1944, Box 171, Harriman Papers.

43. Memorandum, "Remarks by W. Averell Harriman, Mission for Economic Affairs Staff Meeting in London," 4 May 1944, Box 172, ibid.

44. State Department Policy Committee, minutes, 10 May 1944, Box 138, Notter File.

45. Feis, *Churchill, Roosevelt, Stalin*, 339–40; Gardner, *Spheres of Influence*, 185–86.

46. Kimball, *Churchill and Roosevelt*, 3:153–54. See also Feis, *Churchill, Roosevelt, Stalin*, 341.

47. Hull, *Memoirs*, 2:1451–53. See also Adolf A. Berle Diary, 9, 23 June 1944, Berle Papers.

48. Kimball, *Churchill and Roosevelt*, 3:177.

49. Ibid., 3:178–86.

50. Hull, *Memoirs*, 2:1457–58.

51. Kimball, *Churchill and Roosevelt*, 3:278–79, 297.

52. Memorandum, "Staff Meeting at the American Embassy in Moscow," 15 Feb. 1944, Box 171, Harriman Papers; Harriman to Franklin D. Roosevelt, 24 Mar. 44 (draft, not sent), Box 172, ibid.

53. W. Averell Harriman to Lord Beaverbrook, 5 Apr. 1944, Box 172, ibid.

54. Memorandum, "Conversation between W. Averell Harriman and Winston S. Churchill," 2 May 1944, ibid. See also memorandum,

"Conversation between Harriman and Anthony Eden," 3 May 1944, ibid.; and Harriman, "Comments at a Press Conference in London," 4 May 1944, ibid.

55. Charles E. Bohlen to Cordell Hull, James C. Dunn, and H. Freeman Matthews, 16 May 1944, Box 216, Edward R. Stettinius Papers, UVAL.

56. Memorandum, "Conversation between W. Averell Harriman and Franklin D. Roosevelt," 17 May 1944, Box 172, Harriman Papers. See also Harriman to Roosevelt, 29 May 1944, Reel 8, Map Room, Roosevelt Papers; Roosevelt to Harriman, 1 June 1944, Box 172, Harriman Papers; memorandum, "Conversation between Harriman and Vyacheslav Molotov," 3 June 1944, Box 172, ibid; and Harriman to Roosevelt, 7 June 44, ibid.

57. Campbell and Herring, *Diaries of Edward R. Stettinius,* 77–88.

58. W. Averell Harriman to Franklin D. Roosevelt, 11 June 1944, Reel 8, Map Room, Roosevelt Papers. See also memorandum, "Conversation among Harriman and Joseph Stalin and Vyacheslav Molotov," 10 June 1944, Box 172, Harriman Papers.

59. Franklin D. Roosevelt to Joseph Stalin, 17 June 1944, Box 173, Harriman Papers. See also Kimball, *Churchill and Roosevelt,* 3:208–10, 234–35.

60. W. Averell Harriman to Cordell Hull, 21 July 1944, Box 173, Harriman Papers.

61. Kimball, *Churchill and Roosevelt,* 3:253–55, 258–59, 261–62.

62. Feis, *Churchill, Roosevelt, Stalin,* 377–83.

63. W. Averell Harriman to Franklin D. Roosevelt and Cordell Hull, 10 Aug. 1944, Box 173, Harriman Papers. See also Harriman to Roosevelt and Hull, 1 Aug. 1944; and Harriman to Roosevelt and Edward R. Stettinius, 11 Aug. 1944, ibid.

64. Feis, *Churchill, Roosevelt, Stalin,* 385–86.

65. W. Averell Harriman to Franklin D. Roosevelt and Edward R. Stettinius, 15 Aug. 1944, S. F., Box 66, Roosevelt Papers.

66. W. Averell Harriman to Franklin D. Roosevelt and Cordell Hull, 17 Aug. 1944, Box 173, Harriman Papers. See also Anthony Eden to Clark Kerr, 16 Aug. 1944; Hull to Harriman, 17 Aug. 1944; and Harriman to Roosevelt and Hull, 19 Aug. 1944, ibid.

67. Winston S. Churchill and Franklin D. Roosevelt to Joseph Stalin, 20 Aug. 1944, Reel 7, Map Room, Roosevelt Papers. See also Cordell Hull to Roosevelt, 17 Aug. 1944, S. F., Box 68, Roosevelt Papers.

68. Kimball, *Churchill and Roosevelt,* 3:294–96, 309–13.

69. W. Averell Harriman to Harry L. Hopkins, 9 Sept. 1944, Box 194, Harriman Papers.

70. John R. Deane to Carl Spaatz, 2 Oct. 1944, ibid. See also W. Averell Harriman to Franklin D. Roosevelt, 23 Sept. 1944, ibid.

71. W. Averell Harriman to Cordell Hull, 20 Sept. 1944, ibid. See also George F. Kennan to Harriman (two memoranda), 18 Sept. 1944; and Harriman to Franklin D. Roosevelt, 29 Sept. 1944, ibid.

72. Charles E. Bohlen to Harry L. Hopkins, 3 Oct. 1944, Box 335, Harry L. Hopkins Papers, FDRL.

73. Franklin D. Roosevelt to Joseph Stalin, 4 Oct. 1944, Reel 8, Map Room, Roosevelt Papers. See also Kimball, *Churchill and Roosevelt,* 3:341–45; and Stalin to Roosevelt, 8 Oct. 1944, Reel 12, Matthews-Hickerson File.

74. Franklin D. Roosevelt to W. Averell Harriman, 4 Oct. 1944, Reel 8, Map Room, Roosevelt Papers.

75. W. Averell Harriman to Franklin D. Roosevelt, 10 Oct. 1944, Box 32, Map Room, Roosevelt Papers.

76. Gardner, *Spheres of Influence,* 198–206.

77. Kimball, *Churchill and Roosevelt,* 3:352–53. See also W. Averell Harriman to Franklin D. Roosevelt, 11 Oct. 1944, Box 174, Harriman Papers.

78. W. Averell Harriman to Franklin D. Roosevelt, 12 Oct. 1944, Reel 12, Matthews-Hickerson File.

79. Feis, *Churchill, Roosevelt, Stalin,* 389–90, 453–59. See also Kimball, *Churchill and Roosevelt,* 3:357–61, 363–65; W. Averell Harriman to Franklin D. Roosevelt, 14 Oct. 1944, Box 174, Harriman Papers; and memorandum, "Conversation among Harriman and Stanislaw Mikolajczyk and Tadeusz Romer," 18 Oct. 1944, Box 175, ibid.

80. Berle and Jacobs, *Navigating the Rapids,* 460–68 (see also 457, 470). See also State Department Policy Committee, minutes, 13 Oct. 1944, Box 138, Notter File.

81. Lincoln MacVeagh to Franklin D. Roosevelt, 15 Oct. 1944, S. F., Box 54, Roosevelt Papers. See also MacVeagh to Roosevelt, 17 Feb. 1944, ibid.

82. State Department Policy Committee, minutes, 25 Oct. 1944, Box 138, Notter File. See also Stimson Diary, 23 Oct. 1944; and Blum, *Price of Vision,* 393.

83. Edward R. Stettinius to Franklin D. Roosevelt, 31 Oct. 1944, S. F., Box 66, Roosevelt Papers.

84. "United States Interests and Policy in Eastern and Southeastern Europe and the Near East," 8 Nov. 1944, *FRUS,* 1944, 4:1025–26.

85. Edward R. Stettinius to Franklin D. Roosevelt, 2 Nov. 1944, S. F., Box 91, Roosevelt Papers. See also W. Averell Harriman to Roosevelt, 23 Nov. 1944, Box 175, Harriman Papers.

86. Kimball, *Churchill and Roosevelt*, 3:461–66.

87. Ibid., 3:475–77. See also Edgar Snow to Franklin D. Roosevelt, 28 Dec. 1944, S. F., Box 68, Roosevelt Papers.

88. Kimball, *Churchill and Roosevelt*, 3:481–84, 492. See also Minutes of the Committee of Three, 2 Jan. 1945, RG 59, NA.

89. *FRUS: Conferences at Malta and Yalta*, 1945, 450.

90. George F. Kennan to Charles E. Bohlen, 26 Jan. 1945, Box 3, Bohlen Papers.

91. Campbell and Herring, *Diaries of Edward R. Stettinius*, 213–15.

92. W. Averell Harriman to Edward R. Stettinius, 6 Jan. 1945, Box 176, Harriman Papers. See also Stettinius to Franklin D. Roosevelt, 8 Jan. 1944, S. F., Box 91, Roosevelt Papers; and Minutes of the Committee of Three, 9 Jan. 1945.

93. Henry Morgenthau Diaries, 808:294–315, Henry Morgenthau Papers, FDRL. See also ibid., 806:168; and Leahy Diary, 10 Jan. 1945.

94. Dobney, *Selected Papers of Will Clayton*, 108–11. See also memorandum, "Meeting between William L. Clayton and Henry Morgenthau," 25 Jan. 1945, Morgenthau Diaries, 812:209–10.

95. *FRUS*, 1945, 5:986–87. See also Edward R. Stettinius Diary, 7–23 Jan. 1945, Box 29, Notter File.

96. Notter, *Postwar Foreign Policy Preparation*, 372–73, 394, 655–57, 663–64. See also Campbell and Herring, *Diaries of Edward R. Stettinius*, 215–16, 230, 235–37; Mark, "American Policy toward Eastern Europe and the Origins of the Cold War," 321; John D. Hickerson to Stettinius, 8 Jan. 1945, Box 222, Stettinius Papers; and Charles E. Bohlen to Hickerson, 9 Jan. 1945, Box 3, Bohlen File.

97. Russell D. Buhite, *Decisions at Yalta: An Appraisal of Summit Diplomacy* (Wilmington, Del.: Scholarly Resources, 1986), 114–18.

98. Memorandum, "Meeting aboard the HMS *Sirius* at Malta," 1 Feb. 1945, Box 5, RG 43, NA. See also Campbell and Herring, *Diaries of Edward R. Stettinius*, 227–28, 235–36; Hamilton Fish Armstrong to Stettinius, 30 Jan. 1945, Box 719, Stettinius Papers; memorandum for James C. Dunn, 3 Feb. 1945, Box 719, Stettinius Papers; and memorandum for the president, 2 Feb. 1945, Box 278, ibid.

99. Buhite, *Decisions at Yalta*, 49–56; Gardner, *Spheres of Influence*, 229–37.

100. James F. Byrnes, *Speaking Frankly* (New York: Harper and Brothers, 1947), 50–53; Feis, *Churchill, Roosevelt, Stalin*, 564–67.

101. Memorandum, "Conversation between Franklin D. Roosevelt and Joseph C. Grew," 2 Mar. 1945, "Conversations," vol. 6, Joseph C. Grew Papers, HUHL. See also Leahy Diary, 6 Mar. 1945.

102. Kimball, *Churchill and Roosevelt,* 3:579–80, 605–7, 618–19.

103. W. Averell Harriman to State Department, 2 Mar. 1945, Box 177, Harriman Papers; Joseph C. Grew to Franklin D. Roosevelt, 5 Mar. 1945, S. F., Box 91, Roosevelt Papers; Grew to Roosevelt, 6 Mar. 1945, S. F., Box 83, ibid.; Grew to Harriman, 8 Mar. 1945, in *FRUS,* 1945, 5:150–52.

104. Kimball, *Churchill and Roosevelt,* 3:545–51, 560–63. See also Edward R. Stettinius, "Notes for Cabinet Meeting," 16 Mar. 1945, Box 730, Stettinius Papers.

105. W. Averell Harriman to State Department, 25 Mar. 1945, Box 178, Harriman Papers. See also Leahy Diary, 29 Mar. 1945.

106. Franklin D. Roosevelt to Joseph Stalin, 31 Mar. 1945, Box 31, Map Room, Roosevelt Papers. See also Kimball, *Churchill and Roosevelt,* 3:593–97.

107. W. Averell Harriman to State Department, 3 Apr. 1945, Box 178, Harriman Papers. See also Harriman to State Department, 6 Apr. 1945, ibid.

108. Dean G. Acheson to Franklin D. Roosevelt, 4 Apr. 1945, S. F., Box 147, Roosevelt Papers.

109. Franklin D. Roosevelt to Isador Lubin, 6 Apr. 1945, ibid.

110. Kimball, *Churchill and Roosevelt,* 3:622, 627–28, 630.

111. Campbell and Herrings, *Diaries of Edward R. Stettinius,* 317–19.

112. Truman, *Memoirs,* 1:14–17, 23–25, 37–39. See also Edward R. Stettinius to W. Averell Harriman, 14 Apr. 1945, Box 178, Harriman Papers.

113. Minutes, 20 Apr. 1945, Secretary's Staff Committee Records, RG 353, NA.

114. Memorandum, "Conversation at the White House," 20 Apr. 1945, S. F., Box 187, Harry S. Truman Papers, HSTL.

115. Campbell and Herring, *Diaries of Edward R. Stettinius,* 325–29; Stettinius, calendar notes, 22 Apr. 1945, Box 244, Stettinius Papers; Truman, *Memoirs,* 1:74–75.

116. Memorandum, "Meeting at the White House," 23 Apr. 1945, S. F., Box 187, Truman Papers. See also Stimson Diary, 23 Apr. 1945; and Millis, *Forrestal Diaries,* 48–50.

117. Memorandum, "Conversation between Harry S. Truman and Vyacheslav Molotov," 23 Apr. 1945, S. F., Box 187, Truman Papers. See also memorandum, "Conversation between Truman and Molotov," 22 Apr. 1945, ibid.

118. Sherwood, *Roosevelt and Hopkins,* 885–910. See also Truman, *Memoirs,* 1:257–63.

119. W. Averell Harriman to State Department, 28 June 1945, Box 180, Harriman Papers.

120. Kolko, *Politics of War,* 401–3, 575–78.

121. Truman, *Memoirs,* 1:236, 346, 377–78, 384–85 (see also 425–26). See also Millis, *Forrestal Diaries,* 78–80.

122. W. Averell Harriman to State Department, 11 Apr. 1945, Box 178, Harriman Papers.

123. Minutes, 21 Apr. 1945, Secretary's Staff Committee Records.

124. John L. Gaddis, *The United States and the Origins of the Cold War, 1941–1947* (New York: Columbia University Press, 1972), 222–23; Thomas G. Patterson, *Soviet-American Confrontation: Postwar Reconstruction and the Origins of the Cold War* (Baltimore: Johns Hopkins University Press, 1973), 37–56.

125. Byrnes, *Speaking Frankly,* 91–122.

126. Daniel Yergin, *Shattered Peace: The Origins of the Cold War* (New York: Penguin, 1977), 144–46, 151–52, 156–60.

127. Truman, *Memoirs,* 1:551–52.

CONCLUSION. THE POSTWAR ERA

1. Executive Committee on Economic Foreign Policy, minutes, 11 May 1945, Box 776, RG 169, NA.

2. Dobney, *Selected Papers of Will Clayton,* 150–52. See also Executive Committee on Economic Foreign Policy, minutes, 7 Sept. 1942; and Truman, *Memoirs,* 1:475, 478.

3. Minutes, 9 Oct. 1945, Secretary's Staff Committee Records, RG 353, NA.

4. William L. Clayton to Robert E. Wood, 17 Nov. 1945, Box 1, William L. Clayton Papers, HSTL. See also Blum, *Price of Vision,* 662.

5. Division of Historical Research, "State Department Analysis of Anglo-American Financial Negotiations," Apr. 1947, S. F., Box 172, Harry S. Truman Papers, HSTL.

6. Dobney, *Selected Papers of Will Clayton,* 153–61. See also Blum, *Price of Vision,* 526–27; and minutes, 9 Oct. 1945, Secretary's Staff Committee Records.

7. Edward Mark, "Charles E. Bohlen and the Acceptable Limits of Soviet Hegemony in Eastern Europe: A Memorandum of 18 Oct. 1945," *Diplomatic History* 3 (spring 1979): 207–9.

8. James F. Byrnes, *Speaking Frankly* (New York: Harper and Brothers, 1947), 108.

BIBLIOGRAPHY OF PRIMARY SOURCES

ARCHIVES

Columbia University, Butler Library, New York City.

Carnegie Endowment for International Peace Records

Franklin D. Roosevelt Library, Hyde Park, N.Y.

Adolf A. Berle Papers
Harry L. Hopkins Papers
R. Walton Moore Papers
Henry Morgenthau Papers
Franklin D. Roosevelt Papers
Harold D. Smith Papers
Myron C. Taylor Papers
Sumner Welles Papers
John C. Wiley Papers

Harry S. Truman Library, Independence, Mo.

Dean G. Acheson Papers
William L. Clayton Papers
Clayton-Thorp File
Ralph K. Davies Papers
Samuel I. Rosenman Papers
Harold D. Smith Diary
Harry S. Truman Papers
Yale University Documents Regarding the Atomic Bomb

Harvard Business School, Baker Library, Boston, Mass.

Thomas W. Lamont Papers

Harvard University, Houghton Library, Cambridge, Mass.

Joseph C. Grew Papers
J. Pierrepont Moffat Papers
William Phillips Papers

Herbert C. Hoover Library, West Branch, Iowa.

Hugh R. Wilson Papers
Robert E. Wood Papers

John F. Doyle Private Collection. Naperville, Ill.

Leo T. Crowley Papers

John Hopkins University, Special Collections Library, Baltimore, Md.

Isaiah Bowman Papers

Library of Congress, Washington, D.C.

Charles E. Bohlen Papers
Joseph E. Davies Papers
Herbert Feis Papers
W. Averell Harriman Papers
Cordell Hull Papers
Jesse H. Jones Papers
Frank Knox Papers
Breckinridge Long Papers
Leo Pasvolsky Papers
Francis B. Sayre Papers

National Archives and Records Administration, Washington, D.C.

Record Group 43, Records of World War II Conferences
Record Group 59, Records of the State Department
Central File
Dean G. Acheson File
Charles E. Bohlen File
John D. Hickerson File
Matthews-Hickerson File
Alger Hiss File
Harley A. Notter File
Leo Pasvolsky File
Minutes of the Committee of Three
Records of the Petroleum Division

Record Group 80, Records of the Navy Department
James V. Forrestal Records
Frank Knox Records
Minutes of the Top Board
Records of the General Board

Record Group 107, Records of the War Department
Henry L. Stimson Safe File

Record Group 169, Records of the Foreign Economic
Administration
Record Group 218, Records of the Joint Chiefs of Staff
William D. Leahy Records
Minutes
Record Group 353, Records of Interdepartmental and
Intradepartmental Committees
Executive Committee on Commercial Policy Records
Executive Committee on Economic Foreign Policy Records
Secretary's Staff Committee Records

Princeton University, Mudd Library, Princeton, N.J.
Bernard M. Baruch Papers
Harry Dexter White Papers

University of Arizona, Special Collections Library, Tucson.
Lewis W. Douglas Papers

University of Iowa Library, Iowa City.
Henry A. Wallace Papers

University of Virginia, Alderman Library, Charlottesville.
Edward R. Stettinius Papers

Wisconsin State Historical Society, Madison.
William D. Leahy Diary

Yale University, Sterling Library, New Haven, Conn.
Henry L. Stimson Papers

COUNCIL ON FOREIGN RELATIONS DOCUMENTS

Studies of American Interest in the War and the Peace

PERIODICALS AND PROCEEDINGS

Annals of the American Academy of Political and Social Science
Bankers' Magazine
Barron's
Business Week
Commercial and Financial Chronicle
Foreign Affairs

Foreign Relations of the United States
Fortune
Magazine of Wall Street
Oil and Gas Journal
Proceedings of the Export Managers' Club of New York
Proceedings of the National Foreign Trade Conventions
Think
Vital Speeches

PUBLISHED PAPERS AND DIARIES

Berle, Beatrice B., and Travis B. Jacobs, eds. *Navigating the Rapids: From the Papers of Adolf A. Berle, 1918–1971.* New York: Harcourt Brace Jovanovich, 1973.

Blum, John M., ed. *The Price of Vision: The Diary of Henry A. Wallace, 1942–1946.* Boston: Houghton Mifflin, 1973.

Bullitt, Orville H., ed. *For the President Personal and Secret: Correspondence between Franklin D. Roosevelt and William C. Bullitt.* Boston: Houghton Mifflin, 1972.

Campbell, Thomas M., and George C. Herring, eds. *The Diaries of Edward R. Stettinius Jr., 1943–1946.* New York: Franklin Watts, 1975.

Dobney, Fredrick J., ed. *Selected Papers of Will Clayton.* Baltimore: Johns Hopkins University Press, 1971.

Grew, Joseph C. *Turbulent Era: A Diplomatic Record of Forty Years, 1904–1945.* 2 vols. Boston: Houghton Mifflin, 1952.

Hull, Cordell. *The Memoirs of Cordell Hull.* 2 vols. New York: Macmillan, 1948.

Ickes, Harold. *The Secret Diary of Harold L. Ickes.* Vol. 3, *The Lowering Clouds, 1939–1941.* New York: Simon and Schuster, 1954.

Israel, Fred L., ed. *The War Diary of Breckinridge Long.* Lincoln: University of Nebraska Press, 1966.

Kimball, Warren F., ed. *Churchill and Roosevelt: The Complete Correspondence.* 3 vols. Princeton: Princeton University Press, 1984.

Millis, Walter, ed. *The Forrestal Diaries.* New York: Viking Press, 1951.

Nicholas, H. G., ed. *Washington Dispatches, 1941–45: Weekly Reports from the British Embassy.* Chicago: University of Chicago Press, 1981.

Roosevelt, Elliot, ed. *F.D.R.: His Personal Letters, 1925–1945.* 2 vols. New York: Duel, Sloan, and Pearce, 1950.

Sherwood, Robert E. *Roosevelt and Hopkins: An Intimate History.* New York: Harper and Brothers, 1948.

Truman, Harry S. *The Memoirs of Harry S. Truman.* 2 vols. New York: DaCapo Press, 1955–56.

INDEX